THE LONELY QUEST OF UNILEVER'S CEO PAUL POLMAN

THE LONELY QUEST OF UNILEVER'S CEO PAUL POLMAN

JEROEN SMIT

Translated from Dutch by Jenny Watson

 FIRST HILL BOOKS

FIRST HILL BOOKS
An imprint of Wimbledon Publishing Company
www.anthempress.com

This edition first published in UK and USA 2023
by FIRST HILL BOOKS
75–76 Blackfriars Road, London SE1 8HA, UK
or PO Box 9779, London SW19 7ZG, UK
and
244 Madison Ave #116, New York, NY 10016, USA

British Library Cataloguing-in-Publication Data
A catalogue record for this book is available from the British Library.

Library of Congress Control Number: 2023901569
A catalog record for this book has been requested.

ISBN-13: 978-1-83998-892-9 (Pbk)
ISBN-10: 1-83998-892-4 (Pbk)

This title is also available as an e-book.

I recommend that the Statue of Liberty on the East Coast is supplemented by a Statue of Responsibility on the West Coast.

Viktor Frankl, psychiatrist and Auschwitz
survivor (*Man's Search for Meaning*, 1962)

It is difficult to get a man to understand something, when his salary depends upon his not understanding it!

Upton Sinclair, investigative journalist writing
in in 1906, quoted 100 years later by Al Gore
in his film *An Inconvenient Truth*

CONTENTS

*In Rotterdam they're on a rollercoaster. With a heavy heart and widespread
dissatisfaction the 125-year-old 'university of marketing' has to be sold. Will
Polman manage to find safe harbour for a head office in Rotterdam? Do those in
The Hague and the rest of the country understand his mission?*

*Dutch PM Mark Rutte fears that Unilever and Shell will leave the Netherlands,
he doesn't want that on his conscience. Polman also feels the weight of this
historic decision. Yet they seem to be forgetting that the Brits prefer to be
economical with the truth and that to them Unilever's departure from London is
unthinkable.*

*In England they're celebrating it as a shareholder victory, in the Netherlands
they're celebrating it as a victory for democracy over the interests of a handful of
multinationals. But really there are no winners, only losers.*

*Unilever has done the right thing but Polman isn't where he wanted to be.
Through highs and lows, he's battled for 10 years against enduring scepticism
regarding his intentions. The recognition of the pioneer comes too late, yet there
are clear signs that his lonely high road is the right path to follow.*

A NEAR-DEATH EXPERIENCE

Friday, 10 February 2017

How would he like to make $200 million? Paul Polman stares at Alexandre Behring in astonishment. Does his guest truly imagine that he's for sale, that he'd turn his back on his mission for a big sack of cash? Hasn't the chairman of Kraft Heinz done his homework on Unilever at all? Doesn't he know who he's dealing with?

Over the past eight years, Polman has tried to show the world that businessmen need to do the right thing, and that companies whose sole reason for being is to make money no longer have any right to exist. The CEO of Unilever has gone so far as to call his company 'the world's biggest NGO'.

Over at Kraft Heinz, meanwhile, priority number one is making the shareholders even richer and doing so as quickly as possible. The idea of Unilever being taken over by people like that is completely unthinkable to Polman. Is Behring unaware of that or does he just not understand?

It's probably a case of the latter. These kinds of people truly believe that anything and anyone can be bought. The thought makes Polman furious. He needs to make sure he doesn't let his feelings show. Otherwise he could easily fly off the handle completely, and the man sitting across from him would have no idea why. To this Brazilian, doing business is a simple calculation, a game with winners and losers. And the winner is whoever makes the most money.

These are the people who are consuming and destroying the world: businessmen and billionaires all as rich as Croesus who have zero concern for the billions of people who have nothing. They're completely wrapped up in themselves, in increasing *their* already enormous wealth, *their* room to manoeuvre, *their* freedom to operate. They don't understand that with great freedom and wealth comes great responsibility. Are you rich to the detriment of the others who have so much less than you do, or do you use your wealth to help them?

Polman informs Behring that if the takeover were to happen he would regard the sack of cash they gave him as blood money and use every cent to fight against the way people like him do business. In Paul Polman's eyes, a man like Alexandre Behring is a shadow of a person, only half human.

This isn't their first encounter. After the Unilever board reached their decision to sell the spreads division, including brands like ProActiv, Flora and Blue Ribbon, the previous year, the company had put its feelers out to a number of firms that might be interested in buying. They'd reached out to Danone, known for yogurts and snack cheeses, but they'd also approached Kraft Heinz. During a meeting in New York at the end of 2016, Polman had invited Behring to consider a possible takeover of Unilever's spreads division. The meeting had been top secret.

The sale is a delicate matter. Spreads are part of Unilever's Dutch DNA, its identity. In fact, Polman has been wanting to get rid of them ever since 2009. Back then when he had just been appointed CEO of Unilever, he had been confronted with a company that had shrunk in size by almost a quarter over just 10 years. Little remained of what they had once proudly called 'the university of marketing'. He knew there was only one way to get his demotivated employees' heads back in the game. With a simple promise: we are going to grow. Polman, who had built his career at Unilever's arch rivals Procter & Gamble and Nestlé, had promised them that they would be back playing in the same league as those companies within the next 10 years. He promised them they could be just as big as the two firms that had grown to the same size as Unilever in 1994 and later far outstripped them.

He had woken them up, declaring that they could double their turnover to €80 billion. This increase would mostly be derived from emerging economies, countries with billions of poor people crying out not only for personal care and home care products but for a few more luxury food items here and there, such as ice cream or decent tea. Margarine, Polman claimed, would play no part in their ambitions for growth; people in those countries haven't even heard of it. And even in markets like the United States and Europe, where people *do* spread their sandwiches with ProActiv or Flora, revenues have been declining since the 1990s.

Persuading his colleagues they were better off selling those operations hadn't been easy. The Dutch in particular found it difficult to accept. Many of them had started their careers at Van den Bergh & Jurgens, named after the two businessmen Simon van den Bergh and Antoon Jurgens from the Dutch town of Oss, who from 1872 had built their empire manufacturing margarine back when it was the nutritious and, more importantly, cheap alternative to real butter. The factory on Nassaukade in Rotterdam is still physically attached to Unilever Benelux head office. The quayside there has smelled of margarine for 125 years. Colleagues had been at pains to point out to Polman that even though sales were stalling, there was still good money to be made from spreads, and that those revenue streams were necessary to pay dividends and invest in the Far East. The Dutch accuse Polman of disliking margarines and systematically underinvesting in renewing the spreads division over the years. They suspect him of tactical neglect. By now things had reached such a low point that young Unilever talent didn't want to work there anymore. It was only natural that sales had slumped even further. Unilever had milked the spreads operation completely dry.

To Polman, the sale is a no-brainer. He wants to use Unilever to show it's possible to make money by doing good. Moreover, he feels a greater affinity for Unilever's British DNA, which comes from William Hesketh Lever. At the end of the nineteenth century, the founder of Lever Brothers, later Lord Leverhulme, had set out to improve the hygienic conditions of Victorian Britain with the aid of his soap. William Lever is Polman's great hero, the man who understood all the way back then that a company's primary purpose is to serve its community.

Eighteen months previously, Polman had decided to ring-fence spreads and make it a separate division. When covetous financial analysts – the CEO of Unilever insists on calling them spreadsheet monkeys – asked whether that meant spreads were now up for grabs, he'd naturally denied it. Admitting as much would drive down the price. They had formed a new management team and promised to do everything they could to make spreads more profitable. Internally, they resolved to go out under the radar and start looking for a buyer.

At the end of January, Alexandre Behring had come back and informed them that Kraft Heinz wasn't interested in buying the spreads division on its own. It had been a bizarre meeting. The Brazilian had smiled broadly as he asked Polman whether the two of them couldn't come up with something more substantial. He didn't want to get into specifics but seemed to be mooting the possibility of a merger or takeover of Unilever by the much smaller Kraft Heinz.

Polman had been apoplectic. Over the past few years, those on the board had spoken increasingly often of the risk of activist shareholders who bought small shares only to use the court of public opinion to exert pressure on the board. They had never even considered an outright takeover. Who on earth could come up with that kind of sum, a minimum of €130 billion? Let alone construct a bid for a company that's highly difficult to take over in the first place because of the complex Dutch-British structure that's been holding it prisoner ever since its founding.

Right off the bat, Polman had told Behring that he saw little prospect for a deal; the companies were simply too different. He explained to him that Unilever regarded increasing shareholder value as an outcome, rather than its goal. The company, he said, aimed to serve its customers and the society in which it operates as sustainably as possible. He's convinced that this is the only model that works because it brings prosperity to all stakeholders concerned, not only in the here and now, but above all in the future. However, in the interests of being polite, Polman had promised to think about it.

They agreed to reconvene on 10 February. Unlike with the first meeting, which had blindsided him, Polman was able to prepare properly for this second encounter. He spent the 10 days leading up to it visiting Unilever's daughter companies in Asia. Despite his shock and the need to figure out what to do, he had decided that the trip needed to go ahead. Cancelling a trip like this at the last minute would lead to questions and cause a great deal of concern. Once on the road, he'd had time to do his research into his opponent. He read the book *Dream Big* about the founders of 3G Capital, the investment consortium of multi-billionaire Brazilian businessmen behind the attack. In addition to being Kraft Heinz's board chairman, Alexandre Behring is also a managing partner of 3G Capital.

3G Capital's main owners are Jorge Paulo Lemann, Carlos Alberto Sicupira and Marcel Herrmann Telles, enterprising Brazilians who found each other in the 1970s via their shared passion for competition. Whether it's harpoon fishing or growing companies, it always comes down to beating the other person, wanting to be the best and biggest. At the heart of 3G Capital's philosophy is the deeply held conviction that people must be given the space to develop their talents *and* be paid handsomely for doing so. For decades now, Jorge Paulo Lemann, the undisputed leader of 3G, has kept his eye out for what he calls PSDs: *poor, smart and a deep desire to get rich.* These are young, often poor Brazilians whose education he personally bankrolls at the best American universities. After that, they go on to become supremely loyal employees in his company.

3G Capital has spent years trying to consolidate the power of well-established global brands. From banks to beers and from hamburgers to ketchup, the central task is to scrutinise costs. Because costs are like fingernails, they constantly need trimming. Trimming the fat is the quickest way to turn a bigger profit. By rewarding their managers with enormous bonuses tied to those quick results, they've remained highly profitable for decades.

Polman studies the way 3G Capital built AB InBev into the biggest beer brewer in the world via a series of canny takeovers. And how they had then gone on to use the takeovers of first Heinz and then Kraft to build yet another colossal company.

On paper, the mission of Kraft Heinz, a company dominated by 3G Capital and Warren Buffett's investment fund Berkshire Hathaway, which together own 49 per cent of its shares, sounds a little like Unilever's. Kraft Heinz wants to make customers 'rich' by providing them with high quality food at a low price. But in the eyes of the Brazilians, the most important objective is to keep making as much money as possible for the owners, which is to say the shareholders, for as long as possible. You keep to the letter of the law while doing so, of course, but in their way of working the philosophy of Milton Friedman reigns: the social responsibility of business is to increase its profits. If you should happen to get permission from a local government to, for instance, burn down a section of rainforest and if doing so should happen to be highly lucrative, then you would be a poor businessman if you didn't go ahead and do it. Because your competitor would. And if you're worried about global warming and think trees are important then of course you're more than welcome to invest your personal savings in planting more of them. A businessman who wants to save the world isn't a good businessman. That isn't his role.

Buy, squeeze, buy, squeeze. That's how Polman sums up the Brazilians' business model. In the brief two years since taking over Kraft they have scrapped over thirteen thousand jobs at the company. The margin has shot up, in stark contrast to their sales figures. Now that, apparently, there aren't many costs left to squeeze out of the Kraft Heinz conglomerate they are in need of fresh prey, another big, juicy prize to which they could apply this same tactic.

Obviously, Polman has also done his research into the peculiar friendship between Jorge Paulo Lemann and Warren Buffett, and the way they have joined forces in various business ventures since 2013. This was how Buffett, often dubbed the 'most successful American investor', ended up becoming a significant investor in Kraft Heinz, even joining the company's board. Buffett's frequent praise for Lemann's work confuses Polman. Didn't the 86-year-old American like to project an image of a calm, considerate investor interested in long-term results?

Alexandre Behring and his board had agreed ahead of the January meeting that he would only put forward the possibility of a complete takeover of Unilever if he got the impression that the idea would be received sympathetically by Polman. But then what constitutes a sympathetic reception? Doesn't it all boil down to money? In any case, Behring had interpreted the meeting at the end of January as a maybe, an opening to negotiate further. And that's how he represented it to his own board.

In advance of the second meeting with Polman, Behring called Kees Storm. The two men know each other well. Up until two years ago, the Dutchman had been a member of the board at InBev as well as at Unilever. Behring indicated to Storm that his conversation with Polman had been productive, and that he had gotten on quite well with the Unilever CEO. Storm warned the chairman of Kraft Heinz off, telling him that he had misread Polman and that the Unilever CEO would stop at nothing to prevent himself from going down in history as the man who sold off the multinational.

But as far is Behring is concerned, he doesn't get a decisive 'no' from Polman during the second meeting either. And so he presents him with a summary of the plan for Kraft Heinz to take over the entirety of Unilever. Very much to his annoyance, Polman is handed an abridged but well-thought-out plan. Behring talks him through the structure of the new business. He explains how they will cut around a third of costs from the new combination by focusing on Unilever's daughter companies. Behring grins as he declares that the new conglomerate will be the largest producer of fast-moving consumer goods after Nestlé. He tells Polman about their plans to set up headquarters for the new giant in New York.

In order to realise this dream, Kraft Heinz will pay approximately $143 billion (€135 billion) for Unilever. This represents a premium of 18 per cent on the company's current stock market value. Behring underlines the fact that is an opening bid. The same applies to the €200 million they've reserved for Polman too by the way.

The Unilever CEO tells him in no uncertain terms that he sees zero potential in the proposal. He follows this up by saying that the world is changing quickly, meaning it's sensible to look closely at all possible options. Polman also makes it clear that this isn't his decision to make. Obviously, the task of making a recommendation to Unilever's shareholders will fall to the board. They will determine the fate of the company by deciding whether or not to sell their shares to Kraft Heinz. To Behring's mind, he is still yet to hear a firm 'no'; he leaves the deal proposal with Polman and departs.

As soon as Alexandre Behring has left, Polman calls Marijn Dekkers, his board chairman for just under a year. He reads him the proposal. The discussion is brief. Unilever's board isn't interested. The differences in company culture are too great and if there are costs to be cut from Unilever then they are much better off cutting them themselves. They also conclude that the 18 per cent premium is much too low. Dekkers thinks Kraft Heinz is hurting its own cause with such an offer. The Unilever share price was just as high as the price Brazilians are offering only a couple of months ago. It would be relatively easy for Unilever's board to shrug off such an offer and promise the shareholders at least the same value within the foreseeable future. The two men come to the conclusion that Kraft Heinz will have to raise their offer considerably if they wish to succeed.

However, they also realise that *they* need to arm themselves for battle. They decide to summon the Unilever board that same weekend. The small army of bankers, lawyers and PR specialists that have been hard at work over the past ten days will receive reinforcements. They need to estimate the enemy's firepower and weigh up the various scenarios, predicting their outcomes. All this will have to be done in strictest secrecy. If the public gets wind of the takeover bid now, the share price could shoot up, meaning the board loses control of the process. For this reason, they decide not to use the services of the Crowne Plaza Hotel, next door to Unilever head office in Blackfriars, London. They'll set up camp in the Mandarin Hotel instead. Polman reckons his board members will appreciate this. They've often implied that the Crowne Plaza doesn't quite meet with their standards.

Once he's put down the phone, 60-year-old Polman is upset, really upset. It's his fault all this is happening. He's the one at the helm, it's no coincidence that he is the recipient of this unwanted attack. If Unilever winds up being crushed in Kraft Heinz's talons, it will be because he wasn't vigilant enough. If things go badly, it will be his responsibility.

Polman looks out of the window. He's spent over eight years in this office, on the site purchased by Lord Leverhulme nearly a hundred years ago. The stunning art deco head office had been built after his death, in 1933. From the sixth floor, the CEO has a magnificent view all the way from St Paul's Cathedral, only a stone's throw away, to the huge Tate Modern museum, downriver on the other side of the Thames.

No. The story of Unilever mustn't end here. His story mustn't end here. Because right now they are one and the same. Over the past few years, it has become ever clearer to Polman that Unilever is a vehicle for him. It was only in this role that he had realised why he was put on this Earth. He needs to use Unilever to prove that multinationals play a crucial role in solving the big issues of the age. They have to contribute to solving the climate crisis and take responsibility for the enduring poverty in the world.

That's why he'd steered Unilever through a radical change of course. First, he had put a stop to quarterly results publications. Then, in the Unilever Sustainable Living Plan (USLP), he had articulated exactly how Unilever was going to contribute to a more sustainable world. It was a plan with a spectacular 10-year horizon. He promised that by 2020, Unilever would double in size while at the same time halving the environmental impact of producing and consuming its products.

In recent years, he had positioned himself ever more explicitly in opposition to the ways of thinking that dominated the stock market, the approach taken by financial analysts. Not once in those eight years had they asked him a single question about the ambitions or achievements of his USLP. Due to the dominance of short-termism on the financial markets, multinationals have failed to do what they are on this Earth to do: devise solutions for humanity's future needs. Not doing so has placed the world and its ever-growing population at huge risk.

The crisis of 2008 had convinced him that the one-sided, financial analysis of the economy had become far too dominant, and the space for long-term, responsible entrepreneurship terribly limited as a result. The general public had started asking itself whether businesses and businessmen were actually serving the communities that had produced them and justifiably so. He knows what he's talking about. He spent many years poring over financial analyses, starting out as a financial controller at Procter & Gamble and ending up as chief financial officer by the time he left Nestlé in 2008. Back then, he decided he would no longer be dominated by that way of thinking. This was his great battle, a fight for the soul of capitalism.

Obviously, he realised that Unilever couldn't change the system that radically on its own. He'd expended an enormous amount of energy trying to get other companies to join his cause. But more than anything he had tried to gain the trust of governments and NGOs. These kinds of cooperative relationships were the only means by which a company could directly contribute to making the economy more sustainable. This was what inspired him. It was in this world, completely alien to him at first, that he'd learnt his most important lessons.

At the invitation of the United Nations, he had helped to establish the 17 new Sustainable Development Goals (SDGs). He'd worked flat out to get the Paris Climate Agreement off the ground in 2015. He'd worked with the Pope on his *Laudato Si'* encyclical, thereby ensuring that Christ's representative on Earth had understood more clearly that the business sector was the one they needed to harness. Polman viewed himself as the CEO who, by doing all of this, had expanded the playing field for Unilever and the business world as a whole.

He'd had to overcome an avalanche of scepticism. Day in, day out. Inside *and* outside Unilever. He was constantly under suspicion in the financial world and in the media. He was accused of greenwashing. It was all just a marketing ploy, a gimmick for the zeitgeist.

On the other hand, he'd been widely applauded and enjoyed the enthusiasm and the recognition he'd received in the world of NGOs and charities. They regarded him as the first CEO to look ahead, the first they could really talk to. He had been presented with awards in a whole host of countries and by the United Nations, where he had been honoured as a 'Champion of the Earth', the highest award for people endeavouring to make the world more sustainable.

For years, everything had gone well. Unilever's revenues grew, the share price went up and, with some trial and error, the various goals of the USLP were being realised. Polman had long dreamed that the world would reach a turning point in 2016, that they would reach global agreements on the climate, the impact of CO_2 emissions, combatting poverty and promoting gender equality. And, because the company would have been following the goals of the USLP for several years by then already, Unilever would be ahead of the game and profit from the change.

But the world had gone down another path. The Brits had voted to leave the European Union and the Americans had elected Donald Trump president. Trump had gone so far as to withdraw the United States from the Paris Climate Agreement. Polman can't understand it. He feels like a citizen of the world. A citizen of the world who wants to solve the world's problems. Problems that will only keep getting bigger if people, companies and countries start focusing even more narrowly on their own, local interests. That would mean going backwards. Just like with Kraft Heinz, this 'every man for himself' mentality represents a way of doing business that is on its last legs. Why is it so difficult to persuade the world of this simple fact?

Polman looks at the papers laid out before him. He reads over Alexandre Behring's proposal one more time. As a group, his investors have extremely deep pockets. He stops at the name Warren Buffett. The world famous billionaire is probably the one putting up most of the capital, just as in their previous deals.

Polman realises that the next few days are going to be incredibly tense. Kraft Heinz has them at a disadvantage. The company has spent months preparing for this attack, taking its time to line up its resources ready to respond to any number of possible developments. British law also works in favour of the attacker. As soon as an offer has been made that might be of interest to Unilever's shareholders, the management are sidelined. The moment that happens, all kinds of short-term shareholders, mostly hedge funds, step in hoping to bring about a sudden increase in share price and ride the wave to instant profit. Unilever is also barred from talking to its own shareholders in order to convince them to take the side of the current management. In Polman's experience, Unilever will be fighting with one hand behind its back. As far as he is concerned, the British Takeover Code stimulates rather than prevents hostile takeovers. It is designed to assist the buyer and the seller in working together amicably to agree on a fair price. It gives them 28 days to reach an agreement. He hates the British rules.

Polman is under no illusions. His shareholders will go ahead and sell the moment they're offered enough money. Many of the bigger pension funds wax lyrical about the importance of sustainability but if anyone has disappointed him over the past few years it's been those same big investors. They are supposed to secure pensions and insurance policies over the long term but are ruled by short-term incentives. They'll sell their Unilever shares to a company like Kraft Heinz, shrugging their shoulders and saying that they need the returns in order to fulfil their fiduciary duty to provide decent pensions.

He's just finished saying as much to Dekkers. If Kraft Heinz raises their offer, to 35 per cent for example, Unilever is in serious trouble. They have to stop Unilever's shareholders from catching any whiff of those potential stacks of money. But how? Their advisors have already calculated that Kraft Heinz could finance a premium of 35 per cent. They could probably manage much more if they had to. And that isn't solely down to the enormous personal wealth of the four billionaires. Polman knows as much at this point. They can offer that amount because Unilever has relatively little debt on its books. They can add tens of billions of new debt by securing it against the company they're planning to buy.

Suddenly Polman realises. Unilever is going to fund much of this unwanted takeover itself. How has he allowed this to happen? This is a nightmare; it feels like a near-death experience.

Paul Polman looks at the signatures at the bottom of the proposal. He knows only one of the signatories personally. He saw Warren Buffett's name at the bottom of a very different letter eight years ago. Back then, the American billionaire was congratulating Polman on his decision to stop publishing quarterly results and start focusing on sustainable business practices. Polman had been tickled pink, reading the praise from one of the world's most successful investors aloud to various colleagues.

Is it possible Buffett doesn't realise what he's getting into here? Hadn't the American, then Kraft's biggest shareholder, criticised the company's $19 billion takeover of Cadbury's as a stupid deal? That was only seven years ago. Cadbury's is to Kraft what Marmite is to Unilever, a brand so British that nobody is allowed to touch it. Kraft hadn't kept its promise to keep open one of Cadbury's factories and guarantee jobs after the takeover. The name Kraft had been mud in the UK ever since.

For decades, the ageing investor had cultivated his image as an investor interested in long-term value. Hadn't Buffett repeatedly and very publicly claimed to be against hostile takeovers? Fundamentally opposed to them even? The older a person gets, the more sensitive they are about their legacy and their image. Surely that applies to him too? Why would Warren Buffett suddenly be in favour of hostile takeovers? Does that make any sense? Is he fully aware that he's about to get tangled up in just such a fight? Polman suspects the American is being naïve and placing too much trust in the Brazilians.

The Brazilians, meanwhile, have clearly got their teeth into Unilever and have no intention of letting go. But without the financial firepower of Buffett, they won't be able to pull this takeover off. The CEO of Unilever decides he is probably best off targeting the elderly American.

How much time does he have left? A week, maybe two? This is the fight of his life. If he doesn't find a way to keep Unilever out of Kraft Heinz's clutches then it will all have been for nothing. If he doesn't find a way then he will have failed. If he doesn't find a way then he won't have managed to prove that a big, publicly listed multinational like Unilever can do well by doing good.

PART 1

Doing Well and Doing Good, 1994–2007

CHAPTER 1

MEA CULPA, WE'RE COMPLETELY IN THE WRONG

1994–1998

'Whatever Unilever comes up with, we'll be the ones who sell it to the public around the world.' Paul Polman and his colleagues at Procter & Gamble like to make fun of their much larger competitor. The 37-year-old director of P&G's Spanish operation is baffled by the arrogant Dutch-British multinational. What are they playing at over there?

It's the beginning of the 1990s and companies like P&G and Nestlé are swiftly taking over the world. Brands like Fairy and Ariel or Maggi and Nescafé are being sold cleverly, efficiently and on a massive scale using international advertising campaigns. For years, Unilever has been failing to come up with a meaningful response. The company is run by know-it-all local managers, collectively responsible for keeping around two thousand relatively small brands up and running. This is also the reason they haven't managed to turn their takeovers of bigger brands like Calvin Klein, Elizabeth Arden and the US makeup brand Pond's into successes. Those brands demand a centralised, global strategy but there's no chance of getting anything like that off the ground at Unilever, which is hopelessly decentralised.

Polman finds it telling that Unilever calls its category managers based at its head office 'coordinators'. The terms reek of discussion and slow-moving bureaucracy. He often hears Unilever employees complain about the 'matrix' they're all trapped in. This is the complicated mechanism that divides responsibility for results between the regional managers and the category managers. They spend a lot of their time complaining. The Brits, focused on making money from cleaning products like Dove and Surf, moan about the other side of the company. There, Dutchmen make up the majority, with a focus on food products like Blue Band margarine and the Dutch smoked sausage brand Unox. They in turn don't think the Brits grasp the first thing about food.

Food and care, Unilever's two biggest markets, are worlds apart to the marketers. By their reckoning, the decision to buy something to rub into your skin is dominated by the rational, left side of the brain. What you eat is a question of taste and nutrition, that's a more emotional issue and decisions are made using the right side of the brain. So why doesn't Unilever choose one or the other? Whenever analysts ask that question, Unilever gives the same answer: the two belong together, all the products are fast-moving consumer goods and they're mostly sold using the same retail channels, in particular supermarkets.

At Unilever, a great deal of energy goes into trying to keep a whole series of complicated relationships in balance. The company has a peculiar structure, which can only be explained through its history. Sixty-five years on from the merger, the firm still consists of two companies. The Dutch NV and the British PLC each have their own chairman and their own board but the two boards each consist of the same 12–15 people. Their meetings alternate between Rotterdam and London.

Polman can see why the most cherished dream of his counterparts at Unilever is to be appointed manager of an important national market. The two-headed decision-making body means that a lot of power rests with the over one hundred and fifty countries in which Unilever operates. As long as they bring in enough money, the local managers can do pretty much what they please. Within the Unilever matrix they exploit the freedom they have to make their own decisions by investing in all kinds of things. The most important central monitoring of these local operations takes place via financial reporting.

Over at Procter & Gamble, things are completely different, the whole operation rests on strict, hierarchical leadership from company headquarters in Cincinnati. Plans are constantly being devised centrally on how to speed up growth and consolidate power in order to beat their competitors around the world. Everyone has clearly defined duties and is held to account on how they perform them. Those who do well are able to advance quickly. The American company has only been active in Europe for 30 years but it's conquering markets across the region one by one. Successful managers like Paul Polman are the ones leading the way.

Some Unilever managers, particularly the young ones, are jealous of the speed of what they regard as P&G's state-of-the-art marketing machine. But most of them simply shrug at the might of the Americans. Unilever is still the 'university of marketing' in their eyes, anyone who makes it in fast-moving consumer goods can sell anything. At almost €4.8 billion their advertising budget is the biggest in the world. They aren't too worried about the competition. The population of the world is growing and growing wealthier, there will always be demand for trusted food and hygiene brands. Thanks to the colonial pasts of both of its 'motherlands', Unilever is also deeply rooted in developing economies. This local connection is one of Unilever's greatest resources and it views this as the key to its future success.

For many poor people, calling a doctor is simply too expensive. In order to avoid getting sick, they tend to buy the slightly more expensive, branded items Unilever sells. They trust these tried and tested products more than the locally produced alternatives. Furthermore, there are still billions of people in those countries who have yet to even see certain products like roll-on deodorant. Unilever can be the one to introduce them. The numbers for 1994 show an increase in turnover and profit. An annual turnover of around €38 billion is yielding them a profit of around €3 billion. Enough to invest *and* to give the shareholders a slightly higher dividend each year.

The numbers are impressive. But the analysts who follow the sector on behalf of big banks remain unconvinced. They compare the results with those of various other key players in the market. According to their spreadsheets, Unilever is being outperformed by Procter & Gamble, which may be somewhat smaller, with a turnover of around $30 billion, but is almost twice as profitable.

This worries Niall FitzGerald. The ambitious 49-year-old coordinator of washing powders is an atypical Unilever man. The son of a customs officer and a journalist, he had been a member of the Communist Party once upon a time. When a friend was asked to find potential candidates for interviews with Unilever, FitzGerald went along to talk to the company. To his astonishment, he was hired. The Irish Catholic had gone on to advance quickly on the financial side of the company, surrounded by Brits who had mostly studied at Oxford and Cambridge.

The Dutch treat him like a Brit but the fact that he, like them, comes from a small country also means that he can step back and view the often tense Dutch-British collaboration impartially. There's a lot of mistrust behind the veneer of consensus. In FitzGerald's opinion, this lack of trust is caused by his colleagues constantly searching for the other side's hidden agenda. Even though there are continuous discussions and meetings, the various sections of the company – marketing and research being a prime example – often don't work very well together.[1]

The Brits and the Dutch don't see eye to eye. The Brits' biggest issue with people from the 'Low Countries' is that they're too direct; sometimes their bluntness borders on rudeness. They wonder whether the Dutch ever take the time to think about things properly. Dutchmen tell you what they think, expressing themselves loudly and clearly, but they don't seem to realise that this isn't always the most effective approach.

For their part, the Dutch don't trust the British because, in contrast, they never say what they really think. Their British colleagues think it's completely normal to take a decision that's already been made and unmake it step by step once it comes to taking action. When a British colleague says he thinks a proposal is 'very interesting', that usually means that it can go straight in the nearest bin as far as he's concerned. They always *sound* interested and polite but they aren't honest. Whenever they confront them with this dishonesty, they always smile politely and explain that they *are* honest, they're just economical with the truth.

The Brits often give the impression that they think Dutch people are stupid. At least, that's how the Dutch feel. In reaction to this, the Dutch often make furious attempts to get through to the arrogant Brits, an outspokenness that the British regard as vulgar.

At London head office in particular – which, incidentally, the British regard as the only *real* head office – the Dutch are a tightknit club. They feel as if they're constantly having to hold their own against the domineering Brits. One thing that frustrates many of the Dutch is the British ability to spin. The classically educated ones in particular, of which there is no shortage at Unilever, have been trained to command a room with charm, expressing themselves clearly and theatrically. However good their English is, none of the Dutch colleagues can keep up. Sometimes they can't help but switch into Dutch. In response, the Brits then start using their most obscure vocabulary in an effort to shut their Dutch colleagues out of the conversation. Only a handful of them have bothered to learn any Dutch themselves. Language is a perennial handicap. Because it's their native language, the Brits tend to take on the role of secretary during the meetings then go off and write their own summaries of what happened.

The 'top-down' tone of all this is often poorly received by the Dutch. The Brits haven't got a clue about so-called *polder* model, the Dutch culture of discussion and negotiation. They don't understand all the meetings with business associations and their Dutch colleagues' desire to maintain good relations with trade unions. They view unions as the enemy, not to be trusted. All they do is go on strike.

This underlying lack of understanding and tendency towards distrust doesn't help a complicated matrix organisation that requires people's constant sign-off on things. All local Unilever operations are divided between the NV and the PLC, but sometimes they both have a part interest. The total interest of the NV, which falls under Dutch law, has been 55 per cent ever since the companies joined back in 1929. That makes it quite a bit larger than the PLC, which operates under British law. Among the factors that determine which side of the company a daughter company falls under is the colonial past of the country in which it operates. Revenue and profit in Indonesia fall under the NV, the Indian results fall under the PLC. A complex set of rules – the so-called equalisation agreement – ensures that any discrepancies are compensated and the two sides constantly brought into line with one another. The agreement exists to make sure that the shareholders in both companies are treated equally. If it turns out that too little profit is being made on the PLC side to pay the shareholders the same dividend as those on the NV side, the PLC has to borrow money and transfer over a section of the NV so that the profit made there can compensate for the shortfall. For years there has been a great deal of criticism, particularly from analysts and investors, about the lack of transparency concerning results. They think that the company's agility and ability to invest big are being compromised by this system. Unilever always has to pay for new takeovers in cash because it's pretty much impossible to pay in two different sets of shares. Analysts often say it would be better for all concerned if they were to split the company back into two. But the moment this suggestion is made, the Brits and the Dutch start clinging to one another fiercely. Unthinkable!

Despite the moaning and the mutual distrust between them, both sides also recognise that they've complemented one another very effectively for decades. The Brits are good at making plans and discussing in detail what needs to happen. And by the time they are halfway through talking, the Dutch have started taking action. The Dutch are the ones who implement the plans. They know that they benefit from the size and clout of the Brits – their powerful history and their Commonwealth. The access they have to many of the world's markets is a real advantage.

Another practical thing that helps employees of both nations is the simple fact that they share their adventures abroad. Far away from London and Rotterdam, they have to rely on one another. They also share the same appreciation of humour: they know how to laugh at themselves and therefore at each other. They come together in times of stress. Finally, it also helps that more and more managers of other, different nationalities have joined them at the discussion table over the past ten years.

Despite the endless complaining, the majority of the leadership is made up of so-called lifers. These people have worked at Unilever since the beginning of their careers. Unilever is their club. The managers, both the Brits and the

Dutch, have grown up together. Often, they know each other from the student clubs they were in at university, a few of them even lived in the same fraternity house or were in the same class. Some move up the ranks more quickly than others and find that all the shared history they have with their inferiors makes it difficult to bring a business-like tone to this lifelong friendship. Finding the courage to fire a friend who is underperforming is even harder. This means the whole culture is geared around keeping the delicate peace, a constant effort to keep the Brits and the Dutch on the same page.

Those at head office try to nurture this sense of an informal club. It's the glue that holds the company together. Whenever one of the managers, who are scattered all over the world, comes to London, they roll out the red carpet. They fly first class, bringing their whole family with them if they need to. In London, they mostly set up camp at the five-star Grosvenor House Hotel, with their own suite, a stocked fridge and assistants to help them make reservations at restaurants and book theatre tickets. They are driven to these dinners and events in the company Bentley.

The top 100 managers at Unilever are pretty much all the same type of happily married man. They would certainly get some funny looks if they arrived at one of the many social events that accompany company meetings without their wife in tow. Is something amiss? Surely such a challenging career requires both of you to take active part?

They are ambitious men constantly in need of new challenges. The question of who the best person is for a particular position is often fiercely debated. Whenever a Brit is appointed in a top role, the Dutch think they have a claim to the next top role and vice versa. Giving managers new and ideally slightly bigger responsibilities every three or so years keeps them loyal to head office.

The unspoken rule, therefore, is that you attend all the little parties marking new appointments and retirements. The fact that this sometimes requires you to spend 20 hours on an airplane doesn't come into it: you're here! Seeing each other regularly in informal settings means the connection is constantly reinforced. It also helps to know that they can always find a nice, cushy spot for you in the safety of the company even if you don't perform quite so well. This is how they, the Margarine Union and the Lever Brothers, have built a colossus, ever since 1929.

Niall FitzGerald's detergents operation represents 22 per cent of Unilever's annual turnover. But the company lost its position as market leader back at the beginning of the 1990s, even in the Netherlands. In the European detergent market, worth around €7.5 billion, it is Procter & Gamble, established in 1837 through a collaboration between candle manufacturer William Procter and soap maker James Gamble, that rules the roost. Its global brands and dubbed-over adverts seem unstoppable. Because the laundry market is barely growing at all anymore, the increase of market share for one means a loss of market share for the other. Ariel (P&G) in particular now represents 15 per cent of the market in Europe and is almost twice as big as Unilever's Omo-Persil.

All this means that Niall FitzGerald needs a win and right now he's excited about what he regards as a revolutionary discovery. One of Unilever's four large laboratories, Port Sunlight in the UK, has developed a new, organic molecule. This bleach catalyst, which they're calling the 'Accelerator', contains the metal manganese. It allows laundry to be cleaned thoroughly at lower temperatures. To great media fanfare, Unilever announces that it is going to bring about a revolution in the world of detergents. The new washing powder will be called Persil Power in the UK and Omo Power in the Netherlands.

This needs to be a revolution on several fronts because FitzGerald wants to roll out the new washing powder across the whole of Europe more or less simultaneously. Since all of Unilever's local, national managers can feel the Americans breathing down their necks, they agreed. FitzGerald gave the whole operation the codename 'Winnipeg': 'winning over P&G'. A successful roll-out is important to him on a personal level too. The Irishman is about to step up as the 'third man' in Unilever's highest decision-making body, the three-headed Special Committee. This 'third man' eventually takes over from one of the two omnipotent chairmen, in his case as chairman of the PLC.

The small Dutch market will be the first to try out the new washing powder. Omo Power is announced there with big claims. It's concentrated, clothes come out clean at lower temperatures *and* it's environmentally friendly.

Stef Kranendijk swings into action immediately. The director of Procter & Gamble Benelux ships hundreds of boxes of Omo Power to their laboratory in Belgium. What is this stuff? After two days of washing his colleagues can't believe their eyes. Washing at 30 degrees is fine but at higher temperatures clothes are worn to shreds after 30 or 40 wash cycles.

Ed Artzt, the CEO of Procter & Gamble, calls FitzGerald immediately. The arch enemy of Unilever wants the company to stop selling Omo Power without delay. With each 10 degree increase in temperature, the chemical reaction caused by the bleach catalyst happens twice as fast. At higher temperatures, it doesn't only oxidise the dirt, it directly attacks the fabric. The effect is dramatic. People will literally wash their clothes to pieces. And because they regularly change the brand of washing powder they buy, they could easily think it is being caused by Ariel. Artzt tells FitzGerald that he's worried it will cause enormous damage to the whole industry.

When his call doesn't have the desired effect, Artzt and his colleague Roel van Neerbos, P&G's European head of detergent marketing, decide to take a suitcase full of damaged clothes to Unilever's head office in London. They'll show them in person what their powder is doing.

FitzGerald's reaction is restrained. None of this is true, they do good work here at Unilever. Around 9,000 scientists spend over €700 million a year carrying out their own research, much of it of the same quality as academic research. The products are also tested rigorously before going to market. There's nothing wrong with Omo Power, the Americans are just jealous of Unilever's discovery. FitzGerald has also just read the recent, provocative book *Soap Opera* by the *Wall Street Journal* writer Alecia Swacy. In it, she portrays Procter & Gamble as an extremely aggressive player that doesn't shy away from breaking the rules of fair competition. The book gives Ed Artzt, the darling of financial analysts thanks to his doubling of P&G's profits, the nickname Prince of Darkness. FitzGerald is determined not to let Artzt intimidate him. This visit has done nothing but confirm his suspicion that their competitors are crapping their pants: we're onto a winner, full steam ahead!

Stef Kranendijk is pleased when a journalist from the Dutch broadsheet *Het Algemeen Dagblad* contacts him to ask whether Procter & Gamble really believes Omo Power ruins clothes. After consulting with his legal team, he goes on the offensive. Kranendijk thinks it's outrageous to mislead the consumer, who will have trouble spotting the harmful side effects because they only occur after 15–40 washes. He suspects Unilever of taking this risk deliberately, hoping that the consumer will have got their use out of the garment by then.

The headline the next day is 'War of the Washing Powder'. In the article, the head of Unilever Netherlands Willem Selman defends himself: 'Omo Power allows you to wash even more thoroughly at lower temperatures. That is crucially important to the environment. It's our discovery and I can imagine that others in the market are nervous about it.' Unilever has calculated that 60 per cent of CO_2 emissions from washing detergents are caused by consumers washing their clothes at too high a temperature.

But Selman also admits that Unilever hadn't given much thought to the quality of the washed items. The 'tensile strength test', intended to see whether textiles are affected by new powders, wasn't carried out. They only looked at 'washing effect' because, according to Selman, 'damage to the weave simply isn't a problem anymore'. Selman says they are considering taking legal action against their competitor.

News of the story soon goes global, the media embraces the 'soap opera'. After years of being bombarded by infuriating taglines like 'whiter than white' and 'now even cleaner' they take a certain pleasure in announcing the news. The dirtier the fight, the better.

And it does get dirty. Two weeks after the news comes out, P&G sends a stack of photos of damaged clothes out to all the country's biggest media outlets. To his horror, Willem Selman is not only confronted with these dramatic photos the next day in the paper but finds they've sent him his very own package of ruined clothes.

The photos spread all over Europe. Paul Polman is tasked with sending the dramatic images to the Spanish media. He thinks his bosses are reacting rather rashly to the whole situation. But a job's a job and he knows that only 30 per cent of the consumer base is loyal to one washing powder. As soon as a competitor's washing powder offers something new – and they do so constantly – the customers switch over. And because the manganese stays on the clothes, customers could start thinking that the damage to their fabrics was caused by the last thing they washed with, including Ariel. It's this crossover effect they need to avoid.

Polman is in dire need of some success anyway. Procter & Gamble's activities in Spain are a source of worry to the company. He has been tasked with reversing the fortunes of the now practically bankrupt operation. This campaign could help him do just that. It will allow P&G to show that it has the interests of the Spanish consumer at heart.

The situation for Unilever soon becomes hopeless. Only a couple of months after releasing its 'revolutionary discovery', Unilever decides to withdraw it from the market. They are forced to write off the €350 million invested in R&D. Even worse: customer confidence has been dented. And trust is Unilever's greatest asset. A bigger setback is scarcely conceivable. The self-confidence of many Unilever employees is suddenly faltering. How could this happen? Everyone immediately starts pointing fingers. The researchers blame the marketers but they blame them right back. At Rotterdam head office the Dutch blame the Brits; they even fantasise about splitting the company.

With all eyes on the failed launch of the new washing powder, hardly anyone outside the company notices that Morris Tabaksblat has taken over as chairman of the Dutch NV. He and the British PLC boss Michael Perry are now at the head of a company of over three hundred thousand employees. Tabaksblat is taking over from Floris Maljers, another lifer. The two men have known each other for almost thirty-five years.

Ever since the 1980s, Maljers has been aware of the growing pity with which those in the dominant US business culture have begun to regard Unilever. They don't understand the company and view it as a half-finished merger. This

means they often wondered whether the company, or rather the two companies, wouldn't be more valuable as separate entities. At times, Maljers even
thought he saw signals that Unilever was high on the list of some of the big
American takeover specialists' lists of potential targets. He expresses these concerns in a farewell interview with the Dutch broadsheet *NRC Handelsblad*, 'It
seems the only thing that offered us protection was the unusually complex legal
structure, which goes back to the original Dutch-British contracts of 1929. But
that barrier could have been overcome. We were in the remarkable position of
having such a big financial reserve that anyone who bought Unilever for market value plus a takeover premium would have been able to cover a substantial
part of that sum with our own money'.

Maljers believes Unilever has to be more decisive. He spent years worrying about a culture in which local managers were allowed free rein and poor
results weren't addressed. A strategic reorientation is needed in order to create more focus and discipline in the company.[2] Maljers has spent the last ten
years making sure that the firm concentrated on four areas: food, detergents,
personal care products and specialist chemicals. By doing so, he had forced
Unilever to shed numerous operations initiated by the powerful local managers. These ranged from the manufacture of curtains in Scotland to a ferry
service between the UK and the Dutch seaside resort of Scheveningen, paper
factories in Germany, cookbooks in Switzerland, a cruise line in Nigeria and
duty-free shops in the Arabian Gulf States. All of them were sold off.

His successor Tabaksblat wants to keep pushing forward with these
reforms. He also thinks Unilever is a victim of its own conservatism. At the
more responsive Procter & Gamble they focus more closely on what markets
and cultures have in common, rather than the differences between them. They
also place much greater emphasis on technological solutions for those overlap-
ping customer needs. Moreover, poorly performing managers are dealt with
extremely harshly at their American competitor: they are often asked to leave
the company.

The new chairman knows that there are those inside Unilever who look at
Procter & Gamble's financial success with a certain amount of jealousy. But
they also enjoy saying that you have to be a robot – a 'Proctoid' – in order to
work there. Fifty-seven-year-old Tabaksblat, a marketer by training himself, is
glad that Unilever makes space for truly creative people. 'His' company has a
much more playful culture than Procter & Gamble and he likes that.[3] But the
new chairman also thinks his colleagues tend to give up on things too easily.
Issues are left unaddressed. He's jealous of the perseverance of the staff at P&G.
The organisation is like a terrier, the people there refuse to let anything go

until the job is done. Tabaksblat wonders whether the time has come to look critically at their own way of working and chain of command.

The fact the Americans managed to scupper Omo Power has done more than just injure the pride of marketers like Tabaksblat. If anything, the pain felt by many Unilever researchers goes much deeper. One of their number, Hans Broekhoff, is terribly disappointed. The director of detergent research at the Unilever Research Laboratory in Vlaardingen had been enormously proud of the new invention they'd come up with in collaboration with their British colleagues at Port Sunlight. Their team of 200 had spent three years working on it. The goal was to produce an environmentally friendly washing powder. After all, washing clothes properly at a lower temperature means an enormous energy saving. This is exactly what the world needs. In 1994, the same year they are forced to remove Omo Power from the shelves, 'sustainability philosopher' John Elkington sums up the priorities of the future in his three 'P's': People, Plants, Profit. The British business expert had himself been inspired by the Rio Conference two years earlier. In their 'Agenda 21', heads of governments had declared that humanity was at a 'defining moment in history'. Will we continue to allow the gap between rich and poor to grow, to exploit our natural resources and endanger our ecosystem? Or will we resolve to develop the world economy in a sustainable way? That is the challenge facing Unilever's 1,200 researchers.

In terms of the work it does, the R&D department at Unilever is comparable to a university. They even carry out fundamental scientific research. According to the researchers, this depth is crucial because every claim Unilever's marketers make, whether it be about food or care, has to be backed up. You can't mess around. If, for example, you want the support of the medical establishment for ProActiv then you need your own, rigorous research to back up the health claims you are making. You can't buy that kind of support, doctors demand hard evidence.

This is why, for a long time, it was a hard and fast rule that marketers didn't have too much direct contact with researchers. Otherwise they could sway them with short-term concerns like market share and margin. This rule has come under increasing pressure over the last few years, much to the chagrin of Broekhoff and his colleagues. The researchers have also noticed that they are being invited to present their findings to the board much less frequently than in the past. In 1987, research was separated and brought under the various divisions and product groups in order to be able to respond to the market more quickly, placing researchers closer to the market and the marketers. The upshot of this was that the coordinators of the various product groups had been given much greater say over the research being conducted under their auspices. This meant that marketers, who had always been very demanding, now had easy access to the researchers. They could go to them directly whenever they were feeling under pressure from the competition and demand they renew their products. They demanded renewals they could market easily, renewals that could put them ahead of the game. Omo Power had been one of the outcomes of this system.

The researchers now feel that their own company's marketers are making them look like idiots. A man like Broekhoff of all people knows that the new washing powder damages clothes when used at a high temperature. More than that, he ordered the tests himself: after a hundred wash cycles at higher temperatures, all that was left of the socks they'd used were the heels and toes, the rest had been shredded to pieces. The researchers in Vlaardingen had spent the months leading up to the Omo Power launch worrying about the fact that their own wash tests had shown that the powder caused wear at higher temperatures.[4]

Broekhoff had made certain that the test results were shared with England. Various colleagues confirmed that he had pretty much pleaded with the marketers over there not to sell the washing powder with the claim 'suitable for all temperatures'. A colleague who wished to remain anonymous tells *NRC Handelsblad*, 'the whole development of Omo Power took place with a single goal in mind: developing a totally environmentally friendly washing powder. That was our mission and that means you expect it to be presented as such. To our grave disappointment, that didn't happen. The marketing department tried to pitch it to the whole market, which was wrong. They failed to play the environment card and should have settled on the low temperature angle. The failure has blown back on the whole lab'. The proud R&D laboratory, the place where innovation is supposed to come from, went up against the marketers who, under pressure from their competition, forgot all about the interests of the consumer.

Shortly after the Omo Power scandal, Niall FitzGerald confronts the managers responsible. He looks at the 31 sombre, worried faces and makes a calculation. Between them they have almost a thousand years of marketing and R&D experience when it comes to washing powder. A thousand years! All those involved in Omo Power at management level are in the boardroom at London head office for a post-mortem. The charismatic Irishman tells them that none of them will be leaving the room until they get to the bottom of what went wrong. How is it possible that the great and powerful Unilever got it so wrong?

Regardless of the 'who' and the 'why', one thing is abundantly clear: customers don't read the small print on packaging. It's been proven that they barely look at the instructions on how much washing powder to use or what temperature to wash on. They discuss this for hours, why didn't they know that? Why had they been so blind as to push a washing powder that washed so spectacularly thoroughly that it didn't only remove dirt but destroyed their customer's entire garment?

Then FitzGerald has a flash of inspiration. He asks all those present which of them washes their own clothes. He goes first, admitting frankly that he, at least, does not. None of his colleagues put their hands up. Nobody here washes their own clothes. This is when the penny drops. They realise that the whole time they were developing Omo Power they never heard the most important voice because the customer hadn't been included in the process.

FitzGerald believes that he's the one responsible for the biggest marketing blunder in the history of Unilever. He offers his resignation to the British *PLC* chairman Michael Perry. Perry, however, doesn't want to hear another word. He tells FitzGerald that Unilever has invested £350 million in his training, if the young upstart thinks he can simply take this huge investment and go to a rival firm then he's got another thing coming. Now it's time to earn back the loss, Perry says. Get to work!

Robert Polet is pleased that FitzGerald is being allowed to stay. Unilever needs to show more grit if it wants to stay afloat and keep up with companies like Procter & Gamble. Just like Niall FitzGerald, the director of Van den Bergh & Jurgens is frustrated by the lack of entrepreneurial spirit he sees around him. Back in 1992, Polet wanted to start selling liquid margarine. It's healthier because it contains less solidified (trans)fats *and* it's easier to use, you don't get your fingers dirty. But when he tried the official channels, his plans fell at the first hurdle. His bosses thought it was all much too risky. Polet immediately resolved to carry on working on the idea in secret. In a small back room at the factory in Rotterdam, he set up a machine that would produce liquid margarine. He and his colleagues market tested the product they created very carefully. It had to stay under the radar. By the time his bosses got wind of it, the market research results were strong enough for Polet to get permission to bring the new product to market. It became a runaway success.

However, that success by no means meant they were any more willing to listen to Polet now. His suggestion that Unilever should start selling products directly and more quickly to consumers on the fast-growing internet almost cost him his job. The top brass at the company is terrified of Unilever's direct customers, the big retailers. If they found out their supplier was trying to bypass them, the claws would come out. Big retailers like Ahold in the Netherlands and Tesco in the United Kingdom are Unilever's most important clients and Unilever's products have to reach the consumer via their shelves.

Polet isn't the only manager trying to get the message across to his colleagues that things need to change. Some approach the task in rather unconventional ways. Tex Gunning was appointed managing director of Unilever Meat Group in 1995. The 45-year-old accountant is one of the very few high flyers at Unilever who isn't a lifer, he started his career elsewhere. Gunning has been given the task of getting Unilever Meat Group back on track. The profitability of the operation is falling way behind the rest of the company. They're also dealing with a dramatic drop in quality which has already led to a couple of mass product recalls.

As he walks through the production hall, the new managing director can't believe his eyes. Some employees aren't doing anything at all, they just stand around the whole day polishing the machines. It's more like a social club than a place of work. For years, barely anything has been done in terms of training. Gunning immediately comes to the conclusion that they need to cut jobs, at least a quarter of the 1,200 people working there have to go.

He is furious with the previous management. What exactly have they been doing to train their employees or offer them a future? Leaving people to rot is completely immoral, what are they going to do when they wind up unemployed with zero job prospects? They've spent years twiddling their thumbs without any intervention. They've rested on their laurels and taken home a pay check without doing anything to earn it. It's as if they've completely forgotten what quality is. It seems as if the people here in Oss have been thinking 'we're the birthplace of Unilever, nobody can touch us', this whole time.

Gunning invites all 1,200 employees to join him on an excursion. As they board the coaches, some of them think they're being treated to a day out at a theme park. Instead, the buses stop in front of a massive warehouse. As they enter, they hear Mozart's Requiem echoing through the hall. The ghetto blaster is sitting on one of 3,700 pallets of rejected products stacked throughout the space. Leaking tins of sauce, reject sausages, gone-off soup. The stench is unbearable. Above each stack of pallets is a big sign stating the day these unsellable items were produced and whose shift it was. The value of the products, which are about to be incinerated, is printed in bold. Here €75,000, there €100,000, these are enormous sums. A total of around €2 million in unsellable items is about to be destroyed. One of the men in charge of production can't contain his emotions, he throws the ghetto blaster to the floor in a rage. The music stops.

But Gunning isn't scared. He doesn't believe that he has anything to fear so long as he speaks from the heart. He addresses the crowd from an improvised podium. He cuts a strange figure, bundled up in his lamb's wool sweater he doesn't exactly look like a managing director, let alone a managing director at Unilever.

As he speaks, his tone gets brighter. 'What a massive waste. Do you see it? Do you think of yourselves as skilled? Then how is it possible that you produce such poor quality?' He asks the distraught workers to take a walk around the stinking pallets and have a good look at what poor quality means. He wants them to feel it. He wants them to feel ashamed.

Most of the employees are at a total loss. What's this about? What's the point of all this? Don't they turn a decent profit every year? Why didn't anyone warn them they were coming here? Gunning makes it clear to them that the company is slowly but surely going belly up. They've been lazy and as a result the revenue, market share and profit margins of their various products have been falling year after year. The whole thing is their fault. How else have competitors like Campbell and Heinz been able to show double-figure growth over the past few years? Don't they realise that theirs is a massive responsibility? This is about feeding people. 'You're all people too', he shouts. 'Why don't you feel any real connection to what you're doing?'

In Rotterdam, there are many who can't understand why Niall FitzGerald hasn't been fired. A rumour is going round that the Irishman invited the British members of the board to his house to persuade them to secure his position as Perry's successor.

Tabaksblat understands why FitzGerald was saved. In his eyes, Omo Power was at least an attempt to do something new, the people involved stuck their neck out and tried doing things differently. Tabaksblat has no desire for revenge, they don't need a public hanging to make this right. Not least because FitzGerald is a symbol of entrepreneurialism at Unilever. Tabaksblat also believes that it's rarely if ever a case of people sabotaging things on purpose. It's usually the execution that goes awry.[5]

The Dutch chairman decides to focus on smoothing internal relations. But the blunder can't go completely unanswered. Perry and Tabaksblat decide that the planned promotion of FitzGerald to chairman designate, the so-called third man in the Special Committee will be postponed. First, he has to clear up the mess he's created. For the first time in the history of Unilever, there will be no third person in the Special Committee. This decision will have far-reaching consequences.

Over the past sixty years, this 'third man' has frequently been the one to ensure that the two captains at the helm of Unilever stayed on the same course.

Ever since 1929, the three-headed Special Committee has worked to prevent competitiveness from arising between the Dutch and the Brits. The two chairmen, who have thus far been a Dutchman and a Brit, take it in turns to chair the meetings of the board, which reports to the Special Committee.

Naturally, conflict is common. These men, these two egos, haven't ended up top dog by accident. It's down to the third man to defuse the conflict, he acts as a mediator between the two fighting cocks. He tries to synthesise their differing positions neutrally, invites them to take a breath or asks them to put themselves in the other's shoes. The third man is also usually the one who makes notes and manages to summarise a meeting or a discussion in a way that restores peace. He also runs the secretarial pool, which includes the chairmen's personal assistants. They ensure that everything is presented to their bosses just as he instructs.

In order for the Special Committee to work, they have to keep to one inviolable rule: what happens in the Special Committee stays in the Special Committee. Their discussions are a 'black box'. The two men speak to the rest of the world in one voice, even in meetings with the people who report to them. Those are separate meetings. They are never particularly long and have a strict agenda. Only one of the two chairmen addresses the meeting. The two other Special Committee members nod along but don't speak themselves. Interruptions from them are also unwelcome. Effectively, the other two bosses are only allowed to speak if the chairman asks for their opinion on something. This is how they preserve the unity of the Special Committee; no one is ever allowed to walk away from a meeting with the impression that the other chairmen could have a different opinion. The mere hint of discord between your superiors might give you the idea to go to one chairman with your plans and not the other.

By speaking with one voice, the two captains endeavour to make it clear that the Dutch-British firm is one company with one course plotted out for it. That's what they tell the dozens of managers working directly below them too: whether you work for the NV or the PLC, whether you're Dutch or British, whether you're on the food side or the care side of Unilever, you also have to address the world with one voice, no matter where you are or what's going on. We are the leaders because we set the right examples, as we have done for 65 years. This is the only reason Unilever is still here.

Not that people outside the company truly understand it. Who's in charge here? The Dutch media constantly implies that the head of the Dutch NV is the CEO of Unilever and the British chairman his right hand man, while the Anglo-Saxon media portrays the head of the PLC as the only real boss and the

Dutch chairman as second fiddle. Floris Maljers often used to complain that he had never managed to explain properly how the system worked. He used to use the example of a bumblebee, which has a big body and two tiny wings. Anyone looking at it might wonder how it manages to fly, but it does so regardless.

The fact is that this double structure which makes both chairmen board chairman *and* CEO is confusing to many, they can't figure out who the boss is. And even more importantly, they can't figure out who is keeping an eye on that boss.

Tabaksblat doesn't think this construction will be tenable for much longer. In 1992, a British commission under Sir Adrian Cadbury, the chairman of the chocolate empire of the same name up until 1989, drew up new guidelines on proper corporate governance. In England, a model of governance combining executive and non-executive directors, a so-called one tier board, has since become the norm. The most important rule of thumb in that system is that the role of board chairman and CEO can no longer be filled by the same person. Moreover, the board must have a majority of non-executive directors who keep a close eye on the executive directors, including determining how much they get paid.

It's clear to Tabaksblat that Unilever hasn't got these checks and balances in place. At the moment, nobody audits the three-man team in the Special Committee. All Unilever has eight-man 'Advisory Board' appointed by the top brass at the company. They sit in on meetings but have no formal powers or ability to intervene. When asked what exactly the advisory directors do, Maljers had always been clear: they give advice when we ask for it. Nobody has the power to bring the Special Committee to heel, let alone fire them.

But this is 1994, not 1929: something has to change. For his part, Tabaksblat would prefer to go over to a one-tier board: a governing body made up of a couple of executive directors and a majority of non-executive directors who share responsibility for all policy. The non-executive directors would monitor the directors involved in the direct, day-to-day running of the company.[6] Tabaksblat argues that more and more companies, even those in Europe, are bidding farewell to the collegial model of governance and starting to appoint a single CEO with ultimate responsibility for decisions. He situates this in a wider context of increasing individualism.[7] This development is being bolstered by the focus on creating shareholder value, which has for many years increasingly been the dominant paradigm.

The closer attention now being paid to daily changes in share price is creating a growing appetite for straightforward leadership with strong communication. A strong leader is the figurehead of the company. More and more CEOs are receiving a certain amount of media attention as a result; many of them even seek out this celebrity. Tabaksblat does not welcome this development. These star managers are believed to have all kinds of fabulous attributes and praised as miracle workers. If the adulation goes on for long enough, they start to believe their own hype, with all the attendant negative consequences. Even at Unilever, there's a risk of the two chairmen making themselves bigger and bigger, both externally and internally. There's a risk they'll try to become the face of the whole company. Tabaksblat often reflects on this. If that were to happen, the discipline necessary to keep on speaking as one and to give up the limelight in order to take on others' perspectives would be eroded. Doubly so if they were ever to find themselves in troubled waters. And as it stands currently, there would be no overseers to intervene if this were to happen.[8]

Tabaksblat hopes that a one-tier board will speed up the slow decision-making processes at the top of the company. But resistance from the old guard is enormous. They believe that both executive directors, the chairmen of the NV and the PLC, are needed to keep an eye on one another. In their view, this is the whole basis of the successful Dutch-British partnership. As it turns out, the advisory directors aren't particularly keen on taking on any actual responsibility either, they're happy as they are. They get paid handsomely and never have to put their name to any decisions.

Even so, Tabaksblat wants to find out whether Unilever would benefit from conforming to the norm. The lack of any controls on the Special Committee, also known to those at the company as the 'Holy Trinity', isn't healthy. Tabaksblat asks FitzGerald to join him in investigating the issue further.

In 1996, a Nominations Committee and a Remuneration Committee (later called the Compensation Committee) are created at FitzGerald's suggestion. The advisory directors who sit on these committees still don't dare make the transition to a single CEO and a supervisory chairman of the board. They do, however, scrap the role of the third man and replace it with a group of five directors: a category director of food, a category director of home and personal care (HPC), a financial director, a personnel director and a director of strategy and technology. The Special Committee is renamed the Executive Committee.

From now on the 14 'Business Group Presidents' will report to this Executive Committee. Each president will be responsible for the results in their branch of the company. Five of them take care of the two biggest markets, the United States and Europe, which represent 70 per cent of turnover. The rest of them are responsible for the development of the various categories. From now on, the company will be focused on two product groups: food and HPC. They decide to sell off the chemicals division.

To the frustration of many, the 30 years' worth of tensions caused by the matrix remain unaddressed. The chairmen apologise for this in the media. 'Sadly, life is complicated', Perry says. However, colleagues in Rotterdam are pleased Tabaksblat is still there to keep an eye on FitzGerald, who has been appointed *PLC* chairman after a year in the sin bin. He is a much more experienced chairman and able to keep him in check.

A number of Tabaksblat's direct colleagues express concern about the new system, however. Speaking with one voice was just about possible for a three-person team but when the two chairmen, who still have final say, disagree in front of an audience of five colleagues it won't be as easy to keep it a secret. Having two captains and one ship has thus become considerably riskier. In terms of governability, Unilever may have gone from the frying pan into the fire.

The Dutch directors all agree that Tabaksblat's mission to create a more incisive board has stalled. The Omo Power scandal seems to be festering at the root of this too. They think Tabaksblat lost too much of his goodwill and sway in London by apologising for the scandal during a press trip to China. The trip was supposed to have been about China; Unilever had started making some tentative investments there. Yet when the usually guarded Tabaksblat had found himself sitting next to the China boss Alexander Kemner on their tour bus, he hadn't been able to resist talking about Omo. Tabaksblat had gone on to rail against Niall FitzGerald, who had been initially unwilling to admit publicly that Unilever was at fault. Kemner had gone so far as to warn his boss to keep his voice down in the midst of so many journalists, many of whom could speak Dutch. When he was asked what he thought about the Omo Power affair at a press conference a couple of hours later, Tabaksblat decided to be honest: Unilever had been in the wrong.

Colleagues over in Rotterdam believe that 'their' chairman's unprompted mea culpa has restored the unity of Unilever. In London, they see things rather differently. A Dutchman apologising for British shortcomings? It's unforgiveable.

Meanwhile, the Dutchmen over at Procter & Gamble are doing rather well. They have the most 'level 6' positions at the company after the Americans, 10 of the top 300 are Dutch. To Paul Polman this is only logical. From an American perspective, the Dutch aren't all that foreign. They speak good English and seem to have embraced the Anglo-Saxon market philosophy enthusiastically ever since the fall of the Wall. P&G Europe head office is also in the Benelux.

The Dutchmen at P&G all know one another and keep a close eye on each other's careers. After meetings, they all go for a drink. The most successful of them is Durk Jager from Friesland; people say he could be the first foreigner to become CEO of the American behemoth.

Stef Kranendijk likes Paul Polman a lot. Between 1984 and 1987, he worked closely with his Catholic countryman, from the town of Enschede in Twente. He was a marketing manager, Polman was a financial manager. Polman produced the financial models for all the plans Kranendijk was tasked with making. Kranendijk had been struck back then by how keen Polman always was to discuss things and the sheer number of questions he asked. Most of his colleagues in the finance department simply wrote down whatever the marketers wanted from them and went off to do their calculations. Yet Polman, four years Kranendijk's junior, joined in actively with the thought process, wanted to know how marketing worked and tried to find out what made marketers tick. It was clear he wanted to understand the business from top to bottom. Kranendijk had advised Polman to transfer over to the marketing side of Procter & Gamble. It was an unwritten rule that you needed a good understanding of marketing if you wanted to become a managing director.

Polman had said goodbye to his career on the finance side of the company and made a sideways step into marketing. He was put in charge of the nappy brand Pampers in France. It was there he learned that marketing is almost like waging war. You're constantly grappling with your opponent. For example, he and marketer Roel van Neerbos had made a detailed plan of attack on how to usurp Pampers' market position from the perspective of their key competitor Kimberly Clark with the brand Libero. They'd come up with and modelled all possible scenarios, including their effects on the profit and loss calculation. That way they were well prepared to respond to any such attack as soon as it was in the offing. Van Neerbos can also see why Paul Polman is moving up the ranks so quickly. There are very few people who can process, analyse and retain such massive volumes of information. He's also very strong physically, he doesn't require much sleep and always works harder than everyone around him. Most importantly of all, a marketer who also knows the financial side of the company inside out feels like a pair of safe hands to an organisation like P&G.

To most of his colleagues, it's already clear that Paul Polman is on the fast track to the top. In 1996, after making Procter & Gamble's relative small, loss-making Spanish operation profitable again, he had been rewarded with the directorship of their British daughter company, a significant step up. England is P&G's biggest European market and contributes 50 per cent of their European profits.

His office is in Newcastle, a city with lots of heavy industry that played a central role in the Industrial Revolution before falling into decline. Thanks to the economic malaise of the 1990s, unemployment is at a record high. Polman's predecessor, Mike Clasper, is from the region and has spent the past few years setting up all kinds of initiatives designed to boost the economy. As the director of one of the biggest employers in the region, he sits on various boards pro bono, including one of the city's universities and the Newcastle Initiative, a public–private enterprise that invests in improving economic infrastructure. It's expected that Polman will take over these roles as well. So he does.

He immediately feels at home in the charitable sector. Polman, the second of six children, saw the way his parents always selflessly took up for other people. His father did a great deal of charity work, for example helping as many Turkish guest workers in Enschede as he could to fill in their tax return. That was the central message of his Catholic upbringing: always be there for others. And especially for those who have less than you do.

For a long time, his father had two jobs in order to support his family. He had to because when Paul's mother, a teacher, had fallen pregnant with her first child in the 1950s, she had been fired on the spot. That was the rule in those days. Polman still gets choked up whenever he thinks of his father. His role model and greatest hero was only 68 when he died suddenly in 1993. The man had literally worked himself into an early grave to ensure that all his children got the opportunity to go to university. How much he had taught him, how much he has to thank him for.

His father was on the church council, which meant that Polman joined the Catholic scouting organisation in the club house next to the church. Since he did so well at school, always getting top grades – a nine out of ten because, as the Dutch say, 'a ten is for God' – he became an altar boy and later chief altar boy. At home he would go on to build his own altar and pretend he was the priest. He would stand at the front, while his parents sat listening in the pews. One of his uncles, Father Valentinius, who lived in a monastery, often came to visit the family at home. At the age of 12, Paul decided he wanted to be a priest too. His parents supported his decision. For almost a year, he attended the minor seminary in Apeldoorn. It was cold there, Spartan. There weren't many other children. When he got homesick, his parents took him back to Enschede.

After that, he was expected to become a doctor and set out in pursuit of that goal. But despite his excellent grades he wasn't among the students selected for medical school in the annual government lottery. Keen to be well prepared for the year after, he brought all the medical textbooks he would need home and studied them alongside the work he was doing for his economics degree. He needed to study something, after all. However, after three years of not being picked for medicine, his father said enough was enough: he needed to start earning his keep. Polman junior had realised in the meantime that his employment prospects would be greatly enhanced if he continued his studies at an American university. During his undergraduate degree in economics it had become clear to him that the most important new ideas about business and the economy were coming out of the United States.

His father had agreed to help him once again. It turned out that one of his colleagues at the American-owned tyre manufacturer Vredestein, where he worked as an administrator, was prepared to offer his son a spare room in Cincinnati. Once he'd arrived there, Polman had immediately signed up for two postgraduate courses, Finance and International Marketing and Economics. During a module on 'Collective Bargaining with Unions' he had fallen head over heels in love with Kim Strauss, a music major three years his senior who was studying at the conservatory.

As his studies were self-funded, he worked evenings and nights as a Jack-of-all-trades at Procter & Gamble head office. He had always been driven by the desire to show his parents that their efforts hadn't been for nothing, even if he hadn't managed to become a doctor. Procter & Gamble, feverishly working on plans to best their European competition, had immediately offered the hard-working Dutchman a position as a cost analyst upon completion of his studies. He began working there full time in 1977.

When he finished his Master's, his father presented him with a gift, a small Delftware tile. He had a text inscribed on it: 'An economist is still just a normal person.' That little tile is still in a drawer in Polman's office. It's a variant of the saying he so often heard from his parents growing up: never forget where you come from. His mother still lives in the same house. He visits every month. Paul Polman knows exactly where he comes from.

The CEO of Procter & Gamble UK realises that by working for all these good causes here in Newcastle, he can be a little bit more like his father. It will change him from half a person into a whole person. He's a bit ashamed that it's taken him so long, he's almost forty now. But better late than never. From now on, he wants to be the kind of person who serves those who have less than he does. His father would have been proud of him.

CHAPTER 2

TWO CAPTAINS, ONE HELM

1998–2001

Antony Burgmans is mortified. Unilever is about to return $8 billion to its shareholders. How has it come to this? The company's revenue has dropped over 2 per cent in the 1998 financial year. Is there really nothing we can come up with to invest in so that we can grow the business? The fact that Procter & Gamble and Nestlé are still growing exponentially galls the *PLC* vice-chairman. The expansion of the Swiss is particularly irritating to him: they're a European company too, surely they have exactly the same mountain of red tape to contend with?

Many of Unilever's managers struggle with the same question. If we're as big and clever as we think we are, then why is this happening to us? Following the sale of Unilever's chemical operations, which had contributed over €4 billion in annual revenue, Burgmans thinks it's high time for a big acquisition to strengthen the company's food division. They're lacking the big brands there that could profit from Unilever's worldwide distribution network, which, after some trial and error, is now performing better and better on the HPC side of the company. For some time now, he has been lusting after Bestfoods, the US firm with brands like Knorr and Hellmann's. But he won't find any support for his dream. Tabaksblat for one wouldn't dare risk such a takeover, which would cost at least $20 billion, and the situation is not being made any easier now that the profit from the sale of the chemical operations, the $8 billion, is being handed over to the shareholders.

Burgmans has accumulated a tidy pile of shares himself at this point. He has no objection to supplementing his income but he does wonder whether they aren't overly focused on driving up shareholder value in the short term. The British side of the company in particular is placing ever more emphasis on this. Burgmans doesn't think a drastically variable remuneration scheme really suits

Unilever. Does being offered a bonus really make you work harder? It almost feels like an insult: Surely you always do your best? He recognises that there's no escaping it, however: the bonus system is too important to the Anglo-Saxon side of the company. Burgmans realises that he'll have his work cut out for him once he's taken over from the current Dutch chairman and joined Niall FitzGerald at the company's helm.

FitzGerald, meanwhile, is full of regret. Two years previously, he and Morris Tabaksblat promised the shareholders that if Unilever didn't manage to find a good use for the $8 billion within two years then they would get the money. And – surprise, surprise – all the companies they had investigated turned out to be 'too expensive', 'too complicated', 'too risky'; there had always been some reason not to invest. He would never make the same mistake again. Unilever had been hamstrung. In order to stop the tax authorities from taking a big chunk of the dividend, they made an arrangement with the inspectorate to return part of the money in the form of new preferred stocks that would remain on the market for at least five years. Whatever else happens, at least this will improve the share price.

FitzGerald notices that the explicit focus on creating shareholder value is causing a stir across the Atlantic. He's surprised by a call from Warren Buffett. The two men have known each other for some time. One of the world's most successful investors is considering taking a large share in Unilever. FitzGerald is buoyed by the news. When Buffet gets involved in something, it usually means a long-standing relationship and a great deal of money. That would do a lot of good, creating trust and peace of mind. The Irishman offers to lend Buffett any assistance he can. A couple of months later, however, Buffett calls back with the news that after careful consideration he has decided to increase his investment in the razor company Gillette instead. He goes on to joke that *that* market, at least, really *does* grow every day.

Within the company, the old guard in particular are worried. For decades, they'd barely spared a thought for shareholders and nobody had seriously concerned themselves with the share price. It was healthy, and so long as Unilever served its customers, employees and community with its products, the shareholders would have nothing to complain about. Case closed. Sure, sometimes they needed to have a bit of patience, and trust that Unilever would invest in the right things, but one way or another, they'd come up with enough money to pay the shareholders a tidy dividend: a dividend that would grow a little bit year on year.

So where is this creeping fear of shareholder ire coming from? The older lifers have only one explanation: the opportunistic, short-term mentality that is coming to dominate the stock markets. Shareholders transfer their capital with a single push of a button, thereby determining the share price's trajectory and, increasingly, the fate of businesses. It is as if the leadership of publicly traded companies are being given a daily report card. A declining share price is evidence of failing leadership and marks the company out as tempting prey for a hostile takeover and the swift replacement of said leadership.

Bankers and analysts encourage investors to behave in this way by drawing comparisons between companies and their competitors. Little lists appear at regular intervals, showing who's doing best. These days the end of each quarter sees those analysts complaining and making threats if the results aren't up to scratch. As a result, companies like Unilever are increasingly allowing themselves to be steered by the expectations of the financial markets. Any CEO forced to submit a revenue or profit warning because their company isn't going to meet its targets is already as good as gone. The golden rule on the stock market: you keep your promises.

Inside the company, a battle is underway between enthusiasm and distaste. There are a growing number of senior managers at Unilever who have a personal interest in rising share prices; they have become shareholders themselves at this point. For the last few years, their end-of-year salary summary has come with a lengthening list of regulations, explaining the implications of taking stock options or shares from their employer. For the past two years, they have been allowed to invest up to a quarter of their bonus in Unilever shares *if* they agree to retain those shares for five years. As shareholders, these employees want to be paid as handsomely as possible. It's their pensions – their nest eggs – that are on the line.

An 'outrageous example of shareholder capitalism'. This is what the GroenLinks (Green-Left) coalition speaker Paul Rosenmöller calls the share buy-back scheme in the Dutch media. He finds it incomprehensible that a company currently making swingeing cuts to its workforce, which has shrunk by tens of thousands, to 265,000, over the past couple of years, can be giving such a sum back to its shareholders. However, the growing emphasis on the creation of shareholder value can come as no great surprise even to the Left. Dutch listed companies have fallen under the spell of the markets in the recent years too. Some call it neoliberalism, others simply the 'Anglo-Saxon' model. Even huge Dutch banks like ABN AMRO and ING now identify increasing share price as their most important aim. The shareholder comes first. Give the markets free rein. Money is pouring into listed companies. In the previous year – 1997 – the number of Dutch households investing in the stock market increased by 21 per cent, to 1.9 million. That fact alone means that most share prices have risen. As a result, boardroom discussions increasingly revolve around satisfying the shareholder, mollifying the markets. As long as the share price arrow is pointing upwards, they have a license to operate.

Most politicians of a liberal stamp in the 'Purple Cabinet' (a Grand Coalition-style government made up of the social-democratic PvdA and the conservative-liberal VVD under Wim Kok) think this is a welcome development, thank you very much, and are itching to devise regulations that might stimulate this trend even further. As long as share prices keep going up and trust in the economy keeps growing, they'll reap the rewards at the next election.

In reality, what Unilever is doing is simply what has become the norm for most listed companies: tying the financial interests of its managers to the financial interests of its shareholders in the hope that this will spur them on to even greater efforts. The annual reports are focusing ever more explicitly on the approval of the shareholders and foregrounding the company's victories over competitors and other sectors on the stock market.

In the foreword to the 1997 Annual Report published in May 1998, Morris Tabaksblat and Niall FitzGerald excitedly confirm that Unilever has gone up another three places in their reference list of 21 companies. The list features the 20 largest manufacturers of comparable consumer products. When it comes to the 'total shareholder return score', the firm is in seventh place. They claim that 'the greater clarity of roles and responsibilities has led to a release of energy and vigour in the pursuit of improved competitiveness', citing, 'the new measures of value creation'. Offering colleagues more opportunities to participate in the financial growth of the company through stock options will remain a top priority.

This policy has the biggest impact at the top of the company, where more and more people are being paid in shares, and investing off their own bat. In 1996, the 20 top managers at Unilever made an equivalent of €300,000 from cashing in their annual stock options, but a year later the doubling of share prices means those profits are up to €7 million. 'Unilever top brass get stock options worth 1.5 million', scream the headlines of *NRC Handelsblad*. Tabaksblat and FitzGerald had each received 138,000 shares, worth 1.5 million guilders (€2.3 million) on paper. The newspaper sounds almost apologetic as explains to its readers that it is only able to report so precisely on the income of the Unilever management in the first place thanks to a British law. Tabaksblat is entirely at ease with this; he thinks the English system of oversight and accountability is better than the Dutch one.

Only a select few dare to stand against the tide. Jeroen Bordewijk, the man in charge of sustainability for the agricultural commodities arm of Unilever, thinks Tabaksblat is trying to exert too much influence using these financial incentives. Bordewijk, like many of the other mostly Dutch, lifers, values the 'soft' culture inside Unilever: it creates space for quality. By declaring the share price and other quantitative aims sacred, and by attaching all kinds of bonuses to them, the leadership is encouraging bad behaviour. Bordewijk informs his boss that some of the directors of Unilever's operating companies have been unable to resist adding part of the coming year's revenue to the current year's lagging figures in order to hit their targets and get their bonuses. Tabaksblat doesn't take this criticism well and bites Bordewijk's head off, but later sends him a personal letter in which he plays down his irritation. He promises to give the matter further thought and not to let it get out of hand. It's a dilemma for Tabaksblat. He truly believes that more transparency around results, translated into changes in share prices and reshuffles of the personnel responsible, will finally allow him to break open Unilever's antiquated old boys' club.

Being tasked with dismantling this old boy's culture is what finally persuades Arjan Overwater to make the move to Unilever in 1998. He initially had zero interest in joining the old-fashioned corporate club but Jan Peelen of the Executive Committee for Human Resources eventually persuades him to make the move from Coca Cola. He explains to him that the leadership under FitzGerald and Burgmans is about to need someone to translate their vision for the firm into concrete aims, roles and reward systems.

One of his first tasks is to identify how the top 100 employees are paid and analyse the true impact of variable remuneration. Overwater soon finds his prejudices confirmed. The Dutchmen at the top of the company have all known each other for 25–30 years, from the very beginning of their careers, and as such they all watch each other's backs. Precisely the same thing goes on among the Brits. He attributes this to the remuneration policy. On average, each of them gets between 16 per cent and 24 per cent of their salary in additional bonuses. This means that performance has barely any impact on pay.

Overwater suggests raising the bonus cap to 100 per cent and even awarding no bonus at all from time to time. Not everyone will thank him for this suggestion. The growing disparity in bonuses fuels a discussion of the criteria by which these bonuses should be awarded. They are all caught in the same dilemma: which results carry the most weight, the one for the country or region in which they operate, or the one for the category for which they are responsible? Is this really the best way to shake up the inward-looking, indulgent and somewhat lazy culture of Unilever?

'Sure, I'd love to', says Burgmans when Tabaksblat asks him if he wants to take the helm. Tabaksblat realises immediately that Burgmans, at least, believes he is the proper choice.[1] Tabaksblat is choosing this lifer because he proved during his time as managing director of European operations that he was willing to make difficult choices. By closing factories and cutting 20,000 jobs, he had managed to boost the profit margin from 2 per cent to 12 per cent. In Burgmans, Tabaksblat sees the decisiveness the company is sorely lacking. He is a striking, dynamic, solid man, a commanding presence both physically and in terms of his opinions. There is literally and figuratively no getting around him. Tabaksblat also knows that it will take a tough Dutchman to keep up with the charming but domineering FitzGerald. Besides which, Burgmans is a principled manager. He gets positively furious when faced with professional misconduct.

Burgmans and Niall FitzGerald begin their partnership in May 1999. Going forward, all of their decisions will be made together. On one matter they are already entirely agreed: the company is too complex and too fragmentary for proper management, meaning that they are falling further and further behind their competition as a result. The Unilever share price is 30 per cent lower across the board compared to Nestlé and Proctor & Gamble. Anyone who bought shares in Unilever three years previously, in 1995, has essentially made nothing apart from the dividend, while the AEX index – the Dutch stock exchange index – has doubled over the same period.

The august institution of Unilever is increasingly being written off as a company from a bygone era. It doesn't help that investors' heads are being turned by the young, vibrant IT sector. The internet promises a whole new economy while investors see Unilever as an impenetrable conglomerate of companies, which, by definition, means lower value. They also view it as badly run. The top brass find themselves asking: Does the real talent still want to come work for us?

In the early days of their collaboration, Burgmans and FitzGerald struggle with a lack of clear roles, direction and coordination. The thousands of managers under them are primarily concerned with feathering their own nests. The ones that *are* go-getters limit their efforts to their own, local contexts. It's as if they are continuously circumventing the overall system and the overall aims of the company through an informal network. They let each other get on with things undisturbed, don't challenge each other's poor results, and are polite and accommodating with one another by default. Each recognises that they may have to rely on the other one day. In short: they are more concerned with their own careers than with beating the competition.

The two board chairmen are convinced the market will not tolerate this complacency and inefficiency much longer. If they don't take decisive and uncompromising steps then things will keep going south and the 70-year-old multinational will find itself on its last legs. The two chairmen believe that the whole culture of the Dutch-British enterprise needs overhauling from the ground up.

In the spring of 1999, they ask 20 promising young managers with an average age of 32 to build a picture of the consumer of the future. They give them six months to examine all the company's documentation and call anyone they like. What new avenues should the company explore in the new millennium? Burgmans asks management guru C. K. Prahalad to join the project. Prahalad believes it will be multinationals like Unilever, rather than any other companies, that will play a decisive role in raising the four billion people around the globe with an annual income of less than $1,500 from poverty. The Indian businessman is enthusiastic about the ways in which Hindustan Lever, a daughter company of Unilever and, in his eyes, the best-run business in India, is already working towards this goal.[2]

This is one of the main conclusions of this 'Foresight' project: the future of Unilever will lie less and less in the developed Western markets, and more and more in the provision of food and hygiene products in poorer parts of the world, in particular Asia and South America. However, the most important resolution the youngsters reach is deeply unsettling: Unilever must scrap as many brands as possible. Their analysis of the rapidly expanding Brazilian market proves that it pays to concentrate on the 400 biggest brands that make up 90 per cent of revenue. In Brazil, a similar choice to focus on the most important brands has resulted in much higher annual revenues and a 1 per cent improvement in profit margin.

At the end of 1999, Burgmans and FitzGerald announce that Unilever is going to scrap 1,200 of its brands. In their view, these brands are too small: taken together, they only make up 10 per cent of annual revenue. They will either be sold off or mothballed. The remaining 400 brands are now required to reach number one or number two position in their respective markets. In a meeting with market analysts, FitzGerald promises a cost saving of more than £1 billion within three years. He uses Dove as an example. In 1991, the brand was sold in 13 countries, now it is on sale in 75. Back then it was just a soap, now there's a whole range of skincare products. Revenue increased from $350 to $800 million within eight years. This is how it's done.

FitzGerald and Burgmans call their strategy 'the Path to Growth' and make driving up Unilever's rapidly declining revenue the top priority. It must increase by between 5 per cent and 6 per cent each year. Through enormous cost saving measures and increased efficiency the final operating profit will come out almost 4 per cent higher, at 16 per cent. All things being equal, this should allow for double digit annual growth.

Burgmans explains to *Het Financieele Dagblad* that the 'Path to Growth' programme is aimed in the first instance at removing obstacles. We're in a good position, he says, we're leading in our markets, but we waste half our time dealing with the complexity of 1,600 brands in all these countries, with divided accountability, an impenetrable bureaucracy, etc. The European market in particular, which makes up 52 per cent of our revenue, is still much too fragmented. Purchasing needs to be centralised, and around 100 of Unilever's 250 factories will have to close. This means a loss of around twenty-five thousand jobs, nearly 10 per cent of the workforce. The cost of the whole restructuring is estimated at €5 billion. Burgmans is well aware that these numbers could double over the coming years, although he keeps that to himself. Expenditure on advertising will have to increase; €1.5 billion extra is being invested in the remaining 400 brands. Getting rid of those 1,200 brands will mean kissing goodbye to around €4 billion in revenue. 'Cut it, slash it, shut it', concludes the paper.

In April 2000, a couple of months on from the announcement that they will be scrapping 1,200 brands, Unilever buys two well-known American brands. The media describes it as a schizophrenic announcement: on the very same day Unilever buys SlimFast for $2.3 billion, it also buys the ice cream manufacturer Ben & Jerry's for $326 million. 'The two purchases are a curious mix, but strange bedfellows are increasingly common in the battered food industry, where companies are prowling every aisle of the grocery, convenience and health-food store looking for growth', writes *The Wall Street Journal*. 'What Unilever found were two groups of consumers – one that can't get enough ice cream, candy and cookies, and one that buys "better for you" soy-based products, energy bars and vegetable drinks.' Because both of the brands are mostly sold in the United States, analysts anticipate that Unilever will introduce them to the rest of the world. Some analysts are concerned about the high-price takeover of SlimFast. Will they be able to maintain the 20 per cent annual increase in revenue now that Nestlé has announced *its* intention to pour investment into the diet market?

To make the best ice cream in the world, to promote social progress and to provide fat financial benefits for its employees, and – oh yeah – its shareholders. This is the three-fold mission founders Ben Cohen and Jerry Greenfield have been pursuing for the past twenty-two years. Their history reads a little bit like that of William Lever. They started out back in 1978 with a mission to make 'the best ice cream in the world that is affordable for everyone'. The two men want to make the world around them a better place. Ice cream helps, it is the ideal comfort food for keeping your cool in heated discussions. Earning money is an afterthought – second fiddle. At Ben & Jerry's, mission comes ahead of results.

The ice cream makers want to prove that it's possible for a company to heal society while making money at the same time. Ever year at least 7.5 per cent of company profits have to go to good causes. Time and again, Ben and Jerry come up with humorous ways to tie new ice cream flavours to social issues. 'Rainforest Crunch', for example, uses nuts grown and sold by indigenous tribes in Brazil. The ice cream's packaging is regularly used to protest things the founders see as damaging, such as the use of growth hormones.[3] When asked why he is always so confident and why he always believed that his crazy ideas would become reality, Ben Cohen replies: 'It's funny but the more I believe in an idea, the more creative I become.'[4]

The two founders want to expand, 'because the more we grow, the more we can give away'. Their efforts to grow the company have met with varying degrees of success; revenue has increased over the past few years, but their credibility as a successful business has lagged behind, much like their share price. Not all of the shareholders are so socially minded that they are willing to let this lie. Even worse, the newly much-expanded Ben & Jerry's is dependent on Dreyer's for distribution, the same company that's about to team up with Nestlé and start distributing their arch enemy Häagen-Dazs in the United States.

Managers at Unilever have been greedily eyeing Ben & Jerry's for a while now. As the 1990s draw to a close, their company still has no share in the lucrative luxury foods market in the United States, the biggest ice cream market in the world. The takeover of Ben & Jerry's seems like their last chance. In hopes of motivating Ben & Jerry's to allow themselves to be taken over by Unilever, the multinational starts a rumour that they are considering introducing their own new brand.

Ben & Jerry's are stuck between a rock and a hard place. If they want to remain independent, then they will have to abandon their ambition to keep on expanding rapidly, including into Europe. In a dramatic meeting, five of the eight board members vote to sell the company. The decision is all the more painful because Jerry sees selling as 'the lesser of two evils', while co-founder Ben votes against the move.

Ben & Jerry's make enormous demands in the takeover deal. Unilever can only take up two of the eleven seats on their board. The board must ensure that Unilever does not start tampering with the quality of the ice cream or compromising on their social missions. During the battle with Dreyer's, which was also trying to swallow up Ben & Jerry's, Unilever made more and more concessions. Unilever must keep on supporting all kinds of good causes, pour millions into a foundation set up by the founders and keep using expensive, responsibly sourced milk from cows in Vermont. If, at any point, the management suspects Unilever is trying to undermine the philosophy of Ben & Jerry's, they are entitled to start immediate legal proceedings and charge the costs of them to Unilever.

All this is new to the Unilever managers. Usually when they buy a company they get complete managerial control. For this reason, the legal department at Unilever come up with a mechanism by which Ben & Jerry's can still be run as a kind of cooperative. The sole shareholder, Unilever, may, after 'a good faith discussion', hire and fire the CEO but the board of Ben & Jerry's can block the CEO from changing the quality of the product to the extent that it could damage the brand image. However, all Ben & Jerry's managers do have to sign the Unilever Code of Conduct. At the 11th hour, Ben & Jerry's demand that Unilever ensures all full-time employees receive a living wage. Living wages are not based on the legal minimum wage in America but on an estimate of the income necessary to live in a 'minimum of comfort and safety' in Vermont. The board of Ben & Jerry's will set the figure.

'We have saved the heart and soul of Ben & Jerry's', declares CEO Perry Odak when the deal is signed. Going forward, the employees of Ben & Jerry's insist on calling it a merger rather than a takeover. Not everyone is so enthusiastic. Ben Cohen calls the day the company was sold the worst day of his life.[5]

Various colleagues hear Burgmans boasting about this unusual takeover. He claims that Unilever has a lot to learn from the little ice cream company, and that the multinational has been running along the same lines for the last 15–20 years. However, he is actually not all that impressed with Ben & Jerry's when it comes to the reduction of environmental impact. During his first visit to Vermont, he had been proudly informed that they had just removed the bleach from their cartons. Burgmans comes to the conclusion that the people at Ben & Jerry's are all talk and no trousers. FitzGerald goes even further and tells the Americans: 'Your choice is you can do your little thing in Vermont or you can be part of us and we can do it everywhere.'[6]

Analysts complain about all the attention this takeover is getting and call it small fry. However, substance is far from lacking in a top secret deal that has already been in the works for a couple of months. By the end of 1999, mere months after Burgmans's appointment, the idea of buying Bestfoods was back onto the table. The various plummeting share prices across the stagnating food industry meant that the company, with a stock market value of around $13 billion, now seemed affordable. Nevertheless, some Unilever big wigs regarded this sum as problematic so soon after returning $8 billion to the shareholders.

Bestfoods has been on Unilever's hit list for over fifteen years. It is one of America's biggest manufacturers of food products, many of which fit in well with Unilever's categories and markets. With its leading brand, Knorr, it dominates the worldwide market in stock cubes alongside Nestlé's Maggi. Unilever's Royco brand makes barely any impression by comparison. After the takeover, Knorr will instantly become Unilever's biggest brand. Anticipation is high, because the good thing about stock cubes, as opposed to margarine, is that different varieties are used all over the world; they are a route into households everywhere, especially in the less developed countries into which Unilever hopes to expand.

The Bestfoods share price is monitored day to day. In April 2000, Burgmans approaches CEO Dick Shoemate at his holiday home and tells him he's willing to pay 20 per cent over the current share price. A day later, a flabbergasted Shoemate informs him that he finds this offer too low. A higher offer from Unilever is subsequently rejected. But Burgmans doesn't let it go, and two weeks later offers $66 a share (a total of over $18 billion). He adds that he considers this 'serious money' and that it's logical at this juncture for Bestfoods and Unilever to enter negotiations. 'We're surprised they still don't want to talk, given that our offer now stands at 34 per cent over their latest share price', Burgmans tells the *Wall Street Journal*. He promises to take over not only the brands but the management. 'We know them well, they'll get leading roles in the new structure.'

The top brass at Bestfoods is now searching frantically for possibilities to merge with an American competitor. They hold talks with Campbell and Heinz. The fact that they allow news of these talks to leak to the *Wall Street Journal* only helps Unilever's cause. At least now it's clear to everyone that they are in play. Unilever raises its offer by another 12 per cent. In the end, it's the Bestfoods shareholders who signal the company's acceptance of the settlement.

At the end of June, Unilever hands over $73 per share for Bestfoods, a total of over $20 billion, and takes on over four billion additional dollars in debt. Unilever is buying a company of 44,000 employees, 132 factories and $9 billion in annual revenue. 'From a strategic point of view we're extremely well suited; this had to happen', Burgmans tells the *New York Times*.

In Rotterdam especially, the takeover is cause for celebration. Burgmans is putting Unilever's 'Dutch' foods division emphatically back on the map. For years, the 'British' care division has been growing faster, now balance is neatly restored.

However, there are concerns too. Integrating Bestfoods into Unilever will be a Herculean task. In many cases, there are two people for each role, they'll have to choose between managers from Unilever and managers from Bestfoods. It has been agreed that a third of all the managers on the food side of Unilever will henceforth come from Bestfoods. The task of putting all this together and ensuring that the company, bought with $25 billion in loans, quickly starts contributing to the bottom line falls to Patrick Cescau. Sadly the NV/*PLC* structure means they weren't allowed to pay for the takeover with shares.

The news causes shockwaves. It is by far the largest takeover ever undertaken by a Dutch AEX-listed company. The British marketing manager of Bestfoods, Anthony Simon, is inundated with questions from his American colleagues. What are they supposed to make of all this? Simon finds the logic indisputable: if Unilever wants to go further in the food industry, then they need to take a decisive step. You can't build that kind of future on a margarine business that is declining steadily in existing markets and will never get off the ground to start with in the rest of the world.

His colleagues at Bestfoods are also not exactly surprised by the takeover. They know they are too small to break into the group of leading players worldwide, and that to do that you need to join forces. Yet the takeover by Unilever does not sit well with the Americans. They think it's a weird company and firmly believe that Unilever can learn more from them when it comes to management culture than the other way around. They had pinned their hopes on Nestlé, the more capable company in their eyes, but the competition authority wouldn't have approved. They also suspect that the takeover is mostly Burgmans's baby, his effort to expand the food side of the firm. He may have forced it through but does this mean that the other chairman, FitzGerald, is also on board? The Brits are more into detergents and personal care products, are they really going to back this move? And what kind of bizarre structure is that anyway, two captains at one helm? Who's in charge here?

The two-headed leadership model is causing Tabaksblat, himself a veteran with first-hand experience, more concern with each passing day. At one reception and reunion after another he hears about how tensions between Burgmans and FitzGerald have risen to new heights now that their first set of results, for 1999, are proving disappointing. He finds what his successors are doing highly ambitious. Trying to realise the double whammy of increased revenues and improved margins promised in the 'Path to Growth' *at the same time* is simply not going to work. Improving the profit margin requires making savings, increasing revenue demands investment. The chairman of the Dutch firm clearly wants to increase turnover at all costs, while the chairman of the British firm is dead set on beefing up the margin.[7] Tabaksblat keeps his concerns to himself and discreetly warns a small circle of his colleagues: if the two chairmen don't start singing from the same hymn sheet, and keep on pursuing their own agendas, then the company is going to get into difficulties before too long. Once again, Tabaksblat realises how badly the company needs a real board of directors, with a decent number of non-executives around the table. Overseers who can intervene at times like this and get the two men in line, or sack them if necessary.

External observers also note that Burgmans and FitzGerald are setting the bar rather high. You can only achieve both aims – saving and growth – if you have rock solid, household-name brands and a well-oiled internal structure. All of that has to be in place first. And this is one in a long line of time and money devouring corporate restructurings to promise the moon on a stick, why should this one be any different?

Nevertheless, FitzGerald is determined. On an almost daily basis he tells his colleagues, 'you have to walk and chew gum at the same time'. Burgmans, too, believes they can pull it off. For that to happen, however, they'll have to stamp out inefficiency, bureaucracy and laziness in the company as a matter of urgency.

When speaking to his colleagues of the plan, Burgmans draws a triangle with 'direction', 'empowerment' and 'accountability' at its corners. In the middle he writes 'transparency' and 'trust'. He is increasingly coming to the conclusion that Unilever isn't transparent enough in its current form. Even worse: mutual trust is wearing wafer thin. Is enough truth being spoken to power in the company; are the people at the top hearing what's really going on? They need to work on that. But how? Naturally, the leadership retreats Tex Gunning has been on with the margarine division over the past few years haven't escaped Burgmans's notice. Maybe that's the way to go?

By this time, Gunning has managed to build a working cooperation between the 'arrogant Rotterdammers' in oils and fats and the 'Brabant farmers' in meats and soups. Over the course of only a couple of years he has turned the merger of Unilever Meat Group Nederland (the farmers) and the margarine subsidiary Van den Bergh & Jurgens (the Rotterdammers) into a success and Unilever is abuzz with stories about the dynamic manager. Forty-seven-year-old Gunning has a rather unconventional approach. Back in early 1998, Gunning, inspired by the philosophy of the popular management guru Stephen Covey and his 'Seven Qualities for Effective Leadership', had set out in search for ways to challenge his colleagues. Covey claims that changing an organisation begins with changing the individual who needs to be pushed out of their comfort zone and Gunning always relishes doing just that. He shocks his colleagues by dismissing Unilever's hallowed market research exercises as nonsense; they measure today what the consumer wanted yesterday, leading to one inevitable outcome. Gunning has no time for the power of objective analysis, viewed as gospel by Unilever employees. What a load of hot air. He isn't interested in your ability to turn clever analysis into a good story. He wants you to tell him what you're going to *do* with it. Gunning intends to place the question of 'why' at the heart of personal development plans going forwards. If you want to please the public with tasty soup, ask *chefs* what makes a really tasty soup, then go make that. Or ask yourself why you're selling sausage. According to Gunning, the main thing they're selling with Unox sausages – the smoked, cured sausages beloved of the Dutch consumer – is a sense of home, enjoyment and togetherness: *gezelligheid*. They soon come up with the idea of making Unox-branded orange bobble hats and sponsoring the traditional New Year's Day outdoor swim, attended by families and friends across the country. The project gets them a great deal of free media coverage and the sausages are soon back contributing to the company's profits.

They're still making a great deal of money on their most important product, margarine, which has a profit margin of around 40 per cent. The only problem is that less and less margarine is making its way onto breakfast tables. Gunning flies into rages when his colleagues come and complain to him about it, or observe with resignation that it's a declining market. He glares at them as he snaps things like: the market isn't declining, you are! You're all giving up! There are no saturated markets, only saturated marketers! He takes them to the margarine factory at regular intervals to drive home his point. While they're there, he makes them tell him how many people work there, how many families are relying on their sales successes. When the executives, dressed in white coats and hair nets, turn out to have no idea, Gunning strikes. He tells them they're failing in their job; they have to feel responsible for these things too. He has them spend 10 minutes standing at the production line, reflecting on this message so that they'll never forget it again. He often wonders aloud how so many brilliantly talented people can produce such mediocre results.

This type of out-of-touch arrogance cuts Rob Rijnders to the core. He was the first manager of Van den Bergh & Jurgens to come in from the outside, at the end of 1999. In his previous job at Bols Wessanen, Rijnders had looked up to huge, powerful Unilever but his first few months there are extremely difficult. Rijnders has to fight his way in. He is constantly belittled. His new colleagues are lazy. They increase revenue and profit by raising the price but otherwise do very little. When Rijnders comments on this, they tell him outright that they have no intention of listening to some upstart from Bols Wessanen.

After only a few months, he's considering throwing in the towel but on the advice of his father, Rijnders sticks at it. Not least because he is fascinated by Tex Gunning. He thinks he's a tyrant. And what's more, Gunning, just like him, seems to have a strong aversion to the self-satisfaction innate to many Unilever types.

Gunning has organised a variety of retreats to lend power to his message. Trips designed to get the message across to his managers that they need to work on their personal growth. Only if people grow personally can they effect growth in their company. By creating growth in the company, they give *themselves* further space to grow. During these retreats, Gunning had asked his colleagues what it was they wanted to do with their lives and what role Unilever had to play in making that happen. He had explained to them that he didn't want employees around him but real people, happy people. Because 'happy cows give the most milk'. He wanted to get them thinking about their role at Unilever. Are they selling margarine or are they selling health? It's only with the latter that you give your work meaning.

They had been tough trips, physically demanding and emotional exhausting. They created ideal opportunities, mostly sitting around a big fire, to sharing their real stories, their personal life stories. Gunning had set the tone and been honest. He told them about how his father died in Korea when he was a year old, about his mother's grief, his stepfather's abuse, his long stint at a boarding school. He told them about his troubled school career, the effort it took to finance his degree in economics at the Erasmus University in Rotterdam and about his time in the navy, from which he was dishonourably discharged for insubordination. He had learned a huge lesson from all of this, he told them: I won't achieve anything if I keep fighting the system. At the end of his story he had burst into tears.

After that, all the team members had shared their life stories. They had gotten to know each other's true selves, people with talents and shortcomings. Looking so deeply inside one other and bonding as people was an overwhelming experience for almost all attendees. Some were angry, they thought it was dangerous to mix their work and personal lives. What claim did the boss have on their personal turmoil? Gunning annoyed them and they criticised him for being like a cult leader, singing his own praises. But his fans had been in the majority and went to work with new dedication. This was how the top 180 at Van den Bergh & Jurgens had become such a tightknit team, and the results from 1998 and 1999 had revealed an upwards trend.

Back before he began organising these trips, one of Gunning's disciples, 29-year-old Kees Tielenius-Kruythoff, had told him about a member of his old hockey team, Erik-Jan de Rooij. De Rooij was a young anthropologist whose company, MultiLevelTravel, aimed to unlock people's hidden potential by carefully connecting them to other people and putting them in touch with their personal truths. Gunning had invited him to deliver a pitch.

De Rooij had explained that people get in touch with their innermost selves when you immerse them in natural beauty, because the beauty of nature is self-evident and inescapable. You can't stay cynical when you're looking at a waterfall, there is no saying no to it. In that impressive kind of environment, openness to introspection is heightened. This also applies to your willingness to share the things you encounter during the trip with other people. That sharing has to happen in order for you to really connect and get to know one another. After his presentation, Gunning had asked De Rooij whether he had the 'assets' to organise trips like that. De Rooij had no idea what he was asking him but nodded along nevertheless. In order to make doubly sure, Gunning had asked the head of management training to help organise the trips.

Mark Rutte had been delighted with this request. He and a friend from HR, Rob Schaerlaeckens, had analysed Gunning to see what made him such a special leader. It starts with truly getting to know your own values and beliefs. A leader knows the answer to questions like 'why am I here?' and 'what is my mission?' Finally, a leader has to commit to never deviating from these values and remaining clear on them at all times. This only works if he is speaking from the heart, only then is the story persuasive and only then is he unstoppable, regardless of circumstances. Only then can he get others on board.

Tex Gunning seems uniquely gifted when it comes to awakening that kind of leadership in people: bringing them to an awareness of their own intentions. He teaches them to verbalise them, to refine them. He helps the team of young managers around him to get to know themselves in this way until they are able to help others do the same.

The historian Rutte ended up joining Unilever in 1992 basically by chance. As a gifted pianist, he had toyed with the idea of going to the conservatory. A former chairman of the JVVD, the youth branch of the conservative-liberal VVD (People's Party for Freedom and Democracy), Rutte is primarily interested in politics, as he believes it is the best way to effect change. For this reason, he had resolved to build a business career before standing for parliamentary election when he gets to age 50 or so. His interview at Shell didn't go anywhere, but the people at Unilever were interested.

When, during one of their first team meetings, all the new trainees were asked about their ambitions for the future, most of the people there spoke of their dream of one day heading up one of Unilever's national divisions. Rutte stunned his new colleagues when he told them *his* ambition: to be the prime minister of the Netherlands. He made it clear that money wasn't his primary motivator from the moment he was taken on as a trainee at the specialist fats factory in Wormerveer, by indignantly informing the head of HR that he considered bonuses an insult. Mark Rutte always gives his all.

In his first few years as an HR executive, he comes to believe he is not unique in this attitude, and that basically everyone is motivated by things other than money so long as things are going well. He is therefore fascinated to see the way Gunning builds up people's self-assurance and effusively enthusiastic about the leadership retreats to places like the Ardennes and Scotland. During these trips, Rutte often played the role of moderator. He had learned a lot and had fun, seeing himself as a sort of clown whose job it was to maintain a positive vibe. He gets on well with Erik-Jan de Rooij, who praises him as the ultimate facilitator.

Two years later, Burgmans and FitzGerald decide to ask the same young bucks who assisted Gunning to organise their retreat for them. De Rooij is grateful to Rutte, who has since handed over the reins to Arjan Overwater, for managing to get the top brass at Unilever on board with his approach. In order to translate what they regard as the rather physical-intuitive nature of De Rooij's trips along more business-like lines, they ask IMD business school professor Tom Malnight and Annie McKee from Hay Consultancy along to help. These 'world class people' speak the same language as the people at head office and that's a start.

In early January 2001, the top managers at Unilever, a total of 98 people, set off on a voyage to an unknown destination. All they have been told is that they have to report to Ocean Drive in Miami on Sunday morning. It's a strange sight: dozens of sweating men dragging their suitcases on wheels through the powder-fine sand. Most of them have worn suits just to be on the safe side. Confused passers-by ask a police officer whether they could be Cuban refugees on a quest to find freedom in America.

In a tent further along the beach they are each given comfortable clothing and a rucksack. They won't be seeing their suitcases again for another five days. All they are allowed to bring is one item that best reflects their way of thinking. For one it is a photo of his family, for others a book or a small musical instrument.

From there, the men are flown to Costa Rica in 24 Cessna planes. One of the pilots jokes that the Cuban Coast Guard went on alert at the sight of their little squadron. When they reach their hotel, the men frown at the three stars above the door. This gives way to utter consternation. Several of them go back to the concierge desk after checking-in; there must have been some mistake. Someone is in their room! It takes a while for them to get the message that they all have to share. It's been a long time since any of them last had to do that. When Niall FitzGerald returns to his room after dinner that evening, he finds his rucksack out in the hall. His roommate hasn't quite come round to the notion of sharing a room either. Well. The chairman of the board is about to explain it to him. Sharing who they are, getting to know one another, is the whole point of this trip. It is urgently necessary. Not least when it comes to the poor relationship between him and his Dutch co-chairman.

On the second day of their trip, the men visit the Instituto Nacional de Biodiversidad. There they are treated to a presentation about the importance of strong biodiversity, and Costa Rican efforts to protect the environment. After lunch, they are driven to the beach in 32 Range Rovers. Burgmans and FitzGerald, each standing next to one of the enormous campfires, open the floor: Now is the time to get it all off your chest, what isn't working, what don't you like? A litany of misery pours out. People complain about the slow pace of decision making, the lack of growth, the lack of quality leadership. Where do they want to take this company? They talk about each other and about the list of competitors they need to beat, the 'must-win battles' identified by Tom Malnight as crucial to their immediate future. That night they lie six to a tent. They don't have much chance to get on each other's nerves. They're exhausted.

The next morning they wake groaning at 4:30 a.m. Thirty little boats are waiting on the beach. Together, they have to make their way through the roaring surf to a larger boat a little way offshore. Once they're aboard, the atmosphere improves. They join pre-assigned groups of five or six colleagues and begin to share. What have been the high and low points of their lives? What do they still want to do? Annie McKee has set them the challenge of listing 27 ambitions. Making each of them start with a list of personal aims pushes them to verbalise what they hope to achieve in their work too. The exercise subtly connects the personal and the professional. The colleagues surprise each other, it turns out you don't know the people you know half as well as you think you do. Slowly but surely, a co-worker becomes a person, with problems and concerns you can relate to. All this is helped immeasurably by the fact that they've now spent two very rough nights together in a hot climate under strange circumstances. The exhaustion has made them drop their guard.

Afterwards, they hike through the jungle in groups of 10. In the middle of the jungle they make camp and the group leaders tell them their life stories, right from the day they were born. Surrounded by hummingbirds, they tell them who they really are, where they're from, what made them the way they are. Burgmans and FitzGerald are sitting together at the front. Burgmans tells them about his upbringing as the only child of an exacting Dutch father and a British mother. The mother he felt ashamed of as a young boy because she wasn't Dutch. He was often alone, his father was a captain on a merchant ship. His polio meant he was frequently teased at school.

FitzGerald, too, tells them about his sad childhood, how it was dominated by his father who was a customs officer but above all an alcoholic. He tells them about his brother, who died of cancer when he was 11. And about his first love: communism. The fact that he wound up at Unilever basically by accident.

That evening, the men, divided in small groups, really open up to one another and gain a new respect for the person behind the colleague. They laugh, they shed a few tears. They sleep in hammocks in the middle of the jungle. Occasionally one of the hammocks crashes to the ground, but it doesn't matter. The men are completely exhausted, physically and emotionally. On the last morning various top managers stroll practically naked through the camp on their way to use one of the two makeshift showers.

Something profound has happened to these men. Even the head of the auditing department is convinced. Before the trip he had sent a furious email to human resources: you're treating us all like boy scouts, this is unbecoming to Unilever. Now he stands before the group and apologises. If this group of leaders starts focusing on the success of our people rather than the success of the firm, FitzGerald declares, then we can make both things a reality going forward.

On the last day, Burgmans's triangle becomes the main focus. The chairman is satisfied: many things are coming into focus on this trip. Mutual trust has increased, and that should form the basis for clear direction, empowerment and accountability.

Various participants notice, however, that the two bosses, who should be radiating a unity of purpose, are barely looking at each other. They are making all the right noises but their body language shows that the leaders of the NV and the PLC are still at odds. They stand with their backs to each other. Various managers observe that when Burgmans says something, you can tell he is sincere, even if it comes across badly. When FitzGerald says the same thing, it may sound good, but you constantly question whether he really means it.

In the atmosphere of openness, the managers speak up and say that they can see their leaders are not afraid, that they've stuck their necks out for the 'Path to Growth'. Someone observes that they each have qualities that complement the other, the more intuitive Burgmans and the analytical mind of FitzGerald, and that Unilever would be on its way to a golden age if only they could find a way to communicate more effectively. Others note that it's natural for them both to have big egos, but that it's important in their role as leaders that they subordinate those egos to the interests of the company.

Richard Greenhalgh, the UK boss, half-jokingly asks the two chairmen why they don't give each other a hug. At this, Burgmans and FitzGerald look at each other, laughing nervously and even embrace for a moment. But it isn't from the heart. Both of them know it.

Bestfoods veteran Anthony Simon, responsible for cutting brands on the food side of the company, is unenthused by the trip. Of course he enjoyed the honest, personal stories from his new colleagues. They were truly moving. But what was the point? What does spending a couple of terrible nights sleeping in tents together have to do with the work? There is still so much that needs doing and now everyone has been off the clock for five days. And it's costing us an absurd amount of money. Why are they even here? Sure, it's personally enriching but what do you get out of it, concretely? Work is work, and work is about completely separate issues. It just isn't sensible to be buddy-buddy with your colleagues; all it does is confuse people. Simon thinks the retreat is a typical, soft Dutch-mafia initiative.

He completely disagrees with Unilever's strategy for that matter. In his view, ditching 1,200 brands is a fool's errand. There are real gems among them, brands with enormous potential, brands that can generate revenue. As he sees it, his respected colleague Burgmans, the marketer, has been pitted against the finance man FitzGerald. It is he that wants to concentrate on the big brands because managing all the little ones is too hard for him. Too much hassle, too much red tape, too inefficient. All those brands and their markets don't fit on his financial dashboard. As far as Simon is concerned, FitzGerald doesn't know the first thing about marketing. The Irishman clearly thinks that a *global* company should focus on *global* brands, and his thinking ends there.

Simon believes the company is being run too much from the top down, by finance people who throw the baby out with the bath water in their haste to increase profits. Simon is enraged by their secretive, aloof approach, they even seem to look down on the true experts, the marketers. He sees this as a cardinal sin. Simon came up in an American company that focused exclusively on driving up shareholder value, but at Bestfoods the finance people knew their place: they were there to support the marketing executives, not to monitor and question them. Now almost everyone is tied up dealing with this rationalisation plan. There is scarcely space for anything else, they're placing all their bets on the big brands, like the Bestfoods brands Knorr and Hellman's.

When Gunning looks at the two chairmen, he sees two captains stuck in a bad marriage. Maybe that explains why something was off on the retreat. Gunning believes you have to start this kind of process at the top. These two men should have spent an intensive period of time away, finding a way to break through to one another. Only then, once they were speaking with one voice, should they have brought their Executive Committee along and forged a bond between the seven of them, before finally bringing in the big group. That was what he'd done back at Van den Bergh & Jurgens. This retreat had wound up being the 'Niall and Anthony Show' far more than was sensible. Moreover, their message didn't sit well with him: the whole trip had focused almost exclusively on taking responsibility. This was putting the cart before the horse. People only take on responsibility wholeheartedly when they know how they themselves can grow from doing so. Only then does the penny drop, allowing them to harness their personal growth *and* grow the business. He told Burgmans all of this back when the boss asked him for advice but he hadn't taken it on board. To do so would have meant Burgmans allowing himself to be coached by a subordinate who would also be going along on the trip. That would have been uncomfortable but now it had been a wasted opportunity. The clearest thing to Tex Gunning now is that these two men bring out the worst in each other. They cut each other zero slack and are incapable of listening to one another.

The relationship between the two chairmen is deteriorating further and further as time goes on. This is also down to their personalities. Burgmans is blunt, sometimes to the point of being rude, but he means what he says. FitzGerald is charming, brilliant, good in front of an audience, but can be 'economical with the truth', like most English-speaking people. FitzGerald is also all analysis, he follows the Anglo-Saxon tradition of concerning himself more with Unilever's profitability and working in the interests of its shareholders. Burgmans is less interested in the numbers and more of an intuitive salesman. He focuses on the revenue side: the interests of the consumer. Their direct colleagues agree that both of them are remarkably shrewd leaders, albeit with huge egos. They have each poured their heart and soul into Unilever and either of them could lead the company effectively. Just not together. Over the past two years they have done exactly what Tabaksblat feared they might: they have not spoken with one voice.

Jeroen van de Veer has noticed this too. Unilever has just appointed him as an advisory director. At the end of 2001, Frits Fentener van Vlissingen had called him and insisted he take on the role. He told him he could learn a great deal from how things were run at Unilever, the *other* big Dutch-British firm. Van de Veer understands what Fentener van Vlissingen is getting at immediately. For the past two years, he has been board chairman of Royal Dutch Petroleum. This Dutch limited company makes up 60 per cent of the Royal Shell Group, the other 40 per cent belongs to the British Shell Transport and Trading Company *PLC*. The group, which formed in 1907, also has two boards of directors, known collectively as the 'Committee of Group Directors', and it too has been criticised for many years by outside observers. Lack of transparency, the slow pace of decision making, an impenetrable division of responsibilities, these issues come up time and time again not only in the media but in his office. As deputy chairman of the committee, Van der Veer sees reducing the complexity of the huge oil concern as his biggest task. It is urgently necessary; complexity can lead to mishaps.

Van der Veer had been immediately intrigued by the invitation. He knows that Fentener van Vlissingen has been an advisory director at Unilever for 12 years. This makes the former head of SHV Holdings by far the longest-serving member, the paterfamilias. He knows the board's needs and explains to Van de Veer that even if it isn't strictly speaking a board of directors, let alone a one-tier board, building up a formidable cohort of the right kind of people can provide some sort of balance when it comes to the two chairmen.

Knowing that Fentener van Vlissingen was sent to recruit him by one of those two chairmen, Antony Burgmans encourages Van der Veer. Plus, as a Shell man, he could learn a great deal from these marketing men. A meeting with Lord Simon of Highbury, the former head of Shell's competitor British Petroleum and an advisory director at Unilever for the past two years, inspires him even further. Lord Simon is clearly the one who wears the trousers on the British side. Fifty-five-year-old Van de Veer also likes the fact that Simon – eight years his senior and already retired from BP – is firmly above all the Dutch-British bickering. He believes his British opposite number to be an excellent manager and reckons that, as two oil men, they have something real to contribute here. No sooner had he notified them of his acceptance than he was given a place on the Nominations Committee. In light of his years of experience inside the other Dutch-British alliance, he sees this as a logical step. Lord Simon and Bertrand Collomb are the two other external members of this board, which also counts Burgmans and FitzGerald among its number.

In his first meetings with the Unilever managers, the man from Shell notices that tensions between the Brits and the Dutch are running high. During the meetings themselves, everyone tries not to let this show too much, but during the coffee breaks he is repeatedly taken aside to hear what a particular Brit or Dutchman *really* thinks is going on: how *they* think he should interpret statements made by the opposite side. It doesn't take long for him to realise that the advisory directors are forced to rely on individual board members' personal powers of persuasion. As far as he is concerned, this is a clear example of poor oversight. Van de Veer wonders how long it can go on.

CHAPTER 3

MUTINOUS MEN; WE CAN'T GO ON LIKE THIS

2001–2005

Men. The top brass at Unilever consists entirely of men. A fact they rarely give a second thought to themselves, mind you. They like it that way, because despite their various cultures they speak more or less the same language. One in which sharp analyses and clever calculations are king. These men perceive the world as one of markets and competition. He who wishes to remain standing has to destroy the competition, has to want to be the biggest. Above all else, he who wants to keep his clients, employees and shareholders happy has to work like a dog. That's how they end up here.

André van Heemstra is worried about the way the two bosses at the company's helm are frantically plugging away. The Executive Committee personnel director has his work cut out for him too, he has to watch that he doesn't get crushed between these two millstones. Van Heemstra is constantly stuck trying to reconcile the rowing Burgmans and FitzGerald. The ambassador's son acts as a little bit like the third man who maintained balance in the Special Committee over the decades up to 1994. Nowadays, they're feeling his absence. He will have to pull out all the stops; the two chairmen don't even like to sit at the same boardroom table anymore. And Burgmans and FitzGerald aren't having an easy time of it at home either, neither of their marriages have lasted.

Van Heemstra suggests the leadership set an example to the rest of the management by trying to establish a healthy work–life balance. They agree that from now on they will spend 56 hours a week working, 56 sleeping and 56 doing something else. The directors will stick precisely to these hours. Since they often read reports while they're on planes, this time counts as half work. In order to fill the 56 hours of 'doing something else' in the best way possible, members of the Executive Committee can sign up for three sports, or for yoga or tai chi. All they have to do is say when and where they want to spend these hours and everything will be arranged for them. For a while, seven of the eight members of the highest echelon of management keep strictly to their schedules. Only Patrick Cescau thinks the whole thing is nonsense.

Just before they left for Costa Rica, Niall FitzGerald had asked Van Heemstra to ensure that at least 20 per cent of the participants on the trip were women. Van Heemstra had told him that this was impossible, that doing so would be a complete misrepresentation of who was really in leadership positions.

'The trip to Costa Rica with our top 100 in 2001 was a wake-up call; there wasn't a single woman among them. There's been no progress. We asked female managers back in 1991 what they thought of working at Unilever, we've been looking into it for that long. Rather than diversity you have a club of identical men who are always in agreement with each other. That is fatal to creativity, fatal to our "Path to Growth". We need to teach ourselves not to see difference as a threat but as something positive', Burgmans told an interviewer in an internal newsletter.[1]

FitzGerald went on to say: 'If people really don't feel at home in an organisation then they leave an important part of themselves outside the workplace, but it's exactly that talent that Unilever needs.' When asked whether the two chairmen disagreed with each other when it came to this issue, FitzGerald reacted irritably: 'People needn't constantly look for differences between us. When it comes to diversity you won't get a hair between us. We differ in the way that we express ourselves but that's not the case when it comes to content.'

After Costa Rica they decided that they needed an urgent increase in the number of women at the top. Van Heemstra asks a senior manager, Philippine Rhodora Palomar-Fresnedi, to take on the task. He makes her head of diversity. In the 18 months she has been at London office, Palomar-Fresnedi has been shocked. How is it possible that the leadership of Unilever is *this* homogenous? Almost 90 per cent of the products they make are bought by women, remember! Yet she sees the same faces in every office and every meeting. Stale, male and pale. Clever, diligent men who no doubt have good intentions but who she believes have lost touch with reality. This is a text book example of the dangerous *groupthink*, these are men who constantly reinforce each other's one-sided view of the world. When Palomar-Fresnedi asks her male colleagues why there are so few women in leadership roles within the company, the answer is unanimous: women don't want our jobs. The men don't doubt their analysis for a second: in order to build a serious career in a company like Unilever, you have to develop a big 'footprint', you need to have achieved successes in various foreign countries. You need to be able to sell different categories of products in different cultures. In practice, you need to have worked in six or seven different countries overseas in order to earn your seat at the top. That means upping sticks every three years. Men have their families in tow for all of this but women hardly ever manage to get their husbands to follow in their wake in the same way. Those husbands find it difficult to follow their wives around, it almost always mean that they can't have a career of their own. Or worse still, it means they wind up in the 'ladies' program whenever their wife has an important meeting and have to visit a museum or go shopping with all the other partners' wives. These men fear the scorn of their friends, many of whom *do* have successful careers. The upshot of all this is that talented women at Unilever don't progress and often work for years in staff functions at one of the two head offices. At a certain point, these women have the requisite depth – the knowledge – but not the breadth – the experience. So they get stuck, also because by then their male counterparts, who *have* developed said breadth, find it difficult to accept input from anyone who doesn't have the same experience.

Palomar-Fresnedi does find the piles of research Burgmans was talking about in the archives as promised, research that confirms that Unilever urgently needs to tackle this issue. Yet nothing is being done. Palomar confronts her male colleagues with their complacent self-absorption. She asks a colleague with two daughters whether he thinks *his* girls would want to have a job like his later on. While he considers the question she warns him: if the answer is no, we have a problem. She informs the men that the situation isn't anything to do with women themselves, but rather with the fact that their jobs and their way of working are totally unappealing to women.

She also reproaches the men for their narrow-mindedness. Even if they do talk about the meaning of their work – their purpose – now and again, in practice their only concern is the bottom line: revenues, profits and margins. That's the game they're in. Their intentions may be good but they are totally disconnected from the real world and what's happening in it. If they want women to build careers in Unilever then they need to start valuing different things and acting accordingly.

Palomar-Fresnedi wonders how exactly all these identical men think they're going to realise their 'Path to Growth' ambitions. How do they intend to integrate Bestfoods? Palomar tries to motivate her colleagues by harking back to the results of the Foresight Project, which mapped the trends of the coming 15 years. If we're going to be drawing more than half of our revenue from non-Western countries then we're going to need to invest more in diversity at the top and more in local talent. Doesn't the simple fact that not a single woman is making it within so much as spitting distance of the top mean that we're presiding over a total squandering of that talent? Do they really think we're going to be able to fathom the ever-increasing complexity of our markets without diversity?

The topic also comes up at the 16th *Business for Growth* meeting organised by Mark Rutte. In order to ensure that the lessons of Costa Rica aren't limited to participants from the top 100, Rutte is asked to organise sessions for around 500 managers in the summer of 2001. Burgmans and FitzGerald will take it in turns to moderate the sessions, held in a comfortable chateau to the south of Paris.

Burgmans talks about the need to grow. He emphasises the increasing importance of growth beyond Europe and the United States. Palomar-Fresnedi looks around and wonders just how Unilever is going to realise this: more than 80 per cent of the firm's top 100 are European men, 50 per cent are either British or Dutch. The rest is made up of Americans who have come over from Bestfoods, with a smattering of Indians here and there. She notices that here once again the Europeans are making a lot of noise and trying to outdo each other, while the managers with Asian roots mostly keep quiet.

During his presentation, Burgmans asks his audience whether they believe that the leadership of the company always tells the truth. Palomar-Fresnedi is one of the few to raise her hand. Burgmans calls on her. In the moment of silence that follows, the Filipina feels like all the eyes fixed on her are trying to communicate only one thing: keep quiet, don't do it, this is the end of your career. She does it anyway.

'No, you don't always tell the truth', she says. Palomar-Fresnedi states that the leadership talks and talks about improving people's living conditions, but only cares about the quarterly results when it comes down. That the managers focus on those things because they are afraid of being criticised by the bankers and analysts. She thinks the fact that they've been talking for years about the importance of diversity is pure hypocrisy, that there should be more Asians in leadership positions in the Asia teams because that is the only way they'll be able to reach a deep understanding of the local conditions and offer the right products. She reminds them that the firm has been calling for more women in leadership roles for years now. But just look around, how many women are sitting here and how many Asians? They're going nowhere.

When she's finished speaking, the room is silent. Palomar-Fresnedi wants to say sorry for being so uncouth as to speak her mind. She is almost in tears. But then a gale of applause roars through the hall. Colleagues are hugging her.

In the break, Burgmans also comes over and embraces her. He congratulates her for her bravery and invites her to talk further. He wants to find a way for them to work together to improve things.

In order to accelerate the progression of women to top jobs, Van Heemstra suggests that they select 15 career women to coach members of the Executive Committee. In teams of three they can bring the men up to speed on the problems women in the company encounter. In the beginning, the women are highly sceptical: Why do *we* have to talk about that? The men are obviously not used to having this many women sitting in their office, and not at all used to women taking the measure of them. They find the whole thing threatening. The women quickly learn to avoid talking too much about feelings with these men. They try to keep the conversations as concrete as possible. They call them 'brave encounters'. Every quarter they make a report to the whole Executive Committee.

Rhodora Palomar-Fresnedi acts as coach to both FitzGerald and Burgmans. It's painfully obvious that the two men aren't friends, she can see that they are both tough cookies who have difficulty giving each other any ground. But she can also see that they both only want one thing: to keep Unilever united and afloat. These men have been saddled with a decades-old Dutch-British legacy, and there's nothing they can do about that. They will have to figure things out together. She sympathises with the two of them.

In one of their sessions, she quotes Albert Einstein, who once remarked that you can't solve problems with the people who caused them in the first place. She calls on the men to look beyond the people they know and trust. If they want to build the leadership of the future, they will have to embrace 'the other' sitting next to them. She can tell that this message is starting to hit home, and that Burgmans and FitzGerald are realising that the change they desire will have to start with them. Burgmans tells her that he could easily be the last Dutch chairman and recognises that it's important to be open to change at the very highest level.

The rationalisation of the brand portfolio, the cuts and the takeover of Bestfoods each have a deep impact. Overall, turnover goes up 8 per cent in 2001, to €52 billion, mostly because it is the first time Bestfoods counts for the whole financial year. Meanwhile, ferocious cost savings mean that the operating profit also grows by a dramatic 56 per cent, to €5.1 billion. Over the past few years, a total of 100 factories have been closed, 87 companies sold off and 40,000 jobs cut.

The gross profit margin has risen from 12 per cent to 13.9 per cent. When they calculate the balance for the end of year report, the two chairmen are content, 'we are on track to reach our 2004 goals of 5% to 6% overall growth and an operating margin of at least 16% of sales'. Analysts have no idea what to make of the numbers. Is this just the effect of Bestfoods? Has anything fundamental changed? The share price has barely moved.

Now it's time to get serious. This message is repeated time and time again during the sessions in the French chateau. The history, the Dutch-British alliance, the decentralised power, the various products and markets, all of them make it tempting to simply keep on discussing strategy and coordination, to keep bickering forever over who is responsible for what, who has to pay what costs and cynically trying to score points off one other. The top brass all promise each other to stop talking and get down to work. But how?[2]

These days, Unilever managers are feeling success and failure in their own pockets more acutely than ever. Before setting their remuneration each year, the Advisory Board goes to firms like Hay or Towers Perrin for advice. These consultants lay out the remuneration schemes of comparable companies, showing the board what competitors pay their managers. Because everyone is desperate to hire and retain the best people, and because of the deeply held conviction that you need to be paying ever so slightly more than the competition in order to do that, these comparisons lead to a persistent upward trend when it comes to pay.

In its annual report, the board's Compensation Committee under the leadership of Frits Fentener van Vlissingen states that they are convinced that the financial interests of the management need to be tied even more closely to the financial interests of the shareholders. Unilever managers are encouraged to plunge a significant portion of their bonus into Unilever shares, for each share they purchase, the company gives them another. The top managers are required to have invested at least one and a half times their annual salary in Unilever. Members of the Executive Committee are provisionally awarded €500,000 in shares. In 2001, Burgmans and FitzGerald receive €800,000 in shares each. If Unilever makes it into the top 7 of a comparison of 20 firms (based on their three-year rolling average) then they stand to make millions. In this reference group comparison, shareholder earnings, in terms of share profit and dividends, are key. It is also agreed that for the next few years they will only receive additional shares if they remain in the top 11 over three consecutive years. If the company remains in its current position, a disappointing 15th place, then nothing will be awarded. If they make it into seventh place then the men are allowed to cash in 100 per cent, if they make it into the top two, it will be 200 per cent.

During 2002, the margin increases by a further 1-14.9 per cent. Even the profit per share goes up, by 21 per cent. The chairmen proudly report that

Unilever now has 14 brands with a turnover of more than €1 billion, 10 years ago there was only one. Revenue from the 'flagship brands' has increased 5.4 per cent.

They're devoting a lot of attention to these 'flagship brands' but the company's overall turnover has decreased by a shocking 6.5 per cent to €48.3 billion. Analysts are further concerned by the fact that operating profits are also down slightly. Once again, FitzGerald is being asked whether it isn't time to separate the household and toiletries divisions from the much less buoyant foods division once and for all. He repeats the old message: 'We see big advantages in this combination. 90% of our consumers are the same, 70% of the clients and 70% of the suppliers.'[3] In the end of year report, the two chairmen cheerfully declare, 'we're still right on course to meet the aims of our "Path to Growth": a sustainable revenue growth of 5–6% and a gross profit margin of 16% by 2004'.

In order to get a proper idea of Unilever's results, analysts constantly hold them up against those of two of their main competitors. Nestlé has increased turnover by 6 per cent and operating profits by 10 per cent. Procter & Gamble has a turnover growth of 3 per cent and an operating profits increase of 49 per cent.

Meanwhile, Patrick Cescau, responsible for the foodstuffs division, is wrestling with how best to integrate Bestfoods. The pledge to fill a third of management positions at Unilever with people from Bestfoods is meeting with a great deal of resistance. Unileverers can't comprehend it; who has taken over whom here? Cescau asks Kees van der Graaf, member of the European directorate of the foods division, to look at the division of labour in their European operations. With the help of an external bureau, all potential candidates for a position are ranked according to their abilities. For each position, someone from Unilever or Bestfoods is put forward, with justifications for their appointment.

Over the years, Van der Graaf has learnt how Burgmans approaches management. He is well acquainted with his blunt, often unpredictable behaviour. Van der Graaf begins each of their meetings with the easier files, so that he can test his boss's mood. If the atmosphere sours, he always suggests that they reconvene at another time to look at the rest of his queries and suggestions.

This time it goes off without a hitch. Burgmans agrees with his suggestions, but makes it clear to his colleague that he needs to present them to FitzGerald too before they can rubberstamp them. Van der Graaf doesn't understand why Burgmans doesn't take on this task himself. Isn't FitzGerald his opposite number? Don't they speak as one? When he presents his selection to FitzGerald, Van der Graaf begins by saying that Burgmans is already in agreement. In hindsight, he realises that this was a foolish move. FitzGerald immediately has reservations, his plan needs a total rethink. Once again they're losing time, lots of people still have no idea where they are going to be deployed.

Colleagues hear Burgmans complaining about FitzGerald pretty much non-stop. It is taking more and more time to get decisions approved. All important matters require the sign-off of both chairmen. Even Cescau is struggling as a result. The animosity between the two of them means that the unity of the leadership is falling apart. They are working against each other, they can't get along. The much-repeated adage that Brits are too polite to be honest and Dutchmen are too honest to be polite seems to the Frenchman to fit the two characters to a tee. It's becoming a melodrama. He watches time and again the way Niall tries to rope people into starting a project only for Burgmans to pour scorn on it. Like a bucket of cold water. Their intentions are good, but because the two men don't speak each other's language, they never manage to get the managers who report to them on board. They're also making absolutely zero headway with reducing the complexity of the company. The margin is only improving because the costs are going down; the company is in decline.

Unilever is being squeezed on one side by big brands that belong to multinationals like Nestlé and Proctor & Gamble, and on the other by the small, upcoming, local brands. This last trend is largely due to the fact that Unilever itself has shed so many of its small brands.

In order to get all staffing issues within the food division squared away, Cescau poached American Sandy Ogg from Motorola. Once again, a newcomer is awestruck by the ambition of the Dutch-British concern. As far as he is concerned, what they're attempting is not so much a 'Path to Growth' as a reorganisation aimed at achieving more growth through enormous cost-saving. Ogg believes that Unilever hasn't the first idea of how to go about growing. The old, decentralised strategy stopped working a long time ago but trying to move on from that culture and centralise the whole shebang like Proctor & Gamble are doing just isn't working. In Ogg's eyes, what is intended as a 'Path to Growth' is actually a road to hell. How are you supposed to go about disciplining that many managers, all of them set on following their own plan and accustomed to behaving like kings of the castle? He had to ask permission from the Italian boss to *visit*, for Christ's sake!

Ogg can't make head of tail of the 'eleven hallmarks of growth leadership' that the advisors from Hay have set out at the request of FitzGerald and Burgmans. The posters are hanging up all over the office. He understands that Hay compiled the hallmarks on the basis of a series of interviews they conducted with the more successful top managers in Unilever, people like

Rob Polet, Harish Manwani and Tex Gunning. The results seem to be geared mostly towards maintaining the status quo. Working at Unilever is still all about cultivating good connections informally, nurturing them as best you can and trying to gradually improve your working relationships. Ogg finds the whole thing frightfully slow moving and even worse: it keeps the existing personal fiefdoms intact.

Members of the generation of managers that started at Unilever five years previously under the tender care of Tex Gunning and are now making their way through the ranks are also becoming more and more concerned. Conny Braams is wondering whether the 'Path to Growth' isn't a path to destruction. She is the person inside Unilever Nederland responsible for spreads and cooking products. She was also given the task of selling off various smaller brands. Recently, Burgmans has asked her several times whether she has finally managed to sell off the butter brand Zeeuws Meisje. But Braams thinks doing so would be a bad move. She thinks that you need to look at more than just the prestige of a brand, and consider its role in the whole brand category. You may well be able to sell off a less profitable brand but then you are inviting a competitor into your market. A competitor that pays under the odds for your brand – you want rid of it after all – will then invest heavily in what you've spent so many years laying the groundwork for.

She thinks that the whole 'Path to Growth' policy is stupid. It brings in a bit of money but eventually you have to invest further in the remaining brands in order to maintain your dominance over new competitors in that category. Braams thinks that they are centralising too much, with all their attention fixed on the ever diminishing group of 'global brands'. Smaller, local brands like Zeeuws Meisje may not be profitable enough right now but they are close to the hearts of customers in the region.

Braams has also come to the conclusion that Unilever paid way over the odds for Bestfoods. The financial wiggle room to invest in factories and growth is seriously limited thanks to the mountain of debt that now needs paying off. With the help of an indignant media and a number of her Dutch colleagues, Braams manages to protect local Dutch brands like Zeeuws Meisje butter, Robijn fabric softener and Unox sausages and keep them within Unilever. Apparently even Burgmans can't bear to force their sale through.

Kees Kruythoff is still working for Tex Gunning. Under his leadership, Kruythoff is trying to build up the food division in Asia. It is not going well. He too is coming to the conclusion that the takeover of Bestfoods in particular was a gigantic mistake. It isn't just that they paid much too much for the company. In the key growth markets in places like Asia, you can't get anywhere with its products, the goods the American company produces don't fit with dietary habits here. The other thing increasingly causing Kruythoff concern is the lack of unity at the top. During a leadership retreat in Iceland he saw for himself that Burgmans and FitzGerald were not talking to each other. The lack of consensus and unity is snarling up the whole system.

In May 2003, a shock reverberates through the company: they have had to issue a revenue warning. Up until now they have been promising a revenue increase of 5–6 per cent off the back of the leading brands, but now they're looking at a maximum of 3 per cent. This is disastrous news because they have been relying on vigorous growth from the biggest brands this whole time, it's the cornerstone of the 'Path to Growth'. Investors are stunned and the Unilever share price falls like a stone. The company loses 8.5 per cent of its value in a single day. Anyone who invested their money in a share in Unilever four years previously, at the start of the 'Path to Growth', has now lost around a quarter of their investment. Anyone who invested the same amount in Nestlé has seen the value increase around 10 per cent. The same applies for an investment in Procter & Gamble.

The two board chairmen are now coming under increasing fire for both their clashing personalities and the whole structure over which they preside. In the spring of 2003, financial auditors confront the bosses with the limited sustainability of the firm's creaking governance mechanisms. The 'Cadbury Code' and the planned Dutch 'Tabaksblat Code' are demanding ever more insistently that they comply or give justification for why they haven't already done so. Up until now, Unilever had been getting away with it, not least because the agreements it had made were 65 years old at that point. The advisors tell Burgmans and FitzGerald that scandals at Enron and WorldCom in the United States have led to a discussion about the importance of rigorous oversight and to new, stricter laws. If Unilever wants to keep its listing on the American stock exchange then it has to start getting to grips with the new law, the Sarbanes-Oxley Act. This requires that all audit committees at listed companies consist of at least 50 per cent non-executive directors, the ones that oversee the company's financial directors. These must also be experienced business people. For Unilever there is no escaping the fact that they need to have a proper look at changing their oversight structure. The company needs to begin seriously considering appointing non-executive directors, overseers who can fire the executive directors if they don't do their work properly. The auditors joke among themselves after a meeting with Burgmans and FitzGerald that the two men remind them of cousins running a family firm together even though they don't get on. They wonder whether warring cousins will be capable of getting the management structure at Unilever in order.

Among the advisory directors, the lack of cooperation between the two chairmen remains an elephant in the room. This frustrates Wim Dik. He has been part of the Advisory Board for two years and is accustomed to saying what he thinks. It's clear as day to him that the 'Path to Growth' has failed and that the cause of this failure lies with the two men who are both so set on being in charge. How are you supposed to hitch two horses to the same wagon when all they want to do is kick each other? The problem is that all the day-to-day scenarios that highlight this failure of leadership are not part of the Advisory Board's remit. Therefore, they are never officially discussed. Wim Dik knows Unilever intimately. He worked there from 1964 until 1981, when he was asked by the centrist-progressive party Democrats 66 to become their secretary of state for finance. Not being able to intervene frustrates him deeply but he realises that the tendency for those at the top of the company to defend Dutch and British interests means that the dual leadership model is effectively sacrosanct. Unilever is trapped in a model of oversight that offers no way out of this situation. The moment that model is called into question, both sides become terrified that they're losing their influence.

No, he isn't worried about sales or the demand for Unilever products. 'People keep washing and people keep eating', FitzGerald tells *The Guardian* in an interview that summer. He is holding forth about the lack of trust society places in captains of industry. Without naming any names, or alluding directly to the big scandals playing out in the background, such as those at Enron, Ahold and Parmalat, FitzGerald explains that there are three categories of leader: crooks, incompetents and mostly competent leaders. 'The crooks should be driven out, tried and put in jail. The incompetents, once they have manifestly been seen to be incompetent, should be taken from their responsibilities and allowed to do something else. The mostly competent should be judged on what they deliver.' The only problem is that 86 per cent of the public at large currently believes that all bosses in the business world are crooks, while that's probably only true of about 5 per cent of them. FitzGerald warns that if these emotions form the basis of the strengthening of oversight then competent leaders – especially those that like to take risks now and again – are likely to turn their backs on the business world. 'I don't like going home at night to find my kids asking whether I'm a crook.'[4]

Burgmans is irritated by the way his colleague airs his opinion. He questions whether it's sensible. Why does he always need to be in the public eye, giving his views on everything? When FitzGerald explains in the *Financial Times* that family values are important to him, several of his colleagues are furious. The man has just left his wife for a younger woman and is in the process of getting divorced. It's so hypocritical! Burgmans thinks this was clumsy, but recognises that FitzGerald is an Irish Catholic wrestling with his roots. This is obviously just his way of coping.

Burgmans is also disturbed by reports that there is more and more internal chatter about him and FitzGerald not getting along. He thinks they do alright. He notes that it is mostly colleagues just below the Executive Committee, men who haven't quite 'made it', who are complaining about the leadership. Thanks to the major reorganisations over the past few years, opportunities to advance have become increasingly scarce. There are far fewer jobs at the head of the company.

Burgmans feels lonely all the way at the top. He decides to start inviting a few trusted Dutch colleagues, such as Tex Gunning and Kees van der Waaij, round to his house after work. He wants to make sure he still has a feel for what's going on in the organisation. Maybe this informal network will help him come up with some new ideas, find fresh inspiration. Down in his wine cellar, once they've opened quite a few bottles, an atmosphere of openness develops. Burgmans shares his concerns about the future. He's looking for the right next step but he doesn't quite know how to proceed. The men present have never seen him like this; his armour has fallen away. One of the topics they discuss is the question of the dual directorship. Is it still sustainable or is it a relic of another era? The men warn Burgmans not to let anyone outmanoeuvre him. They talk about the possible necessity of going over to a single CEO. But who should it be?

In the corridors of London head office there are whispers that FitzGerald, aged 58 and in service at Unilever for 35 years, with now almost eight years as chairman of the PLC board, is getting his ducks in a row. He is reportedly eyeing up the chairmanship of the media company Reuters. His recent appointment as Non-Executive Director lends credence to the rumours.

FitzGerald promised himself back in 1996 that he wouldn't stay on in his job for more than eight years. If he hasn't managed to achieve what he wanted to by then, then that's too bad. Staying any longer isn't an option. He knows what power does to people and doesn't trust himself to resist its pull. More so than that, however, he fears growing bored. By 2004, it'll be high time for something new. FitzGerald put this agreement with himself in a sealed envelope and gave it to a legal advisor, asking that they make sure the letter be returned to him in 2003. The Irishman is also worn out from the never-ending struggle with Burgmans, of course. They are nothing alike. It's a case of finance versus marketing, culture versus nature, details versus the big picture, analysis versus intuition, focus on profitability versus focus on revenue, charm versus bluntness. His mother taught him a long time ago that the key to success was to learn to value the best attributes of the people around him. In the case of his most important colleague, Antony Burgmans, he has never managed it.

When the top 25 men at Unilever gather in Limerick in November 2003, the mood is sombre. It was FitzGerald who suggested they organise this meeting in his hometown. HR executive André van Heemstra suggested that they have the 12 Business Group presidents and a dozen staff directors – the echelon that reports to the Executive Committee – gather in groups of four or five under the leadership of one of the committee's members, and vent their spleen. Afterwards they will be asked to think of some solutions. FitzGerald can well imagine what the result will be but doesn't tell Burgmans. He suggests that they give the idea a chance and Burgmans agrees.

The next day, the six Executive Committee members, Clive Butler, Chief Financial Officer Rudy Markham, Keki Dadiseth, Patrick Cescau, Charles Strauss and André van Heemstra, present their groups' conclusions from the previous day to the two chairmen. They have not discussed these in advance. The reproaches are bitter. You don't listen to us, too much is being left unaddressed. You shove things under the carpet because you don't like having to deal with each other. We can't go on like this. Mutiny is in the offing. The five groups have reached the same, irrefutable conclusion completely independently: we don't want two bosses anymore. It is crippling the organisation. If it was up to the group of managers immediately below the Executive Committee, Unilever would put an end to its long-cherished dual directorship at the earliest opportunity.

Confronted with this resounding rejection, FitzGerald and Burgmans realise they have to take action. If these people are all having the same experience then their collaboration has failed. Even if they don't feel that way themselves, and are certain that they have been working towards the same goal over their years together despite their differences of opinion: holding together the company they both so dearly love.

This conclusion is easier to accept for FitzGerald than it is for Burgmans. The Irishman is due to leave Unilever in September 2004 to become the chairman of Reuters. One year before he is officially due to retire, FitzGerald announces in Limerick that Patrick Cescau will succeed him as the chairman of the *PLC*.

No further decisions are taken but speculation runs wild. Those present in Limerick come away with the impression that FitzGerald intends to head

Burgmans off at the pass by pushing forward Patrick Cescau as the first CEO of the whole company. Cescau is a finance man through and through, just like FitzGerald. Someone cracks a joke that makes its way round the whole company: a Frenchman like Cescau has two advantages whatever happens – he isn't Dutch and he isn't British.

For Burgmans, the future is now uncertain. He is a few years younger than FitzGerald and isn't due to retire until 2007. Naturally he wants to become the first CEO of the whole of Unilever himself once FitzGerald leaves. Various people at the meeting think this is a logical wish, a way to spend his last few years erasing as CEO the failure of his collaboration with FitzGerald.

Before they return home, the men have a kick about. Green versus Red: and team of mostly Dutchmen with Anthony as captain and a team of mostly Brits led by Niall. The Greens miss a penalty, the final score is 1:1. They can't help but laugh at the result.

Three months later, Burgmans surprises Kees van der Graaf with an invitation to take Cescau's place as the man responsible for the foodstuffs division. Van der Graaf can't fathom what's happening, this means Burgmans passing over a whole layer of more senior managers. That same morning, a few minutes before his first meeting with his new team, Cescau's secretary tells him that he's too busy to supervise the handover.

The meeting is a dramatic one. Men who had been above Van der Graaf in the hierarchy mere hours earlier are aghast. When he goes to the front of the room and tries to begin the meeting, they ignore him and stay where they are, chatting with a handful of their colleagues in the corner of the office. Van der Graaf feels like he's the wrong man, in the wrong place, at the wrong time. The crowning moment of his career has quickly become the most disastrous too.

Robert Polet is convinced that Burgmans is trying to sure up his own position by appointing a trusted confidant. Polet also makes it clear to Cescau that he doesn't believe he has anything meaningful to contribute. He thinks that the Frenchman is first and foremost a technocrat, not someone who can lead an organisation from the front: a political animal, primarily concerned with his own position.

Although Van de Graaf's former boss Polet is one of the people who stands to suffer most from this bizarre appointment in the eyes of his colleagues, he himself is no longer especially concerned. He's about to announce his new job. The Unilever lifer, director of the ice cream and frozen foods division, is about to become CEO of the fashion house Gucci. Forty-eight-year-old Polet is desperate for freedom. After 26 years at Unilever he is tired of the protracted meetings. Tired of people who come up to you afterwards and say that they actually agreed with you but didn't dare say so because they were afraid their boss would hold a different opinion.[5] Tired of the endless, suffocating intrigue. How are you supposed to reach a decision with 20 of you making it? This culture had frequently had him at a loss. He'd hear that an important resolution had been reached and when he asked who had reached it, the answer would be 'the meeting'. But how does a *meeting* make a decision? Whose vision lay behind it, who would take responsibility? Polet is glad to have a way out.

Eight years previously, he and Tabaksblat had failed to make a one-tier board system a reality, now Niall FitzGerald was pressing ahead with it. After the meeting in Limerick he told Burgmans he was going to instruct the Advisory Board to ensure that Unilever had just one CEO going forward, and a board with a majority of independent, credible non-executive directors alongside him or her. He also informs Burgmans that he is going to nominate Patrick Cescau as the first CEO. The conversation is an awkward one for FitzGerald.

Van der Veer and Lord Simon are happy with this decision. It is abundantly clear that they can't carry on as they have been. Much damage has been done in recent years by the fact that these two men were incapable of pulling in the same direction. But also by the fact that there was nothing that the advisory directors could do about it in practical terms.

The men create a Corporate Risk Committee to look into governance. Since he is about to leave, FitzGerald won't be sitting on it. Antony Burgmans, already a member of the Nominations Committee, is invited to join. However, it becomes clear very quickly that they have no intention of carrying Burgmans forward as the first CEO. In their eyes, the debacle of the past few years means that wouldn't be logical. It's time for a breath of fresh air, a new pair of hands. They need to plot a new course and clear away the wreckage. Starting May 2004, they want Patrick Cescau to take over as the single captain at Unilever's helm. They view the fact that Cescau is French as a great advantage. More to the point, he's a finance man, and reducing costs remains the top priority. Burgmans rolls the dice and gives his colleagues his blessing. He suggests that he stay on as the first chairmen of the new one-tier board for the coming two years. He thinks he has a right to the role, he's not officially due to retire until then. FitzGerald is horrified when he hears of this; he'd advised Van der Veer and Lord Simon to make Burgmans board chairman for no longer than a year. As far as he is concerned, two years is much too long. Burgmans won't make it easy for Cescau, not least because Burgmans will treat this chairmanship as a full-time job. But apparently this is the price they have to pay to turn the advisory directors into a one-tier board and Cescau has explicitly told Burgmans that he is ok with the arrangement as long as he stays away from the day-to-day running of company. That will now be Cescau's task.

The recently published Dutch 'Tabaksblat Code' warns of the risks associated with former executive directors wielding power from beyond the grave. Turning departing executive directors like Burgmans into non-executive directors is very much inadvisable. Burgmans understands his predecessor's concerns but defends the new division of responsibilities by asserting that this, after all, is an exceptional set of circumstances. He has been asked to oversee the transition to a new form of governance. The interests of Unilever are at stake and aren't these kinds of codes meant to be broken now and again?

With a heavy heart, Burgmans concedes that there are no other options but to pursue a new course: 'We didn't react quickly enough to difficult market conditions and increased competition. The structure in which the two chairmen were also both Chief Executive worked well for 75 years. In order to improve the governance of the company and the effectiveness of the organisation, we have now come to the decision that the firm will actually better served by *one* chairman, a non-executive director responsible for leading the board of directors, and by *one* executive officer responsible for operational activities.'[6]

When Burgmans and FitzGerald explain the results of their wrangling to the top 150 leaders in the company, some in the room chuckle. Miracles *do* happen; for once they agree on something; there's a first time for everything. When Burgmans sees the relief on their faces, he jokingly tells them that since he and FitzGerald are now getting along so well they would like to explore the option of them staying on together for another year or two. The whole meeting hall falls around laughing: no, no thank you. Relief reigns.

They try to keep the positive mood going a little longer in their last co-written introduction to the annual report, for 2003: 'We're pleased to have managed to increase share profit by 11% in what was a challenging year. We have met or exceeded our aim – to keep share profit growth in the low double figures – in every year of our "Path to Growth" strategy.' They direct attention to the fact that the net profit margin is almost at the desired level of 16 per cent, currently sitting at 15.7 per cent, that the number of brands with over €1 billion annual turnover has tripled to 12, and that the 400 largest brands are good for 95 per cent of revenue as opposed to 75 per cent five years ago. They've closed 140 factories and cut almost fifty-two thousand jobs. Unilever has become a good deal more profitable.

In the same period, however, the business has shrunk by about 10 per cent. Revenue has dropped even further, from €47.7 to €42.9 billion. The men see this as disappointing but understandable. They point once more to the fact that the 'Path to Growth' was developed in order to rationalise the company's operations and free up resources to support a select number of large brands. 'It would be all too easy to lose sight of what we have achieved. Our intention is to have achieved or exceeded all or close to all of these ambitious aims by the end of 2004.'

Analysts frown as they read this: the one aim they won't have met is the most important one; more than anything, all companies have to increase revenue in order to have any right to survive long term. Only a year ago, FitzGerald and Burgmans had still been insisting that they were 'on the right track' to achieve a turnover growth of 5–6 per cent. Further on in the report, SlimFast and the margarine division are identified as the biggest stumbling blocks. It is costing Unilever more and more effort to bring the admittedly still profitable artificial butter to market. The men are in total agreement, however, that SlimFast was a bad investment from the word go.

Under their leadership, the company has spent five years expending a huge amount of energy on getting the shareholders on side: without success. Trust has actually decreased. Anyone who invested €10,000 five years ago when the 'Path to Growth' was announced is now €1,500 poorer on paper, whereas a similar investment in P&G, Nestlé or Danone would have delivered a share profit of around €1,500. Someone who invested two years ago *would* be better off, however. The price of Unilever shares (NV *and* PLC) has been above that of the AEX and FTSE indexes since December 2001. In a comparison of shareholder benefit across the 20 companies in their reference group, Unilever is in sixth place, which means that the directors can cash in 100 per cent of the shares awarded to them in 2001.

This may be the reason that Burgmans and FitzGerald opt to appear in a photo together, smiling, one final time: 'With her trusted brands, talented people and inspiration mission, we believe that Unilever is stronger than ever. We are preparing ourselves for the next phase in our strategy. All over the world, 150 million times a day, people are choosing our brands because they help them to feel good, look good and get more enjoyment out of life. We sum this up in the word "vitality". Consumers are citizens too and they demand that companies live up to ever higher standards of accountability. We are proud of our reputation for good management practices, transparency, and commitment to society and the environment: we see the name Unilever as a valuable asset. By the time we celebrate our 75-year jubilee in mid-2005, our packaging, letter heads and name tags will all display the Unilever name.'

It's as if the gods are laughing at them. In his final month as Unilever chairmen, FitzGerald, the man who has spent the last five years making sure that

Unilever's primary focus was keeping its shareholders happy, is forced to issue a profit warning. It's the first one in the company's history. The firm had been anticipating a profit increase of 10–15 per cent. Investors can now expect a maximum of 5 per cent. In a press release, FitzGerald and Burgmans prostrate themselves, calling the results unacceptable. It is FitzGerald's final message. There aren't many Dutchmen at his leaving party in London.

Analysts wonder aloud what these latest disappointing results will mean for Burgmans's position. A choir of experts pipe up, saying the company has done too much cost-cutting over the past few years and invested too little in its own products and in advertising. CFO Rudy Markham tells *The Economist* that the firm is struggling to remain competitive and desperately needs to boost its credibility with investors after seven disappointing quarters.

In order to emphasise internal unity and put a stop once and for all to suggestions that the firm would do better to split, management decrees that all subsidiaries will carry the Unilever name going forward. The only problem is that the brand Unilever only really exists on the stock market. Consumers barely know it and even employees mostly work for brands like Dove, Magnum or Persil. Other than the shareholders, nobody seems keen on the brand, let alone the two industrial chimneys connected by a thin line that now form the 'U' in the Unilever logo.

At a shareholder meeting, company representatives explain that Unilever no longer wants to be some hands-off holding company, and that the firm wants to step into centre stage with a new logo and make clear exactly what it stands for. From now on it's all about 'One Unilever'. As Burgmans explains: 'We want to take responsibility as a company for society and the environment. We want to bring vitality to everyday life. That sounds very ambitious but it's been at the heart of what we do from the very beginning. We are just trying to make it more visible. And we believe that we're on the right track.'

Director Clive Butler is the mastermind behind the term 'vitality'. He suggests that they place this at the centre of Unilever's new mission: 'We add vitality by anticipating the daily needs of our customers, whether in terms of food, personal care or hygiene. We help people to feel better, to look better, and to get more out of life.' The new logo is a chunky 'U' containing a palm tree, a sun, a hand, lips, waves, a bird, a fish, etc. Symbols that are supposed to sum up the company's 25 most successful products. From a distance it looks solid and reliable, designer Wolff Olins explains, from close up you can see the diversity.

Burgmans is glowingly enthusiastic. This logo, which will soon appear on the packaging of every single Unilever product, expresses Unilever's connectedness with society. This 'U' stands for products made in the most sustainable way possible. He gave this commitment to sustainability concrete form in his Rotterdam office by installing a huge aquarium filled with Cape seahorses. These tiny creatures are threatened with extinction so Unilever is financing a breeding programme set up by the Blijdorp maritime research centre based in the Rotterdam Zoo.

Most of Burgmans's colleagues miss the business-like impression given by the previous 'U'. They think the new logo is too soft. We're supposed to be a business, aren't we? Where is the dollar or euro sign? During the internal presentation, men on all sides whisper that Burgmans is obviously trying to show off his feminine side. Others like the logo. With it, Unilever is making clear that the company has a duty to care for nature, for people and for the world. The fact that it is responsible for the well-being of its customers but also for the sensible management of the finite supplies of raw materials necessary to create its products.

Retired Unilever director Hans Eenhoorn, now a member of the board at Ben & Jerry's, manages to persuade Burgmans that an exception has to be made for the ice cream manufacturer. The Americans are still very much getting used to Unilever and the changes it's making to their company structure, they aren't ready to put the Unilever logo alongside the portraits of their beloved founders on their eccentric packaging. More to the point, Eenhoorn says, it's not at all clear that Unilever can force them to do so. It was agreed during the takeover that they could chart their own course, after all. The American ice cream makers are still stubbornly insisting on calling the takeover by Unilever a merger. Eenhoorn points out the advantages of this to Burgmans: if they embark on some ludicrous course of action of which Unilever disapproves, then it's an advantage *not* to have the 'U' on Ben & Jerry's packaging.

In February 2005, in a hotel in Vevey, Switzerland, Paul Polman hastily summons his immediate subordinates. They have no idea why. Is their boss going to announce a new promotion? Forty-eight-year-old Polman's career has been going from strength to strength over the past few years. Since his takeover as president of Procter & Gamble Western Europe four years ago, revenue has almost doubled to $15 billion, in part because of the acquisition of German company Wella. Is Polman being given a spot directly under the CEO and chairman Alan George Lafley? Lafley is 58 and has only been in the job four years, but maybe he's already busy lining up Polman's next big challenge?

People are singing Lafley's praises. Procter & Gamble is growing quickly in terms of both revenue and profitability. Dutchmen inside the company think that Lafley is mostly just executing the aggressive growth strategy put forward by his predecessor Durk Jager, their countryman who was fired out of the blue in summer 2000. Where Jager failed due to his haste and clumsy communication style, Lafley is a communicator par excellence. He is able to motivate people in ways no one else can. At the beginning of this year, he rolled out the 'two moments of truth strategy' for this very purpose. Everyone is trained to manage as well as possible the two 'moments' in which everything needs to go to plan. The first moment is the one where the consumer is standing in front of the shelf, in which they decide in three to seven seconds whether to go for a Procter & Gamble product. The second moment comes once they're back at home, when the product is used. If everything goes to plan there, then the consumer comes back for more.

The Dutchmen miss Durk Jager. Will Polman, another Dutchman, even be allowed to step into his shoes? He was very close with Jager. That is a disadvantage now, of course. There are also whispers that Jager's tumultuous departure a few years earlier means that no more foreigners will be hired for top jobs. Americans only from now on. On the other hand, Polman was named European Business Leader of the Year by the *Wall Street Journal* last year. That must have made an impression in Cincinnati, surely. Thanks to him, European operations are growing more quickly than the rest of the organisation.

Polman also misses Jager. He regarded him as his mentor. He is no fan of Lafley's and is convinced that he is the one who screwed over de Fries twice back to back in 2000 by surprising him with unexpected profit warnings. It had been a Roman tragedy, in which betrayal played the leading role. The fact that Lafley had been made chairman of P&G a mere year after taking over from Jager as CEO also bothered Polman. But then they find that sort of thing perfectly normal in the United States.

The opportunism of his colleagues back then didn't sit right with him either. Polman had thought it only logical that nobody had any right to additional remuneration during lean times but his colleagues had not agreed with him. A low share price is the best of all moments to get a share package, they reasoned, because then they'll rise again all the more rapidly. He no longer wanted to work in an environment filled with so many Judases. By 2001, Polman was feeling so jaded that he'd resolved to take voluntary redundancy. But then Lafley came knocking. The boss of P&G Europe was leaving, did Polman want the job? Hiring someone from outside was not an option, and his experience in Benelux, Spain and the UK made him the ideal candidate. Polman told Lafley that he only wanted to do it if he had full autonomy, a clear final say and as little contact as possible with Cincinnati. Lafley had agreed to his terms.

Looking back on all this, Polman thinks that he was overcautious and took the coward's way out by not quitting. Now he's being punished for it. Because despite the agreements made back then, head office in Cincinnati is diverting more and more power into its hands. Worse still: Bob McDonald is becoming more and more powerful. Polman has a burning hatred for the worldwide head of detergents. And it seems it's mutual. McDonald creates a layer of bureaucracy between Polman and head office. A head office that is making more and more of the decisions. They're playing games in which he has no interest in participating. Polman refuses to work for McDonald, refuses to communicate with him at all. This leads to a massive conflict. Unsustainable conflict. He realises that there is no way he's ever going to make it to CEO of Procter & Gamble.

As he stands before his troops, his colleagues realise that something is terribly wrong. Polman looks defeated. He tells them that he is about to be replaced effective immediately. The news is explosive. A rumour immediately goes round that McDonald has falsely accused him of something and that Polman hasn't managed to come out on top in the ensuing struggle.

Polman's friend and colleague Robert Jongstra seeks him out in his hotel room straight after the dramatic announcement to ask whether he can do anything to help. But Paul Polman can barely take in what Jongstra's saying; he can't get any words out and seems completely overcome with emotion. After giving his heart and soul to Procter & Gamble for 26 years, his employer is kicking him to the kerb. The press release has already been sent: 'Mr Polman has announced that due to personal reasons and the desire to pursue other interests that he will be retiring effective immediately.'

Suddenly he has time on his hands. Time to play sports, time to think and time to read. One of the first books on his 'to read' pile is *Touch the Top of the World* by blind mountaineer Erik Weihenmayer. In it, Weihenmayer described his ascent of Everest. Polman calls him, wanting to tell him how impressed his is. This is a man who doesn't recognise any limits on his abilities. Polman loves this. Weihenmayer enthusiastically invites the unemployed Polman to join him in climbing Kilimanjaro in Kenya. Polman suggests that they make a real event out of it. In the end, eight blind mountaineers receive an invitation to make the ascent in a team of 26.

During the expedition, Polman is deeply moved by the willpower of the blind climbers. He realises that it isn't all that bad being blind so long as you see what's important in this world. It is much worse to have your sight but not see the things that matter.

On the last evening of their seven-day expedition, Polman stands up during dinner and announces that he intends to create a foundation dedicated to improving the lives of blind children in Africa. In advance of the trip, Polman had visited schools for the blind in Kenya and realised how difficult their situation was. Without help, their lives remained highly limited. He wants to donate braille machines that will allow them to take part in lessons and become full members of Kenyan society.[7]

Polman, his wife Kim and Erik Weihenmayer will form the board of this Kilimanjaro Blind Trust. He and Kim fantasise about being able to pursue the venture full time. Polman doesn't need another job in order to find the money, and he's had his fill of head offices and the political games people play in them.

But then his friend Peter Brabeck-Letmathe calls. The big boss at Nestlé asks him whether he'd like to come and work for him. Polman turns down the offer but Brabeck persists and asks whether he'd consider coming on short term as a consultant. Polman has zero desire to do that either. At a third meeting, Brabeck asks him to be his right hand man and become CFO of Nestlé. For Polman, who began his career in finance at P&G all those years ago, this has an exciting ring. Brabeck doesn't say so in so many words but this opens up the prospect of him taking over his CEO position one day. It also means they can stay where they are in Geneva. Polman's wife Kim is taken aback by the news. She reminds him of the scandals at Parmalat, Ahold and Enron. It's the CFOs that end up in court, her husband could be about to wind up in jail. Polman tells Brabeck that he's keen to go ahead but jokingly adds that any possible risks will be on the CEO.

The *Wall Street Journal* observes that the appointment of an outsider to this important post is highly unusual for Nestlé. Usually they only appoint people who have been working for the company for 25 or 30 years. The newspaper goes on to speculate that it has something to do with the disagreement Brabeck had with his shareholders earlier that year. They disapprove of the fact that he is both CEO and board chairman of the Swiss giant. He's wearing too many different hats. Brabeck told them he saw it as necessary in order to make headway. The shareholders eventually agreed on the condition that Brabeck would hand off the CEO role to someone else within two to three years. He'd probably have to do so in any case; a law is coming in that will require him to. The newspaper quotes as analysts saying that they hope Polman will bring the dynamic culture of P&G with him to Nestlé.[8]

Former colleagues are surprised that Polman is returning to his old profession. Others understand it. Robert Jongstra tells *NRC Handelsblad* that Polman 'sucks in numbers and translates them into opportunities. He is always on top of the numbers, which means that he can prop up his proposals extremely well. That way you make decisions more quickly, but you see a plan through over a longer term because you know it's well-founded'.

The president of the World Business Council for Sustainable Development (WBCSD), Björn Stigson, is also enthusiastic: '[Polman] doesn't believe that you can judge the market value of a company simply on profit margin anymore. He thinks that the valuation is increasingly dependent on brand value, reputation, and the way the organisation is put together.' Polman led a working group for the WBCSD that worked with young people to look at ways in which companies can live up to their responsibilities in terms of climate change and energy use.[9]

Unilever-man Kees van der Graaf tells the same paper: 'I think he's an exceptional person. He knew about our search for a cure for my son's muscular disease, FSHD, and rang me a while back to say that he was going to be running the Paris marathon and wanted to do it to raise money for our foundation. He brought in €10,000 in donations for us.'

Paul Polman has become addicted to long distance running at this point. He gets up at 6 a.m. a couple of times a week to go running for an hour. He wanted to run a marathon for his 50th birthday and he made it happen. The new CFO of Nestlé is determined and resolves to do better at following his internal compass in his new job. He won't expose himself to political intrigues ever again.

CHAPTER 4

A FRENCH BOOKKEEPER PUTS SHARE PRICE CENTRE STAGE

2005–2007

'Why is it that we take so little pride in what we're doing? Why are we always looking longingly at what's working for Procter & Gamble or L'Oréal? Why do we want to be something we're not? I have no idea whether this lack of pride is just the result or actually also the cause of our recent struggles. Let's start concentrating on what it is we do better than anyone else: providing good food, supporting vitality.'

Nihal Kaviratne glances at Antony Burgmans and Patrick Cescau. He's worked with them for decades. The brand new board chairman and chief executive officer have asked the Indian head of Home & Oral Care in Asia to share his personal opinions with top 200 leaders in the company. During this 'O be joyful' session on 8 February 2005, Unilever is celebrating its 75th birthday in a very fitting location: Port Sunlight, the place where William Lever produced his first soap 120 years previously.

It's going to be Kaviratne's last appearance, he's retiring this year. He's been at Unilever for 40 years. 'The reasons for our success and the causes of our failures over the past few years seem to me to come down to a series of paradoxes. We made a very simple business unbelievably complicated. The complexity means that we remain inward looking. Right now we're celebrating the savings we made as part of the "One Unilever" concept but we're forgetting that we created those costs ourselves. These internal battles have frustrated me the most. Beating competitors like Procter & Gamble was a piece of cake compared to the internal battles we've been having with one another.'

The man known by colleagues as 'the great unifier' warns them: 'The fall of Rome teaches us that change brought about by personal interests is the beginning of the end. Of course we need to change, even if it's just to keep the barbarians from our doors. But I also believe that a matrix organisation can function brilliantly, so long one maintains two solid lines. Compare it to the way a family works. Children learn that they have to go to their mother for some things and to their father for others. When the child goes to the mother for something that comes under the remit of the father, you simply have to tell the child, "sorry, you have to go to your father for that". I believe successful change can't be about power but about mutual trust in a team made up of different members.'

Naturally, the firm publicises the idea that it wants to use its products to improve the lives of its customers and thus make the world a better place. But Kaviratne has learned never to think of Unilever as an altruistic operation, the survival of the company always comes first. He is sick to death of critics who believe that the world is being destroyed by pollution and over-consumption and that the world would therefore be a better place without Unilever. All sustainability begins with combatting poverty through the creation of prosperity. So long as there is poverty in the world, it cannot be made sustainable. Companies like Unilever play a crucial role in combatting poverty. As an Indian, he knows all about this. Unilever can lift up the world *and* turn a decent profit doing so, that has to be the point of departure here. In order to realise this aim, however, the company has to invest in innovation. They need to renew their products. Kaviratne is therefore more and more concerned by the diminishing importance of the R&D department within the company: 'It pains me to see trust in the capacity and integrity of this important element of our greatness being eroded the way it has been since the Persil Power crisis.'

He warns the new leadership in friendly terms that 'the top is living under a microscope, their behaviour is being sharply observed; inconsistencies appear bigger than they are. Of course it's important that the leadership is made up of a diverse mix of people. But here lies another paradox: the fruits of diversity can only be reaped if unity is number one. Do you remember the hug our colleague Greenhalgh managed to get out of FitzGerald and Burgmans in Costa Rica? When have we seen the same since? Why do we separate our discussions of business plans and company culture? Why don't we bind them together, like DNA in a double helix, like our yin and yang? It's crucial that we pick leaders who are motivated by the things they help create, rather than what they get for doing so. Humility is the most intangible of the virtues but it's also the most important.'

Kaviratne closes by saying, 'I've learned three key lessons from all the leaders I've worked for over the past forty years. The central thing is a tireless search for truth, rooted in the humble acknowledgement that the limits of your knowledge are nothing more than the limits of what you don't know. This means you need to possess a personal readiness to take responsibility the moment thing go wrong. Finally, you need to have discipline necessary for delaying gratification. Leave that low hanging fruit to others, a leader aims at the fruit that is highest and most difficult to reach.'

'One Unilever'. That is the message the new CEO emphasises continuously. The company, still officially two companies, is battered and divided but it now needs to transform under the leadership of one CEO into a single company of the future. For Patrick Cescau, the wishes of his shareholders are the primary point of departure. As long as they support his leadership, the share price will stay up and the company will be able to keep running self-sufficiently. He is well aware that the shareholders want to see results immediately. Their patience is wearing thin. For the past eight years, the share price has been hovering around €20 a share. The heads of the Foundation Unilever Trust Office (Stichting Administratiekantoor Unilever), which controls the issuance of depositary receipts for the Dutch NV, made no bones about confronting Cescau and Burgmans with their projections that a splitting of Unilever into a food company and a HPC company would deliver shareholders a value increase of 15 per cent. Shareholders would no longer have to pay a premium for investing in an impenetrable conglomerate.

When the consultant who produced this projection observes half-jokingly that the main function of this amalgamating of all activities is as a protection measure – because, after all, how do you separate eggs once they've been scrambled? – Burgmans is offended: food, HPC products belong together.

In their co-written letter in the 2004 end of year report, Cescau and Burgmans bear their souls. 'At the end of our five-year Path to Growth period we are not where we set out to be. Despite many achievements in simplifying the brand portfolio, in increasing margins and capital efficiency, in restoring financial flexibility and in many other areas, we do not end this period of Unilever's history with the level of growth we wanted. This is not because our portfolio is incapable of growth. Our portfolio is strong, and is capable of generating the growth we need, but we have not been fast enough in reacting to toughening market conditions and increased competitive challenges. Our overriding objective is to return the business to healthy growth. We recognise that we must also be smarter and more disciplined in execution. We remain completely committed to delivering Total Shareholder Return in the top third of our peer group.' In 2004, Unilever has slumped from sixth to fourteenth position.

Cescau is glad that they're in crisis mode. He tells *The Independent*: 'The profits warning has had a liberating effect on them. We had to recognise that we were not as good as we thought. That makes you humble and, at the same time, is a motivation for change. No human being wants to be a loser. Employees ask me if the changes could not be made more quickly.'

Naturally he too has heard the joke about him only getting the top job because he was neither a Brit nor a Dutchman. Patrick Cescau is able to laugh at himself. As far as he's concerned, though, his appointment as CEO *is* proof of the fact you no longer need to be British or Dutch to be appointed to a top position. If a Frenchman can become the boss of this Anglo-Dutch multinational then from now on talent is going to be the deciding factor. Isn't that encouraging? Cescau, who has been living in London for years by this point, can sense insecurity: the Dutch employees in particular are worrying about their position. To him this is only logical: the Netherlands is a small country, and in terms of absolute numbers a lot less talent comes from there. The Brits have a much less to worry about on that front. There's simply more of them.

Less complexity, more trust and more cooperation. Cescau realises that he's facing exactly the same task as his two predecessors. The only difference is that now there's a lot less time to get things up and running. For the 57-year-old Frenchman the solution is as complex as it is simple: he needs to make sure that all these independent little chieftains learn to depend on one another. They need to start trusting each other and working together. No amount of pretty words or little trips to Costa Rica is going to make that happen. It's going to require a radical shift in the balance of power. Cescau wants to detach responsibility for development of brands and categories entirely from the development of national markets and relationships with buyers. Going forward, he wants to map all the product–market combinations in each country and decide from London where the potential for growth lies, and where it doesn't. Difficult decisions will have to be made in each of the countries; many companies will have to merge in order to make the whole national operation more manageable. Now that he's the only one making executive decisions, he can do what he has long believed to be necessary. For years now, all these local Unilever managers with their personal fiefdoms have been doing little more than profiting from the two warring bosses at the top.

The mergers mean many managers will have to relocate in order to keep their jobs. If it was left to Cescau, 40 per cent of the top jobs would be scrapped. That alone would drastically reduce complexity and the opportunities for bickering over who's earning what and where. He realises that this means declaring war on dozens of colleagues who have built their own business empires within Unilever. This makes him sad, somehow. Once you're in your 50s, you no longer welcome change, you want to find ways to secure your personal status quo, to reinforce the identity that you've built for yourself and in which you have invested for all those years. You want to keep all that intact. But Cescau is resolved: this has to happen. He is happy to hear a number of younger colleagues express their support. They see the potential and want to make it a reality.

The division and business group structure is completely dismantled. Cescau reduces the number of managers in the top two levels from 18 to 8, the so-called Unilever Executive. In addition to the CEO, this includes a CFO and a head of human resources. Two top marketers are added to oversee the development of the brands in the two categories: 'Food' and 'Home and Personal Care'. They will be responsible for innovation, brand positioning and communication. Responsibility for the profit margin lies with three regional presidents (Europe, North and South America, and Asia, Africa, Middle East and Turkey). Cescau leads this executive committee. The CEO, CFO, Europe boss and head of HPC, together with nine external, non-executive board members, form the highest managerial body in the company. These are the two identical one-tier boards, one for the NV and one for the PLC, both under the leadership of Antony Burgmans.

Even the Dutch NV is now suddenly given a one-tier board. This is unusual because Dutch law does not accommodate such an arrangement, only making provision for a separate board of directors, the so-called two-tier board. Sven Dumoulin, board secretary of the NV, eventually manages to make the case for Dutch companies being allowed to opt for this Anglo-Saxon form of oversight going forward.

Two shareholder meetings, two systems of incorporation and securities law with multiple supervisory bodies, two accountancy organisations and two tax systems, it still represents a lot of work and costs a lot of money. Burgmans wants to tackle that straight away. After years of criticism from analysts and investors regarding the complex and inefficient Anglo-Dutch construction, they have decided to experiment with alternatives.

Shell, the other Anglo-Dutch multinational, put an end to its own, similar dual structure earlier that year. The direct impetus for the move had been the so-called reserve scandal. The oil company was forced to admit that it had been too generous in its assessment of its own oil reserves. These turned out to be 20 per cent below what they had reported. The loss of face was comparable with the Persil Power incident at Unilever. Regulators fined Shell £83 million and loudly questioned whether the management at Shell was still fit for purpose. The firm consisted, just like Unilever, of a British and a Dutch company, with two shares in the NV and *PLC* and comparable governance issues. Shell promised to reform.

It was Jeroen van der Veer who ended up with that particular task. After only a couple of weeks of research, the committee he was leading came up with the idea of separating the company's legal domicile from the location of its head office. That way, they could do justice to both the British and Dutch legacies. Van der Veer has discovered that the Brits were rather attached to their *PLC* status and like being able to say that one of the biggest companies in the world is British. Their prominent place in the most important British share index, the FTSE, is also terribly important to them. The logic of this escapes Van der Veer, but he respects the sentiment. The Dutch are more concerned with employment opportunities. What's more, the Netherlands has an exemplary business environment, even when it comes to taxation. The location of head office determines the top rate of tax.

Luckily for Shell, the Dutch tax authorities recognised that the *PLC* shareholders would have no desire to suddenly start paying a 25 per cent dividend tax. Dutch investors can have that tax deducted but since this tax doesn't exist in the United Kingdom, it isn't deductible for the Brits. In order to avoid them being stung with this tax on dividends, Shell sets up an arrangement by which their so-called B-shares are made exempt from dividend tax. The company makes no secret of this either, it is a ruling, a custom-made agreement with the tax authorities of the kind often made by individual companies. These are mostly given a duration of five to seven years. Given that there have been rumblings among politicians in The Hague about scrapping the dividend tax for a while now, Van der Veer is confident that the issue will resolve itself within the not too distant future. And as it turns out, the issue only grows more contentious over the next few years. Van der Veer becomes so busy dealing with it that he misses four Unilever board meetings.

Just like FitzGerald and Tabaksblat 10 years previously, Burgmans is working with advisors to find out if and how the complicated legal set-up of Unilever can be simplified. The project is called 'Skyline'. At first he fantasises about moving the head office to Rotterdam. He believes the Dutch model of governance, with its consideration of the interests of all stakeholders involved with the company, to be better suited to Unilever than the British model and its focus on the interests of shareholders. Over the years, transfer of more and more functions to London has irritated Burgmans. But in order to make Unilever into a Dutch NV he would need the agreement of 75 per cent of the investors in the British *PLC*.

Burgmans meets frequently with the Dutch finance minister Gerrit Zalm and his state secretary Joop Wijn to talk about the business climate in the Netherlands. During one of these discussions, they are joined by the mayor of Rotterdam, Ivo Opstelten. The government officials were interested. Naturally they'd love to bring Unilever over to the Netherlands entirely, and with a Dutch chairman in place, this would be a good time to do it. They speak of a 'rational feeling of Dutch patriotism'.

But moving to Rotterdam would mean overcoming one huge obstacle: the dividend tax. In their examination of the 2006 Tax Plan, Zalm and Wijn state that they see no long-term future for the dividend tax. However, they also emphasise that a complete scrapping of the tax wouldn't be appropriate. In the lower chamber of the Dutch parliament, secretary of state for Finance, Joop Wijn of Christian Democratic Appeal (CDA), summarises it thus: 'Getting rid of the dividend tax would cost us €1 billion net. What's more, this is a tax levied on foreign taxpayers. So scrapping it would mean giving foreigners a tax break. What we *can* do is ensure a real-terms profit overall by looking at things like the rate of tax, for example. We need to strike a good balance between budgetary constraints, legal necessities and an attractive business climate, but the message to the business world may well be that we don't see this tax surviving long term.' The secretary goes on to announce a reduction of the tariff from 25 per cent to 15 per cent.

When he talks about the tax not 'surviving', Wijn means that while he himself has no plans to scrap it, he assumes that the dividend tax isn't going to survive the European process of tax harmonisation. He sees it as unfair for a Dutch investor to be able to deduct the tax as standard while a foreign investor in the same company is barred from doing so. Judges in various legal cases have already ruled the tax discriminatory. But so long as this tax exists, the secretary of state will use it as a bargaining chip in tax agreements with other countries. Even a rate of 15 per cent leaves him with some room to negotiate. When it comes to this kind of tax deal, he's particularly proud of the one he has reached with the United States. People on all sides are pleased with the arrangement. Through it, Dutch businesses with American parent companies are exempt from paying the dividend tax.

Wijn understands Unilever's problem. Since the United Kingdom doesn't have dividend tax, they've got nothing with which to bargain. Unilever will simply have to wait for Europe to solve the problem. Burgmans dreams of making Anglo-Dutch Unilever a purely Dutch company are put on ice. In the annual report, he writes: 'After an in-depth analysis, the executive committees have reached the unanimous conclusion that Unilever's current, dual structure will, with some important adjustments, meet the needs of the firm in the near future very well.'

Cescau, another man who has spent his entire career at Unilever since starting there in 1973, has leapt head first into the day-to-day running of the company. As he sees it, dreams about 'building' brands are being given more priority than is sensible. In an interview with *The Independent*, he says, 'We built a story around a brand such as Cif. We painted a romantic picture and forgot that clients only want to know whether the product kills bacteria. The challenge lies in the stores. With the advance of own-brands and discounters [such as Lidl and Aldi], we have to do much better there.' Retailers such as Carrefour, Tesco or Ahold tell him 'that when we lose a share of the market somewhere, we don't fight back but restructure. We have forgotten how to fight to the death for market share. That is why our organisation now consists of two groups: brand builders and the group that does business with commerce. A competitor used to call it a division between "poets" and "farmers". Our country managers should no longer make all types of objection against packaging or advertising campaigns. Other people in the company will think about brands. They only have to take the brand, bring it to the market and sell it.'[1]

As Kaviratne expressed in his 'O be joyful' speech, many of the marketers think it's a shame brand renewal has centred on emotional matters for so long, rather than on improving functionality. Where are the real breakthroughs and product innovations? For years now, Unilever has limited itself to selling 'a good feeling', claims that are above all aimed at extending the lifespan of a brand. That in itself is becoming more and more difficult.

All this empty branding leads to things like them launching five different deodorants brands in the Netherlands and the account managers of Lynx, Dove, Vaseline, Impulse and Sure all having their own individual profit and loss calculations. They are limping from fad to fad. If a competitor is doing well with a product containing aloe vera, then R&D is tasked with developing something with aloe vera in it. In the Netherlands alone, a brand like Sure spends about €10 million per year on advertising in the hopes of inducing the customer in the shop to reach their hand an extra 10 centimetres for Rexona rather than their competitor Nivea. At this point they're shelling out 60 per cent of the retail price of the product on adverts aimed at appealing to emotions. Some people at Unilever are likewise disturbed by the global policy to move from roll-on to aerosol deodorants. The idea is to tempt the customer into buying a deodorant he can spray all over his whole body, rather than just on his armpits. Research has shown that spray deodorants run out twice as fast on average as roll-ons or stick deodorants. None of this is exactly what you'd call sustainable or environmentally friendly.

Cescau's colleagues are often struck by his financial wizardry and the way he concentrates so exclusively on ways Unilever can make money in the short term. The Frenchman intends to manage the 400 brands from London. The goal is to reach the number 1 or number 2 position in every market across the board. Heads of national divisions are going to have to sell products that have been developed centrally. The space to give an opinion on them, to tell London that a particular product or a particular piece of packaging is not going to work in a particular market, no longer exists. Since the national managers *are* responsible for their results, this is no doubt going to be a source of pain; they're going to have to achieve those results using products over which they have had little to no say. They'll be asked for their opinion a couple of times in the early stages of development but that's it. Only the sales divisions still report directly to the national managers, all other functions, from buying to marketing, report over their heads to London head office.

Approaches to advertising are dictated centrally, from the content of adverts to their placement on television, in publications and on the internet. Internally there is a lot of criticism. Aren't the marketers being held at too great a distance from the market? They need close proximity to the end client, the consumer, in order to understand what speaks to them. A marketing boss in Singapore doesn't understand the first thing about the Vietnamese consumer. Isn't this approach detrimental to the 'speed to market'?

By bringing Unilever more and more emphatically into the marketplace as an umbrella brand, the brands with which the consumer is familiar are made subordinate. This can be damaging. The sauce brand Bertolli has traditionally made customers feel special and superior compared to the cheaper brand Knorr but now that they are increasingly being confronted with the fact that both brands belong to Unilever, they are placed on an equal footing and the space to distinguish oneself is diminished.

Cescau has no qualms: 'the centralisation of our business under the leadership of three regional presidents will mean we can really start to implement our vision as "One Unilever" from now on. The levelling out of top management leads to simplification, clarity and well-defined responsibilities.' His colleagues suspect that if he got his way, Cescau would limit them to 20 huge, global brands.

Simon Clift, the freshly appointed chief marketing officer, is enthusiastic about the new 'U'. After all, Unilever is the biggest brand in the world that nobody has ever heard of. The firm needs to make a calculated shift and start steering things from the centre. By doing things like bundling advertising campaigns, currently managed locally, in together, he can take them to the big advertising and media companies, make demands and ask for discounts. The local managers naturally fear losing their autonomy, and it will indeed be reduced. They need to start thinking of themselves as Unilever employees.

Patrick Cescau has kept Sandy Ogg by his side throughout his rise to power. The American is now André van Heemstra's successor as head of human resources and an important sparring partner for Cescau. On two things, however, both of them are in absolute agreement. When structure and culture come into conflict, culture is the priority. Shifts in culture are what make way for change. Furthermore, even though the 11 characteristics of leadership Hays put together are probably logical, there are too many of them. No one can remember all that. Something else needs to take their place.

Ogg asks Cescau what three or four things he thinks need to change in terms of colleague behaviour. He gets his answer within a few days. Cescau wants to shift from a local to a global focus, from excuses to real accountability, from an internal to an external orientation, from debate to action and from independent working to working in teams. Global, Real Accountability, External, Action and Team: we need to make Unilever GREAT again.

Cescau makes good on his promises immediately and puts an end to the tradition of the yearly 'O be joyful' gatherings. Why do we celebrate our successes every year? What successes? In their place, he intends to organise sober leadership conferences. The first one is held at a hotel in the London borough of Paddington. There, Cescau sets out the situation in stark terms. He makes it clear that he is going to make difficult choices in their brand and market portfolios. He is going to be merciless in these decisions and will tolerate no dissent. He has asked the most important 'kings' inside Unilever, including both the bosses of countries like Italy and Brazil and the man responsible for ice cream in the United States, to respond to the 'GREAT' proposal. He emphasises that it is precisely the fearful protection of individual independence and lack of internal codependency that caused the 'Path to Growth' to fail. Sandy Ogg sees the way the men are wrestling with the new terminology. Their every action demonstrates that they have absolutely zero desire to relinquish their independence. He watches them digging their own graves, securing their own departure from the company.

Ahead of his second leadership summit at the beginning of 2006, Cescau prepares a pep talk. He wants to assure his faltering colleagues that they've turned the corner, and that the medicine is taking effect. He also wants to make it clear that they're not there yet. 'A year ago, we were losing market share. The valuation of our brands wasn't in the region we had hoped. Our communication was ropey at best. Our innovation was fragmented and weak, we were looking inwards and had lost sight of our clients and customers. We were barely growing.' He can't say it in so many words, the numbers aren't out yet, but Cescau is alluding to the most concrete evidence of their improved position: a 3.1 per cent growth in revenue over the past year.

He adds that even outside observers are watching Unilever closely: 'A. G. Lafley, the CEO of Procter & Gamble, took the trouble to tell me that they're keeping an eye on what we're up to. We're doing better in various market research exercises too; in the United States, satisfied customers have put us in fourth place, *ahead* of PepsiCo, Colgate and Nestlé. We should be proud of that. It shows what we are capable of. But we aren't there yet, Nestlé is growing twice as fast. P&G, Reckitt, Danone and L'Oréal grew in Europe while dealing with the same structural problems we were. If we really want to make Unilever great again, it isn't enough to go from loser to competitor, we need to want to win again.'[2]

Cescau tries to empathise with his people: 'we're in the middle of a transition and transitions are always messy. Not everyone understands what has to happen, or how they should behave. There are still tensions that indicate complexity and lead to far too many meetings, too many trips, too much asking for information. In short: there is still too much energy being directed internally. But please consider also that Unilever has never before formulated a strategy for the entire world with so much detail and focus.' He swipes at the generation of managers that preceded him: 'Before, we had a hundred different strategies that amounted to nothing. Now we have *one* strategy for the whole firm. It is going to ask a lot of you all. We are going to ask you to put money you've brought in at the disposal of colleagues. There will no longer be any freedom to make your own decisions with it. In this new reality, we are going to win together, not individually. For many of us, it will be the first time we have to bring meaning to phrases like "mutual reliance". This doesn't just require you to start thinking differently but to start *behaving* differently. This is the only way to build the kind of trust we can all get behind.'[3]

The Frenchman emphases that changing a culture isn't easy: 'I see people struggling, they just can't get used to the new power relations. That applies to us in the leadership team too. We need to internalise them. That isn't just about our head but about our heart too. This mutual reliance is extremely difficult in the beginning, but once we too recognise the need for it, to feel the desire to be part of something bigger, then it's going to flow smoothly.' Of course, Cescau doesn't forget to hammer home what all this is intended to lead to: 'I want this company to be in the top 30 per cent of its peer group. This is possible. We need to get active. To radiate vitality. In everything we do.'[4] Many of those present notice that Cescau has lost a considerable amount of weight.

Burgmans wants to strengthen his supervisory committee. Observing the need for a tough finance man in his one-tier board, he asked Kees Storm to step in immediately as the chair of the Audit Committee. The former CEO of Aegon, the Dutch life insurance multinational, compliance officer at firms like Belgium beer supergiant InBev and Dutch airline KLM, had been approached by Burgmans before, back in 2001. Back then, Storm had been under fire as board chairman of Dutch supermarket group Laurus, and entangled in a legal case resulting from mismanagement that ultimately led to the collapse of the company. Now that he has been cleared of all charges, he can accept Burgmans's invitation. Yet Storm clearly remembers wondering aloud what his role in the Advisory Board would be. Board member Wim Dik had told him not to expect too much from the mostly advisory role.

It quickly becomes clear to Storm that the leadership of the company is still getting used to a serious one-tier board. He immediately clashes with CFO Rudy Markham. Kees Storm wants to take away the press release announcing Unilever's quarterly results and proofread it before it goes out. Markham tells him this is impossible. The lawyers have vetoed it. They are afraid something might get leaked. Markham will have to take back the press release after five minutes. Storm welcomes Markham to the brave new world of an actual board and audit committee. He demands the press release and won't give it back.

Storm is proud of this new, prominent role but doesn't enjoy the first meetings. It isn't exactly pleasant here. He doesn't like the fact that they've organised everything right down to the last detail. His access to the company numbers is monitored endlessly; there is a whole assortment of lawyers and controllers whose job it is to decide what he's allowed to see. They each seem to have gone over the numbers three times with a fine-toothed comb. Storm sees right away that they've got too many people being paid too much to do this work. It's one of the first numbers that really concerns him: at 15 per cent, Unilever's indirect costs are at least twice and sometimes three times as high as equivalent costs among their competitors. When he remarks on this, everyone is in total agreement with him, those costs need reducing drastically. Great, so why isn't it happening then? What's stopping them?

Storm has recently joined the board at InBev, a beer brewing company that was created in 2004 out of the merger of Belgian Interbrew and Brazilian AmBev. There's a completely different vibe there. Things get tough sometimes, but the Belgians and Brazilians maintain a culture of friendship throughout.

They are a team. When it comes down to it, they'd walk over hot coals for one another. Under the leadership of two demanding Brazilians, the place is bubbling over with plans. They want to become the biggest beer brewer in the world. They fantasise about taking over the American beer giant Anheuser-Busch.

Of course, Kees Storm realises that there are big differences. Unilever has to contend with a variety of different shareholders and their respective opportunistic sentiments. InBev belongs to 3G Capital, a company owned by a couple of big, dominating Brazilian shareholders who are able to make snap decisions and who have announced their intention to enjoy their majority ownership for years to come. Storm is especially impressed by Jorge Lemann, the 67-year-old Brazilian billionaire who sets the tone at InBev as majority shareholder. Storm is fascinated by Lemann's approach. For him, the power of meritocracy is sacred. You have winners and you have losers. Workers in the bottom 10 per cent in terms of performance should be fired each year to make room for new blood. Anyone who does well, who keeps their feet in the world of markets and competition, is lavishly rewarded. The top 15 per cent can be awarded as much as five times their salary in bonuses.[5] And those employees have to invest the overwhelming majority of that sum in shares in the company, thank you very much. Plus you don't just get that given to you. Anyone leaving the office after 12 hours of hard work does so to sarcastic applause and people asking whether they're a part-timer. Lemann believes in his model, he dreams of making it the benchmark for companies in the twenty-first century.[6]

In a frank interview with the *FEM Business*, a weekly magazine for business professionals, Cescau explains that his role as ultimate decision maker is very demanding: 'It has meant me having to change a few things. It helps that I'm utterly persuaded of the need for me to make those difficult decisions. That gives me peace of mind. Once I know that it's the right thing for the company, the pressure lifts.' He tells them contentedly that Unilever's share price has risen 18 per cent since his appointment. Unilever lent it a helping hand by buying up half a billion euros' worth of its own shares. Cescau shares his intention to do that again this year.

Cescau is most concerned about their European operations. 'I can't expect my shareholders and customers to keep footing the bill for inefficient organisation. The company needs to become more successful and grow.' In response to rumours that he is under pressure from 'corporate raiders' and is looking at breaking Unilever up into a food concern and a personal and home care company, he says: 'If I don't do it, maybe they'll do it for me, is that it? That implies that a split would be for the best. I believe the combination is more valuable. But I do want our current portfolio of companies to start working harder for us.'[7]

In his first end-of-year report as chairman of the Unilever board, Burgmans expresses his pride that his initiative of nine years previously, to work together with the World Wildlife Fund towards sustainable fisheries, has resulted in all fish fingers being prepared using sustainably caught fish as of 2005. Of all the fish Unilever processes, 60 per cent is caught sustainably. The mission of the Marine Stewardship Council (MSC), to raise this to figure to 100 per cent, will have to happen without Burgmans and Unilever, however. The European activities related to frozen foods are mostly being sold off. Revenue is not growing quickly enough there. In a press release, Cescau states, 'it was a difficult decision but the sale is the best way for us to create value.'

As the board member responsible for food, Kees van der Graaf thinks this is nonsensical. He fought to retain the frozen foods division. During the sale negotiations it came to light that the division was the most profitable of its kind in Europe. So what is this really about? Deep freeze foods belong in Unilever, not least from the standpoint of their ambitions for sustainability. In Van der Graaf's eyes, it's the most straightforward way to keep food fresh over a long period. Since vegetables are often frozen on the day they are harvested, it keeps the vitamins in.

Van der Graaf has had heated discussions with Cescau and Burgmans about this, accusing them of a lack of vision and of being too impatient. An irate Cescau tells him he doesn't want to hear the word 'vision' coming from his mouth ever again. The chairman of the board tells him he doesn't want to talk about this again until Unilever has lived up to the expectations of the analysts for eight consecutive quarters. That has to be given top priority for now.

Van der Graaf realises that the finance people within the company, who were already so dominant, have become even more powerful. Whenever he ends up in a discussion with his bosses about the future of Unilever, and points out to them the importance of making sensible long-term decisions because without them the company won't go anywhere, they respond by telling him that a lack of short-term results will have the same result. Without profit, the share price will drop, we'll be sold off and we won't have a future anyway. We need to sort that out first.

It annoys Van der Graaf that the board meetings are now almost entirely dominated by this financial agenda. At the top of that agenda is ensuring that the analysts who monitor Unilever are never unpleasantly surprised. To this end, an external bureau goes to the ten to fifteen most important analysts before each set of quarterly results is brought before the meeting, to ask them what figures they are expecting. The board then takes the average of these projections as the point of departure for their discussion about possible improvements. Everything is geared towards making the analysts happy in the hope of getting a 'buy this share' declaration from them.

Van der Graaf is getting very tired of this. And the board is no picnic on a personal level either. The directors come in with an opinion and focus on getting it heard. There is barely ever any actual discussion because everyone is fixated on striving for a consensus. He does like the fact that Burgmans uses the informal moments to try and work on the chemistry between members. He usually brings a general topic to the table, something to do with technology or a geopolitical issue, and asks directors specialised in the topic to give their opinion. Those are moments in which they listen to one another properly. After all, there's a wealth of expertise at this table.

The fulltime presence of Burgmans at head office regularly raises eyebrows. Various colleagues notice that he seems to have a lot of time on his hands; he often drops into one of his colleagues' offices unannounced to have a chat. Isn't a chairman supposed to maintain a bit of distance? To stay out of the CEO's way? Cescau is on the defensive, he thinks that Burgmans is trying to push his own agenda, especially when it comes to appointments. The chairman constantly offers Cescau unsolicited advice. In order to restore the balance between Rotterdam and London a little bit, they agree that Burgmans will put in more appearances in London and Cescau more in Rotterdam.

In the 2005 annual report, Burgmans congratulates 'his' CEO. After years of decline, turnover has stabilised at €39 billion. Cescau emphasises that the company needs to concentrate even more on personal care products and on emerging markets. For the first time in their history, these products outweigh the whole West Europe market and make up 38 per cent of revenue. Cescau is proud of the fact that the majority of the key markets now report directly to the Unilever Executive. He expects the company to have made around €700 million in savings and for this to rise to as much as €1 billion during 2007. 'But the biggest benefit for us is that we now have "one face" for our customers and consumers, as well as being faster and more disciplined. In other words we are fit to compete.'

Responsibility for addressing the company's stagnating European operations now falls to Kees van der Graaf. The expansion of discount supermarkets is leading to pressure on prices. At the same time, Unilever is making too few good innovations to justify a higher price. Overheads are also far too high, and there are too many factories.

Van der Graaf uses the summer of 2006 to put together a plan for Europe. He and his colleagues take stock of their situation. The basis for this is a matrix of almost two hundred cells. Inside are the 12 product categories linked to the 15 regions in which the company operates. Some large countries, like Germany, Great Britain, China, India, Russia, the United States and France, form a region in themselves. They decide to concentrate on the 'cells' with more than €100 million in turnover. These are divided into product–market combinations that need to grow, and in which Unilever should therefore invest: product–market combinations that should be managed in such a way that they bring in money for the rest, and so-called cash cows. The first exercise fails, in the end there are too many cells that require investment. A second attempt is more successful. The finance colleagues are buoyed and start counting the profits immediately. With a little time left over, they decide to make an estimate of risks and score all the product–market combinations as either high, medium or low risk. They also judge which combinations will be easy, or perhaps impossible, to manage. The summary looks good.[8]

But that evening, just as he's finished ordering a hamburger from room service at the Crowne Plaza hotel next to head office, Van der Graaf begins to have misgivings. The summary looks good but what lies behind it makes him uneasy. Something isn't right here. He decides to go over his notes from the afternoon. Western Europe is dominated by combinations that mostly need managing as cash cows. The money they make from them should be reinvested in combinations in Eastern Europe. But all those combinations are marked as 'high risk' and 'possibly manageable' – right down to the ice cream operations. Van der Graaf realises there is only one possible conclusion: they can't do it. And he realises something else: this is going to come as an enormous shock. The European division has so far managed to just about meet the stated aims, but that's only because they've been savvy when it comes to massaging the numbers. He can no longer escape making radical decisions.

He spends the rest of the night working on a plan. Once he's finished, at six in the morning, he summarises it on a single sheet of paper: production costs must be drastically reduced. The same applies to indirect costs. Twenty-five factories will need to close. European costs must be reduced by 30 per cent, which means laying off 25,000–55,000 employees. Unilever will have to carry on shedding non-essential activities, in particular more of their small, local brands. They need a Europe-wide IT system and a European purchasing operation in Switzerland. The number of daughter companies per country needs to be reduced to one. The total cost of this reorganisation: €3 billion.

By 6.40 a.m., Van der Graaf is sitting outside Patrick Cescau's still-empty office, sheet of A4 paper in hand. He knows that his boss is usually in the office before eight. He wants to talk to him before his meetings start. He manages to catch him. For a moment, after he begins his presentation, Van der Graaf thinks he's about to be fired. But the opposite happens. Cescau listens attentively, then writes down a list of names on a scrap of paper and asks Van der Graaf to get to work on his plans with these trusted people. They agree to keep the plans secret until September. This way, Van der Graaf will have time to refine them in consultation with some external advisors. Van der Graaf feels empowered, he's ready for this fight. He knows that the regional and national managers in particular are not going to like this further shift in power and cash flow. Not one bit.

That's okay. Most of them understand the necessity. Van der Graaf's main problem is Cescau. No matter how hard Van der Graaf pressures him, the matter is never given serious attention in board meetings under the leadership of Burgmans. This means that decision making is always deferred. Cescau is hesitating. He explains to Van der Graaf that he fears Burgmans won't be willing to take on this enormous restructuring. Maybe this proposal is too dramatic to put before the departing chairman, who's due to leave in April the following year. Burgmans should be able to leave while the sun's shining.

Cescau thinks this should be a matter for the new chairman of the board. But *he won't be* joining until January. Meanwhile, the people who report to Van der Graaf are getting impatient. They reproach him: Wasn't this urgent? We're ready, eager even! Hurry up and give us the green light! Van der Graaf tells Cescau that this delay is costing the company piles of money per day. If they don't get started until the beginning of next year, they're looking at a loss of at least €100 million.

Kees Storm would like to speed things up a bit too. Everything just keeps getting held up by the bureaucratic matrix organisation. Whatever you do, whoever you make responsible, they can always point to someone else. But he also thinks Kees van der Graaf should stop complaining and do more to get this on the agenda himself. If you're in charge, you need to be willing to take a stand. That doesn't happen often enough. Storm thinks that Cescau is a clever, amiable man, but not the powerful leader they need to make decisive interventions.

Storm finds the top dogs at Unilever fairly toothless in general. He watches with a heavy heart as Cescau suffers under the dominance of Burgmans. Burgmans, meanwhile, doesn't seem to like Cescau being at the controls day-to-day. When Burgmans gets angry, Storm watches as Cescau almost physically recoils. Nothing is being achieved like this. It's high time for a new chairman to come in and ring the changes.

And they're working on it. With support from Jeroen van der Veer and Lord Simon, Antony Burgmans has embarked on the search for his successor. Executive recruitment company Egon Zehnder has been tasked with finding the first ever independent chairman of the Unilever board.

CHAPTER 5

OUTSIDERS IN CHARGE

2007–2008

Mike the Knife. That's what the Swedish press calls him. Michael Treschow takes it all in good humour. He knows where it comes from. Since 2002, he has mostly been in the news as the chairman who presided over the rescue of leading telecoms company Ericsson. In just 18 months the company laid off 31,000 of its 85,000 employees. Treschow doesn't lose any sleep over it. In a recent interview with *Business Week*, he stated, 'Restructuring is a part of daily life. If you don't do it every day, [the mess] piles up.' He believes in the power of good analysis and never asks himself whether or not something is going to work. He sees this as a betrayal of the process: we'll cross that bridge when we come to it.

After a stellar career in business, Treschow is now the chair of the Swedish association of employers. The call from David Kidd at Egon Zehnder doesn't surprise him. A couple of months previously he had applied for a similar role at an even larger company at the request of this executive recruiter. In the end, they had gone for someone a couple of years younger. From that moment on, those same guys at Egon Zehnder had naturally had him in their sights, he had become their business.

It had been Kidd's colleague Joost van Heyningen Nanninga's idea to put out some feelers with Treschow about the role of chairman at Unilever. The briefing from Lord Simon, Antony Burgmans and Jeroen van der Veer had made it clear to the headhunters that it couldn't be a Brit, a Dutchman or an American. The first two nationalities were still too contentious and an American would not understand the European basis of Unilever sufficiently. Van Heyningen Nanninga believes it's important at a company like Unilever, where all important functions have been carried out by Unilever veterans for over eighty years, that an incomer doesn't start throwing his weight around straight away. Coming from a small country, a reserved Swede will fit the bill well and not be perceived immediately as overly threatening. Swedes also speak good English and are internationally orientated. The fact is, though, that *this* Swede has never worked in the fast-moving consumer goods market. However, that could give him an edge; a good chairman needs to make decisions objectively and, above all, avoid playing CEO. People from the same business background can seldom resist the temptation.

Naturally, Treschow is interested in becoming the first outsider to step into the role. It's clear from his very first conversation with Lord Simon that things at Unilever aren't going well. They are still too inward-facing. Simon insists that the company isn't innovative or enterprising enough. Even worse, there's not been enough growth for a long time. Simon suggests that Burgmans's successor will have to pull off a transformation. The new chairmen need to create an atmosphere of growth: significant growth. Jeroen van der Veer agrees. The top boss at Shell is impressed by the quiet, affable Swede, and by his solid track record. He could really make a difference at Unilever.

The Swedish engineer Treschow is immediately intrigued by the over a century-old credo 'doing well by doing good'. He sees it as a good principle, and one that can be a source of pride. Pride is a requirement for success, because only those who have pride in their work make the necessary contribution. As far as he's concerned, this kind of company origin-story or raison d'être doesn't have to be true, so long as it works. He gets the impression that this kind of pride has been thin on the ground at Unilever over the past few years.

Treschow, the 63-year-old son of a major in the Swedish army, suspects that Burgmans wasn't really capable of giving Cescau the space and support he needed. He looked over his shoulder constantly, criticising his decisions. It must have been an impossible position for the Frenchman. In reality, Burgmans had always been and remained his boss. No, it hadn't been wise bumping Burgmans up to chairman. He's the last person you can ask to take a step back from daily running of things and focus on listening. Burgmans has been too involved in operational matters for too long to actually be able to listen properly. And that's a chairman's most important job: listening and asking lots of questions.

Cescau isn't involved in Treschow's appointment, he had one conversation with him and was asked afterwards whether he thought he would be able to get along with the Swede. It seemed to be no problem for the Frenchman.

'We are delighted that Michael Treschow has agreed to succeed me as the first independent Chairman of the Boards of Unilever. When these changes are implemented we will have finalised a complete restructuring of our corporate governance arrangements. This change process was initiated in 2004 and it involved the elimination of Advisory Directors, the phase-out of the dual leadership system, the adoption of a one-tier board structure and the appointment of a fully independent Chairman of the Boards.' Antony Burgmans sums up the state of play in his last annual report, in March 2007. He traces a few long-term trends: turnover in Western Europe has declined from 65 per cent to 34 per cent of the worldwide total, developing countries now make up 40 per cent. Fifteen years ago, 25 per cent of turnover consisted of products that had nothing to do with fast-moving consumer goods. Now Unilever is focusing on 400 brands, rather than 1,600. Twelve of those brands create turnover of more than €1 billion per year and together make up 55 per cent of turnover. The growth in personal care products is nothing short of spectacular: from 4 per cent of turnover in 1972 to 28 per cent today.

While Burgmans speaks of a company that is rock solid and completely prepared for the future, Patrick Cescau opens his message a few pages later rather differently: 'We are on a journey to restore Unilever's competitiveness and growth potential. That journey is ongoing. The improving top-line performance recorded during the year suggests that the wide-ranging changes we made to the business in 2004 and 2005 – both to our organisation and to our strategy – were the right ones for Unilever.' At the last minute, the CEO takes a swipe at the chairman who's about to leave: 'I also believe that we will look back on 2006 as the year when the business regained its confidence and self-belief after the setbacks of recent years.'[1]

Michael Treschow is congratulated from all sides on his appointment. The Swede also receives a friendly message from a certain Paul Polman. He can't recall ever having met the Dutchman. And indeed he hasn't. But Polman has made it his habit to send out 10 handwritten notes every day. Sometimes to acquaintances, sometimes to people he doesn't know, often on the occasion of an important or noteworthy appointment in his sphere. And so, Treschow receives a card with warm congratulations from the CFO of Nestlé.

'Patrick Cescau, Unilever's chief executive, seems to be gradually winning back the confidence of investors, although as one shareholder recently put it: "Unilever is a bit like Pirates of the Caribbean 3: it could be so much better than it is."' Cescau's first two years are summarised in the *Financial Times*. The Unilever CEO has invited analysts at Sanford C. Bernstein & Co. to challenge the leadership of Unilever with a 'provocative analysis'. The apparently well-informed newspaper is only too happy to oblige and summarise the findings of the analysis: if the company were better managed its profits could improve considerably. They see no potential in splitting up the company and instead emphasise the need to bring in people from outside as quickly as possible:

people who can overturn the bureaucratic stilted Unilever culture and make it dynamic. The company needs to learn to be more transparent and informal and to communicate less defensively with shareholders and the rest of the world. Cescau's task is clear: get to grips with a business culture that is still exhibiting a lot of bureaucratic tendencies.[2]

The *FT* quotes from a meeting with Andrew Wood, an analyst at Sanford C. Bernstein. Wood has been following Unilever's fortunes for years and put in an appearance during the senior management seminar, speaking to 20 successful managers handpicked by Sandy Ogg and Patrick Cescau as leaders of the future. People like Alan Jope, Kees Kruythoff, Peter ter Kulve, Jan Zijderveld, Keith Weed, Simon Clift and Nitin Paranjpe spent two weeks together at the Four Acres training centre under the leadership of C. K. Prahalad, identifying Unilever's priorities for the next few years.

Just like the young managers from Project Foresight eight years previously, these 20 'leaders of the future' search the whole world for inspiration. A visit to the 22-year-old Facebook boss Mark Zuckerberg makes a particularly big impression. Asked whether he really thinks that Facebook will generate income from selling adverts online, the American replies with a chuckle that he had hoped the Unilever managers would be the ones to give *him* that answer.

Online market research is the first of their three recommendations. The increase in internet usage means that Unilever can't escape the necessity of collecting and compiling all the information about their customers in a single central point, in order to get to know them better. The second recommendation concerns further commitment to emerging markets. There are billions of people in those countries who have yet to buy their first stick of deodorant. Concerns about what the planet can tolerate, in terms of both production and consumption, are named as the third recommendation. It is in Unilever's DNA to engage rigorously with such questions. Various colleagues wonder whether Cescau, with his sustained focus on improving quarterly results, is really going to go down that road.

Are you all one hundred per cent certain that you are in the fast-moving consumer goods market? To everyone's annoyance, Michael Treschow repeats the question over and over again. Even though people warned him, he is constantly surprised: what a ponderous, navel-gazing crew of people this is. Why aren't they profiting from their deep-rooted, global presence in the way they should be? In preparation for his new role, Michael Treschow dove head first into every aspect of Unilever. He is completely unimpressed. The Unilever bosses seem to be defined by a lack of resolve. In fact, no decisions are made at all, because after each so-called resolution the discussion begins. They talk endlessly about what the decision means and who exactly is responsible for it. He finds a perfect example in Kees van der Graaf's suggestions about how to make swift and significant changes to the European operation. They have been left to one side for far too long. Treschow realises that Burgmans has no desire to leave just after the announcement of a big reorganisation. This is the first place he's going to need to make a start.

Van der Graaf himself is tired. He's been waiting with baited breath in anticipation of the approval of his plans to dramatically restructure Europe for almost six months at this point. The same story emerges in the 360 degree feedback Van der Graaf receives on his own performance. The colleagues reporting on Van der Graaf criticise him for going along with his colleagues in the board too much. Meanwhile, his direct colleagues on the board criticise him for the opposite, for listening too much to his subordinates. While his plans lie neglected he's having to motivate his colleagues to meet their targets.

Van der Graaf works between 80 and 100 hours a week and feels guilty for doing it. Back in the summer of 2005, meditating on a mountain in Montana, he had promised himself he would change, that he would devote much more of his time to family and friends, as well as to the FSHD foundation and the search for a cure for his son's illness. Back then, he had expressed his concerns to Cescau. He told him about his diminishing love for Unilever and the lack of family intimacy in the company. The Frenchman had advised him to organise his schedule better and to cross out everything that didn't contribute to his three greatest priorities.

Clearly, that hasn't worked. In a conversation with Cescau, Van der Graaf once again declares that Unilever is no longer *his* company: that it's too much about making money, about short-term results, about coaxing up the share price. Cescau is firm. This is the reality in which Unilever has to operate. And he, for one, has no regrets. They come to the same conclusion: maybe it's a good idea for Van der Graaf to step down. The only thing Cescau wishes to avoid is him stepping down at the exact moment that the reorganisation is announced. That would be too dramatic. They agree that he will stay on until May 2008 to make a start on it with them. After that, his successor can finish the task.

The knowledge that the end is in sight gives Van der Graaf the peace of mind to keep going for the final stretch. Cescau asks him to explain his situation to Treschow himself and ask for his approval. Van der Graaf thinks that's for the best. He has no idea what the appointment of the Swede is all about, how would someone with that background understand the world of Unilever?

But he's pleased that the arrival of Treschow means most of his plan can finally be implemented.

The announcement that Unilever's Europe division is going to make almost 10 per cent of employees redundant in order to raise the operating margin to 15 per cent boosts the share price by 4 per cent. But to many analysts it sounds like a repeat of old tactics. Hadn't they promised the same back in 1999 with the announcement of the 'Path to Growth'? Back then they had set aside €5 billion for restructuring, this time it's €3 billion. They had just managed to reach their target back then, only for the margin to fall to 13.7 per cent again afterwards. Once again, it's all about restructuring, closing factories and cutting costs. Where are the plans to actually start growing? Are we seeing the hand of the new chairman Treschow in all this, wonders the *Financial Times*. That would be a shame. The company needs to grow much more rapidly if it wants to get into the same league as its successful competitors in terms of results; they are growing twice as fast.

Treschow careens from one nasty surprise to another: at each board meeting, two people take notes, one for the British PLC and one for the Dutch NV. And it seems the whole company is set up like that. Everything twice. He is also deeply frustrated by the sheer number of presentations: the piles of Excel printouts that are handed round. The new CFO, Jim Lawrence, originally from General Mills, makes the whole thing much too complicated, presenting in such excessive detail that you lose track of what he's even talking about. And then there's the interminable complaining: the Brits and Dutchmen going on about what belongs to whom, which part belongs where. There is constant conflict over the distribution of titles and responsibilities. When Treschow asks them whether there isn't another way of doing things, he's told to get used to it: this is what it's like here, it's how it developed historically.

He notices that lots of people are busy with all kinds of projects at the same time. That looks interesting but functions as a smokescreen. Treschow regards himself as a hardliner when it comes to a clear sense of duty. He wants it to be crystal clear who is responsible for what and holds no truck at all with complicated matrices to manage shared responsibilities. That leads to nothing but trouble, with people having to get together to agree over tasks only to disappear one by one. He agrees entirely with the findings of the Bernstein analysts: what Unilever needs most is fresh blood. With this management in charge, the company is never going to win the war.

The layer below the top management is in agreement with Treschow. Jan Zijderveld, responsible for the Middle East and North Africa, believes that Cescau and his 'One Unilever' message have saved the company. He has made it clear to the outside world that Unilever won't be split up despite its weakened state, that it is *one* company, with central purchasing, *one* sales apparatus and *one* route to the customer. This has given Unilever space to breathe. But Zijderveld also realises that the Frenchman is a bookkeeper first and foremost. In his search for areas to create value, he is endlessly confused by complicated matrices with blue lines, red lines and dotted lines. A plethora of lines that all eventually lead to Cescau himself. And in the meantime, the company isn't growing fast enough.

'Doing well and doing good', thinks Cescau, emphasising that financial success must remain in first place. Only a successful company can be a responsible company. 'In the old days, we mostly created functional surplus, then emotional surplus, and nowadays social surplus. We create additional value for society and, crucially, make good returns for our shareholders too.'

Fine words, but as far as Marc Engel sees it, the last component is dominating proceedings. Cescau appointed the Dutchman as director of purchasing. Engel has been working at Unilever since 1990. He is rising through the ranks but for years now has had to explain to family and friends at parties why on earth he is still working at Unilever. What kind of company *is* it, what does it stand for, is it even growing anymore? Don't they mostly make unhealthy food, washing powder and unnecessary ointments? And for the past ten years, the share price has been going nowhere, so it's not making you rich either.

Even when he turns the conversation to their sustainability efforts, the criticism wins out. It's great that Unilever is going for one hundred per cent sustainability in tea production but wouldn't it make more sense to take over production of tea directly? Making tea production more sustainable would have been much easier if Unilever hadn't sold off almost all its plantations. The same is true for palm oil.

From Engel's perspective, the company has mostly been led by finance men, people like FitzGerald and Cescau. By their calculation, it was always sensible to sell off assets, to reduce the balance: it led to an immediate gain for the bottom line.

Tex Gunning no longer believes in all this. His colleagues notice that he is becoming cynical. He has no respect whatsoever for Cescau, who he doesn't think knows the first thing about marketing. In his eyes, opportunism is running rampant. He is leaving Unilever after 24 years to become the CEO of Vedior. Even Peter ter Kulve, head of the growing ice cream business, feels like he spends his days working solely on the share price. If it goes up, then they all profit, but you need more than that to run a company. In their opinion, Cescau has done little else other than reduce lots of costs within the company. He even took money from the pension pot, which had risen to 200 per cent of final salary thanks to the steep rise in the return on investments. He was well within his rights to do that, but doing so makes pensions less future-proof; after all, share prices can drop steeply too.

Ter Kulve is worried about their strategy. Even if they question whether Cescau has a proper understanding of brands and customers, managers like him want to talk to the CEO of Unilever about them. The exchange of ideas isn't there. Meanwhile, Unilever, steered centrally by the product category managers in London, is beginning to look more and more like Procter & Gamble. Does that really suit the culture of the company? Aren't we just going to end up going from 'hopelessly local' to 'hopelessly global'? Cescau's obsession with P&G doesn't inspire confidence among his critics. Ter Kulve wonders how long they can keep going like this. What is it that makes Unilever unique? Start doing something with *that*!

Cescau is mostly unaware of all this. He's content. The share price has risen by almost 60 per cent within three years. That sounds more impressive than it is. After the dot-com crash, investors looked for safe investments, for shares in companies that won't suddenly collapse. Companies that make things people are always going to need, like food and hygiene products, are a safe bet. The share prices of Procter & Gamble and Nestlé also grew considerably, by 34 per cent and almost 70 per cent, respectively. They are all profiting from the rapid expansion of emerging markets too, particularly in Asia. Hundreds of millions of people in India, China and Indonesia are suddenly earning enough to buy laundry detergent, deodorant or the occasional bar of chocolate.

Cescau is proud that revenue has increased by 5.5 per cent during 2007, compared to 3.8 per cent in 2006, the first whole year of his tenure. This growth is almost entirely down to the emerging markets, where revenue has grown by 11 per cent. They now account for 44 per cent of the total; three years ago it was only 36 per cent. Sales of household and personal hygiene products in particular have increased enormously. The fact they have sold off various activities means that turnover has only gone up 1.5 per cent, to around €40 billion. Reorganisations and sales of divisions have meant a 17 per cent reduction in workforce, from 206,000 to 171,000 employees.

'We have a new strategy, we have a new structure and we have a new way of working. But all that means nothing; it's about the people who are going to realise all this, which is why we have brought in new blood throughout the company. We are even making progress when it comes to diversifying the leadership.'

During the third leadership summit, this time in the Dutch village Noordwijk, Cescau is intent on underlining all they have achieved. His assessment: 'We're saving more, we're refining our portfolio even further and we're bringing "One Unilever" deeper and deeper into the organisation.' He sounds almost relieved as he says, 'we've modernised our governance; we've now got a truly independent chairmen for the first time ever'. 'Of course, not everything is going to plan yet, but I'm asking you all to be patient and keep persevering. And to take a moment to think about everything we've already achieved. Last week our shares reached the highest price in our history. In only three years, we have increased the value of this company by 20 billion euros, let me say that again: 20 billion euros.'[3]

The subject of diversity is once again back on the agenda too. Little has been done since the Costa Rica trip with the 100 male top managers six years previously. The Frenchman Cescau isn't particularly interested in changing things but that only makes the Swede Treschow all to more determined. To him diversity in leadership is essential: if you only have people with the same point of view then you don't have the capacity to see that the world around you is changing, for that you need to ask the right questions. Those are only asked if you have put together a diverse team. Sandy Ogg and Treschow are in complete agreement on this issue. They try to identify the causes. Ogg is surprised that a company so diverse in terms of nationality and skin colour falls so dramatically behind when it comes to the percentage of women in leadership roles. Last year the intake of new junior colleagues was 56 per cent women. Yet when it comes to advancement to senior positions, they fall away in droves. One level up, it's 39 per cent women, the next 27 per cent, 17 per cent after that. Of the top 100 in the company only 8 per cent are women.

Ogg regards this as an enormous waste of talent and assets. He is convinced that the company would make far fewer mistakes across the board if there were more women in leadership. This would particularly benefit a company like Unilever; after all, 86 per cent of their products are bought by women. It's clear to Ogg that this many men must, by definition, design the wrong products and commission the wrong adverts; these kinds of mistakes must be happening on a grand scale. He manages to persuade Cescau to tackle the issue as a matter of urgency. The CEO allows Ogg to instruct the top 100 in the company to appoint a woman to their team within the following 18 months. The message: one woman in your team is only the beginning, two is better and three is how many are really required. He calls the project 'One More'. It is given top priority.

Ogg tells these top 100 they are all going on a list on the wall in his office from which he intends to cross off their names one by one. If your name is still on that list in 18 months' time then you no longer have a future at this company. The outburst of anger is immediate and overwhelming. Many men claim not to be able to find any good women, they want an extension or an exception. Ogg speaks with them personally and tells them that 50 per cent of the human race is female. They'd better look more carefully.

More complaints roll in. The yearly assessment of salary levels at Unilever in comparison to equivalent companies reveals that they should actually be 5 per cent higher in order to remain competitive. However, with the sense of crisis still in the air, Cescau wants to keep costs down and has resolved to put a salary freeze in place.

At Ogg's suggestion, they also address the travel budget, reducing it by 50 per cent. The leadership of the company is now required to substitute as many meetings as possible for video conferences. Ogg quickly calculates that five video conferencing devices can lead to a saving of €5 million in tickets and hotel costs per year. A hundred more of those devices are ordered. Here and there, Ogg receives positive feedback from colleagues who tell him that their marriage is benefitting from them spending more evenings at home. Ogg realises that this measure could also work well for female colleagues, who are often less keen on travelling for their careers.

He has only been CEO for three years so far, normally he would be able to continue in the role for another two. Yet Cescau is turning 60 in September, which will mean he can apply for his pension. He is in two minds. As far as he is concerned, he has succeeded in bringing about the large-scale modernisation that was necessary; Unilever's new structure is up and running. Overseeing the next phase properly would require at least four more years and that's just not viable. He made a commitment to his wife and children to finally make more time for them. A conversation with his senior managers reveals that the powers that be inside the company wouldn't be averse to him leaving slightly earlier than planned. The board gives Patrick Cescau exactly the nudge he needs to take early retirement. It is agreed that as of 1 January 2009, after over three years in charge, he will pass the baton to a new CEO.

Paul Polman, by this point 51 years old, is finding everything at Nestlé very much to his liking. But he tells the magazine *Twentevisie* that he still follows everything that goes on at Procter & Gamble very closely. 'Even if it's only to keep a close eye on my pension', he chuckles. He claims he had actually been planning to retire completely when they gave him the chop.[4]

When asked whether he is about to become the new CEO of Nestlé, he explains that Nestlé is set to transform itself over the next few years into a company dealing in 'food, health and wellness'. 'That's a tall order. I have discussed my plans with the board of directors.' He continues, laughing: 'But I tell each of them to pick the other one.'

Polman is more eager to talk about how he managed to get 200 Nestlé employees to run the Geneva Marathon. In order to provide them with the requisite mental fortitude, he invited an American Vietnam veteran who travelled the world in a wheelchair to come and talk to his people. All 200 colleagues then had to sign a contract promising to complete the 26.2 miles. It took the last ones over seven hours to make it back but they were met with applause from the others. Polman explains: 'You can motivate yourself by telling as many people as possible what it is you intend to do. Do it with friends or for a charity. If you back out then, you get yourself into difficulties.'

Polman is praised for his work as Nestlé CFO. Journalists and analysts speculate that he is being groomed for the next step. That would be remarkable. Up until now, Nestlé has also only ever appointed old hands to the top spot, men with decades of experience under their belts. Peter Brabeck-Letmathe has been in post for almost eleven years. While Unilever revenue was shrinking by almost 25 per cent, Nestlé's was growing under his leadership by around 50 per cent, to $83 billion. Brabeck-Letmathe asks Polman to throw his hat in the ring to replace him. In an interview with *Fortune*, he explains why the producer of Nescafé and Maggi has been so much more successful than competitors like Unilever and Kraft: 'In the 90s there was a paradigm that only "focus" would lead to operating efficiency. It meant selling off lower-margin businesses and not investing in new markets, so that there would be an instant improvement in EBIT. Almost all of my competitors followed this. But we saw that with focus, there was a danger that you would not be able to get long-term growth. We looked for a different model. We wanted to combine a certain complexity with operating efficiency. That way we could have top-line growth improvement and long-term margin improvement. This is biology – the day you stop growing you start dying. If you focus and focus and focus you will end up in the hands of somebody else.'

Brabeck-Letmathe explains how he brought individual divisions with a high level of autonomy together using a big IT-platform (Globe), designed to keep the whole company working in unison. 'When we were a 50 billion company, we changed to get to a 100 billion company. To get to be a 200 billion company, we had to change structure again. The businesses are all different. I can't run ice cream the same way that I run Nescafé. I had to think how to ensure we could get organic growth of 5–6 per cent, which is very high for the industry. Now we have 27 brands with sales of more than CHF 1 billion each. Without Globe, we wouldn't have been able to become a 200 billion company.'[5]

There is also criticism. Brabeck-Letmathe is both CEO and chairman since 2005. More and more stakeholders wonder if there is not too much power in the hands of one man. Where are the necessary checks and balances? As has been done in the UK and the Netherlands, adjustments have been made in the Swiss governance code recently. It is allowed to combine the roles but preferably not.

In the run up to Nestlé's announcement of who is to become the new CEO, the Swiss press is convinced that Paul Polman is in with the best chance. Most analysts also think it will be him. He is regarded as the man who has made Nestlé run more efficiently over the last eighteen months, the man who got the Globe system up and running effectively. *Forbes* reports enthusiastically that everything is going so well under Polman's financial leadership that Nestlé will buy back $21.1 billion in shares over the next three years. His erstwhile mentor at Procter & Gamble, Durk Jager, adds fuel to the fire and tells the marketing platform *Ad Age*, 'he is a big-picture man. He is [a] future and results-oriented manager who cuts through the bureaucracy, the politics. He is a good marketer with interest in innovation.'[6] Polman's biggest competitor is Paul Bulcke. This Belgian has headed up the company's American activities over the past few years, with more than twenty-eight years in service at Nestlé in total.

Brabeck-Letmathe tells *Fortune* that it has been a very careful and intensive process. Over the past few months, both candidates have presented their vision for the future of Nestlé to the members of the board individually. There have been meetings with the families of the two candidates. He also informs the journalists that the outcome of the selection process was unanimous.

The board of directors chooses 53-year-old Paul Bulcke. Brabeck-Letmathe denies that the fact Polman was an outsider had been to his disadvantage. 'No. He has very high values. If we had been perhaps in a crisis or you would have to do fundamental changes in a short period, perhaps his personality would have been the right one, but this company is not in crisis.'

Investors have other ideas. The Nestlé share price drops 8 per cent. Polman too is deeply disappointed. He had been through intensive discussions with Brabeck-Letmathe and thinks that there *is* a great deal that needs changing. To hear Brabeck-Letmathe tell it, the turn to 'food, health and wellness' is already complete and his successor simply needs to keep following the course he has laid out. Polman realises that this is really Brabeck-Letmathe trying to preserve what he himself has built. He finds this disappointing. The thing he least understands is his boss asking him to take over Bulcke's old job, to resolve the issues the Belgian couldn't fix in the United States once and for all. Irritated, Polman asks Brabeck-Letmathe why he appointed Bulcke as his replacement when he was so clearly failing in his duties.

Polman's heart is no longer in it. First the palaver at Procter & Gamble, now this let-down. All that energy lost to political wrangling, to constantly watching your back. He is tired of the constant cycle of meetings and asks himself once more whether he still wants to work in a big company where people spend the whole time trying to make themselves feel safe and secure. Why don't people just do what they need to do? Off their own bat. Because it's necessary.[7]

Every so often he thinks: Why didn't I just become a doctor? And even more occasionally whether he shouldn't give it a go now. One of those doctors of tropical medicine who tries to save human lives under difficult circumstances, those are the real heroes in his eyes. His work for the Kilimanjaro Blind Trust gives him a lot of satisfaction. It's the closest he comes to the real thing.

So what to do now? Is he still on the right path? He rereads one of his favourite books: *Man's Search for Meaning*, by Viktor Frankl. Frankl was an Austrian philosopher who wrote this little book shortly after surviving the Second World War in four concentration camps and coming to the conclusion that a successful life isn't about obtaining pleasure, consumption and the avoidance of pain, but about finding meaning. Man therefore shouldn't ask himself what the world has to offer him but what he has to offer the world. The meaning one finds is always related to the other, to stepping beyond the self. The more a person is willing to efface himself by dedicating himself to a task, or to loving another, the more human he is and the more he realises his potential.

These words touch Polman anew every time he reads them. This is the essential truth. But what does he have to offer the world?

Michael Treschow has asked Sandy Ogg to help him find Cescau's successor. Ogg thinks it's logical for Cescau to depart early, the man deserves a medal, albeit a bronze one. He saved the company by the skin of its teeth. To go for gold, and get the show truly back on the road, the company now needs a much more charismatic leader. Internally, there are three logical candidates: Harish Manwani, Vindi Banga and Michael Polk. CFO Jim Lawrence thinks he belongs on that list too.

Treschow notices that his colleagues are assuming the new CEO will come from among their own ranks. He's not so sure. With the support of Lord Simon and Jeroen van der Veer from the Nominations Committee, they decide that at the very least the internal candidates need to be compared to the talent on offer outside Unilever. When this leads to criticism, Treschow asks provocatively why the Unilever bosses aren't up for the challenge. If they're so good – the best company in the world – then what have they got to be afraid of?

Treschow asks the headhunters who paired him with Unilever to start a search. David Kidd and Joost van Heyningen Nanninga are instructed to look for a CEO who will fully commit to growth. Treschow tells them at the outset that there is a high chance Unilever will appoint someone from outside to this position for the first time in its history.

Lord Simon adds to the requirements. He wants the new CEO to dare to look further ahead. It bothers him that so many leaders in the business world develop ideas that are too small and look for quick solutions. They don't look more than three years or so ahead. Simon sees this short-term thinking as an indicator of laziness. The changes necessary to be successful in the long term are drastic and require much more time to prepare. They require a leader to change the mindset of a company and open themselves up to a completely new way of doing things, to developing new capacities. Simon wants the new CEO of Unilever to dare to make plans with a timescale of at least five to ten years.[8]

The executive searchers start looking through their files for a second in command who would like to start playing first fiddle somewhere. They quickly alight on Paul Polman. In the President Wilson Hotel in Geneva, David Kidd talks to Polman, telling him that they are looking for a boss for a big player in the world of fast-moving consumer goods. Polman plays hard to get. He and his wife Kim are making plans to expand their Kilimanjaro Blind Trust operation into more countries. He tells Kidd he has no more interest in the world of big business.

That being said, he returns for a second meeting, during which Kidd tells him that the company concerned is Unilever. Now his interest is piqued after all. Polman sets up meetings with Jeroen van der Veer and Lord Simon. One Saturday morning, on his way to visit his mother in Enschede, he drops by for a coffee at Van der Veer's house in Wassenaar. In the hour and a half he's there, Van der Veer notices that his guest possesses many of the qualities and attributes he put on his list. He's got plenty of relevant experience, lots of energy, has thought things over carefully and clearly regards the health of a company as top priority. The Shell boss likes the fact that Polman isn't solely focused on lining his own pockets. It seems he combines the American way of doing business with a sharp awareness of what is customary in Europe. And it's clear he wants to be the boss for once after the way things ended at Procter & Gamble and Nestlé. They speak about the need for Unilever to grow for real. The word 'sustainability' doesn't come up.

During the meeting with Treschow, the subject is the same; they talk about growth, about dominating the market. Treschow sees in Polman a desire to be the best. They click. The Swede is impressed by Polman's humility, his primary driver isn't money. He isn't a macho man. He also doesn't express any negativity towards his former employers. He tells Treschow there's a lot to be done but that he sees this as providing opportunities too. In an effort to moderate his enthusiasm, Treschow tries to tell him about the less positive aspects of their situation. In doing so, he realises that the fact Polman has worked for Unilever's biggest competitors is a mark against him. How can you just dive in and work for a company you spent years at P&G and Nestlé making unkind jokes about?

In both conversations, Polman makes it clear that he left Procter & Gamble on less than positive terms. On the Unilever side, efforts begin to establish exactly why that happened but they never manage to build a clear picture. Van der Veer assumes that Nestlé managed to get to the bottom of it a few years earlier, otherwise the Swiss would never have made him CFO. He lets the matter lie. Kees Storm is also enthusiastic, he tells Polman all about the dramatic increase in turnover at Unilever, and about their shrinking market share over the last ten years. Polman promises to do something about it without delay.

The advisors from Egon Zehnder spend months getting a total of seven candidates through the assessment process. If the best internal candidate and the best external candidate end up with the same score, the company will select the internal candidate by default. This won't be an issue in this case. Polman quickly emerges as the big favourite.

Although he hasn't lived in the Netherlands for 33 years, Polman is still another Dutchman. Some former directors wonder whether this is sensible. Has the company moved beyond its Dutch-British tensions? In years to come, Unilever will mostly be growing in emerging markets, in countries like India, Indonesia and China. Isn't it time to make one of the superstar Indians the boss? But on the other hand, what would having an Indian as CEO mean?

Veteran Nihal Kaviratne doesn't believe that is a conceivable scenario for the Brits. Wim Dik agrees. Unilever is an icon of the Western business world, it wouldn't be fitting to place an enterprise like that in the hands of someone from Asia. The company isn't ready for it yet. Dik thinks Unilever have struck it lucky with Polman, who is almost as enthusiastic about the company as Dik himself. Nestlé were foolish to bring in such a person on the promise of making him the boss and then not do it, thinks Dik. They're going to live to regret it. He realises that after his careers at Procter & Gamble and Nestlé, Polman is actually embarking on his third 'Unilever'.

As a mark of respect, Treschow calls Brabeck-Letmathe, his opposite number at Nestlé, to tell him that he's taking Polman off his hands. The Swiss chairman is laconic, wishes Treschow and Polman every success with their collaboration and also tells him there had never been any intention of making Polman boss at Nestlé. At the end of the day, he wasn't a true insider.

PART 2

Doing Good and Doing Well, 2008–2016

CHAPTER 6

ONLY RESPONSIBLE COMPANIES GO THE DISTANCE

September–December 2008

Two weeks after the announcement that Paul Polman will be the next CEO of Unilever, the American investment bank Lehman Brothers files for bankruptcy. The financial crisis is an unavoidable fact; worldwide, share prices are collapsing. Trust in stock markets, banks and big business is plummeting to an all-time low.

Polman embraces the crisis, 'I'm pleased it's here. This is Darwin at its best. It's great to start a job at a time of uncertainty. It requires me to implement measures for the business to become stronger. When there is a lot of wind even the turkeys can fly, but with no wind it's only the eagles. I'd hate to be a turkey.'[1]

Fifty-two-year-old Polman gives his first big interview to *Portfolio*, the student newspaper at his alma mater, the University of Cincinnati. 'The significant events we have seen in the financial markets are affecting us all, and it is clear that politics and public policy will need to drive the solution rather than Wall Street alone.' The business world needs to start acting too though, Polman says. 'Creating a better world is equally important for business, which simply cannot succeed in societies that failing.' He underlines the important role they have to play in tackling issues like poverty, global warming and water scarcity and challenges his old business school to incorporate more socioeconomic elements into their curricula. He cites his hero Viktor Frankl, who said in a speech back in the 1960s that the Statue of Liberty on the east coast of the United States should be matched by a Statue of Responsibility in the west.

Polman tells his student interviewers, 'You can achieve anything you want if you are passionate about it. And you can do well by doing good. It was the Dalai Lama who said: "If you seek enlightenment for yourself to enhance yourself you miss the purpose. If you seek enlightenment for yourself to enable yourself to serve others, you are with purpose."'

The man who is going to become the first outsider CEO of Unilever, on 1 January 2009, thinks it's a good interview. He frames the cover of that issue of *Portfolio* and hangs it on the wall of his office back home in Geneva.

Paul Polman can't wait. From 1 October, he wanders around the two head offices. His new colleagues joke that he must be the most expensive intern they've ever had. An intern who behaves like a student. At London head office, they regularly see him hunched over his desk in a tiny back office for days at a time. Studying, reading, writing. He is immersing himself in everything; he wants to know it all. He also spends a great deal of time at the library in Port Sunlight. Before bed, he's reading three inches-thick volumes of Unilever's history. Various employees who chat to their incumbent boss are impressed. Polman already knows more about the history of the company than many of his new colleagues who have been working here their whole lives.

While the banking crisis dominates the news in the background, and more and more people get pulled into the disaster, Polman comes across the book *So Clean*, a portrait of Lord Leverhulme, the founder of British Lever PLC. A hundred years ago, William Lever became convinced that a company only had a right to exist so look as it provided well for society. After all, it was society that made the business possible. Lever is described as a man who was much more committed to this ideal than his enterprising contemporaries.

In the course of his research, Polman naturally also comes across the margarine manufacturers Van den Bergh & Jurgens. But he finds the two businessmen who form the basis of the Dutch history of Unilever are much less inspiring. Before they merged in the second decade of the twentieth century those families mostly seem to have spent a lot of time and energy fighting one another.

William Lever, on the other hand, was a pioneer, a true contributor to world progress. Polman thinks it's inspiring that Lever wanted to share his wealth and was more than just a businessman. As a liberal member of parliament he brought about the introduction of the first 'Old Age Pension' in 1908. By guaranteeing his workers' jobs and continuing to pay their salaries, he provided the most volunteers of any company to fight the Germans during the First World War. To Lever, making money was a means, not an end.

Thomas Dreier, a contemporary and friend of Lever, described an exchange between the businessman and a banker in 1891, 'When the banker reproached him that he could make at least $3 million by floating his company on the stock market, William Lever looked at him in bewilderment. "Do you really think I could ask $3 million from the investing public for a company that is five years old and could go under at any moment thanks to the competition it faces?" The banker was equally stunned: "Why in the devil should it bother you what happens after your company goes public, so long as you've got your money? Make money, that's my motto." Lever shook his head pityingly: "Be of service, that's my motto. And so it seems that we must part ways, we can't do business under such different banners."[2]

With a selection of big banks currently quaking in their boots, Polman reflects that William Lever had it relatively easy. Not making his company public meant he never had to deal with outside shareholders. Polman doesn't have that kind of room to manoeuvre. A mere couple of hundred yards up the road from Blackfriars, the head office of Unilever in London is the financial centre of Europe. Concerns are growing by the day there. Suspicion of the banking system is so great by this point that people are worrying it will collapse completely. Governments are pulling out all the stops trying to keep that from happening.

This terrifying situation inspires Polman. He realises that the world would benefit now more than ever from businessmen like Lever. Especially right now, when it's becoming clear that companies are being driven far too much by a logic of opportunism, by the short-term calculations and avarice of bankers, by analysts and by Wall Street. In their heads, it's solely about making money, everything comes down to the quarterly results and the share price. As far as Polman is concerned, this is the biggest reason people are losing faith in bankers and multinationals: they don't work for their community, they only work for the winners.

He thinks bankers should remember their place and start making themselves useful again. Banks should help companies finance their efforts to make the world a better place for everyone. Companies whose main aim is to make money have no right to exist. That should be the biggest takeaway from the last twenty years. The time has come for a company like Unilever to start acting as a role model. This is about things like food and hygiene; Unilever has the proper DNA. Doing well by doing good; Lever found the right formula 120 years ago. It's a magnificent ideal. But where has it gone? Where are the William Levers in the Unilever of 2008?

They are often buried deep inside the company. Various colleagues, often lifers, having been trying to hammer home the importance of sustainability for 20 years at this point. Notably, they are often chemists and researchers, people who started in the firm's vast R&D departments. They think Unilever should take more responsibility for the world in which it operates. Chris Dutilh is just such a person. When he hears that Polman used to be a senior figure at Procter & Gamble, he can't help but think of the Omo Power scandal. The chemist, responsible for environmental management at the margarine subsidiary Van den Bergh & Jurgens, had been deeply disappointed that the ever more power-ful and impulsive marketers hadn't been willing to listen to their colleagues in the R&D department. As a result, a washing detergent that would have been good for the environment thanks to its energy saving properties had flopped.

Dutilh has been working to make manufacturing processes at Unilever more sustainable ever since 1988. He was inspired by the Brundtland report 'Our Common Future'. Back then, in 1987, it had been made explicitly and painfully clear for the first time that the big, global environmental issues were the result of poverty in one part of the world and the totally unsustainable pro-duction and consumption of ever increasing volumes of products in the other. The commission appointed by the United Nations under Norwegian chair Gro Harlem Brundtland was the first to make a clear shift from a world in which it's all about 'me, here, now' to a world in which 'they, there, later' also comes into decision making. As Brundtland put it: 'Sustainable development responds to the needs of today without endangering the ability of future generations to meet their needs.'

Chris Dutilh believes that a company like Unilever most of all needs to know what its impact on the environment is, and what the real costs are. Seventeen years previously, he started developing a so-called 'life-cycle analy-sis' for Van den Bergh & Jurgens' activities. Such an LCA would identify and measure all the environmental implications of a Unilever product, from use of raw materials to energy consumption to the processing of waste.

Dutilh was inspired in this by the environmentalist Wouter van Dieren. Environmental organisations like Greenpeace were becoming more and more concerned about pollution caused by detergents. Van Dieren thought that Unilever needed to start taking the environmentalist movement seriously, and that the traditional, top-down approach of their marketers – the 'we know what's good for you' attitude – was seriously misguided. He advised firms like Procter & Gamble and Unilever not to stand in opposition to the growing resistance of environmental organisations but to start working with them.

The 1990 'From Grey to Green' report, written by colleagues of Dutilh, was the first to state that Unilever needed to start working harder to drive down pollution. 'The deterioration of the environment is causing growing con-cern among the general public and is going to keep attracting the attention of governments who want to capitalise on it to win votes. It's a foregone conclu-sion that all industries are going to have to deal with more and more questions about the levels of pollution they cause. Companies with brands aimed at the masses can expect particularly close scrutiny from the media.' The authors of the report immediately follow this observation with a warning: 'Despite the interest in "going green", there are very few indicators that a significant section of the public would be willing to pay a premium for "environmentally friendly" products.'[3]

The bar was already being set high almost twenty years ago: 'When it comes to making our activities more sustainable, we believe in a "from cradle to grave" approach. Since Unilever only "produces" 10 to 20% of the pollution in the supply chain itself, the company's focus must be on addressing the other 80 to 90% of environmental impact that comes from our suppliers and consumers. That requires enormous investment and long-term work.'

Polman had naturally come across the MSC. This collaborative link with the World Wildlife Fund was the first thing people brought up whenever anyone at Unilever uttered the word 'sustainability'. He is impressed by the efforts made by Antony Burgmans and André van Heemstra 13 years previously. He notices that once again it was an NGO that spurred the company to action. An angry letter from Greenpeace had set the ball rolling back in September 1995. The NGO was poised to accuse Unilever of depleting fishing stocks in the world's oceans. They threatened to call for a boycott of all frozen fish products from companies including Langnese-Iglo. André van Heemstra was the head of this German daughter company of Unilever, the fourth largest fish processor in Europe.

Greenpeace had recently brought Shell to its knees in the Brent Spar case. A frightened Van Heemstra asks his PR firm, Burson-Marsteller, for advice. They in turn had just had a visit from Michael Sutton, head of the Endangered Seas Program at the World Wildlife Fund. Sutton was looking for a large company willing to set up a fishing equivalent of the wildly successful Forest Stewardship Council (FSC). The FSC had been set up in 1993 by a couple of NGOs and quickly won the support of governments and international business. Wood with the FSC quality mark comes from woodland managed according to sustainable standards. Any timber company that wants to get FSC accreditation has to cooperate with independent inspections of their work methods.

The PR company asked Van Heemstra whether Unilever would consider working with the WWF. His boss, Antony Burgmans, responsible for all European ice cream and frozen food activities, was immediately intrigued by this suggestion. Burgmans had been concerned for a while. The Food and Agriculture Organisation of the United Nations (FAO) had calculated that

70 per cent of worldwide fishing stocks were nearing exhaustion or only barely being replenished. For Burgmans this development was a drastic example of what the English call 'the tragedy of the commons'. Because everyone is free to focus solely on their own interest without restraint, the things that are important to all of us run out. Because we as individuals have a tendency to prefer personal interest over a (small) negative effect for the sake of common interests, we all end up shooting ourselves in the foot.

Burgmans had asked his colleagues what they would think of Unilever working with an NGO. Could a profit-driven company and a charitable organisation really join forces? Half of them thought it was a bad idea, saying that these kinds of accountability were the remit of governments. And what would something like this cost, for that matter? Would people even understand it? And what would the government think of all this? Let's stick to what we're good at: a company should follow the law and focus on making money. Unilever would be taking on costs that their competitors don't need to, the shareholders would never stand for it.

Burgmans disagreed. If governments are doing nothing, and it looked in this case like they were, then that doesn't mean you just keep merrily fishing away until everything is gone. Those last, rare fish would also make you a pile of money. But after that it's over. For everyone. A scenario like that would have drastic consequences for the world and the environment. And for Unilever. The company would have to go looking for other ways of making money for its shareholders.

Without consulting with his bosses, Burgmans invited the Swiss director-general of the WWF, Claude Martin, out for dinner. Martin had been guarded, his colleagues would probably think Burgmans was just out for what Unilever could get. But the Dutchman had spoken with passion about the tea plantations in Kenya, inviting him to come along and experience the unspoiled nature there. The ice had been broken. Martin reflected that the question was less why Burgmans thought as he did than why other leaders *didn't* have such foresight.[4] And so, in 1996, Unilever and the WWF teamed up to found the MSC.

Back at Unilever, Burgmans had been particularly pleased with the support of his fellow director, Iain Anderson. In a lecture in 1997, Anderson, a marine biologist and long-time head of the R&D department, had sketched out what Unilever's ambitions for sustainability should look like. 'Last year we sold enough shampoo to wash every head in the world three times and enough toothpaste to brush every person's teeth once a month. So there is evidently still room for growth. But we need to be careful. Consumers identify our industry as the primary agent responsible for the future of the environment. They question whether or not we can shoulder this responsibility.'

Anderson told them that Unilever needed to ensure its suppliers began manufacturing more responsibly and its consumers began consuming more sustainably. 'This is new to us. We will need to bring on collaborators in order to make real change possible. It's important for us to start collaborating with partners who increase public trust and thereby contribute to the acceptance of what we as an industry are trying to do. That is going to be a key element if we want to make progress with sustainability.'

Anderson suggests that citizens' growing concerns about the environment are going to mean that they start consuming in accordance with those worries. 'Unilever needs to help them to do that. We believe we *can* help, by working with all kinds of third-parties in the way we do with the MSC. In order to make all this possible, it's important that this topic is placed higher up the agenda among our employees, and especially the decision-makers in marketing, R&D and supply chain-management. We're only just getting off the starting blocks, we see that now.'[5]

At the top of the company it's not only Burgmans who is worried right now. Jan Peelen, head of the food division, is also concerned. He worked in Asia for a long time, and the attractions of selling a couple of deodorants a year to each Chinese person are obvious. But doesn't the impending freedom to do so bring with it huge responsibility to reform the way those products are being produced and consumed? If those billions of people start consuming in exactly the same way as we do in the West, then the burden on the planet is going to grow exponentially.

Since August 1997, Peelen has been working with a team including Jan Kees Vis, a young biochemist, on an internal report in which they claim to be 'making the link between sustainable development and the creation of shareholder value for the first time'. 'When it comes to understanding consumers, we are better positioned than anyone else. By delving deeper into the concerns of our consumers when it comes to all kinds of sustainability issues, we can add value to our brands and products, thereby making money for our shareholders.' The two men, both raised in the Reformed Church, were setting the bar high.[6]

Peelen had tried to get his boss, Morris Tabaksblat, on board. But he was rather more cautious. In Leiden, during a lecture at the annual conference of De Veer-Stichting, a reputable summit for Dutch and Flemish 'shapers of society' and students identified as potential leaders of the future, Tabaksblat expressed the opposite view: 'It's a fundamental mistake to think that businesses can fill a moral vacuum that arises because governments and ethical-religious organisations fall short. These institutions, which have to answer the big questions of the twenty-first century at a national, regional and global level, are paramount. Companies have no mandate to do the same, and aren't equipped for it either. One can demand of corporations that they make a modest contribution to solving the world's problems by acting responsibly. But one must first and foremost ask them to fulfil their most important societal task adequately: creating prosperity.'[7]

Shortly before he retired a year later, Tabaksblat announced that Unilever would be concentrating its efforts on the sustainable products market. 'In the future, the consumer should be able to make the choice for sustainably produced products more often', he tells *De Volkskrant*. The company, along with partners like the Agricultural University of Wageningen, intends to develop standards for sustainable agriculture.

Various pioneers at Unilever laid the groundwork for this long ago. Hans Eenhoorn had exploited his significant autonomy as boss of Unilever Austria in the mid-1990s to set up a line of organic peas and spinach. Colleagues said he was mad, warning that the market was too small and the production process too expensive. But Eenhoorn persevered, and not without success. It turned out that the demand *was* there. Various supermarket chains even set up their own organic grown-brands.

In the years that followed, people inside Unilever set up dozens of projects aimed at reducing waste, saving water, switching to less polluting fertilisers and saving energy in agricultural production chains. Despite the increasing focus on profitability in the late 1990s, technicians like Jan Kees Vis and Jeroen Bordewijk were given space to make production processes for palm oil, tea, tomatoes, spinach and peas more sustainable. It helped that they could often show that more sustainable meant more efficient, so that these efforts could deliver substantial cost savings.

Reading about all these efforts of his new colleagues Polman is suddenly reminded that Procter & Gamble asked him to write the foreword to *their* first Sustainability Report back in 1999. In the piece, the then 43-year-old marketer had started out by apologising for the fact he had no experience with managing environmental issues or social problems. 'As a business manager with no experience directly managing environmental or social issues, I approach the subject of sustainability based on a career in finance, marketing and business management. My experience over the past year of integrating sustainable development into a business has been one of tremendous insight and learning, tempered by a solid dose of reality.'

He had then underlined the importance of P&G looking at the world through the eyes of consumers and taking into account their desire to build a better world for the future, calling sustainable development an 'entirely new paradigm of what is possible'. However, he was also cautious: 'It is difficult to focus on a new concept when that concept does not have a clear definition or success models linked to business growth. Therefore, one of my biggest challenges has been to make sustainability relevant to business in a way that my fellow P&G business leaders will understand.'[8]

Back then, Polman had clearly been inspired by Brundtland's definition: 'Procter & Gamble must strive to better quality of life, now and for generations to come.' He had also warned of regarding sustainability as a marketing tool and opening themselves up to accusations of greenwashing: 'it needs to be about social equality, combatting poverty, good food, the quality of life of women. More than a billion people don't have access to safe drinking water, three billion people don't have adequate sanitation, more than 3 million children die every year from illnesses related to contaminated water. [...] These are big issues and concerns in which we can make a difference.'

In the summer of 2000, Burgmans, who had now replaced Tabaksblat as the chairman/CEO for the Dutch Unilever NV, had invited Jeroen Bordewijk to Rotterdam to give a presentation to a handful of CEOs, including the leaders of Kraft, Danone and Nestlé. These men had been coming together for 20 years at this point, to discuss non-competitive issues and exchange ideas in private. Burgmans and Bordewijk, responsible for increasing sustainability in the agricultural supply chain, wanted to suggest that they make collective agreements regarding the sustainability of raw materials production. Kraft turned them down flat. The Americans were uncertain as to whether sustainability was within the remit of business at all: Shouldn't the government manage this with laws? But Unilever, Danone and Nestlé decide to set up the Sustainable Agriculture Initiative (SAI) Platform, an independent non-profit organisation aimed at making agriculture sustainable. This time without the participation of NGOs.

In the meantime, NGOs had taken the lead when it comes to the growing concerns about the impact of the palm oil industry on the deforestation of countries like Malaysia and Indonesia. Unilever is the world's largest consumer of palm oil. So in 2001, when the WWF went looking for a partner to make this fast-growing industry more sustainable, it quickly landed on them. The director of sustainable agriculture, Jan Kees Vis, went on to play a major role in the organisation of the Roundtable on Sustainable Palm Oil (RSPO). Producers, traders, retailers and NGOs gathered together to investigate how they could use the certification to make all palm oil products completely sustainable by the year 2020. During the summit, Vis reflected that it was a bitter shame that Unilever, the biggest consumer of palm oil in the world, had sold off its plantations over the previous few years. The company had increasingly become a cash-flow generating machine.

Hans Eenhoorn had noticed it too. In his view, taking over Bestfoods in 2000 had been their biggest mistake. And Unilever might have known that it would be. In their 1999 strategy document the Bestfoods management had openly written that they wanted to become the best food company in the world: 'and being the best means striving to optimise shareholder value'.

Eenhoorn advised the Unilever board in 2002 to pay more attention to 'consumers, who are increasingly worried about the health of the ecosystem in which they live, and in which their children will have to live'. These consumers' fears are barely translating into changes in habits of consumption. In his report, Eenhoorn wrote, 'they are worried, they feel a bit guilty, but mostly they feel powerless. The consumer of today is asking companies like Unilever to behave responsibly on this issue.'

He had suggested they involve all of Unilever's 'world brands' in caring for the environment. Not just the handful of 'green' brands. According to Eenhoorn, that would mean having to change something deep in the culture of Unilever: so far it had mostly been sustainability specialists concerning themselves with this topic. 'From now on, the whole management of Unilever should feel like dealing with the environment and sustainability is within their comfort zone. It needs to become second nature to them. That includes also all the marketers who work here.'

In a response to his report, the leadership indicated that they think it's a good idea to invest in the 'environment mind-set' of all Unilever employees. As for what this might mean for their own roles, the two chairmen, Burgmans and FitzGerald, were reserved. Realising the enormous financial ambitions of the 'Path to Growth' is taking up all of their attention. They recognised that the plan is missing the environmental dimension. 'We'll be better off introducing a more substantial contribution on this topic in the next company plan (after 2004).'[9]

Polman notes that the leaders of Unilever are consistent in putting out a message of sustainability, even in years in which they don't manage to grow the company. In an interview with *The Guardian* in 2002, the freshly knighted Sir Patrick FitzGerald says that he's proud Unilever is listed in the ethically responsible share index, the FTSE4Good. 'In time people will take the FTSE-4Good seriously. It won't be for soft, social reasons, though. It will be because people will understand that if you don't operate responsibly wherever you are, your ability to operate in those places will diminish. I do get upset when people have a go at multinationals if they include us in that, because I know what we do. Whether in Birmingham or Bangladesh we apply the same principles. We tend to be setting the standards in environmental, safety and wage-rate terms wherever we are. My business is everywhere in the world. It is in the interests of my business to find the way to get more development of wealth and prosperity because 85% of the world's population lives in the developing world.'

A year later, FitzGerald was set a challenge by Barbara Stocking, Oxfam's UK director. She wanted to investigate the extent to which a multinational really contributes to reducing poverty. Oxfam and Unilever decide to do a study together into the impact of the company on poverty in Indonesia. 'Strange Bedfellows in Times of Globalisation' was the headline in the *Financial Times*. 'It takes a good deal of courage, some would say foolhardiness, for a multinational company operating in impoverished parts of the world to open its internal documents to scrutiny by campaigners for fairer globalization.' This feels like a good move to the newspaper.

It took a lot of effort to arrive at a narrative that was acceptable to both parties. Oxfam in particular was dead set against Unilever abusing their collaboration by expressing one-sided conclusions publicly.[10] Every sentence had been weighed and considered several times. Here and there, Unilever received a morsel of praise: the 3,000 employees in Indonesia are paid more than is required by law. And, thanks to its small product sizes, Unilever ensured that its products (mostly washing powder, soap and toothpaste) were affordable to 95 per cent of the Indonesian population. But the most significant criticism was that Unilever's 300,000 independent dependents – on the one side farmers and on the other side small shop owners – were scraping a living. Their working conditions are often appalling. They earn nowhere near a decent income, despite efforts to provide a living wage, an income that can support a family, to as many people as possible.

Oxfam made it clear that Unilever needed to wield its influence more strongly if it wanted to ensure better pay across the whole supply chain. Only then would the company really make a difference, only then would the living standard of up to a million people be improved. The NGO also couldn't resist observing that Unilever is resistant to having a discussion about the enormous amount of money it still spends on advertising. Wouldn't that be better spent making its products more affordable?

Back then, Unilever had responded by saying that it would intervene where possible, for example by teaching farmers to form cooperatives and thereby reduce their dependency on middlemen who would try to exploit them. But the company also pointed out that it would require many more actors working together effectively to really address the poverty issue in Indonesia. Change was needed at the structural level. Unilever can't bring that about on its own.

In the foreword to the report, newly appointed Patrick Cescau said, 'At times it has been hard for our managers to find their values and behaviours subjected to such sceptical scrutiny, and to see their achievements, when operating in a complex business context, so lightly passed over. I hope that this text will contribute to a greater understanding of the links between wealth creation and poverty reduction.'[11]

Polman gets the impression that sustainable thinking has fallen by the wayside during the three years of Cescau's leadership; the Frenchman doesn't seem to spare much of a thought for the issue. His interest seems to have only belatedly been awakened. However, he did once deliver a rousing speech on the topic during an address to students at the INSEAD business school in Fontainebleau, France, where he himself had been a student. He had said that governments and NGOs were slowly but surely realising that the business world had a role to play in solving problems of climate change and reducing poverty around the world. He had gone on to call on INSEAD to pay much more attention to this topic going forward. 'If sustainability is beginning to form the heart of more and more companies, then it needs to stand at the centre of education too.' Cescau had referred to a study that showed that only 8 per cent of business school students learned about social and environmental issues during their time at university.[12]

It was at INSEAD that Cescau had proudly made the announcement that by 2015 all Lipton tea would be supplied by sustainable producers. 'I have no doubt that this decision will transform the tea industry worldwide. It will improve the quality of the tea and raise the incomes and living standards of almost 1 million tea farmers and tea pickers. Overall this will benefit around 2 million people currently living below the poverty line.'

For Cescau, thinking about sustainability had started with his concern that Nestlé and Procter & Gamble seemed to benefitting from marketing their products much more explicitly as sustainable. In the summer of 2005, this had prompted him to ask Tex Gunning to look into whether Unilever was sufficiently concerned with 'corporate social responsibility'.[13] After only a couple of months, Gunning came to a painful conclusion: it was a mess. Although there were a wealth of programmes, definitions and initiatives within the company, there was no sign of a united front, let alone a consistent strategy. One thing was clear: sustainable thinking had not been internalised.[14] The initiatives were not connected to brands. Not a single brand had established how it needed to proceed in order to purchase sustainably, and no goals had been set on that front either. Gunning concluded that sustainability needed to be introduced to each and every brand. For each product, he wanted a clear answer to the question, 'what is the sustainable role of this brand in the lives of the people who buy it?' Two of the biggest brands, Lipton and Dove, are selected for this so-called brand-imprint-process.

Gavin Neath had welcomed this assignment. The boss of Unilever in the United Kingdom, a marketer down to his bones, had recently decided off his own bat that it was high time to pursue sustainability. The immediate impetus to do so had been a meeting with the former American vice-president Al Gore. During a seminar at Oxford, Gore had screened his film *An Inconvenient Truth* and shown his audience very persuasively that human beings were devouring the Earth. He impressed on them the need to take personal responsibility for what was happening. The encounter with Gore had a profound impact on Neath. As far as he was concerned, the crucial question for Unilever's future was how to renew their brand by integrating pressing social, economic and environmental-technical considerations.[15]

Michiel Leijnse was tasked with working this out in the case of Lipton. At Ben & Jerry's, the veteran marketer had learned that sustainability needed to be woven into production process at a fundamental level, from raw materials to final product. He believes this is possible and that it is the moral duty of Unilever to pursue it. Tea production in particular brought all the world's miseries into sharp focus. With a market share of 12 per cent, Unilever is the largest tea company in the world. Lipton alone is worth two billion euro in annual revenue. For years, the market has been plagued by rampant overproduction and low prices, leading to a lack of investment. Tea has become a commodity, there is little that differentiates one tea from another. This downward spiral frustrates every effort to speed up the process of making tea production sustainable. The levels of poverty among the millions of small-scale tea farmers and the often seasonally employed tea pickers are enormous.

Along with Jan Kees Vis, Leijnse quickly realises that Lipton's sustainable image will only be credible if it is endorsed by an independent third party that certifies tea. They had invited the Rainforest Alliance to be this party. The NGO, set up in 1987, made it its aim to conserve biodiversity by encouraging sustainable ways of living, campaigning for better use of agricultural land, promoting honest business practices and encouraging responsible consumption.

Getting Unilever's top managers on board had proven too difficult for Leijnse. Up until now, sustainability had mostly been treated as niche market, to be filled here and there with specialist brands such as Ben & Jerry's: products for which they could also ask a higher price. Leijnse wanted to transform the Lipton behemoth into a sustainable brand. What's more, he wanted to do it without passing on a higher price to the consumer. He spent five months discussing the costs and benefits of these plans. The intention to start paying farmers millions of euros more per year so that they would be able to produce more sustainably was particularly sensitive. By definition, that would place pressure on Unilever's profitability.

The top dogs were finally persuaded to go along with the plans by the promise that Unilever would increase its share of the global tea market. By setting this example as the leading company, it would become the new standard, putting an end to tea as a cheap commodity. And because Unilever was going to play a leading role, it would reap the biggest profits. In 2010, it was agreed that all tea imported to Western Europe would be certified by the Rain Forest Alliance. All Unilever tea would have to be produced using sustainable methods by 2015 at the latest.

Meanwhile, Jan Kees Vis was also trying to make headway with the Roundtable for Sustainable Palm Oil. Unilever needed to be in a position to make the switch to 100 per cent certified palm oil in 2015. They wouldn't manage it any sooner. Thanks to the still highly limited supply of sustainably produced palm oil, the price of certified oil quickly rose to a couple of hundred dollars more than the standard $450 per tonne. That has a profound effect in a company where growth in profit per share has becoming the guiding principle. Vis explains to the *De Volkskrant* that this is only the beginning. What most concerned him was the knowledge that the demand for sustainable palm oil was only coming from the European market. In China and India over two billion people use palm oil for cooking. The roundtable doesn't cover this market. 'The question is whether you can persuade these people to buy sustainable palm oil. These people don't buy more expensive, sustainable branded products.'[16]

Amid these developments, Gavin Neath is becoming more convinced of the importance of sustainability and the scope for Unilever to get ahead of the curve. At times he has shared these ideas with outsiders. In his pitch, he explained that all brands needed to start fully integrating sustainable goals in order to become future proof. This forces marketers to look much more carefully at the broad impact of their product on the world. Do they know the CO_2 emissions associated with their product? What about the way in which their product is produced, who it's made by and for what price? How does all that fit together? Do they meet the World Health Organisation guidelines on fat, sugar and salt? Can water and energy consumption be more efficient? How much packaging is required and can it be recycled? And how can these products contribute to solving poverty and public health issues? Four billion people still have no access to clean drinking water.

Neath sets the bar remarkably high. He thinks that marketers need to learn to look beyond the desires of their consumers, who want something high quality, affordable and good for their own health. They need to look further, at this same person's growing concerns as a citizen when it comes to social issues and the environment. They need to learn to add value on that side of things. Of tea, Neath says, 'we saw that what was happening wasn't right. The distributor and the marketer make the most, while the poor tea picker doesn't make enough. It's interesting to see how the consumer reacts when you try to restore that balance. Rationally, the consumer recognises that there is a company concerning itself with the welfare of those people. They then make a new emotional connection: because this tea is grown and traded fairly, it will taste better too.'[17]

At the end of 2006, Unilever is the first company to be given a new Dutch award for social responsibility, recognising it as the best in integrating sustainability in the industry. The prize is awarded by the Association of Investors for Sustainable Development (VBDO). Chris Dutilh, Unilever's manager of sustainable development, is asked to accept the award.

Dutilh was pleased with the prize but would have preferred more recognition for his work within Unilever itself. Progress was obviously much too slow. In England, the Stern Review had just been published to enormous dismay. This commission estimated that a temperature increase of between five and six degrees Celsius was now becoming a reality. Nicholas Stern, the commission's chairman, called the fact that markets based on supply and demand had never taken this gigantic environmental change and its associated risks and costs into account, the biggest 'market failure' of all time. Without action, the costs of climate change worldwide could amount to a loss of 5 per cent of GDP per year for an as yet undetermined period. Stern declared in various interviews that the costs of doing nothing would increase rapidly; acting now is cheaper in the long run.

As Polman prepares to take over, a proud Patrick Cescau gives him a list of all the achievements he's made. In 2004, basic revenue growth was still only 0.4 per cent, in the three years that followed it rose to an average of over 4 per cent. Profit per share increased from €0.87 to €1.79. The work force was reduced by 24 per cent to 171,000. Polman isn't particularly impressed. Compared with its competitors, Unilever hasn't done that well at all. More concerning still: Cescau's narrow focus on cutting costs and increasing profits has meant that he has neglected to invest in brands, people and factories.

With 'One Unilever', Cescau has taken an important step in streamlining the company. But the Frenchman has mostly concentrated on the chassis, rather than on the engine repairs needed to get the whole thing moving. Polman recognises that Cescau didn't have much freedom to do much else. He must have spent the first two years with his predecessor Antony Burgmans looking over his shoulder, and he was saddled with the inheritance of the overpriced takeover of Bestfoods. As Polman sees it, Cescau never managed to get Unilever up and running again. A truly integrated, global approach is still nowhere in evidence.

He has heard various colleagues complaining about Cescau's lack of marketing expertise. They regard the sell-off of the American detergents activities two months previously as potentially his biggest blunder. The American washing detergent activities, responsible for a billion in annual revenue, have been sold to a private equity firm for over a billion dollars. Cescau had defended this sale by claiming that it frees up the resources for Unilever to 'strengthen our leading position in this category in the rest of the world'. Polman sees it as a sign of weakness, not at all good for the self-esteem of his new colleagues. Why can't Unilever make a go of it in Procter & Gamble's home market? You can't just drop what you've been doing in the United States and keep going everywhere else, the American market is too important, too dominant and too much the trendsetter in terms of product renewal.

It's clear to Polman that he's going to have to ensure the people here get excited about their futures at Unilever. He's going to have to make sure that they share his vision and believe in the prospects for the company's growth. They're going to have to invest in both brands *and* people, and it is going to take a few years for Unilever to reap the fruits of this investment. But this has to be his first message. He is going to ask for a commitment to the long term, including from investors. If Unilever keeps sprinting breathlessly from quarter to quarter then his plans for growth are never going to get off the ground.

As he prepares for his new role, Polman makes contact with a number of his new colleagues. The call with the top boss of Asia, Africa and Central and Eastern Europe is tense. Harish Manwani, who is also non-executive chairman of Hindustan Lever, would have liked to have been made CEO himself. It's a good conversation even so. Manwani tells him that he has organised a farewell dinner for Patrick Cescau in the magnificent Taj Mahal Palace Hotel in Mumbai. Perhaps Polman would like to come?

The original plan had been for their group of around thirty-eight guests to dine in the garden of the five star hotel. However, since rain is forecast, they end up in a dining room next door to a wedding. At 10.30 p.m., just as the CEO of Unilever Pakistan has finished telling them about growing fears of renewed Taliban activity, they hear what they think are fireworks. At first they assume that the wedding guests next door have brought along a few bangers. But the fireworks don't let up. Then they hear screams: heartrending screams.

At that very moment, a dozen terrorists from the Islamic Lashkar-e-Taiba movement are making their way through the hotel shooting and killing. As the young men gape at the splendour, their leaders are screaming at them from their mobile phones not to get second thoughts: 'Shoot! Be brave, brother, don't panic, if you die, your mission will have been a success. Allah is waiting for you in heaven! Take them all out, you never know when they're going to strike back! Do it, line them up, shoot them in the back of the head!'[18] Dozens of hotel guests and members of staff are murdered.

In the little dining room where the top bosses at Unilever India and Pakistan are celebrating the handover from Cescau to Polman, the staff have locked the doors and turned off the lights. The terrorists try the doors but soon move on. In the room next to them, guests at the wedding fall victim to the shooters, as do hotel guests in the garden.

Paul Polman is lying on the floor next to Unilever veteran Nihal Kaviratne. Kaviratne has a mobile phone which allows him to watch live television. CNN reports that the management of Unilever is trapped in the hotel. They call the London head office and ask them in whispers to tell the news centre not to repeat that information.

They lie there for hours. Paralysed by fear. They use tablecloths to screen off part of the room as a makeshift toilet area. Most of the guests remain composed. As one of the older guests starts to hyperventilate, the others gently calm him down again.

Patrick Cescau is painfully aware that these people are in danger because they have come to give him a good send off. Even worse, most of them have brought their wives and partners with them. His own wife Ursula is right beside him. He feels the adrenaline racing through his body but it gives him a strange sense of calm. A feeling of responsibility dominates his emotions, it's very important that he doesn't panic. He, his successor and the Indian leaders all try in whispers to reassure their respective people.

They pass around a bottle of Lagavulin whisky. Paul Polman never drinks whisky but the liquid helps to keep his nerves in check a little. He's glad that his wife Kim isn't here with him, she had a cello performance she couldn't rearrange. He has already called his brother and asked him to reassure her.

As he lies there, he looks back on his life. He thinks about its fleetingness and the need to do something meaningful. What about the world need to change so that these kinds of things don't happen anymore? What can he do to bring it about? To him, there is only one conclusion: create a world without poverty. After all, it is the key cause of these kinds of terrible attacks. The stubborn and ever-expanding gap between rich and poor. It's becoming more visible too. That's what makes these people so desperate that they are willing to do terrible things like this.

Leena Nair is also there, lying on the hotel floor beside her spouse. Nair is director of Human Resources at Hindustan Lever. The Indian woman is overwhelmed by a feeling of immense clarity: life is a gift. A gift you have to make the best of. If she survives this, she's going to come back to that insight every day.

Just like Polman, she is deeply impressed by the manager of the hotel staff, who is also locked in the room. This young woman, Malika, is constantly busy reassuring her guests, holding their hands and fetching water for them. When her mother calls her, Malika calms her down by telling her that it isn't her hotel that's under attack, and that her mother can go to bed.

By 6 a.m. there is so much smoke coming into the room that it's clear they can't stay there much longer. Malika leads them safely through various rooms, including a couple of bedrooms and a kitchen. Eventually, they are spotted by firefighters. As the tallest person there, Polman tries to smash a high window using a chair. In the end, the firefighters manage to create an opening. One by one, they are able to climb out.

Malika lets them all know that she is her party: she's responsible for operations, so she'll be the last to leave. When the men, the leaders of Unilever, protest, she shakes her head. It's not up for discussion. Leena Nair is struck by the fact that there are so many good people in the world, people capable of so much more than they think they are.[19]

Over the course of four days and twelve attacks, the terrorists murder 174 people. There are 31 victims in the hotel, mostly in the garden and among the wedding guests. On the sixth floor, in the hotel suite next to Polman's, hotel manager Karambir Kang's wife and two children, twelve and five, are shot dead. Kang had worked tirelessly throughout the night to rescue his guests. This affected Polman deeply. The whole time his wife and children could have been in danger, this man had remained focused on his guests, watching over them. After his brush with evil, and with his own death, Paul

Polman is suddenly deeply convinced that the good in people will always win out. It has to.

Late that afternoon in Holland, shortly after Polman has been freed from the hotel and transferred to a safe house, Jan Kees Vis receives an email from him. The man who is about to become the boss of Unilever has read one of his articles about the enormous importance of sustainable agriculture in the combatting of hunger and poverty in an industry newspaper. Polman tells Vis he thinks Unilever needs to dedicate even more energy to this issue.

CHAPTER 7

GROWING, GROWING, GROWING
[...] AND DOING GOOD

December 2008–January 2010

Patrick Cescau receives a standing ovation. He has just addressed his top
200 managers at The Grove, an impressive hotel just north of London that
was once a favourite haunt of Queen Victoria, for the very last time. This is his
farewell. The Frenchman invites his successor to join him up on the podium.
The men laugh as they shake hands. Cescau asks the trim Dutchman whether
he'd like to share his first impressions with the group.

Sitting in the first row, Paul Polman had reflected on the fact that the people sitting behind him had been throwing these sorts of parties for decades. At
Procter & Gamble and at Nestlé they had made fun of these 'O be joyful' summits, the cosy old-boy's atmosphere in which Unilever managers congratulate
themselves and tell each other how wonderful they are. This annoys the new
CEO. Why do these people think they're so fantastic in the first place? What
he's encountered over the past few months has been anything but.

Polman is going to be honest with them about that. But first he tells them
a bit about himself. He puts up a couple of family photos and tells them how
important family is to him. After that, he gives them both barrels. The new
CEO asks: Who is it you're working for? You're all more concerned with yourselves than with the company. He speaks of an inward-looking culture, a company with many personal fiefdoms and privileges. And he warns them: that
isn't a good thing, it's dangerous. The way you work, the priorities you set?
They aren't working. You call yourselves marketers? You seem to be accountants, constantly focused on the numbers. You can't steer a company entirely
on the basis of financial results. Success comes from somewhere completely

different. It has to do with entrepreneurship. Where is your entrepreneurial spirit? Where is your ambition? Things aren't working as they are. It's going wrong.

You could hear a pin drop. Polman realises that he has to rein himself in. He has learned that these kinds of confrontational messages are only taken on board when he shows sufficient respect for the people concerned and for their history. Wasn't it the management guru Jim Collins who wrote that as a leader you had to cherish the core before you could strive for progress, you had to understand before you could be understood? It's important that his new colleagues feel safe with him. And so he goes on to compliment Cescau and dwell on the enormous potential of a company with such a magnificent history. He expresses his respect for William Lever. This fantastic DNA means they have a wealth of possibilities.

The applause is thunderous. It's clear: Unilever has a new boss. Afterwards, some of those present tell each other that this might well be the best speech they've ever heard, of Martin Luther King 'I-Have-A-Dream' quality. Polman came nowhere close to sticking to the pre-agreed 20 minutes.

The next morning, the managers identified two year previously by Cescau and Ogg as leaders of the future present their strategic recommendations to Polman. They talk about the need to digitise, invest further in emerging markets and engage more explicitly with the issue of the planet's dwindling resources. Kees Kruythoff finds Polman's reaction a touch lukewarm, he doesn't really seem to be interested in their perspective. Simon Clift suspects that the new CEO wants to be the one to decide what needs to happen, at least at first. They can understand that.

During the first annual Christmas get-together with company veterans, Hans Eenhoorn wants to make sure that the new boss knows who he is and where to find him if he needs him. Although he's paid by Unilever, Eenhoorn has been working for the United Nations for some time now. He's helping them to investigate the role big business could play in ending world hunger. When Eenhoorn introduces himself to Polman, he presses into his hand a short story written especially for him. In it, Eenhoorn describes Polman on Christmas Eve contemplating his situation before sitting down to dinner with his family.

'Absently, he stares into the open fire. The flames remind him of flashpoints around the world in the turbulent year of 2008. [...] Naturally, the food crisis is being overshadowed by the financial crisis that has sent billions of dollars up in smoke. Madness, he thinks. There are a billion people starving on this earth and at the same time there are a billion people who are still so rich, despite their losses on the financial markets, that they are getting ill from an excess of food. Obesity, cardiovascular disease, diabetes, forms of cancer, all of them illnesses of prosperity. Suddenly, Unilever's message of vitality comes to mind. Doesn't Unilever have partnerships with the World Food Programme, UNICEF and the World Health Organisation? Isn't Unilever involved in the Global Alliance for Improved Nutrition (GAIN)? We've got brands like Stork and Knorr than can be fortified with vitamins and minerals, Annapurna Salt with added iodine, not forgetting Lifebuoy soap, of course. What's more, with our large workforces in India and Africa, where the problems are the biggest, we're closer to the issue than most other companies. [...] Suddenly the UN secretary Ban Ki-moon is standing beside him. He points to the star and says: "Paul, bring a little bit of light into this dark world, you're the one who can do it. Take one or two countries and show everyone it can be done." In the distance he hears his wife Kim calling him: "Paul, come and sit down, Christmas dinner is ready!" Seldom has a meal ever tasted so good.'

In an email sent the same night, Polman tells Eenhoorn that he found it a stimulating story.

On the eve of his first board meeting, Polman sleeps in the former bed of William Hesketh Lever, the late Lord Leverhulme. Now there was a man after his own heart. He relates to Lever. Some of the same words recur across all descriptions of him: decisive, impatient, relentless, resolute, energetic, sharp, electrifying, tireless, a deep hatred of laziness, ruthless, occasionally cutthroat.

It's a sleepless night. The bed is on the roof of Thornton Manor, the stately home where the Lever family has lived ever since 1888. Lever was a health nut, who slept outside in the belief that the fresh air would help keep him in good health. Even if that meant a bit of snow on his bedcovers now and again.[1] Kim Polman had gotten the picture after about half an hour and gone off to find a warmer bed. Michael Treschow has more luck dropping off, the chairman is sleeping a floor below, in Mrs Lever's former bedroom.

Thornton Manor is a few miles away from Port Sunlight, the place where Lever established his first soap factory after seeing from a passing train 'how near to hand the water and the railway were'. Between 1885 and 1925 he and his brother James built an empire based on the sale of soap, mostly from this very site.

Lever wanted to create prosperity and support housewives by lightening their load and helping them to improve their health and attractiveness so that they could get more out of their lives. That was a remarkable mission in Victorian England. In the second half of the nineteenth century, every second child died before its fifth birthday. Lever resolved to make the best soap available to as many people as possible for the lowest price. Whenever people suggested that he could make more money by lowering the quality, he became furious: 'If we could improve our soap by adding gold then I would do it!'[2]

William Lever had not been a highflier at school. He dreamed about a career as an architect but his father, a strict, Protestant teetotaller, had needed him in his grocery wholesalers. He set his son to work wrapping mountains of soap in greaseproof paper. On his 16th birthday, William received the book *Self Help* as one of his gifts. In it, author Samuel Smiles called on the individual to focus on improving themselves, building character and committing to doing good while resisting materialist impulses. 'The spirit of self-help is the root of all genuine growth in the individual; and, exhibited in the lives of many, it constitutes the true source of national vigour and strength. National progress is the sum of individual industry, energy, and uprightness, as national decay is of individual idleness, selfishness, and vice. Schools, academies, and colleges, give but the merest beginnings of culture in comparison with it. Far more influential is the life-education daily given in our homes, in the streets, behind counters, in workshops, at the loom and the plough, in counting-houses and manufactories, and in the busy haunts of men.'[3]

William Lever was gripped by this, he would start doing good. In 1884, he left his father's wholesale business and threw himself into the soap trade. Lever was convinced that rising living standards would mean people not only buying more eggs and butter but more soap too. An expert in trademarks and patents gave him a list of names Lever could apply for a patent on. He plumped for 'Sunlight'. Lever thereby became one of the first businessmen not to use his own name as his brand name.

In 1909, he told an advertising executive: 'The normal method of selling among manufacturers of patent medicines is to attract attention and make a strong impression on the public. When one reads their brochures, one thinks that one is suffering from all the illnesses in the world at the same time. We need to achieve this same hypothetical effect when it comes to our soap.'

In the early years, he bought soap from manufacturers and stamped the name 'Sunlight' into it. However, after seeing his soap heaped chaotically in parchment paper in the window of a grocer's shop, he resolved to pack his soap in an exclusive little cardboard box from that day forth.[4] The box also meant he could print his brand name prettily on the front. When his suppliers showed no interest in this new approach, Lever resolved to start making his own soap. He rented a small soap factory in Warrington and took on two employees: a chemist and a soap boiler. Within a year, the 20 tonnes of soap they started out making per week had become 450. Lever employed the latest American advertising methods, using huge posters to show that Sunlight could make a marked improvement to the daily drudgery of housewives' lives. The company grew quickly and soon expanded abroad. Import duties forced Lever to set up factories in Germany and France, the United States, South Africa and Japan, and even in Vlaardingen, near Rotterdam.

Lever, a devout protestant and later a fanatical member of the Freemasons, was impressed from an early age by the fact that his success was mostly down to the efforts of his employees. As soon as he started turning a profit, he started to wonder: Whose money is this? Could I have made it on my own? He regarded the company as a family for which he had to provide. 'I am not a lover of money as money and never have been. I work at business because business is life. It enables me to do things. I can see I can see finality for myself, an end, an absolute end; but none for my business.'[5]

This family needed a stable basis, a good home. This is where, according to Lever, the most valuable things in the universe are created: a healthy mind and a healthy body. The wrong sort of house made the wrong sort of employee and the wrong sort of citizen. For this reason, in 1888, he built not only the factory but 800 houses, a library, a hospital, a church and various sports facilities for his employees. He had been inspired in this by a visit to the Agnetapark model village in Delft. There, 15 years previously, the Dutch industrialist Jacques van Marken, founder of the company later known as Gist Brocades, had had houses built for his workers. Lever in no way regarded this as philanthropy, but rather as an investment in his company. What was good for his workers was good for his business, and therefore for him, the owner.[6]

A 70-hour week was normal at that time, but an eight-hour working day seemed fair to him. If you paid your employees enough, then they would no doubt produce just as much. Plus paying them more meant they spent more, and a portion of it would go on soap. However, Lever did believe that this free time should be well spent. His employees were required to work constantly and consistently on becoming better people, just like he did. The teetotaller thought it is only logical to keep a close eye on behaviour outside the factory. 'A good workman may have a wife of objectionable habits, or he may have objection-able himself, which make it undesirable to have him in Port Sunlight.'[7]

Eventually, Lever, who was knighted in 1920, controls 60 per cent of the British soap industry. These 200,000 tonnes of soap per year made up two-thirds of his revenues. Founded on an investment of approximately £20,000, his business, made up of more than two hundred subsidiaries, was worth £130 million by the 1920s. But Lever wanted more. He bought the ice cream factory T. Wall & Sons, a paper factory and a chalk mine. He invested in factories in Niger and Indonesia. Then he turned to margarine.

Just as Van den Bergh & Jurgens had once been appointed by Napoleon III, the emperor of France, who was looking for a 'beurre économique' to feed his hungry soldiers, Lever was set on the margarine trail by the British government. When imports of Danish and Dutch butter lapsed following the outbreak of the First World War, the British government asked the Lever Brothers to dedicate themselves to producing margarine. Since soap and margarine are derived from the same raw materials, William Lever was immediately enthusiastic.

Lever thus became a direct competitor of the Dutch Margarine Union. But even though his company was growing, its profitability soon declined. Troubled by a drop in the margarine market, Lever said to a colleague: 'I am very distressed by our margarine position, our quality ought to be irreproachable. I know that Van den Bergh is putting a strong press advertising campaign out on their Blue Band.' He wished he had the confidence to do the same but confessed to having been 'as big a wobbler as any'.[8] The problems were piling up and various bankers were concerned. Francis D'Arcy Cooper of the accountancy firm Cooper Brothers & Co. was asked to put the numbers in order. He found various skeletons in the family firm's closet and in 1921 forced Lever to hand over his company to a Special Committee. Cooper himself took a leading role in this committee, alongside the founder, his two sons and two co-directors.[9]

In 1925, Lord Leverhulme died, as it happens, of complications of a cold he'd been trying to ignore. Four years later, D'Arcy Cooper accepted Anton Jurgens's invitation to investigate the potential for Lever Brothers and the Margarine Union to combine forces. After the Brits established that the Dutch were making very poor quality soap and the Dutch concluded that the British margarine was inedible, the two parties realised that they might be able to learn from one another. Plus buying in their common raw materials, like palm oil, together would certainly bring its own advantages in terms of costs. And so it's decided that the two companies would merge just like the two Dutch families who made up the Margarine Union had done a few years previously.

Various British and Dutch fiscal requirements determined the structure. 'If no considerations other than practical considerations of manufacturing and trading were involved, the objects of the parties could be achieved by one company [...] but in order to avoid multiple taxation it has been found necessary that a Dutch company should be formed to hold the shares to be acquired in Dutch companies and an English company [...] to hold those to be acquired in English companies.'[10]

The influence of the Lever Brothers is evidenced in the decision to have Unilever's two executive boards appoint a Special Committee. Dutch and British interests will be represented equally in this overall board. And so, on 2 September 1929, the Dutch-British multinational Unilever is born. The value of the total complex of plantations, tropical trading companies, whalers, oil plants, refineries, hydrogenation plants, soap and margarine factories, grocery shops, fishmongers and numerous other businesses is estimated at an astronomical one billion guilders or €18.2 billion today.[11] Five weeks later the stock prices plummeted as the stock market collapse began and the company, one of the biggest in the world, was confronted with a severe, years-long economic crisis.

As Polman travels from Thornton Manor to Port Sunlight, just like Lever a hundred years previously, on his way to his first board meeting in January 2009 he feels a deep connection to the firm's founder. Lever was way ahead of his time. Most of his contemporaries, the Mellons, the Carnegies, the Rockefellers, made their enormous fortunes before discovering the importance of charity. Lever opted for shared prosperity from the beginning. He was a true leader, a man with an aim, who would let nobody divert him from it. Polman is well aware that his responsibilities are a little different. In the British context especially, the owners are the boss. Creating shareholder value is central. He isn't under any illusions: when the chips are down, even the shareholders who claim to think long term will go for the instant return.

And as it happens, that return isn't looking so good. Buffeted by the miseries of the 2008 financial crisis, the share price is barely scraping €14. Anyone who invested in Unilever back in 1997, in the era of Morris Tabaksblat, has made zero share profit in the 12 years since. But this has its advantages for the new CEO too. The only way is up.

Polman has resolved to spend most of his time listening. He asks his fellow directors to summarise their personal values: What is it they stand for? He also asks how they see Unilever, he wants to hear where the problems lie. One person talks about the company's excellent products and providing for customers, the next focuses on disappointing profits per share. Everyone present shares one priority, however, and that's growth. Unilever has to start growing again and start selling more products. For higher prices if they can.

This won't be popular. Sales in Europe and the United States are all but stagnant. Those markets are saturated. Even worse, supermarket own brands, often well tailored to local requirements, are gaining ground. In terms of quality they rank barely below Unilever's flagship brands. The growth will have to come from emerging markets, just as it has over the past few years. That will take work. How is Unilever going to remain afloat in a world that is increasingly 'VUCA': 'Volatile, Uncertain, Complex and Ambiguous'?

Polman uses the VUCA acronym constantly. He is worried about the dominance of all the managers who are caught up in their personal calculations and focusing most of their attention inwards. He notices that in a company that has shrunken considerably they have a tendency to make themselves seem big. In a VUCA world you are soon out of the running if you don't look beyond your four walls.

The board follows the CEO's reasoning and agrees that they will have to invest a great deal of money over the next few years, in people as well as brands. Money they will only see a return on a few years down the line. They will have to explain to the shareholders that Unilever needs time. Polman suggests that they underscore this message by announcing that Unilever will no longer be reporting its results every quarter. He says that all the promises, half promises and declarations drive him mad, first they have a good summer and sell more ice cream, then it's a bit rainier again and profits aren't up to snuff. They need to give up on this constant slog to secure short-term wins. Let's make a firm statement, he says, and put an end to this nonsense.

Kees Storm is dead set against this. He thinks that shareholders have a right to information at all times. One of his fellow directors, the American Charles Golden, agrees with Storm. But the majority think this is a revitalising idea; they are impressed by the bravery of the new CEO. Storm realises that they like the board to speak with one voice at all times at Unilever, they don't like this difference of opinion. Nevertheless, he refuses to give up his position and suggests that they therefore simply accept that they don't see eye to eye.

The announcement, 10 days later, goes down like a lead balloon. The day Polman's appointment was announced, the share price went up 6 per cent, now it drops 6 per cent. Analysts castigate them: How can a big firm like Unilever so explicitly disrespect its shareholders? How can it insult them like this? They are offended on their own behalf, too. In order to analyse, they need new numbers constantly, as many as they can get their hands on. They are also taken aback. Isn't Nestlé's former CFO a finance man through and through?

At a stroke, the 3.1 billion total shares in the company, 1.7 billion in the NV and 1.4 billion in the PLC are worth only €42 billion. Roughly seven times the profit. Polman shrugs it off, the markets reacting fearfully doesn't surprise him. Of course the analysts are up in arms, they write about quarterly figures, this is their bread and butter.

At the press conference, he explains why he doesn't feel like playing along with this charade any longer. Companies that put out new projections every quarter only to have to revise them later lack credibility in his eyes. Leading a company in order to reach financial targets is stupid: 'That results in the management doing the wrong things. This is an unusual time, I think that more companies should follow our example.' He goes on to joke, 'I also thought: if I want do this, now's the time. I figured I couldn't be fired on my first day.'

Polman is excited to receive a kind message from one of the most successful investors of all time. Warren Buffett has sent him a short letter in which he congratulates him on his decision. If the American, one of the richest men on the planet, is known for anything, it's for his long-term vision. The 'Oracle of Omaha' thinks that you should value shares based on their intrinsic value and the achievements of the past, and practice patience, placing your trust in management even if you're keeping a close eye on them as you do, of course. According to Buffett, a management team primarily focused on achieving short-term, quarterly results almost always makes decisions that turn out badly for the health of the business in the long term. You have to get out of that mindset. Paul Polman has his blessing.

In the 2008 annual report, Polman pays compliments to his predecessor and thanks him for the transformation he set in motion: 'Cescau replaced the engine while the car was running.' At the same time, Polman makes it clear that they've got their work cut out for them, 'our costs are not yet at competitive levels. There is still much work to do. We are not yet winning in enough of the key categories and geographies in which we compete. Market positions and brand strength are two key determinants of long-term earnings capacity. So we need to do better. Our priority in 2009 will be to get sales volumes growing again, both sustainably and profitably.'

Polman emphasises that costs now urgently need to come down in order for them to be able to invest heavily in the business. It's also clear where these cuts must come from. In the emerging markets especially, the company is sailing full speed ahead. The market there, now worth over 40 per cent of revenues, grew by 14.2 per cent in 2008. In order to free up as much capital as possible for investments, Polman announces that salaries will be frozen for the time being. The travel budget will be reduced by a third too. Anyone who really has to fly will have to do so in economy.

His first trip is to South Africa. The boss there, Gail Klintworth, has a problem: the washing detergent brand Omo is haemorrhaging market share. Polman wants to show his colleagues that when there is a crisis somewhere, he will be there to help. On the return journey, he makes a stopover in Kenya to visit the largest tea plantation still under Unilever ownership. Kericho has been tagged for potential sale. He can see that his predecessors have cut costs at the plantation as much as they possibly could over the last few years. As a result, working conditions have worsened and the quality of the tea has plummeted. Polman wants to reverse this process: Kericho will not be sold. He explains that trust among consumers is being eroded because they don't know where the things they eat, drink and rub on their skin come from. By keeping a plantation like this inside the company and investing in it, it must be possible to produce a quality tea that will appeal to conscious consumers.

Polman thinks that many of his managers have got their priorities all wrong: they spend most of their time calculating what the direct financial impact of their plans will be for the consumers. That is a one-way road to ruin. Unilever needs to grow, which means it needs to invest in growth. If we start selling more good products, we won't have anything to worry about, we'll be able to create and cover all kinds of costs. In his first few weeks he introduces a list of nine operational indicators: customer satisfaction, quality of products, quality of distribution, etc. They dub it the '9 for 2009 list'. These criteria will be decisive in future analyses of how things are going. Polman is closely involved. He asks all of the leading figures in each country and each category to send him a monthly email in which they tell him how things are going in terms of each product–market combination, the three biggest issues in need of fixing and what they need in order to fix them. This way, he forces the regional and national managers to work together with the category managers and come up with a single assessment together. By responding quickly and knowledgeably to these reports, he commands a great deal of respect.

He works non-stop and is soon spending around ten nights per month on an overnight flight. Wherever he goes, Polman wants to talk to retailers and customers. This is all very new to the managers he meets. Cescau kept his distance and seemed to have little interest in consumers, steering the company according to financial priorities. Polman decides that from now on, no one with a purely financial background will be appointed as a national manager.

Pascal Visée is this kind of finance man. As 'group treasurer' he optimises the revenue streams for the whole company and reports to the CFO Lawrence. Visée is deeply impressed with the level of engagement he sees from the former Nestlé CFO. Polman answers every email within twenty-four hours. When Visée asks him how he does it, Polman explains that he simply doesn't go to bed until he has answered all his mail. And yes, sometimes this costs him a couple of hours at night. Some colleagues feel so guilty when they hear this that they decide not to email him anymore. Surely the man has to sleep some time?

During his first encounter with the new CFO, Visée presents the advantages and disadvantages of a potential merger between the NV and PLC. The topic remains on the agenda at Unilever mostly thanks to continued pressure from outside interests. On the basis of 15 criteria, Visée has set out the pros and cons of a Dutch or a British head office, respectively. The Dutch option narrowly wins out in terms of plus points. Visée emphasises that there is no real rush to embark on such a course. The complicated double nationality is still regarded internally as an excellent protection against hostile takeovers. Polman informs him that the NV–PLC debate is at the bottom of this list of priorities.

They call the event 'Finish the Dinner'. The group who survived the terrorist attack on Mumbai a little over three years previously returns to the same hotel. In part, they want to recognise what happened to them, but the main purpose is to thank the staff for their courageous actions. Hotel general manager Karambir Kang is present, having previously being asked whether he would like to go and work elsewhere, in another hotel. After all, this was where his wife and children were murdered. But Kang has opted to stay, he feels a drive to repair this place for that very reason. Contributing to its healing makes him feel better.[12] This time, Kang is sitting at the table with his staff, being served by the Unilever top brass. And this time they are in the garden, the room they were in back then is being renovated along with the rest of the badly damaged hotel.

Polman addresses those present with tears in his eyes. He feels a kinship with these people, these fellows in misfortune. He knows that he has made friends for life here. He is very grateful for that. As Polman is speaking, it starts raining gently. Nihal Kaviratne believes this is a good sign, a ritual cleansing from above has blessed this gathering.

From India, Polman travels on to Indonesia. He is on his way to visit Jan Zijderveld. The man responsible for South-East Asia takes his boss into the interior. He wants to show him what the decades of engagement and investment from Unilever have yielded. He notices that Polman is moved by what he shows him. He clearly hadn't realised how deep into every level of this developing society the company reaches, how it enables more and more people to wash themselves, brush their teeth and enjoy an ice cream. The future growth of Unilever lies at the heart of societies like this, that much is clear. By 2020, it is possible that as much as 70 per cent of Unilever's turnover will come from this part of the world.

In collaboration with Sandy Ogg, Polman has mapped out what the most important roles with Unilever now are and from which positions the most value is created. Anyone who compares those two lists can see what isn't working. How can it be that most of the managers in the company are evaluated as top performers while the company as a whole is a notable under-performer? On the back of this inventory-taking, Polman invites 70 managers to join him in developing a strategy for growth over four intensive sessions. Taking the potential in the emerging markets as their point of departure and looking at Unilever's two biggest competitors, that are now far outstripping the company – Nestlé boasts a turnover of over €90 billion, Procter & Gamble is headed for $80 billion – they reach a drastic decision. Over the next ten years, Unilever must strive to double its turnover, to €80 billion.

This ambition is received enthusiastically at the executive board meeting, but the immediate debate rests on whether Unilever can do this. And what would this cost in terms of environmental impact? Chairman Treschow quickly calculates that Unilever sells around 800 million products in Sweden each year, this would mean an abrupt increase to more than a billion, and all the additional packaging that would entail. What are the true costs of this ambition? They resolve that this growth cannot be at the cost of a greater negative impact on the environment.

To Storm this is all well and good but he remains sceptical. He would very much like to hear how Unilever is going to reduce costs. They can't raise prices in order to realise this growth in turnover, so the company will have to become much more efficient than it is now. Storm warns them to bear in mind that there are no good long-term results without consistently good short-term results.

Wim Dik pushes back. He thinks Polman should be given space to operate. Dik sees it as only logical for Unilever's costs to increase, since they're investing in good people and in the proper treatment of those people. As it happens, Dik himself is set to profit from this investment. He is about to start his last year as auditor and is looking forward to being invited back for this kind of event for many more years to come. Obviously, it's expensive to invite all the former directors and their partners to a party or reunion twice a year on Unilever's dime. But this party circuit exemplifies the company. This is how you maintain a stable of well-disposed ambassadors who will help advance Unilever's interest in all kinds of places.

Polman gets his way: they have yet to attach a specific number of years to the plan but Unilever will focus on trying to double in size and separating the environmental impact from the growth of the company. This they will have to reduce by half. During a big 'city hall' event in London, Polman announces that 'One Unilever' will be replaced by his 'Compass' strategy. The waypoints are summarised in four 'wins', a variation on the previous 'must-win battles', 'we are going to win with brands and innovation, we are going to win in the market place, we are going to win with people and we are going to win through continuous improvement'. The CEO announces that Unilever's turnover will double. The applause is deafening, everyone is enthusiastic. The message that environmental impact is going to have to be halved at the same time barely makes it through to his audience.

That's going to be a challenging puzzle whichever way you slice it. Director Jeroen van der Veer asks researcher Louise Fresco to come and talk about the possibility of her joining the Unilever board. An academic like her is unusual within Unilever's leadership but maybe she will be able to help them. Fresco has worked for FAO, the United Nations Food and Agriculture Organisation in Rome for a long time. She is an honorary member of SER, the most important advisory body to the Dutch government, and as a director at Rabobank she has experience of the business world. When asked what she can contribute, the professor of biological production systems at Wageningen University says that she bases her conclusions solely on the facts and always demands to see proof. A fellow director points out that Fresco also writes opinion columns in *NRC Handelsblad*, one of the Netherlands' top broadsheets, isn't that a risk? She views this question as ridiculous, she is professional enough to be able to keep the two separate, thank you very much.

Fresco enjoys writing and does so prolifically, including novels focusing on social issues. In *The Utopians* her protagonist says, 'what motivates me is nothing more than the sense of responsibility I feel for what my generation has done in its laxness and striving for individual freedom to the cost of social cohesion and shared social responsibility'. Her message fits with Unilever's mission. In a recent, sell-out Ted Talk she warned, 'I understand the resistance to industrially produced food, the suggestion that it pollutes the environment, I understand the growing attraction of small-scale artisan production. But it is nonsense. Only cleverly industrialised food production will be in a position to feed the whole world safely. And this by no means needs to be polluting; it is simply a question of more and better research, and of innovation.' Fresco underscores this message time and again: globalisation doesn't mean that there is one, large market now, so much as it means that there is only one world.

Polman and Fresco hit it off immediately. In their first ever meeting they talk about Africa, starvation and the impact of climate change. Fresco is pleased to hear Polman say that the business model of the future has to be a green approach to the economy. He wants every one of Unilever's product categories to set sustainability targets and take care of those responsibilities. Fresco is surprised, this is really progressive. She accepts the invitation to become a director.

Fresco is pleased to hear that Ann Fudge has also said yes. Unilever asked her once before back in 2006 but she quickly backed out when she discovered that former CEO Antony Burgmans had taken on the role of chairman. Governance at Unilever had clearly not been in order back then. But now it is. This African American businesswoman, high up at Kraft for many years, has had various roles in compliance and learned a value lesson from them: as soon as a board starts concentrating on profit per share, things go amiss. It's the beginning of the end; you soon see improper behaviour. Her first impression is also that the finance people are still dominant inside Unilever.

Paul Walsh, the long-time darling of the stock markets as CEO of Diageo, one of the biggest manufacturers of spirits, is asked to join the board alongside Fresco and Fudge. Kees Storm is especially keen on this addition, Walsh is a man who can be relied on to push the importance of healthy results.

After a long wait, Ben Cohen and Jerry Greenfield get to meet the new Unilever boss. The politically minded founders of Ben & Jerry's had send Polman a personal cry for help as soon as he was appointed in 2008. In doing so they had bypassed two levels of Unilever hierarchy. This had not gone down well. Cohen and Greenfield were deeply concerned about the future of their company. In the presence of their direct boss Michael Polk they hope to get Polman's agreement to keep the factory in Waterbury open. The board of Ben & Jerry's already sent a furious letter to the Unilever top brass a couple of months previously when the announcement came that the ice cream factory was operating too inefficiently and therefore needed to close. Didn't Unilever promise the staff there a living wage and decent treatment?

Dissatisfaction with Unilever is profound on several fronts. Over the past few years, the quality of the ice cream has been threatened by efforts to economise on ingredients. The ice cream has been over-aerated, they'd removed too much of the fat content. Unilever has reportedly even tried to make the pieces of chocolate, banana and nut smaller. This is a cardinal sin: that was their whole starting point back in 1977. Because Ben Cohen had problems with his sinuses that meant he couldn't taste very well, Jerry had decided to stuff the ice cream full of pieces of the primary ingredients, so that Ben could chew on the flavours, as it were. It turned out to be a billion-dollar idea, the whole basis of their success.

Around eight years after the takeover by Unilever, the two former hippies have come to the conclusion that even though Unilever is a professionally led organisation, it fundamentally doesn't grasp the ethos of Ben & Jerry's, the first social enterprise in the United States. They fear that Unilever is going to destroy the Ben & Jerry's brand.

The board shares this concern, writing, 'our board stands united behind the three-part mission [...] we see business as a powerful force for social change [...] we are all aware of the complexity of redefining business from the Milton Friedman perspective to the Ben & Jerry's perspective. [...] We know that it is not simply a matter of trade-offs, it is not simply a matter of a program here or there, it is not philanthropy, and it is not building a brand.'

The letter contains a long list of demands. The stipulated profit margin should be reduced by 4 per cent; they need additional funds to bring on extra staff responsible for implementing the social mission; they need to hire an independent 'social auditor'. 'It is a philosophy of how we run our business day to day, keeping a social justice and environmental on the table as we make all of our decisions for a profitable business.'

The two businessmen and the top manager have a good conversation. Polman promises Waterbury will remain open. But the summary of the discussion Michael Polk circulates after the meeting does not satisfy the founders one bit. They believe he is clinging to a vastly inflated profit margin. Trapping their company within Unilever's suffocating matrix means that their revered three-part mission is doomed. The two men inform Polk that they intend to take legal action if Unilever doesn't keep to the agreements made during the takeover. They only back down when Polman emphasises that the ice cream manufacturer doesn't need to reach these profit targets for the time being.[13] The Unilever CEO resolves to give their quickly expanding daughter company some room to follow its own approach, the mother company probably stands to learn something from it.

During his first shareholder meeting in May, Polman is cautious. He tells his shareholders, 'The company is standing, the wiring is good; my task is to get some current flowing through those wires. Because however well my predecessor did optimising the product portfolio, the fact is that the turnover has remained stagnant at €40 billion. That has to change.' Polman chooses his words carefully, 'In these quickly changing conditions we need to place our customers and our clients back at the heart of what we do. I promise that large-scale revenue growth can be achieved profitably and sustainably and that this is the surest way to create value for you, my dear shareholders, in the long term.'

In his first media appearances, Polman emphasises his humble background. He tells the *Financial Times*, 'I keep things very simple, that's why I like consumer goods.' And no, he isn't surprised that the share price has dipped 17 per cent since his appointment. He explains to the *Financial Times*, 'As far as I'm concerned, quarterly numbers are Pinocchio numbers, a way of playing hide and seek with the analysts. I don't see any necessity for them. People like Warren Buffett don't bother with them either. Let them judge me on the actual results.'

When asked by McKinsey Consultants, who are interviewing him for their quarterly magazine, what the most important lesson he has learned has been, he answers, 'I think the first thing is [to be] purpose driven and [to have] values – that, I think, is very important. And [what] I think over my career is, if your values, your personal values, are aligned with the company's values, you're probably going to be more successful longer term than if they are not. If they are not, it requires you to be an actor when you go to work or to be a split personality.'

'The second lesson, I think, that permeates all of this is the importance of people. At the end of the day, especially where we are sitting right now in positions of leadership, it is the quality of the people, the investment in people. And long ago – I think I have understood perhaps a little bit later in my career than you normally want – in the beginning, you're self-centred. But at the end, you understand that if you invest in people, they invest in you, and your business is going to be successful. I think you've learned the lessons from the last year and a half – what greed and mismanagement, to some extent, can lead to.'

The journalist notices that Polman's name is written on his business card in braille. Polman proudly explains that he runs marathons to raise money for his Kilimanjaro Blind Trust. Over the last week alone he and his son Christian have raised $70,000 for this worthy cause. When the journalist looks concerned, he laughs: 'Oh don't worry, I started when I was 48 [...] the big advantage of starting at that age is that your joints are already about as knackered as they can get.'[14]

Unilever is going full steam ahead. Turnover is increasing, mostly of its own accord but also because of a significant takeover in September 2009. Sara Lee had announced its desire to sell of 'body care products' like Sanex and the Dutch baby care brand Zwitsal. These are brands that Polman can get excited about. He knows this world inside out. He understands it; this is the realm of Procter & Gamble. More exciting still, seven years ago he had actually investigated this company as a potential acquisition for P&G. He and his colleagues had looked at products on the shelves in various stores then gone to the Sara Lee head office in Utrecht to open discussions. While there, he was forced to come to the conclusion that a takeover just wasn't on the cards. Now things are different. It's clear to him that this sector of Unilever is going to yield more in terms of growth over the next few years than the foods division. This takeover will provide them with dominant market positions in various European countries. With brands like Prodent and Zendium Unilever will become the market leader in toothpaste in countries like Sweden and Hungary overnight.

In the end, Unilever pays €1.3 billion for Sara Lee in exchange for €750 million in new revenue. A wave of excitement runs through the company. Their new boss is willing to risk big takeovers in order to support their growth objectives.

Meanwhile, Gavin Neath is hard at work getting Unilever on the path to sustainability. The pledge to half environmental impact is going to be a big ask for the company. He wants to talk to director of purchasing Marc Engel about increasing his input. Neath refers him the promise they made in 2008 in response to a campaign from Greenpeace, to ensure that all their palm oil is certified as sustainable by 2015. At the time, the NGO had exerted pressure in the most ridiculous way. All across Europe, activists dressed up as orang-utans had demonstrated outside the offices of companies they held responsible for deforestation as a result of their growing demands for palm oil. Deforestation was running out of control, including in parts of Indonesia that were the last remaining habitat for orang-utans. Their sights were set mostly on Unilever, then the largest consumer of palm oil with 1.3 million tonnes purchased per year. The 'orang-utans' gathered outside reception at Blackfriars head office. Since the whole Executive Committee was away in the United States, it was Gavin Neath, the UK boss and the man responsible for developing Unilever's sustainability policy, who had come down to talk to the protesters. Neath, son of a diplomat, was shocked. Obviously he knew that Unilever was the biggest buyer of palm oil. But for whatever reason he had not quite made the link between this and deforestation. Within a couple of days, Unilever had promised to help their suppliers to make their product sustainable and to only buy in certified palm oil by 2015.

Neath had asked Greenpeace to show him the problem. In the skies above Sumatra he was confronted with the sight of massive gashes spreading across the tropical rainforest. His sense of urgency had only increased as a result. There is no time to lose. Neath now wants to hear from Marc Engel what Unilever can do, what Unilever *needs to do* in order to make palm oil sustainable. They've made a start: in November of the previous year they had purchased their first palm oil with a sustainability certificate.

The director of purchasing, however, has no desire to hear a sermon from Neath. He is wrestling with his numbers, the price of oil is all over the place. He has to give that priority for now. Neath understands that Engel is under huge pressure. So he asks him to go and see what is happening on the plantations with his own eyes the next time he is in Asia. Engel does so a couple of weeks later. From a helicopter, he sees the crazy pace at which vast tracts of the Indonesian rainforest are being bulldozed to make place for palm oil plantations. The misery with which he is confronted sends a shiver down his spine. It's clear to Marc Engel that this can't continue. He thanks Neath for bringing him to this insight. The director of purchasing will pursue the issue of sustainable palm oil production fanatically from now on.

Neath then invites Engel to join him and a dozen other colleagues in thinking about how Unilever can best approach making their business model more sustainable over the next 10 years. In order to answer that question, they need to find out what the total environmental impact of Unilever is currently. They decide to carry out two dozen lifecycle assessments across the whole of Unilever. These will cover 70 per cent of the Unilever business.

The foundation is already there. The work of Vis, Broekhoff, Eenhoorn, Dutilh and many, many others has resulted in a whole range of insights and initiatives over the last twenty years that contribute to the improved sustainability of purchasing and manufacturing at Unilever. The current lay of the land is summarised in the report 'Sustainable Development 2008, An Overview'.

Polman is impressed and writes in the foreword to the report: 'We are increasingly bedding sustainable thinking into the day-to-day activities of our brand management and R&D teams. We have done this through a simple tool called Brand Imprint. What we are learning is that operating in this way is bringing us hard business benefits. Our quest to run the company more sustainably is fuelling our innovation pipeline, delivering cost savings and above all winning us the hearts (and wallets) of the growing number of customers who want to be reassured that the companies from whom they are buying their products are sourcing, manufacturing and marketing them in a responsible and ethical fashion. Much of this thinking was already well embedded in Unilever; it's my intention to build on Unilever's leadership in this area.'

The report sums up the targets they have already met. Between 1995 and 2008, Unilever reduced the CO_2 emissions released during its in-house manufacturing by 39 per cent, the water consumption of its own factories declined by 68 per cent, as did the amount of waste produced. Over the last six years, Lifebuoy soap has reached 120 million people with its message about thorough handwashing. The aim is to have helped one billion people in this way by 2012. And now, at the end of 2008, half of all the Lipton tea sold in Europe is Rainforest Alliance certified.

The accountancy firm Deloitte signs off on the numbers with a 'limited assurance' certification. A standard assessment of a company's accounts receives 'reasonable assurance' certification. The accountants don't see them as having reached that standard yet. They carry out a few of their own sample audits but mostly have to rely on the details Unilever gives them.

Combatting deforestation is also on the agenda at the Consumer Goods Forum. Founded in Paris under the motto 'Better Lives Through Better Business', this initiative sees the CEOs and chairmen of the 50 biggest manufacturers and retailers of consumer products gather twice a year for two days in order to make concrete agreements intended to contribute to improved safety, better health, higher quality standards and a focus on sustainability.

Paul Polman is full of enthusiasm, this kind of collaboration is indispensable for creating the level playing field Unilever needs to develop their sustainable business model. Unilever is big, but not big enough to bear this burden alone. It's essential that competitors and clients work with them.

At the Consumer Goods Forum, he runs into Marc Bolland, the CEO of Morrison's Supermarkets. When they met before, six months previously in Davos, the two of them had been in agreement that sustainability lives or dies by transparency. Bolland has been concerned for years about the lack of urgency among both retailers and manufacturers when it comes to sustainability. Everybody seems to be caught up in their own short-term concerns.[15] Back in 2006, when he left his job as a manager at Heineken, the Dutchman had been asked by Patrick Cescau to come and head up Unilever's European division. He had even alluded to the possibility of him eventually succeeding Cescau. But Bolland had opted for the more immediate top job at Morrison's.

The two Dutchmen are in complete agreement on the issue of sustainability: if you've found something that works, you have to share it with the whole industry instead of keeping it to yourself. Otherwise progress will be too slow. They note that American competitors in particular have a big problem with that.

Polman is bubbling over with ambition *and* enjoying himself. Over the past few years he has often wondered whether he wanted to spend the rest of his life working at these kinds of big companies. All the energy that is wasted in them on political games and keeping an eye on each other. He wanted out. But now he's glad he embarked on this adventure. It's energising him. Eighty per cent of the world economy rests on the business world, so this is where it has to happen. This is where innovation takes place. This is where he can provide an answer to the big questions societies and governments are asking of dominant multinationals: Are you here for us, for society, for the world of the future, for a sustainable environment? The financial crisis has had a detrimental effect on this front, a great deal of faith has been lost, the answers need to come quickly now. Polman sees winning back this trust as his most important task. This is the key. Now that the business is growing, there is space to carry out a new mission, a calling, a 'responsible strategy'. Unilever needs to lead the way on this; it needs to be a force for good.

His own brief history as CFO of Nestlé helps him. Without that experience he would never have been able to do what he's doing here. At Nestlé he learned that as leader of a company you always need to explicitly look from the outside in. Your vision needs to be tested constantly against that of the world at large. After a merger, for example, you can learn from the company you've taken over, rather than parachuting in your own people to tell that company what to do from the top-town.

At Nestlé, he had spent a couple of years working on bringing Corporate Social Responsibility out of the realm of PR and charity and bedding it into strategy and the company's approach to doing business. That needs to happen at Unilever too. Really he would have preferred to fulfil this CEO role at Nestlé: the people there are better, the culture of the company is more evolved. You need to do less explaining there. The hand Polman has been dealt at Unilever is less favourable. But their competitor doesn't seem to be exploiting their relative advantage. Modest, much like the Swiss themselves, the guys at Nestlé didn't exactly seem to be planning to publicise their plans for sustainability. Do they even have a plan? Paul Bulcke didn't dare go for a 10-year strategy, or really intervene, Polman thinks he's too restricted by the company's history. That creates opportunities for Unilever. It also creates opportunities for Polman.

The damage caused by abolishing quarterly results is tolerable. The share price has started rising again, and bringing investor confidence with it. Kees Storm even admitted at one of the board meetings that he had been wrong, Polman had chosen the right path. That had been a beautiful moment.

The more he thinks about it, the more enthusiastic he gets. Unilever produces around one hundred and fifty billion products per year and operates in 190 countries, it is therefore big enough to shake things up in order to stay ahead of the pack in terms of transformative change. As the biggest buyer of palm oil and tea, and one of the biggest consumers of plastic, with the ambition to double in size, it is Unilever's logical moral duty to start caring more effectively for the world, by doing the right thing and trying to make people's daily lives more sustainable. That needs to be the company's calling, and that of all its employees. They have to prove that this is possible, that you can do well while doing good. Just like William Lever.

Polman enthusiastically tells the *Financial Times* about what his job looks like day to day. 'I'm about 30% of the time here or in Rotterdam. I'm about 20% in outside activities and I'm about 50% in the organisation out there.'

He recognises that the aim to double the size of the company and reduce its impact on the environment at the same time creates tensions: 'But you see, you cannot go on in this world the way we're doing. We're already consuming right now about 1.3 worlds [in terms of resources]. But the road to well-being doesn't go via reduced consumption. It has to be done via more responsible consumption. [...] So that's why we're taking such a stand on moving the world to sustainable palm oil. That's why we work with small-hold farmers, to be sure that people who don't have sufficient nutrition right now have a chance to have a better life. Because at the end of the day, I think companies that take that approach have a right to exist.'

The journalist almost falls of his chair in amazement: What are shareholders supposed to make of this narrative? Polman answers, 'if you want to attract the right investor base long term, it's increasingly easier to have those discussions, to explain a socially responsible business model', he says. 'They look at more numbers than just the balance sheet and the income statement. [...] It's not either results or responsibility, it's both/and. [...] It's doing good and doing well, which I don't see as a trade-off.'

Now his ideas need to be turned into a reality. Polman has asked Gavin Neath and Karen Hamilton to help him set out his plan on paper. They form the team that focuses on sustainability at head office. On the basis of the existing work done by platforms like the SAI and the RSPO, they need to work with the departments of R&D, marketing and purchasing to create a list of defined, measurable sustainability targets. These need to be easily quantifiable, so that people across the business can measure progress and share a sense of common responsibility. External parties, in particular NGOs, also need to be able to use them to form a clear judgement. Hamilton and Neath will spend the next few months collecting materials and writing snippets of text, which Polman will provide commentary on.

Neath is excited. This would never have been possible before. In the era of the Dutch-British chairmen you would have needed the agreement of both of them, and you would never have got it. And Cescau's heart had never been in it when it came to this issue. It's going to be a mammoth task to get the majority of their colleagues on board, they won't be easier won over by a piece of work produced by the London office, but with this energetic CEO signing off on it, maybe this will end up being something after all.

In January 2010, in a speech to the World Economic Forum in Davos, Polman rails against opportunistic, short-term orientated investors. He accuses them of frustrating companies' long-term financial needs. Referring to hedge funds, Polman says, 'They would sell their grandmother if they could make money. They are not people who are there in the long-term interests of the company.' The room falls silent for a moment; is this really the CEO of a listed company speaking? They don't say this sort of thing, surely?

Polman's colleagues are likewise alarmed by these sorts of pronouncements. Is this really sensible? He's making himself, and thereby Unilever, the enemy of the world of high finance. That won't make their work any easier. They are increasingly coming to the realisation that in opposing the existing culture of the financial markets Paul Polman is setting the bar high, very high. In his first year, he made it clear that he expects those around him to set the same high standards he does. Polman scolds anyone who questions this for being stuck in old ways of thinking, for not having the courage or energy to challenge these systems. He thinks they are being lazy.

If there's anything Polman despises, it's laziness. He repeatedly makes it clear that those in Unilever's leadership are not allowed to complain. It is unfathomable to him that some people apparently apply their talents more easily to securing their place in the hierarchy than to creating the value they need to create. It is a privilege to be allowed to do this, to be allowed to shoulder this responsibility. It is only logical that you are guided entirely by the interests of others, those who often have much less than you do.

Polman is convinced that laziness evaporates the moment you know what it is you have to do in this world, and particularly *for* this world. Capturing this passion means no longer having any doubt that you can do good *and* make good money doing it. If you regard work as a means to make money, you can forget it. You need to be passionate in the way an artist is, they don't doubt themselves, they are motivated from head to toe to make what they are driven to make. Day and night. Only then are you authentic in your leadership and only then do you no longer need to compromise between your beliefs as a person–father–citizen and your beliefs as a manager. It requires a great deal of energy, time and attention but you *can* realise this unity of perspective.

Polman is certain Unilever's success will be driven by people with this kind of deep-rooted conviction and these kinds of values. The books *Authentic Leadership* and *True North* by the Harvard professor Bill George have inspired him in this over the past few years.

Jonathan Donner, the man responsible for leadership development at Unilever, recognises this. During a seminar at Harvard last year, he had ended up in a conversation with Bill George, who told him about his new course in authentic leadership.

It's clear to Donner too that a leader must recognise and figure out what the 'decisive questions' in this life are for him. Only once you know why it is you're here do you find the courage to lead from inner conviction. Donner wants to challenge the Unilever top management to do the same.[16] He and four of his colleagues did a training course with George to test the water. It was a big success. For Miguel Veiga-Pestana, responsible for relationships with governments and NGOs, the course was nothing short of a revelation. As an eight-year-old he had learned that the biggest challenges lead to the biggest changes in life. He and his mother had fled from Madeira to the UK without his father's consent. They had 10 pounds in their pocket. This event inspires him to endeavour to make the world a better place in everything he does. He had started out in politics but came to Unilever nine years ago to continue his career. After this course, his calling is crystal clear: when he goes home in the evening, he wants to do so knowing that he has made a contribution to a more sustainable world. He promises himself he will try to eventually take on responsibility for all sustainability at Unilever. If that doesn't happen, he'll go and work for a non-profit.[17]

Polman is immediately buoyed up by these reports. Bill George is an old acquaintance. Back when George was the head of Medtronics, about eight years previously, he had invited Polman, then still the boss of P&G Europe, to visit the factory on Lake Geneva and give a talk to the Medtronics staff. At this factory they mostly manufactured pacemakers. After the tour, he had asked Polman to sit in on a session with a client. The woman's story had moved Polman to tears. She told them that without Medtronics she would no longer be alive; the company, these people, had saved her life. George had explained to Polman that he regularly invited in clients like her. He wanted to drive home to his people the reason why they were doing this work.

Polman calls George and tells him he needs leaders around him who are really engaged, who don't behave like calculating employees at work but like real people, people motivated by the destination. Just like him. Polman wants the top brass at Unilever to be trained in this. George is naturally only too pleased to oblige.

But who needs to be trained and what should this training consist of? A fair number of Unilever managers are pretty pleased with themselves. Are they really open to learning something new? In consultation with Treschow, Polman decides to invite an external agency, MWM Consulting, to assess the top 100 closely and compare their qualities with those of the competition. Where do they stand? How would they do outside Unilever? How much would they really be worth? For his colleagues, this process will clearly take some getting used to. It almost sounds like a gesture of mistrust. A couple of people bring it up with Treschow: Why is this necessary? The board chairman shuts them down quickly: If you all think you're so good, why should you worry?

Two consultants from MWM interview everyone and make a 360 degree analysis of each of the managers. They set out all their capacities and compare them to an external benchmark. The scores are dramatic. Most of the managers come nowhere near the skill level required for similar functions at rival firms.

Even Polman and Treschow are alarmed by these results. For some of the managers this will result in training. If they know what's good for them, the rest will be taking a long, hard look at themselves. What they see should convince them of the need to reflect and start looking for their 'true north', for the answer to the question of what their calling is.

CHAPTER 8

IT'S NOT A JOB, IT'S A CALLING

February–November 2010

She wanted to be a journalist, writing about the widespread injustice in South Africa. But back in the 1980s it was too dangerous. She simply didn't have the courage. So Gail Klintworth went in search of a regular job. Unilever stood out; it was a company that had been refusing for decades to conform to the South African apartheid laws and clearly stuck to its own social agenda. It carried on doing business on its own, non-racist basis in the deep conviction that by doing so it would contribute to solving the problem. Unilever even gained support from the opposition. The boss of Unilever in South Africa, Niall FitzGerald, was asked by trade union leaders to visit Nelson Mandela in prison now and again. The leader of the resistance against apartheid wanted to be well prepared for the day he would become a free man.[1]

Gail Klintworth built a career at Unilever. Now she sits in the chair FitzGerald occupied over twenty years previously and has been personally invited by Polman to take part in the first version of the four-day Unilever Leadership Development Programme.

Polman had insisted on the leadership programme carrying the Unilever name. The name needs to be central at all times, in order to make it clear that what they are doing is unique, that this is their party and not anybody else's. For this reason, Bill George had asked co-author Nick Craig to come up with a bespoke programme for Unilever. The outcome is defined: in four days' time, all participants must know what their calling in life is. They must have found their purpose.

Craig and Donner are very nervous. Are these people, successful by all societal norms and convinced of their own success, really going to open themselves up and be vulnerable? Will they really talk about the most dramatic experiences of their lives with their colleagues?

By way of introduction, Craig gives his own journey as an example. He tells them that after reading Bill George's work, he decided his aim in life was to 'wake you up and finally bring you home'. He wants to help as many people as possible access their core, so that they are capable of finally going and doing what it is they need to do. He promises them that getting to know your purpose is the basis of everything. Participants who are uncomfortable with this approach are told this must mean they are doubting whether Unilever is still the right employer for them. If this is the case, they need to speak to their line manager about where might be a better fit for them.

Craig tells the course participants that they cannot escape this. They live in this VUCA world, this world without sure footing, without any certainties. That means there are no clear markers for them to follow and therefore no option but to turn inward and reflect, to look for inspiration. By doing so, you learn what your gift to this world is.

That 'internal compass' is all the more important now it's clear that Unilever is only going to get results by collaborating intensively with other interested parties like governments, competitors and NGOs. This is the point Miguel Veiga-Pestana has always made. In order to be able to combine forces, you need them to trust you. They aren't going to do that simply because you work for a multinational, in fact they distrust multinationals by definition. But they will trust you if you can get across to them that you yourself really want the change, that you see it as your personal mission. That creates a common frame of reference and the trust that is crucial to success.

A 'collective insight' should help these participants to open up during the course. A couple of days before it starts, they had all received a wake-up call when they were confronted with the analysis the two MWM consultants wrote about them. The unforgivingly formulated conclusions about their qualities and how they work in comparison with what is asked of people in similar positions outside the company are painful for everyone. For most of them, the analysis ends with the same biting conclusion: you think you're ready for the next step but you won't get there like this. Everyone is falling short. This hits home. Craig discusses this assessment with each of the course members. He sees how shocked they are and how, one by one, they're opening themselves up to what is to come.

Many great philosophers come along on the first day. The Greek philosopher Aristotle is quoted as being the first to assert that the wealthy upper class, the elite, profits the most from freedom and has the moral duty to make sure that this freedom is placed in the service of an equitable sharing of prosperity. Craig reels off a number of Polman's inspirations, from Nelson Mandela to Mother Teresa and the Dalai Lama. The ubiquitous leadership guru Jim Collins also is quoted: 'are you an ambitious "level 4" leader who tries to win over his team with grand narratives and lots of charisma, or are a "level 5", who never shows off, stays calm, and makes it clear that it isn't about you, but about listening to others, the organisation. Do you look to the horizon, or in a mirror?'[2]

The course members have to help each other. They are sorted into small groups to get closer to what's meaningful to them by completing questionnaires and trying out various analytic techniques. Eventually each of them has to begin each sentence with: 'My calling to become a leader is [...]'

Craig emphasises that anyone keen to get an idea of what a life with purpose can yield should read the work of Viktor Frankl. 'Purpose is like a pair of spectacles, when you look through it, your live gains meaning.' He also warns them: if your calling makes you too serious and boring, then there's something wrong with it. You've only found your goal in life when your inner child starts to laugh. That child represents energy, curiosity, insight and total dedication. Everything revolves around finding that 'true north'.

Most of the Unilever managers don't find this easy. They have to drill right down. They have to interrogate each other, do all kinds of case studies and exercises but most of all they have to learn to look within. Why is it they do what they do? They do also enjoy this process, however. It's about the 'why', the essence of what they're doing. Their daily cares keep them trapped in the how and what of their work. To them this is like group psychotherapy. They share a great deal, they cry a great deal.

Time and again, Craig has to explain to the Unilever managers that they shouldn't reduce this journey to wanting to grow the market share or beating the competition. 'If you could be fired for it, or let it lie by taking retirement, then it isn't your calling. You're calling is a deep well, it never runs dry.'[3]

The trainer is well aware that this isn't easy for these analytically inclined people. How does the boss of Hellmann's mayonnaise make the link between his job and his personal calling? It's only logical that many of the participants dream of being the boss of Ben & Jerry's or the head of Unilever Thailand. Even at Unilever it's fairly easy to unite calling and results in that kind of position. The boss of Unilever Pakistan is a prime example. By ensuring that a growing number of people have access to simple things like toothpaste, Unilever is helping many of his still destitute countrymen to look after their teeth. Unilever's turnover in Pakistan is growing by between 10 per cent and 20 per cent per year. For course members in that situation, it's not hard to think in terms of a win-win scenario.

Jonathan Donner believes it is important for Polman to show himself and join in. When he tells him that the participants are expecting him to come and tell his real story, the CEO is initially rather reserved. But when one of the participants asks him man-to-man, he can't hold back. He tells them about his parents, who had to save every last penny so that their children could go to university but were always there for them. He tells them about his father, who worked himself into an early grave, and how sad he was not to have gone on holiday to Enschede with the family for Easter 1993, a few weeks before he died. There were still so many things he wanted to talk to his father about.

The tears stream down his cheeks. He also tells them about his childhood dream of becoming a priest and the fact that he often wishes he had become a doctor. He'd still prefer it. He tells them about the life lessons he learnt as P&G director in Newcastle, about the horrors of the attack in Mumbai and about his deep conviction that most people are good. The CEO tells the group that they won't be surprised to hear that his calling is to fight for the people who ended up down on their luck, and who can't do anything about it.

His colleagues are impressed. Up until now their CEO has mostly come across as a rather harsh, super hardworking, demanding boss. Now they are seeing him as a person and they feel a strong connection to him. After Polman has finished speaking, each of them presents their personal calling to the group. Donner hopes Polman's presence will be the cornerstone of the course.

Gail Klintworth leaves the course brimming with enthusiasm. 'My participation in ULDP was transformational. It helped me understand that sustainability and improving people's lives are my driving strengths. I wanted a role that merged sustainability and business to prove that sustainable business is the only viable model. My new role is the perfect fit, but I wouldn't have been brave enough to take it had it not been for ULDP.'[4]

In order to avoid the huge bureaucratic Unilever machine tempting them to fall back into old habits, they have resolved to ask the course members back at regular intervals to other sessions to act as examples and challenge other managers. In addition, a second, two-day coaching course will teach them how to motivate other people to go in search of their own calling. A third training course will focus on collaboration with a strong focus on results. The whole programme will be spread over three years. That way, the managers can thoroughly anchor their personal calling in their daily work. It is agreed that the whole top 100 will have verbalised their calling be the end of the year. If not, they'll leave the company.[5]

Some of the old hands, particularly the Dutch ones, are strongly reminded of the leadership retreats they went on with Tex Gunning 13 or 14 years previously. The charismatic boss of Van den Bergh & Jurgens has always wondered aloud why such excellent people produced such mediocre results, only to conclude with a broad grin that 'the happy cows really do give the most milk'. Gunning took them to challenging locations in Scotland, Iceland and Jordan. There he ran them ragged, before challenging them to tell their life stories. Gunning thought his colleagues needed to become better people before they could become better leaders.

Polman doesn't care for such comparisons. In his eyes, Gunning didn't help the business get anywhere. He spent too much money on exotic trips, seemingly just so that they could spend time somewhere remote, philosophising about the question of what it means to be a good person. Back then, it had been all about personality cult, which had stood in the way of the focus on doing the work. Gunning had started styling himself as some kind of guru. Polman wants absolutely nothing of the sort, it can't be about him. He is nothing to do with it. He can very well imagine that had he been present, he would have been on the same page as Gunning when it came to content, but that's not what it's about. It all comes down to whether you end up any more effective in your work. You're a manager who's falling behind schedule with work. If you're not a good person, you have a totally different problem. Unilever can't solve that for you. In the Unilever Leadership Development Programme, Unilever managers have to learn what motivates them and how they can harness that to advance Unilever and therefore the world. If what motivates them doesn't fit with Unilever then Polman wants them gone. If you want to become a better person, go do it somewhere else.

Doing well by doing good: that is the task Polman's Unilever managers need to take away with them. Where will the company be in five years, what role will you be playing in it? It's great you've found your purpose, now integrate it will Unilever's business model. Over the coming years, this company needs to prove it can be a force for good, one that lifts up not only consumers and citizens but the whole of society, and earns enough money while doing so making sure shareholders have nothing to complain about.

'Freeing up energy so that we can build a better future for us all', 'focus on the good', 'dare to be who you are', etc. From Conny Braams to Jan Zijderveld, from Marc Engel to Alan Jope and from Gavin Neath to Peter ter Kulve: all of them head off in search of the right words with which to commit their calling to paper. Some are more enthusiastic than others. Some, like Alan Jope, forget their purpose within a few days, others think about it almost every day.

All of them submit a report on their journey to Polman. He reads them and gives them extensive individual feedback. The CEO uses this information to move many of them to other roles. In a short space of time, almost half of the top 100 are given new responsibilities. Polman sends Alan Jope to China, for example. The Scot has absolutely no desire to go but is told: you have to, that's where you'll be able to grow.

Simon Clift is also weighing his options. The way Polman wants to alter the role of chief marketing officer doesn't suit him at all. Clift would much prefer to work on advertising content. He is proud of the contributions he has made to the Dove and Lynx campaigns. The Brit isn't particularly impressed with Polman. He doesn't seem all that interested in what other people think or feel, let alone persuaded of the necessity to listen to them. Clift has already seen the CEO's reaction to key colleagues tendering their resignation: he didn't so much as ask them why. Polman obviously regards sharing his vision and getting others on board with it as his main task. Anyone who wants to join him is welcome, the rest are welcome to leave. That even applies to new applicants, who have sometimes come from the other side of the world to introduce themselves. Polman readily gives them a 90-minute slot but barely asks them any questions, all he wants to hear from them is whether they subscribe to *his* vision.

In Clift's opinion, Polman is also quick to anger when he thinks the people around him don't understand him or aren't working hard enough. The 52-year-old marketer calculates that he has made enough money to spend the rest of his life enjoying himself and decides to resign. It comes as no surprise to him that Polman doesn't react to the announcement that he'll be leaving Unilever after 25 years. In fact, Polman is happy Clift is going. He thinks he's a typical British windbag, full of hot air. God knows there's still plenty more of them taking up space at Unilever. He asks the consistently hardworking marketer Keith Weed to be Clift's successor.

Gavin Neath and Karen Hamilton are working hell for leather. They have to get the USLP down on paper. Each text they send to Polman comes back to them with endless crossings-out and corrections. Polman keeps insisting they concretise the plan, there have to be clear, measurable goals in there. Otherwise it can never be incorporated into the daily running of Unilever and will be perceived as theory by the staff at the head office. The piece needs to focus mostly on growth, the growth of sustainable business. If there isn't enough about that in there, Polman won't be able to sell it to the shareholders.

Miguel Veiga-Pestana reports to Neath and is asked to think about Polman's role as the promoter of the USLP inside and outside Unilever. Veiga-Pestana was there back when Neath first started a conversation with Greenpeace about the link between palm oil deforestation and the disappearance of orang-utans.

He thinks Hamilton and Neath make a powerful duo. Hamilton is the intellectual engine, Neath is the seasoned Unilever man, who has built up lots of pull thanks to having been the boss of Unilever-UK. Neath knows exactly which buttons he needs to press and how best to press them. He has a formidable network inside Unilever.

Neath experiences exactly what Miguel Veiga-Pestana has so often predicted: when you're authentic, even NGOs take you seriously. During the drawing up of the plans, Neath has a large number of discussions with various NGOs. He speaks to John Sauven, the director of Greenpeace in the UK, at least once a month. They'll never say they wholeheartedly approve of what Unilever is doing, but they do help the company. They sharpen the plans and objectives. Neath is grateful to the NGOs, without them Unilever would never have come this far.

Veiga-Pestana sees the fact that Polman is from outside the company as an advantage, it means he can come in with a clean slate and make radical changes. In order to get the rest of the firm on his side, he thinks Polman should follow the example of the consummate diplomat Neath. It's not just a matter of *what* you say but of *how* you say it. Polman should act under the assumption that Unilever's buyers, salesmen and marketers won't be looking forward to this narrative. They won't understand it. To get them on board, therefore, he also needs to be humble, he should listen at least as much as he talks. And he needs to be transparent, open about what's going wrong. He needs to be willing to ask for help. That way he'll win people to his cause who are also comfortable with showing vulnerability.

The narrative Polman will offer those outside the company quickly takes shape. To begin with, Veiga-Pestana produces short summaries of all kinds of reports from NGOs and organisations like the OECD. He puts together a list of 10 points containing everything Polman needs to know in order to defend his position. This soon stops being necessary. The roles have even reversed, Polman asks Veiga-Pestana why he hasn't cited certain studies yet.

In the spring of 2010, Unilever gets a new CFO. Jim Lawrence only managed to stick it out for two years. That last year under Polman hadn't been pleasant. Polman had earned his stripes as CFO of Nestlé, a much larger company. He tested Lawrence, cornering him at every opportunity. Treschow also began to lose patience with the American and thought Lawrence made everything overly complicated with endless Excel spreadsheets. Didn't he realise his reports no longer saw the wood for the trees? In Treschow's eyes, Lawrence was the weak link in the chain. Over the past year, his colleagues have been laughing about the rumour that during his first meeting with Polman, Lawrence had told him he thought he was a nice enough chap, but that he, Lawrence, had obviously been the more logical candidate for CEO. His departure is soon arranged. Discretely, of course. Lawrence is allowed to step down as a so-called good leaver, with all the associated financial advantages. The announcement of his departure comes as no surprise to anyone.

The choice of successor, however, is something no one sees coming. Forty-one-year-old Jean-Marc Huët is the great grandson of Sam van den Bergh, one of the founders of Unilever. Paul Polman had to pull out all the stops to get Huët to come to Unilever. He even went to speak to Huët's mother in Geneva before approaching him. Executive searchers from Egon Zehnder supervised the process.

Jeroen van der Veer, now entering his final year as non-executive director, is the head of the Nominations Committee and delighted with the appointment of the new CFO. Van de Veer thinks he's a solid professional, a man of great substance. Kees Storm, chairman of the Audit Committee, is also pleased. Lawrence was a typical bookkeeper, just like him; choosing Huët means opting for a more enterprising financial director. Storm is impressed with Huët's brain power, and that's saying something. He hopes Huët will make sure that Unilever embarks on a couple of big takeovers. Those will be necessary if they are to realise the promised turnover of €80 billion by 2020. As a former Goldman Sachs banker and in his later role as CFO of Numico especially, he has proven himself as a dealmaker. In the latter function he made a personal profit of around €32 million by selling Numico to the French company Danone.

Among the top brass at Unilever, rumours are flying around about his remuneration package. Huët spent two years as the financial director of the pharmacy giant Bristol Myers Squibb, which had offered him a lot of prospective additional earnings. These must have been compensated. He receives £2.6 million in Unilever shares and £680,000 cash. He is then given an additional almost £800,000 in order to look for a house in London. Huët has to get to work immediately. Unilever is set to take over Alberto-Culver, the makers of personal care brands like TRESemmé and VO5, for $3.7 billion.

André van Heemstra is pleased. He has managed to persuade Polman to join him and Miguel Veiga-Pestana for a two-day trip to the United Nations in New York. After his retirement from Unilever, Van Heemstra dedicated himself to the question of how companies can do more and be more effective in protecting universal human rights. In New York, they will present their findings with the title 'How you can do business with respect for human rights'. Their point of departure is the work of John Ruggie, the special representative of the secretary general of the UN on the issue of human rights and multi-nationals. How can companies act against, for example, criminality, slavery and child labour and make sure all workers are treated fairly and equitably, wherever they are in the world? Harvard professor Ruggie is trying to devise rules of play that will empower companies and governments to make clear agreements on the matter.

This is turning out to be a difficult task. Ever since Kofi Annan fired the starting pistol for the Global Compact Initiative in Davos in 1999, calling on the business world to engage in a sustainable way with the big questions facing the world, a fierce debate has been raging. Can companies feel at all responsible for things like universal human rights? Multinationals tend to think they should behave like good citizens of the country in which they are based, and that the norms and values of that country should determine their behaviour. If, for example, a country doesn't have any existing laws concerning the living wage, then why should you start paying it off your own bat? Multinationals see universal laws as dangerous because they pose a threat to their competitiveness.

The previous year, a determined Ruggie had formulated an actionable 'principles-driven pragmatic framework'. In it, companies were called on to respect human rights wherever they are in the world and to ensure that instances of abuse were addressed. Dutch companies like Rabobank, Fortis, KLM, Shell and Unilever, united under the 'Global Compact Network Netherlands', had committed to this framework. They regarded this work by Ruggie as a call to arms for them to set out how they themselves could start working on these issues. In their presentation in New York, Chairman Van Heemstra and researcher David Vermijs show how companies can best pose questions to themselves about the way they approach human rights. By doing this, they get a clearer picture of how they can increase their efforts not only on behalf of their own employees but also for the safety of their products and relationships with their suppliers.

Kofi Annan's successor, UN secretary general Ban Ki-moon, is enthusi-astic. After the presentation, he invites Polman to come and meet with him, setting aside 15 minutes in his schedule in order to make his acquaintance. The meeting lasts an hour. The two men get on well.

Veiga-Pestana is pleasantly surprised by this enthusiasm; he believes whole-heartedly in these powers joining forces and is well aware that the people at the United Nations would rather be seen dead than as constrained by the interests of multinationals. Suspicion is still the dominant mood on both sides. He can see that if anything Polman regards this as an incentive to make the material his own. He tries to persuade Polman, who has the tendency to take on everything himself, to limit himself to the issues in which Unilever can really make a difference. Making sure nobody goes to bed hungry anymore, food security, seems to him to be a clear priority here. When they discuss it together, they quickly come to the unsettling conclusion that the whole system will have to be fundamentally changed in order to realise this aim.

A couple of months after the meeting with Ban Ki-moon, Polman is invited back to the United Nations to take part in a panel discussion about how to organise the sustainability agenda. A study carried out by advisors at Accenture shows that 93 per cent of the 766 CEOs they interviewed believe sustainability is important to the future success of their company. Proper education and combatting climate changes are also identified as key issues. They are in no rush, however. In answer to the question of how long they think it will take for sustainability to be completely integrated into their 'global footprint', a little over half of the CEOs say it might have happened in 10 years' time. Polman thinks this needs to happen quicker. Much quicker. Those in the room respond enthusiastically to his call to action. On the podium, he is surrounded by NGOs, government officials and academics. He is the only CEO and he is enjoying the attention.[6]

Well, well, finally a CEO of a large multinational who understands the issue. Nico Roozen reads the USLP with a rising sense of excitement. He is glowingly enthusiastic. The director of Solidaridad has been on the lookout for a clear ethical motivation that will allow NGOs to start working more intensively with the business world for a long time. He thinks Paul Polman is the first CEO to have laid out a successful business case for sustainability. Finally, a company is explaining clearly that its first responsibility is to the society in which it operates. This is an agenda for growth driven by the environment. Only by working on its environmental footprint can the company achieve the value creation it has promised its shareholders.

Roozen believes in the power of the market. The son of a flower bulb farmer sees no alternative. But as a social democrat he is also convinced that three things are required to ensure this market generates better, fairer results: a government that sets clear guidelines, strong NGOs and a business sector that has integrated sustainability into its approach. Unilever's plan is an excellent example of this.

In the foreword to the USLP, Polman writes: 'We have ambitious plans to grow our company. In fact, we want to double our sales. This growth will create jobs and income for all those whose livelihoods are linked to our success: our employees, our suppliers, our customers, our investors and hundreds of thousands of farmers around the world. But growth at any cost is not viable.

By 2020 we will help more than a billion people take action to improve their health and well-being. By then we will have halved the environmental footprint of the making and use of our products, and enhanced the livelihoods of hundreds of thousands of people in our supply chain.'

As he reads this, Roozen does reflect that it is a shame Unilever sold off almost all of its plantations over the previous 15 years, thereby transferring all the risks to hundreds of thousands of mostly small-scale farmers. Unilever is now basically nothing more than a buyer of raw materials, how are they going to do all this? Making the supply chain more sustainable is precisely the question Solidaridad, best-known as a Fairtrade certification brand, has been focusing on since 1969. Roozen is looking forward to working intensively with Unilever and with Polman to realise the aims of the USLP.

It is a breathtakingly ambitious list of goals. In 2020, the production and consumption of Unilever products will emit 50 per cent less CO_2, consumers will use 50 per cent less water while using Unilever products, waste due to this consumption will have halved, 100 per cent of all raw materials will be sustainably grown and 500,000 subsistence farmers will have been sustainably incorporated into the supply chain. Half a billion people will be helped to access affordable, safe drinking water. Fifty million people will take better care of their teeth. In 2020, the total weight of packaging will have been reduced by a third, and in the 14 biggest countries 15 per cent of packaging will be recycled. The litany of good intentions goes on for page after page: less salt, less sugar, fewer calories, in total there are fifty more or less measurable aims.

In the USLP document, the company claims to be taking this course of action because it's what consumers want. Enthusiastic references are made to the success of Lipton and Ben & Jerry's: sustainable brands are prestige brands. The same applies to Unilever's direct clients, more and more supermarkets are embracing sustainability and Unilever will support them in this. The company points to potential for considerable savings: 'Managing our business sustainably reduces energy use, minimises packaging and drives out waste. It not only generates cost savings, it can also save the consumer money.'

Finally, the document emphasises that almost half of the company's turnover comes from emerging markets, this is where growth is going to come from and this is where they will face the biggest challenges when it comes to sustainability: deforestation, scarcity of drinking water, poor provision of sanitation. 'In the face of these dilemmas it would be irresponsible not to commit ourselves fully to the development of products and processes that make a sustainable increase in prosperity there a possibility.'

Polman is proud. He thinks that with this initiative, Unilever is going much further than companies that talk primarily about creating sustainable value. In the text that accompanies the plan he writes: 'It is no longer enough to say that you are contributing to a better world. You need to be part of the solution and help to turn the tide. Instead of thinking about how you can use society to achieve success, you need to think about the question of how you can contribute to a successful society.'

Neath has 143 versions of the USLP on his computer. He believes in Polman and the high standards he sets. There's a lot of talk about leadership in the business world but this man makes good on his promises. The fact that he has made it crystal clear to everyone else at Unilever that this is what he wants means that it is possible. In terms of content, it has turned into a solid vision. A vision that there is really no saying no to. The enthusiasm from the R&D department is already palpable. The people there come alive when, for example, they are asked to make a product that requires 70 per cent less water. Because in this respect the USLP goes a lot further than companies with similar plans. Unilever wants to engage not only with its production methods but with the impact associated with using their products.

Of course, Neath has some concerns too. Like his colleague Karen Hamilton, he has his doubts about the marketers in particular. They are going to have to let go of the idea that sustainability is something you can profit from directly. Consumers are not going to pay extra for it. Of all his colleagues, they will be the last ones to embrace the USLP. Marketers are soon complaining that they can't see a good advertising angle. It's going to be a long road. Neath thinks that setting aside 10 years for it is logical.

Polman wants to avoid implementation of the USLP falling solely to the sustainability department. Keith Weed, the new boss of Marketing and Communication, is therefore given combined responsibility for both marketing and sustainability. He is tasked with helping drive home to everyone that the USLP needs to be placed at the heart and in the core operations of the organisation. Weed himself remarks: 'In many companies, the head of sustainability is a guy with a beard and sandals urging people to save the planet. We wanted to signal that sustainability was not about "corporate social responsibility" as an isolated activity. It was everyone's responsibility. So we abolished the CSR office to underline our belief that marketing and sustainability were two sides of the same coin. It was a belief [that] became reflected in our strategy.'[7]

Internally, there have been urgent warnings against sharing a concrete timeline for any USLP objectives. Those outside the company will measure the company's success against them year after year, along with the ambition to reach €80 billion in turnover. Polman isn't afraid. Of course, the chance they'll reach all of these aims by 2020 is small. They are dependent on a huge number of external factors over which Unilever has no control. Everyone knows that, don't they? Surely no one can deny that? Every bit of progress they make is a win and will be perceived as such. Polman regards the USLP as more of a philosophy, a way of thinking through which the company can hold itself accountable. He is convinced that the USLP, and therefore the future of Unilever, lives or dies on honesty and transparency. In the introduction to the USLP, Polman says: 'Delivering these commitments won't be easy. To achieve them we will have to work in partnership with governments, NGOs, suppliers and others to address the big challenges which confront us all. Ultimately we will only succeed if we inspire billions of people around the world to take the small, everyday actions that add up to a big difference – actions that will enable us all to live more sustainably.'

The reactions in the press are mixed. In *Het Financieele Dagblad*, Klaas van Egmond, professor of environmental sciences at Utrecht University, says that Polman has got the message: 'As a reaction to globalisation consumers are turning away from big companies.' 'An increasing number of consumers expect companies to save the rainforest and keep their packaging to a minimum', states Herman Wijffels, professor of sustainability and environmental change, in the same newspaper. Even the chairman of the Dutch investors' association (VEB) Jan Maarten Slagter responds positively: 'This isn't altruism. What Unilever is doing is in the long-term interest of the company and the shareholder.' The newspaper reports that Polman also wants to enter discussions with Prime Minister Mark Rutte in order to introduce the Unilever business model to the civil service. 'In order to make progress', Polman claims. Van Egmond suspects Polman is betting on support from the political world.[8]

The *Financial Times* commentator is a bit more sceptical. Will Polman's message be understood properly? He was at the presentation of the USLP and describes what took place. Upon being asked what the shareholders were supposed to make of the USLP vision, Polman answered: 'Unilever has been around for 100-plus years. We want to be around for several hundred more. So if you buy into this long-term value-creation model, which is equitable, which is shared, which is sustainable, then come and invest with us. If you don't buy into this, I respect you as a human being, but don't put your money in our company.' The commentator sees this as highly suspect: 'What was so striking is that Mr Polman said this in the week the *Financial Times* reported his company's shares were lagging behind both competitors' and the market.'

When he is confronted with this fact, Polman, much to the annoyance of the journalist, shrugs his shoulders and says, 'We certainly don't want to attract the investor base that wants higher and higher and quicker results against targets that we put out every 90 days.' The *Financial Times* reporter wonders: 'What are we to make of this suggestion that short-term shareholders get lost? Mr Polman's appeal to shareholders to take the long view is admirable, but I felt nervous about his own long-term prospects. Even the most patient investor eventually needs a decent return. If Mr Polman fails to deliver that, he may run short of supporters who understand his language.'[9]

Polman tells *NRC Handelsblad*: 'We are stealing from the future. People in developing countries have the right to the same prosperity as we do. And what happens if the global population grows by two billion people over the next few years? We have to go over to a new way of doing business on the basis of responsible growth, sustainable growth, green growth – call it what you like.'

When asked whether he is acting out of economical or ethical motives, Polman answers: 'The two overlap. In the end, a company is only successful if it is in step with society. The consumer wants sustainable products, without this coming at the cost of price, quality or flavour. A company that is good for the consumer, for its own employees and their concerns, is inevitably good for its shareholders. Over the past two years we have been praised for our approach. Our share price is stronger than the average in the sector.' In response to the question of whether Unilever's plans go far enough, he replies: 'That judgement ultimately lies with the consumer. If we convince *them*, we will show the competition that this is the best way of growing. By the time they understand that, we'll hopefully already be two steps ahead.'

CHAPTER 9

COLOURS TO THE MAST

November 2010–October 2011

Paul Polman and Chris Dutilh want the same things but working together is out of the question. The man who was one of the first to start tracking the environmental impact of Unilever products almost twenty-five years earlier is being let go. The start of the USLP marks the end of one of its founders.

Kees van der Waaij has to bid farewell to him in December 2010. This does not sit well with the chairman of Unilever Netherlands; it gives him a seriously bad feeling in his gut. Van der Waaij thinks Dutilh's a wise and enthusiastic man, years ahead of his time in his commitment to the world. But he also knows him to be stubborn and awkwardly impatient. A rigid man who doesn't always pick the right words. Why can't he simply play along a bit?

Dutilh has seen this misfortune coming for a while. For a long time, he had a lot of space to operate. But over the past year he has been carefully kept out of all discussions around the USLP. He is increasingly working from home, opposite Amsterdam's Central Station, because his work space in the Rotterdam office is being commandeered for other matters. Foreign guests visiting the manager of sustainable development at Unilever Netherlands can't believe their eyes when they enter Dutilh's third floor back office. The tiny room is filled with glass display cases full of Unilever products and enormous piles of documents. It may look chaotic but Dutilh knows exactly where everything is.

Over the past few years, people have told him time and again that he doesn't know the first thing about marketing. The chemist thinks they're completely mistaken but he understands why they reproach him. He has always been convinced that the quest for sustainability is most often scuppered by marketers only interested in how they can make money from it. The essence of sustainability is beyond them. This message is never gratefully received.

His wife had warned him and questioned why it is that he's so cynical. Dutilh had explained to her that when it comes to sustainability he truly doesn't believe it's possible to link up the results- and process-orientated sides of a company. They are two different worlds. Last summer he was informed that his service was coming to an end.

Dutilh has never spoken to Polman. But he firmly believes that what the new CEO wants is simply not possible. With this new mission Unilever will attract a lot of young talent with good, fresh ideas. That is an important upside. But turnover won't increase by attaching sustainability claims to their products.

With a vision for sustainability, you're aiming for citizens, but you get your revenue from consumers. According to Dutilh, all people are familiar with two systems of reward: a masculine system and a feminine system. The first focuses on harvests, on setting goals and achieving them, quickly, through measurement and precision. The mission is clear: as much as possible. The feminine system is all about sowing crops, giving them water and attention, weeding, nurturing. The aim here is: enough at the right time. Dutilh doesn't believe we are capable of merging the two systems. The role we take on, that of citizen or consumer, determines which system fits.

As a consumer, the individual mostly want things to be safe, healthy and cheap. This is the realm in which a company like Unilever operates, the realm of the calculator. As a citizen, the same individual wants a healthy environment for their children and an end to world poverty. This is the domain of norms and values. People won't take them from a company, says Dutilh. A company that claims to be able to make money following the correct norms and values is not credible. When it comes to these matters, people trust other people, friends and family, sometimes politicians, but not companies.

In Dutilh experience it is probably only right that people place their trust in people like Paul Polman, who are authentic in their ambitions. But that doesn't mean they'll automatically place the same trust in the CEO of Unilever, who claims they should trust Unilever's products. That's where Polman gets into trouble, according to Dutilh. You speak about values and norms with those close to you and expect politicians to say inspiring things. Dutilh thinks perhaps the American economist Milton Friedman was right after all: the behaviour of a company changes because citizens express their concerns and elect politicians who have to anchor those concerns in the law.

The function of Dutilh, the manager of sustainable development, is coming to an end. Anniek Mauser is appointed as the sustainability manager for the Benelux countries. She is tasked with helping the marketers integrate the goals of the USLP into their work. When it comes to this, Dutilh is forced to concede that his bosses are right: he isn't capable of doing that. He had indicated that he'd like to remain involved with Unilever's sustainability efforts in another capacity but the company hadn't seen any potential there. And so the veteran was dismissed after 33 years of service, only a couple of years before his retirement date.

Mauser thinks this is a sad turn of events, but she understands how it came about; her predecessor's cynicism meant he put himself out of the running. More importantly still, she fundamentally disagrees with his claim that it's impossible to profit directly from attaching sustainability claims to products. To her this is a dated position. She has been working for Unilever for eight years at this point and has seen the gap between 'citizen' and the 'consumer' in the same person getting smaller and smaller. In her eyes, the two points of view are beginning to overlap, simply because the individual is coming to understand that the two are related.

Mauser ended up at Unilever mostly by chance. After completing her doctorate on the environmental reform of the Dutch dairy industry in 2001, she had fantasised about building a career in an NGO. Hans Eenhoorn had invited her to come for a meeting at Unilever. The sustainability economist had realised she might be able to have even more impact there. She worked with Jan Kees Vis on increasing the sustainability of agriculture supply chains. Gavin Neath's rationale became her own: the consumer-citizen's awareness that tea pickers are paid properly makes the tea taste better. Mauser views Paul Polman as an example, an authentic leader who has managed to meld these two conflicting perspectives of consumer and citizen into one logical whole.

Joost Oorthuizen also struggled to understand Dutilh, and thought that he frustrated many of the opportunities to work together. From 2008, Oorthuizen had been the first director of the Initiative for Sustainable Trade (IDH), a collaboration between the Dutch Ministry for Collaboration on Development, and a number of NGOs and workers' unions. By bringing different parties together, the IDH was supposed to speed up the implementation of 'responsible business practices'.

Big businesses find it difficult to work together directly: Unilever isn't about to ring Nestlé to see whether they can team up on sustainability. These companies are constantly in search of credibility. IDH wants to help them and has a pot of money from the government, around €30 million, to put to this purpose.

Oorthuizen, himself the holder of a PhD in water management and public–private investment from the University of Wageningen, is constantly on the lookout for what he calls 'business world pals'. It isn't exactly going well. He finds it tricky to tell whether a company actually wants to start operating sustainably or is really only interested in greenwashing for the sake of appearances. The IDH director is brimming with enthusiasm for the USLP and for Polman. He is fascinated by the company's pull in the palm oil and tea industries. Oorthuizen is impressed with the way Unilever is leading the way when it comes to making tea products more sustainable. The IDH helped the Rainforest Alliance, with whom Unilever is now working, to develop a new certification standard for sustainable tea.

This is sorely lacking. Oorthuizen has visited numerous tea plantations. Abuse, exploitation, child labour – there are few places in the world in which you can find so much misery in one place. The deprivation is shocking. The fact that Unilever has proven to be willing to pay the tea pickers and farmers above the going rate for their tea fills him with hope. Oorthuizen knows it is almost impossible to make up for these extra costs by imposing a higher margin. The enormous wealth of teas available is still growing, which means the price is only being driven down. He wants to help Unilever gain more influence over the sector. By getting tighter control over supply, the quality of the tea and production costs, the production process can be made more sustainable. And of course, in doing so Unilever gets a highly marketable story.

Oorthuizen is also pleased with Michiel Leijnse, the man responsible for the global development of the Lipton brand. He finds it fascinating that someone who speaks as an expert on sustainability is rooted entirely in the business world. He doesn't come across that very often. With IDH's help, Unilever can profit handsomely from the fact that it's the first multinational to take significant steps. Oorthuizen believes it is possible; that all the tea Unilever uses could be produced sustainably within a few years. With Unilever's effort, IDH should be able to bring more stakeholders to the table. Oorthuizen sees it as his task to push the envelope a little further in each of these meetings. He thinks Unilever actually needs to go a lot further and commit to paying a living wage across the whole supply chain.

The key players in Dutch business community suddenly want to know all about their previously little-known countryman. Who is this guy, how is he doing all this? How is he combining the role of CEO with the role of eco-warrior? Speaking invitations pour in.

'Call it naïve but I'm remaining positive', Polman tells interviewers from the employers' union VNO-NCW, who are doing a profile on him ahead of his appearance at the annual Bilderberg conference. The men are impressed by the magnificent view of the Thames he has from his office window. Polman says he finds the view humbling and that he'll never forget where he comes from saying in his native Twente dialect: 'Never forget yer house number, the address where you were born.' He quotes the American president Harry Truman: 'It's amazing what you can accomplish in this life if you do not care who gets the credit.'

When it comes to the importance of the Netherlands to Unilever he is very clear: 'a couple of percent of our turnover in the Netherlands. The future of the company lies in the Far East, that's where most of our new customers are. But the Netherlands still makes up a strong component of the company's culture. For my part, I follow Twente FC more closely than I do Dutch politics. Even if we've got an old Unilever-man, Mark Rutte, as prime minister now. I'm proud of that, we need to insure that this cabinet succeeds. There's no sense in only being critical.'

After Polman finishes summarising the aims of the USLP, the interviewer decides that he sounds like the chairman of an NGO. Polman replies, 'I am a member of several NGOs. But it is companies that create value. I regard being allowed to work for this company as a tremendous honour. My motivation isn't a higher final profit or higher share price, nobody remembers that. I want to leave behind a better world. Establish a new business model. Make a difference.' When asked whether he'll quit if he doesn't reach the sustainability targets, Polman is insulted: 'Failing to meet them is out of the question. It might be that we don't reach every single one of them. Scope for progression will then lie in the ones that we have managed to hit. Because what's the alternative? We're talking about something that's extremely difficult. If it was easy, someone else would already have done it. You need to take risks.'

At the World Economic Forum a week later, Polman reserves special ire for shareholders who continue to insist on focusing on the short term. 'The average holding of a Unilever share in 1960 was 12 years; 15 years ago it was about 5 years, now it is less than a year, sometimes half a year.' He calls this phenomenon interesting but to him it's incomprehensible: 'the same consumer who is demanding change is encouraging that behaviour because it is their money and their pension funds that are chasing that shorter-term return'.[1]

Earning money is going well. Unilever is still going full steam ahead. Over the course of 2010, revenue has risen by 4.1 per cent. However, Polman is especially proud of the underlying volume growth of 5.8 per cent, the highest in over thirty years. This is mostly coming from Asia; there, the turnover has grown by over €1.5 billion over three years, to €5 billion. The man responsible for this, Jan Zijderveld, feels like Unilever is flying. That's how well it's going. Polman asks him to turn his attention to the stagnating European sales market.

From now on, the financial ratios will be accompanied in the annual report by results achieved in the framework of the USLP; they'll share the same two pages and be typed in the same font. Emissions of CO_2 are down, less waste has been produced and they have used less water. Polman is still far from satisfied: '2011 will be a challenging year and we need to quicken the pace of transformation if we are to stay ahead. I have every confidence in the 167,000 wonderful men and women of Unilever. They achieved some of the best results in the company's recent history while staying true to the values that make Unilever such a special organisation. It is a tribute to them that 2010 ended with Unilever being named Most Admired Company of the Year in a poll of industry peers.' Even the usually reserved Treschow waxes lyrical: 'This was a significant achievement in a world struggling to come to terms with an economic crisis.'

The board chairman had been immediately enthusiastic about the USLP, of course consumers are going to become more and more attached to brands that suit them and on the costs side, too, the USLP will contribute to Unilever's overall results. Not all of the board members had been convinced straight away. Kees Storm, Jeroen van der Veer and especially Paul Walsh had asked pointed questions: How are you going to measure all this, how are you going to make it concrete? They warned Polman he was making the business vulnerable: investors will think poorly of you if you promise something and then don't deliver it. There was also a heated debate about tying managers' remuneration packages to the targets they were required to hit for the USLP. Treschow, like Polman, thinks it's logical for this to only make up a small part of the variable remuneration. If we all believe that profits and results are going to grow as a result of the USLP then it's self-evident that these bonuses should be tied to that rather than directly to the aims of the USLP in the first instance. You have to trust that you can make good money from doing the right thing. That is the essence of doing well by doing good.

Sandy Ogg is pleased with the way Polman is seizing this opportunity. He would never have got an USLP like this off the ground at Procter & Gamble; Americans don't understand this kind of thing at all. He sees the way this sustainability narrative is being lapped up across this organisation, the way Polman is almost intoxicating large groups of colleagues. This is exactly what Unilever needed after the somewhat uninspiring years under Cescau. The Frenchman was good in small groups but he lacked the charisma for a large audience. He had found it almost uncomfortable to place himself in the foreground. But he had been the logical insider for the unavoidable restructuring of the company. Polman has no need to do that anymore, he can motor along full speed ahead in the car Cescau refurbished for him.

Sometimes Ogg misses his old boss, however. In one-to-one situations he finds Polman charming but not at all as effective. If you go into his office with your own idea or agenda, you pretty much always leave disillusioned. Polman just talks, he doesn't listen. He doesn't ask a single question. Sandy Ogg weighs up his options. The American-born HR boss wants to go home; there's an opening for him at the private equity firm Blackstone so he leaves Unilever for good.

The interviewer from *Management Today* shares some of Ogg's misgivings. In spring 2011, he describes what happens when he tries to interview Polman: 'His speech is like a fast-flowing, undammed river, drowning interruptions or digressions until he has had his say. He's a forceful arguer and trying to get a word in the other direction feels like swimming upstream.'

In the interview, Polman lays out his vision with passionate: 'The focus on delivering short-term shareholder value has led to widespread addiction to quick artificial highs – rather like a junkie hooked on heroin or a financial trader on cocaine. The ultimate cost of short-termism was the financial crisis of 2008–9. Too many investors have become short-term gamblers. This meant that companies started behaving differently, with all the consequences that brought with it. To drag the world back to sanity, we need to know why we are here. The answer is: for consumers, not shareholders.'

Polman explains that the world needs a new way of thinking. That is something many people don't appreciate, even journalists are lacking. 'I hate to say it, but the FT has been the least supportive newspaper. Some of its reporting has been poor.'

'Too many people think in terms of trade-offs, that if you do something which is good for you, then it must be bad for someone else. That's not right and it comes from old thinking about the way the world works and what business is for: Milton Friedman's optimisation of short-term profits. We have to snap out of that old thinking and move to a new model. We need to start viewing things differently. Take Persil Small and Mighty, a concentrated detergent that uses less packaging and is cheaper and less polluting to transport. It washes better, at lower temperatures, using less energy, he says. Everyone benefits. There will always be cynics who ask: "If you miss one target, will you still be the CEO?" But these people are spectators. We say: "We can't do this on our own, so be part of it." In that spirit, I think we can do well and move the world to a better place.'

He reminds the interviewer that he is working on this 15 hours per day: 'I still wonder what my life would have been like as a doctor.' When the interviewer joshes that he certainly wouldn't have been making £2.8 million a year, Polman gives him a fierce look: 'You can't link money with passion and success. My family was always clear life was about more than money.' He goes on to say: 'I say to my kids – don't be driven slavishly by a job title, only to find out when you get there that your ladder is up against the wrong wall.'[2]

In the Dutch business magazine *Quote*, his proud brother René Polman is induced to give a lyrical portrait of the man of the hour: 'He's good with people. He gets in the mix everywhere. Wherever people are, whoever they are, they always ask me how Paul's getting on. From the custodian of a parking garage in Madrid up. He is dedicated to them. If one of the copier guy's relatives is sick, Paul sends them flowers. Often he emails me in English and adds at the end "I am at the airport in Hong Kong" or something, just to show how busy he is. And really he has no time to himself anymore. Even if he does call our mother once or twice a week.'

According to Polman's friend Joost Nijhuis, the basis of his success lies in Jacobus College, the school they attended together in Enschede, run by the Carmelite monks: 'There they taught us about intrinsic values and norms, a specific business culture of "ora et labora", prayer and work. More than once I've wondered, what does Paul have that I haven't? But when I visited his office in Geneva, I saw the answer hanging on the wall. A collage of private messages of thanks from teams and task forces he has worked with. These weren't superficial American thank you cards, but truly inspiring, warm messages of thanks. Then I thought: you're a man who gets involved everywhere. Not one of these self-styled silverbacks trying to dominate the business jungle, not a macho man in some testosterone-fuelled environment, like former ABN AMRO CEO Rijkman Groenink. No, Paul is the kind of CEO the world today needs.'

Childhood friend Marcel Zegger thinks that if Polman had become a priest he would have fought his way up to pope.

In May 2011, Dutch prime minister Mark Rutte, IMD professor Tom Malnight and Paul Polman stand beaming together on a stage set up at Unilever's headquarters in Rotterdam. They have agreed to take part in a public discussion to mark the publication of Kees van der Graaf's book, on the importance of purpose in the business world. Polman pays Van der Graaf, who retired shortly before Polman arrived at Unilever, a compliment: he had been a frontrunner in the company, clearly driven by a higher purpose.

During the panel discussion, the question arises of whether the still dominant 'old-boys' board member type is capable of understanding the meaning of purpose, of helping 'their' CEO to reach his calling. Isn't a different type of director required? The moderator asking the question quotes INSEAD management guru Manfred Kets de Vries, who claims that all leaders in the business world are insecure overachievers suffering from narcissistic personality disorder and that it's therefore sensible to appoint a psychiatrist to every board of directors going forward. The men on the panel laugh and wonder whether it absolutely has to be a psychiatrist, but agree that more diversity in that area would definitely help to speed up the implementation of USLP-type initiatives.

Up on the podium, Polman tries to persuade the other Unilever veteran, Rutte, of the need for the Dutch government to embrace the Unilever model. The prime minister is engaged, his love for his old employer is still strong. He responds jovially but is immediately on his guard too: he can't stand companies that try to be lobbyists. A prime minister must remain above the fray.

A month later, Polman invites Rutte's predecessor to breakfast. He had first met Jan Peter Balkenende two years previously at a dinner at Jeroen van der Veer's house. They had discussed the changing role of big business and agreed unanimously that the business world needed to take on a leading role in addressing big societal problems, in a time in which governments were generally withdrawing. With respect to this question, Balkenende had long been impressed by CEOs like Peter Bakker from logistics service provider TNT, and Feike Sijbesma from chemicals and nutrition company DSM. Theirs was the example to follow. This was why, in April, he had agreed to an invitation from Pieter Jongstra, the boss of Ernst & Young in the Netherlands, to start lobbying for a higher place for 'corporate social responsibility' on the political agenda.

Polman and Balkenende both find it remarkable that so many Dutch companies have been leading the pack in their sectors' various sustainability indexes. Dutch companies have their roots in the way of thinking traditional to the so-called Rhineland Model, taking all stakeholders into consideration, and still doing well in terms of global competition. Balkenende and Polman share the experience that getting Anglo-Saxon business contacts to join this conversation is seldom possible. If anyone raises the issue, these people loudly claim to care about these other stakeholders, but often when you ask follow-up questions and want to know what they are actually *doing*, they don't get much further than reeling off charity projects.

We're much better at that here. Balkenende and Polman agree that they will try to bring the CEOs of leading companies like DSM, Heineken, AkzoNobel, KLM and Shell to the table. They want to find out whether there is a way to unite these powerhouses and put the Netherlands more firmly on the map by doing so.

In 2011, Paul Polman's message shakes the world. After years of crisis, dominated by disappointment and distrust, people are hungry for a new sound. As Unilever's figurehead, Polman suddenly becomes the face of an enormous promise, the promise of a new, sustainable big business. His colleagues responsible for taking on new people are the first to notice this. Unilever's power to attract new talent is enormous, over the past year they've received more than a million open applications.

Even though by now Polman has made it sufficiently clear that coddling the shareholders is no longer the number one priority, and that they need to be patient, he still keeps a very close eye on stock market trends and Unilever's share price. After 30 years of working for publicly listed companies, he knows that a consistent drop in share price can quickly lead to him being sacked. He still needs the timely support of the shareholders, they give him his license to operate. The share price needs to keep going up consistently enough to keep them content.

He pulls it off. When he discusses the share price, Polman constantly refers back to the low point of a little over €14, a couple of months after his appointment. In two and a half years, Unilever's share price has risen over 65 per cent. The most important British and Dutch share indexes, the FTSE and the AEX, went up in the same period by 60 per cent. Yet the share price of his two previous employers, Procter & Gamble and Nestlé, rose much less quickly, by only 30 per cent during the same period.

This gives him confidence. Polman knows this valuation has nothing to do with his plans for sustainability, they're the one-to-one result of their improved margins and the now quickly growing turnover. The fact that financial analysts pay absolutely no attention to the USLP in their enthusiastic discussions of how things are going at Unilever is something Polman finds a crying shame. But mostly just stupid. They are still looking at the economy in the same old way. But that will inevitably change once it becomes clear that the cost of doing nothing now is going to be much higher once the current inequalities in the world lead to bigger problems. Which they will do soon. It's important to get a proper grip on these risks as soon as possible and turn them into tangible numbers. Then these number-crunchers will be able to include them in their analyses. But we're not there yet. In order to keep the results looking healthy, his next move is to keep streamlining operations.

The Unilever matrix is once again being revised. The 242 product–market combinations of Cescau's era are reduced to 32. The top 150 is reduced at a stroke to a top 40. From now on there are only four product categories – food, ice cream/tea, personal care and home care products – and eight geographical clusters. The managers of these eight markets will report to Harish Manwani. He becomes Unilever's first chief operating officer (COO), responsible for increasing sales and profits. Three out of the four men who thought they were the ideal successors to Cescau, Michael Polk, Vindi Banga and Jim Lawrence, have since left the company. Only the faithful Manwani has remained.

Naturally, he had been disappointed once it became clear that he would not become the first Indian CEO of Unilever. But he understands why Polman was chosen. His own appointment to COO also makes sense: Manwani has been with the company since 1976. He joined because it was the most successful company in India even back then, visible everywhere when it came to increasing prosperity and the welfare of millions of people.

Manwani has worked almost everywhere, knows everyone and knows every corner of the company. In reality it is now his task, and the task of the regional managers, to manage the balance of profit and loss over the short term. The heads of the four product categories have to work with R&D to come up with a deluge of new products and developments. In that sense, they are also responsible for the sales and profits of the future.

'Who would have thought that one of the world's most powerful chief executives would be advocating a transformation in society far more radical than any mainstream politician', writes a surprised *Guardian* interviewer in the introduction to yet another profile of Polman. Polman, who would be more likely to vote for the left-wing PvDA than the conservative VVD if he still lived in Holland, explains: 'Some people sometimes accuse me of being a socialist but I am a capitalist at heart. But what I want is a sustainable and equitable capitalism.' This, according to him, will only come about if the business world starts working more intensively with NGOs and governments. 'If we hit all our targets on this plan, but no-one else follows suit, we will have failed miserably. In the past we might not have talked to Greenpeace or WWF, but now we are on the phone with them every week.' He calls on governments to think about legislation that could encourage shareholders to keep hold of their shares for longer. 'There could be different share structures where dividends attract a higher tax rate depending on how long you hold shares.'[3]

Polman tells the interviewer how, at the request of UN secretary general Ban Ki-Moon, Unilever and the people from the UN Global Compact Group have come up with a resolution on improving collaboration between the United Nations and the world of big business.

In this resolution to improve collaboration, they claim that the first obstacle to overcome is the enduring mistrust between the UN and big business. Next will be the big differences in culture and approach. It's important that the business world embraces the United Nations universal values, as described in the Global Compact. More transparency is also needed in terms of their approach; concrete topics will need to be identified on which they can work together. A clear framework is needed that enables both parties to record the results of their collaboration unambiguously.[4]

Addressing an audience of civil servants, politicians and NGOs in Amsterdam, October 2011, Polman says that the fact that more than eight hundred million people are still going to bed hungry is a scandal. 'We will have to work together even more intensively in order to ensure food security around the world.' Standing in the meeting hall of the Westergasfabriek cultural centre in Amsterdam, an old gas works, he tells those gathered about the USLP and about the coalition between the world's biggest companies, which decided in the Consumer Goods Forum that they will put an end to illegal logging by 2020. By then they will no longer buy any soya, palm oil or paper derived from illegal sources.

'It's a mammoth undertaking but a desperately necessary one since 16% of global warming is a result of illegal logging. We are working actively and gladly with the WWF, Oxfam, Greenpeace and governments to realise this aim.' Polman calls for a shared Marshall Plan. 'Investment in the food market needs to increase by 50%, governments and business need to put those €80 billion on the table.' He sees a central role for the Netherlands in all this; its business community is showing leadership on the global stage when it comes to sustainability.

But the new Dutch government, 'headed up by committed leaders like Secretaries of State Ben Knapen and Henk Bleker, supported by the Bernard Wientjes, the head of the Dutch business and employer's organisation VNO-NCW', also needs to get its hands dirty, Polman claims. 'By showing willingness to take on a key role in the issue of food security, the Netherlands is making a wise decision. When it comes to IT, the whole world thinks of Silicon Valley but does the world know that the Netherlands is actually a sort of "Sustainability Valley"?'

Paul Polman can't participate in the panel discussion. He needs to attend the funeral of one of his predecessors and commemorate his life: 'Morris Tabaksblat, his enormous achievements will live on in our memory.'

Secretary of State Ben Knapen can't stay either, the Director-General of International Cooperation Rob Swartbol takes his chair. Both men are deeply impressed by the vision of the enthusiastic Unilever CEO.

CHAPTER 10

BUT WE CAN'T DO THIS ALONE

January 2012–March 2013

He says yes straight away. When Ben Knapen calls him in January 2012 to ask him whether he wants to take on the task of thinking about the challenges facing the world on behalf of the United Nations, Paul Polman doesn't hesitate for a second. Ban Ki-moon, the secretary general of the UN, charges a 'High-Level Panel of Eminent Persons' with formulating new, sustainable development targets. Knapen and Polman agree to meet so that the secretary of state for European Cooperation and Development Cooperation can explain why the government wants the CEO of Unilever of all people to represent the Netherlands in this important UN panel.

Sixty-one-year-old Knapen, of the centrist CDA party, had been a journalist and newspaper editor, then a director and later a journalist once more. As South-East Asia correspondent for his old newspaper *NRC Handelsblad* back in 2006, he realised that although there were still lots of poor people in the world, there weren't really any poor countries anymore. In his analysis, the direction of the economy in most countries is decided by a growing group of middle-earners. The main job of governments is to create the basic conditions that ensure that as many people as possible get a fair shake. They need to make sure that people are investing and consuming responsibly and sustainably, that there is a safe, credible legal system and that taxes are being paid. Citizens and businesses will then determine together whether their economy flourishes. Knapen concludes that in order for this to happen, countries need businesses that aren't just chasing a quick buck but will pour their profits into pursuing the greater good.

As a member of the Scientific Committee for Government Policy (WWR), he has therefore made a strong case for a paradigm shift when it comes to the use of development funding. In 2011, the WWR presented a recommendation to the government on the subject: *Less pretention, more ambition: development assistance that makes a difference.* On the basis of a literature review and 500 interviews, including with former Unilever directors Hans Eenhoorn and Jeroen Bordewijk, the WRR calls for the greater involvement of the business world and predicts that 'along these lines, the Netherlands can regain its voice internationally'.[1]

The Netherlands spends around €5 billion on development every year, around 0.7 per cent of its GDP, and is therefore the fifth largest donor in the world in terms of percentages and the sixth in absolute terms. It was the Dutch economist and Nobel Prize winner Jan Tinbergen who had calculated back in the 1960s that the gap between rich and poor in the world would close if all of the rich countries handed over 0.7 per cent of the GDP to the poorest countries. But the WWR determines that these billions barely have any effect in a world in which cross-border investments have increased by an average of 30 per cent a year between 1982 and 2008, to a total of around $1.7 trillion. The by now approximately eighty-two thousand multinational companies in operation worldwide are playing a central role in distributing this wealth.

The WWR report is well received by the members of the first cabinet formed by Mark Rutte, himself the head of the centre-right VVD party. The motto of the cabinet, sworn in in October 2010, is 'Freedom and Responsibility'. The VVD and the centrist CDA are the majority parties but the right-wing, populist PVV party promises to vote with them on specific issues. Ben Knapen, now a CDA secretary of state, is pleased with the way his remit has been included in the coalition agreement: 'Within the budget for development cooperation there will be a strong expansion of opportunities for big business. Developing the private sector will be a priority, as will contributing to reaching the Millennium Development Goals.'

A bigger role for the business world when it comes to combatting poverty, this will be the approach the new government backs. Knapen immediately sees an important function for partners like Oxfam Novib, Solidaridad and IDH: NGOs that keep creating space for combining efforts with big business. He calls on them to take on the role of moral accountants and tell companies how they measure up when it comes to their sustainability initiatives.

Many colleagues overseas struggle with the Dutch secretary of state's ideas. They see the logic but worry that their role as the custodians of development funds will become more or less superfluous if this distribution of wealth is left to local market forces going forward. Knapen had been pleased that an agreement had been reached during the big UN meeting in Busan, South Korea, that 'international cooperation can no longer be viewed as a relationship between rich and poor governments, but as a complex interaction in which many more parties, including the private sector, have a role to play. International development needs to open itself up to the role of the private sector.'

Back in the Netherlands, Knapen's main challenge is keeping their tacit partner the PVV (Party for Freedom) on side. Their leader Geert Wilders wants to put an end to the 0.7 per cent rule. He thinks it's a waste of money more than anything else. Knapen thinks that strictly speaking Wilders is right but he defends the rule because you can't simply cut aid off dead. The changing role of wealthy countries will take a while to come to fruition. Knapen also knows that this 0.7 per cent serves an important PR function. At the United Nations in New York there's no skipping over the Netherlands when it comes to important appointments.

The secretary of state therefore hadn't been surprised to find a letter on his desk from Ban Ki-moon, inviting him to nominate a member of the High-Level Panel charged with formulating replacements for the Millennium Development Goals that would expire in 2015. The panel will consist of 27 members and be headed up by the presidents of Indonesia and Liberia and the prime minister of Great Britain. It's clear they expect the Netherlands to nominate its own prominent politician too.

The secretary of state had asked the acting director-general of international cooperation, Rob Swartbol, to help him come up with a candidate. Off the cuff, Swartbol suggested Paul Polman. He knows the Unilever CEO has spoken to him a number of times at the United Nations in New York and saw him give a speech there. He noticed that Polman never explicitly positioned himself as a defender of his company's interests during these conversations. The opposite was true if anything, he seemed truly invested in combatting poverty and in climate issues.

Swartbol believes that since then, Polman has come to play a central role in breaking through the stereotypical glass ceiling between governments and NGOs on the one hand, and big business on the other. Sure, multinationals had until recently been viewed as the enemy, companies that plunder the world's resources for their own gain. But the civil servant doesn't doubt Polman's intentions, he thinks he is authentic and trustworthy. He furthermore notes that the CEO of Unilever is keen to learn about the world of development cooperation, listening hungrily for insights.

Knapen was immediately taken with the idea. Placing the boss of a multinational like Unilever in such an important forum for the first time in the history of the United Nations allows the Netherlands to underline very neatly the importance of the role of the private sector. The secretary of state had immediately agreed their plan with his British counterpart Andrew Mitchell.

After all, Unilever is a Dutch-British company and it would be a shame if the Brits, whose Prime Minister David Cameron will take up one of the three chair roles, didn't support the move. But Mitchell had been in agreement.

Knapen had also asked his own prime minister whether he thought it was a good idea. He knew that Rutte still maintained good relations with his first employer. Mark Rutte was immediately enthusiastic. He knew Polman well and believed that he would perform the task superbly. However, Rutte did warn his secretary of state that questions might arise surrounding the size of the Unilever CEO's salary. You don't exactly associate an income like that with development aid.

In their meeting to make the collaboration official, Polman and Knapen agree that the UN's Millennium Development Goals have been successful. Between 1990 and 2015, more than a billion people have been lifted out of extreme poverty. From now on, helping the remaining 800 million people who still go to bed hungry each day will primarily require cooperation between the public and private sectors. Knapen reiterates the Dutch cabinet's ambition to increase the role of big business in reaching this goal. He explains that Polman will receive automatic support from the Dutch delegation to the UN in New York, but that otherwise he has no burden of responsibility to the Dutch government. Following the Dutch nomination, he will be invited by Ban Ki-moon to participate as an individual and can proceed without interference or having to seek approval. The secretary of state has every confidence in Polman, not least because the CEO is about to be surrounded on all sides by 27 political heavyweights; they will check the star manager if he starts pursuing his or Unilever's interests too egregiously.

It's a mammoth task. An end to poverty, bigger economic growth, less social inequality and sustainable environmental development, these are the most important issues that have to be rendered in concrete aims for the coming 15 years. The panel must present its findings in June 2013. The members of the panel will meet five times in all, for a couple of days each time. The plan is for Polman to head up a series of consultations for the international business world, taking their temperature in terms of what they see as their role. The CEO of Unilever will soon be spending around twenty hours per week on this. Over the course of 2015, the 193 United Nations member states will have to approve these new targets.

An enthusiastic Polman explains to his board that this is a logical role for him. This way he can make sure that the field of play changes, that there is more room for Unilever's sustainable approach because sustainable thinking will be codified in various areas of law and governance. The USLP can only

succeed if other companies start following Unilever. For that they need governments and NGOs to act as a catalyst.

Polman asks Gavin Neath, who is poised to retire, to assist him full time
with this new task. All the members of the panel have a 'Sherpa' to fine tune
their work and make preparations for the summits. Neath can see immediately
that Polman is prepared to give this his all. Unilever's gospel needs spreading,
souls must be saved. And the whole world along with them if possible.

Neath is right. At the World Economic Forum in Davos, Polman is onstage
presenting the cooperation between eight big Dutch firms that he has organised
together with former prime minister Jan Peter Balkenende and Feike Sijbesma,
the CEO of DSM. The founder of the World Economic Forum, Klaus Schwab,
is in attendance. Under the banner of the Dutch Sustainable Growth Coalition
(DSGC), Heineken, Shell, KLM, Unilever, DSM, AkzoNobel, Philips and
FrieslandCampina are joining forces to explain to the world that traditional
growth strategies measured in economic and financial terms are too limited
a concept. Solving big social and environmental problems demands an integration of sustainable growth into strategy and operations across the whole
economic chain. In that way, profitability, social progress and environmental
sustainability are linked together. Polman takes the initiative. He made the
urgent case to his fellow CEOs for the importance of the right mindset. You
can only get this message across if you are an authentic leader and there is no
discrepancy between what you say and what you do. Polman had told them
enthusiastically about the Unilever Leadership Development Programme and
the search for one's 'true north'. And he suggested to his Dutch colleagues that
they place three words at the centre of their presentation of their plans. *Shape*:
the eight participants link financial profitability to integrated sustainable business models. *Share*: the DSGC members will endorse this way of thinking at
both the national and international levels. And *Stimulate*: they will stimulate
and influence government policy that makes this possible.

Polman is well aware that all these experiences outside Unilever mean that
he is now a lot further along in his thinking than most of his colleagues at
Unilever. After all, they're mostly preoccupied with selling Magnums and bottles of Dove. In spring 2012, he asks Gail Klintworth, Unilever's first chief
sustainability officer, to think about kick-starting change inside the company.
Polman and Klintworth estimate that only about 10 per cent of Unilever managers really understand what it means to integrate sustainability into daily
operations. Sixty per cent are reluctant, are uncertain or don't understand it
yet. Around 30 per cent of their colleagues are stuck in the old ways of thinking
and will never budge. Unilever needs to get rid of them.

As Klintworth sees it, the conversation inside Unilever can no longer be dominated by the old opposition between business and good causes. This opposition is paralysing. But she is also aware that her colleagues don't know any better and that 'culture eats strategy for breakfast'. Once something has rooted itself into the culture of a company, it is nigh on impossible to change it. The step from verbalising your personal calling to actually daring to change your approach to work isn't easy – it doesn't happen automatically. For that to happen, you need to have the courage to take risks. In order to make a start, you have to trust yourself to let go of old, familiar approaches.

In endless meetings with her fellow managers, Klintworth asks people to think in terms of their 'shields' and their 'swords'. 'Shields' refers to defraying risks, knowing that your costs are about to double and become more than you can deal with if you don't act now, for example as a result of strain on the environment. 'Swords' refers to recognising opportunities, developing new products for consumers who are themselves increasingly realising that something needs to change. Klintworth returns time and again to her central question: Is Unilever capable of delivering these people products that fit with their concerns and beliefs, products they don't have to pay more for and which they can use without having to think twice?

The director of sustainability is well aware that it will be impossible to unite the various silos within the huge, bureaucratic Unilever machine under a single, shared goal. It's the making of new connections that presents opportunities. Colleagues in R&D, marketers and buyers will have to have a different conversation with each other. Sadly, everyone has the tendency to keep anything they achieve to themselves, to funnel savings they've managed to make, for example as a result of a new approach, directly into their own profit and loss calculation. That's good for their personal bonus and for their career. If you put that money into renewing products or processes, in collaboration with other company departments, then it's uncertain to what extent any potential result will be attributed to you.

In order to make some headway in this regard, Klintworth tries to celebrate those 10 per cent that are true believers, the 'early adopters', putting their successes front and centre in order to inspire the rest of the organisation. It's not all that important to her whether these people are doing these things because they want to save the world or because they think it will make them money. So long as they do it, and are clear that it's the only way forward. For example: category managers now need to do what Polman is doing with the Unilever brand with their own brands.

It helps Klintworth that people are asking her colleagues about Polman's vision increasingly often. Privately, at things like birthday parties, this is a good thing, it gives them a sense of pride. It's even better when educational institutions and governments ask Unilever employees to come and talk about the USLP. It helps spread the message further and massages people's egos. Sometimes Klintworth arranges herself for a conservative colleague to receive an invitation from a university to talk about sustainability as a business model. She very much enjoys what happens next. In order to keep up with a panel of big names, they have to immerse themselves in the material and a couple of lights finally go on. Their ego does the rest.

It frustrates her enormously that as a member of the London staff she is not really listened to, especially by colleagues 'in the field'. Even though she was the head of Unilever South Africa, she is told that she is out of touch with the business side of things. Formally, she also reports directly to Keith Weed. As a marketer, he can spin a great yarn but in her eyes he lacks any idea of what needs to happen internally. She isn't the only one who thinks so. Her colleague Miguel Veiga-Pestana also thinks that Weed is a true old-school marketer, without the first inkling of what sustainability means. He has to explain to Weed what human rights are and why it's important for a company like Unilever to care about them.

Klintworth notices that it's mostly men complaining. Sometimes they tell her candidly that when they talk about the subject, their friends start questioning their manhood. They simply don't think this sustainability stuff is manly enough. What's more, their performance each month is measured on their concrete results: market share, margin, and so on. That's the main thing Polman asks about when he comes to visit too. So the USLP is being passed over in the larger Unilever vision, nobody is translating the plan into concrete goals for their brands and markets. Worse still, when the tangible results fall short, Polman can get really angry and disappointed.

In order to inspire the staff in their personal transformations, Polman has made it a habit to send the Unilever top brass some appropriate reading ahead of each of their conferences. This spring, the top 40 receive the book *Capitalism at Risk: Rethinking the Role of Business*. In it, three Harvard professors explain that the role of big business has to change following the financial crisis, and that it needs to concern itself much more explicitly with the society in which it operates.[2] Inside the front cover, Polman writes a personal thank you note: 'Your leadership in adapting Unilever towards sustainable growth is highly valued. We have a fantastic chance to show that living according to the USLP leads to a fantastic business, warmest wishes, Paul.'

Luckily the numbers stay healthy and Unilever keeps growing. Reflecting on 2011 in the annual report, Polman says: 'Underlying sales growth of 6.5% was ahead of our markets.' After being at the helm for three years, Unilever's turnover has increased by almost €7 billion, to €46.5 billion. It's moving from a company fit to compete to one that is fit to win. This growth is still coming from growing prosperity in Asia, the hundreds of millions of new consumers buying shampoo, deodorants, ice cream, etc.

As far as Polman is concerned, it's all systems go; now Unilever needs to make headway. He proudly points out that 86 per cent of Unilever employees are 'very satisfied' with their work and their employer. The number of women in senior management positions has increased by 5 per cent over five years to 28 per cent. He begins the first USLP report, on the 2011 financial year, in a belligerent tone. 'If we realise our aims but no one follows us, then we've failed. That's why we're working with the Consumer Goods Forum, the World Economic Forum, The World Business Council for Sustainable Development, NGOs and governments to drive coordinated, cross-sectoral change.'

In *The Guardian*, Polman explains the first USLP results. In the first 12 months, the volume of sustainably purchased agricultural products has doubled to 24 per cent. He explains that the plan has already had a profound impact on how staff at Unilever work: 'When we look at our supply chain, we think about smallholder farmers, we think about women and employment, we think about land rights, we think about biofuels and because we think about this holistically, our plants are getting better, our sourcing is getting better.' No, he doesn't think that Unilever is being too ambitious: 'The word over-ambitious does not exist when you look at the challenges we have to solve. We have been extremely ambitious and this has moved us out of our comfort zone.'

He admits that it won't be easy for 'old-school CEOs' to start operating in a world that asks for cooperation and vulnerability. 'It is not always obvious how to do that and for some people it is easier than others. It requires a level of transparency and some are more comfortable than others doing that.' He then begins what the journalist calls a 'damning' critique of companies that claim that they are fulfilling their duty to society by concentrating on serving their shareholders: 'too narrow a model of Milton Friedman's old thinking. The world has moved on and these people need to broaden their education with the reality of today's world.'[3]

They aren't doing this enough, according to Polman. To his great annoyance, the analysts in attendance at his presentation of the Unilever financial report once more fail to ask him a single question about the USLP. He explains again that a fundamental change is taking place as a result of the financial crisis. We are going from a society based on rules to a society based on principles. He refers to the small but thankfully growing group of companies that subscribes to this idea and names Patagonia, Heineken and Nike. Polman says that he is most concerned by the lack of cooperation with governments. They are constantly paralysed by elections, which makes it really hard to make agreements with them. No, Polman isn't trying to criticise the British government directly: 'There is not a week goes by when I am not with policy makers. This position gives me access to these people and then it's a responsibility to leverage that.'

Polman's philosophy finds its earliest supporters in the academic community. Stronger still: Unilever seems like the logical company to realise a successful sustainability strategy. Robert Eccles, professor of management practice at Harvard, observes that companies that have been trying to take on social responsibility on a voluntary basis since 1993 are making better results, both in terms of their profitability and the trajectory of their share price. The results are best in sectors where the clients are individual consumers and companies compete on the basis of brands and reputation. If it's a business sector in which the products produced are dependent on large quantities of natural resources, then this is even more the case. The reason: 'High Sustainability firms generate significantly higher stock returns, suggesting that developing a corporate culture of sustainability may be a source of competitive advantage for a company in the long-run. A more engaged workforce, a more secure license to operate, a more loyal and satisfied customer base, better relationships with stakeholders, greater transparency, a more collaborative community, and a better ability to innovate may all be contributing factors to this potentially persistent superior performance in the long-term.'

The researchers have divided 180 companies into two groups of 90 'highly sustainability' and 'low sustainability'. They notice that the management of the first group are rewarded much more explicitly for hitting sustainability targets. They determine that sustainable companies pour a great deal of time and energy in maintaining relationships with as many stakeholders as possible. Such relations are 'based on mutual respect, trust, and cooperation that require significant time to develop'. In other words: 'effective stakeholder engagement necessitates the adoption of a longer-term time horizon'.[4]

The research is discussed enthusiastically in Rio de Janeiro in the summer of 2012. Twenty years after heads of government gathered there and made a joint declaration stating that humanity was at an 'all-important crossroads', the present-day main players in the issue of 'economy and environment' are coming together once again for Rio+20. The delegates determine in endless sessions that the world is careening in the wrong direction at breakneck speed. For 10 days, governments, companies and NGOs try to reach agreements. But the representatives of the 192 countries don't get much further than a non-binding declaration in which all parties promise to strive for a sustainable world.

Paul Polman receives a storm of applause when he says that the shocking lack of ambition on the part of the politicians inspires him to work twice as hard to get results in collaboration with NGOs and other leaders in the business world. 'The declaration lacks specificity, clear dates, funding and accountability.' He quickly corrects himself: 'Criticising never leads to anything. The final text has a lot of good elements and there is a declaration for the oceans and a starting process for the Sustainable Development Goals. We'll have to be the ones to provide them.'

Under the headline 'Captain Planet', Polman tells the *Harvard Business Review* that he is satisfied: 'We have more than 2 billion consumers using our brands every day. And increasingly they are connected, which gives us opportunities to involve them and communicate with them. Part of our model is to turn our company over to them to some extent. In the past, consumers might have been tempted to say, "I have my little sustainable Lipton tea bag, but what difference does it make? Especially when my neighbour doesn't and drives a big SUV to boot." But now we're able to show consumers that it does make a difference. Two billion of you are drinking tea. So ask for sustainably sourced tea, because you can become a force for good. If 2 billion want something, companies will change.'

He also emphasises the need for this: 'Some estimate that the total profits of the consumer goods industry could be wiped out in 30 years if no action is taken.' Concerning his own role, he says: 'The biggest challenge is to keep your humility. The moment a CEO starts to justify how good he is and talk about all the things he's achieved, it's probably time to go.' He isn't thinking about that yet: 'A lot of the challenges we face require forming coalitions with NGOs, governments, and industry partners. When we went public with Unilever's sustainable living plan and audacious targets, people worried that we would attract criticism. Actually the opposite has happened, because we went out there with a human face and made it clear that we don't have all the answers. We made it clear that if others felt these things were important, they could help us and join us and be part of the solution. Unfortunately, politicians have become too short term in their thinking. Most lack any courage and just want to get re-elected. In the U.S., in particular, politicians seem to have a limited understanding of, or interest in, how the world functions.'[5]

And that's turning out to be a handicap, American big business dominates the world in which multinationals operate. They regard governments as the enemy and a competitor is a competitor at the end of the day. *When Core Values are Strategic* confirms the same thing. In this book, 36 top managers, almost all of them Americans, explain why they found the recipe for their success at Procter & Gamble. The P&G alumni network that commissioned this book promises that any resulting profits will be donated to good causes. The by now quite successful Paul Polman is not even named in it. P&G obviously wants to stop people from getting the impression that there is a relationship between Polman and P&G and therefore between P&G and its competitor Unilever.[6]

The timing of the book is far from ideal. In the same month, Bob McDonald, appointed as CEO by A. G. Lafley in a meteoric rise in 2009, announces 5,700 redundancies and cost-saving measures of $10 billion. The man Polman refused to work for is making deep cuts to the company. Ten per cent of all jobs not involved directly in the production of shampoos, nappies or razor blades are to be scrapped.

Concerned shareholders have been asking for such measures for months at this point: costs need to be reduced urgently in order to increase profitability. A chorus of analysts determine that Procter & Gamble is overly dependent on the mature American and European markets, only 35 per cent of their revenues come from emerging markets.

For years, P&G outdid its competitor Unilever in the then growing European and American markets. Now the roles are reversed and Unilever is growing much more quickly in the emerging markets, at this point 56 per cent of turnover comes from them. In these markets Unilever almost caught up with the overall much larger Procter & Gamble, whose revenues exceed €86 billion. To Polman this is proof that his former employer, from whom he parted on such painful terms, is on the wrong track. That buoys him up.

How do we go from a world dominated by 'markets and competition' to a world dominated by 'markets and morals'? Polman gives a couple of speeches almost every week and dozens of interviews per year in order to spread this message. His communications advisors don't always get to direct these efforts, sometimes they aren't even in the room while he's being interviewed. They are frequently caught off guard by the results of these often antagonistic encounters. Polman regards most journalists as sceptical, conservative forces. He also believes them to be superficial and often poorly prepared. The media seem to be in constant search for things that aren't going well, they have no real interest in writing about positive developments. He doesn't understand that, how can anyone be against his ambitions? Surely, everyone has something to gain from them?

In an interview with Gerard Reijn, the editor of the Dutch broadsheet *De Volkskrant*, he does little to disguise his irritation with his interviewer's scepticism: 'Why does sustainability always have to be talked about as something negative? It's clear to everyone by now that philanthropy isn't fixing anything. By teaching children to wash their hands, we prevent two million children from dying. Then we sell more soap and make more profit. What's wrong with that model? Obviously people are programmed to think in oppositions. You against me. Winners against losers. Lost term against short term.' He switches to English, 'If you get paid a lot, you must be screwing someone. Get out of this mind-set!' And back again, 'If you try to keep doing everything the same way, nothing ever changes. If you keeping living in your own little world, nothing gets solved. Apparently people find this more difficult to understand in the Netherlands than in other countries.'[7]

When asked why Unilever only banned battery farmed chickens after the Dutch animal rights' organisation Wakker Dier started a campaign, Polman says: 'You obviously view the world from a Dutch perspective. But what you say isn't true. We have always taken the initiative. Years ago, we were the first to start using free-range eggs in our products: where was this Wakker Dier then? And nowadays the whole EU uses nothing but free-range hens for eggs. By the end of this year, we'll already be using 60% free-range pigs for our Unox-brand smoked sausages. Ben & Jerry's only contains fair trade ingredients. If you looked at how the cows we use for our products lived. [...] Man, you'd want to be a cow yourself.'

The journalist, who thinks that Polman is starting to remind him even more of Marlon Brando in *The Godfather* thanks to his slightly hoarse voice, wants to know how sustainable it is for Polman to have earned €5.8 million in the previous year. 'That's another typically Dutch question. We are trying to increase the incomes of half a million small-scale farmers. In India we're working with 400,000 small distributors, the "Strong Mothers" (Shakti), so that they don't go hungry anymore. No other company is doing that. Everyone thinks it's just fine for a footballer who scores a goal to earn €10 million. The salaries of the Unilever directors are low compared to other companies. Look at the top-100 companies and you'll see as much. And we haven't raised our salaries for three years. You don't get good directors by paying them the same as a tea-picker.'

Raising as many of the often destitute tea pickers as possible out of poverty is supposed to be one of the success stories of the USLP. Unilever promised back in 2007 that all their tea would be produced sustainably by 2015 and certified by the Rainforest Alliance. Lipton, the biggest brand, should lead the charge. And on their own tea estates at Kericho in particular, there can be no doubt about the sustainability of working practices. This is where they need to set a good example and they have invested heavily there for this reason. From free healthcare and schools for the children of employees to a specially trained 'wellness worker' who, supported by four assistants, should function as a first point of contact for any disagreements. The results of all this have been an increase in yield of 4 tonnes per hectare, almost twice as much as the tea plantations in India produce.

The Foundation for Research into Multinational Enterprises (SOMO), a foundation mainly funded by governments, has heard Secretary of State Knapen's call to arms. They are prepared to evaluate the efforts of big business when it comes to sustainability. On the basis of interviews with hundreds of 'tea workers' on eight certified plantations, including Kericho, the NGO determines in October 2012 that working conditions are still problematic.

'It is not the intention of this study to hinder the increased adoption of sustainability standards by finding and exposing shortcomings. Indeed, and as previously noted, at first sight this trend appears to be a promising and laudable development. Yet this study finds that critical and thorny issues such as freedom of association and the right to collective bargaining, discrimination, corruption and sexual harassment are not being addressed properly, if at all. The raison d'être of standards such as the Rainforest Alliance standard system is largely to provide consumers with confidence that products have been produced ethically and with respect for the environment. Based on this study's findings we cannot but conclude that RA does not seem capable of delivering any real guarantees on decent working conditions.'[8]

Unilever responds aggressively in a press release: 'If SOMO intends to improve the living and working conditions in the tea industry, we believe publishing this report will have a counter-productive effect. The tea plantation at Kericho is almost 50 miles long, 16,000 people work there: we would never pretend that nothing ever goes wrong there. We take any allegation of this nature very seriously and have met with SOMO twice to ask them for evidence to back up their claims in their report so we can take immediate action, but regrettably they decline to do so. As part of our Rainforest Alliance certification, we have to meet almost 100 environmental, social and economic standards on an ongoing basis. We believe that the living and working conditions at Kericho are among the best you will find anywhere in the East African tea industry. Unilever does not own or operate the Indian tea plantations mentioned in SOMO's report. We require that all our suppliers comply with Unilever's Supplier Code and have a track record of taking serious action against those which don't. If SOMO's accusations are found to be true, we will act to correct them.'

'Hallmark for "unethical" tea', reports *NRC Handelsblad*. 'Abuses on Unilever's tea plantations despite certification' screams *De Volkskrant*. Polman is frustrated to realise that Unilever is going to need to be more proactive when it comes to this battle in and with the media in years to come. A publicly listed multinational that makes billions and pays its leadership millions is not going to win the trust of NGOs or the media quickly, let alone be perceived by them as a force for good. That trust will have to be gained step by step. This is also the price you pay for transparency. Being open about your affairs is always painful in the short term. This won't be the last bit of negative press. Far from it.

'He is the chief executive of a multinational corporation, but Paul Polman sometimes sounds more like a spokesman for Occupy Wall Street. The boss of Unilever agonises about unemployment, global warming and baby-boomer greed. He puts some of the blame for these ills on the most influential management theory of the past three decades: the idea that companies should aim above all else to maximise returns to shareholders.'

The influential British weekly *The Economist* admits in November 2012 that the fact that 80 per cent of managers intend to save on R&D and advertising in order to be able to reach their promised short-term targets is worrying. But the magazine of conservative opinion brands the solution Polman suggests ridiculous: 'Many critics of the shareholder model embrace a "stakeholder" model instead, but this is too vague to be much of a guide. Who are a company's stakeholders, and how should their competing interests be weighed against each other? No one knows. The great virtue of a share price is that it provides a clear external measure by which managers can be judged. Rather than junking shareholder value, companies should tweak it. Offer shareholders bonuses for holding shares longer than a certain period of time. Giving managers ordinary shares (rather than options) which they cannot sell for several years aligns their interests even more closely with those of ordinary shareholders. As Bill Clinton once said of affirmative action, the best way to deal with the shortcomings of shareholder value is to "Mend it; don't end it."'[9]

Unilever's shareholders aren't too concerned. The share price has all but doubled since Polman's arrival, to €29 per share. Polman is especially proud of having managed to halve the number of shares in the hands of hedge funds to 5 per cent. Apparently they no longer see any appeal in short-term speculations.

Year 2012's sparkling results make much more of an impression on the market than SOMO's concerns about working conditions in Africa. Unilever reports proudly in a press release that 'turnover increased by 10.5%, taking Unilever through the €50 billion barrier, a significant milestone to becoming an €80 billion company. We have grown by nearly 30% in just four years. Growth was broad based – across all our markets and categories – and high quality, with a good balance of price and volume. Emerging markets continued to be the prime engine, growing for the second consecutive year by more than 11% and now accounting for 55% of total business. Growth was ahead of our markets, with approximately 60% of the business gaining share. Personal Care and Home Care showed double digit growth, in line with our strategic priorities.' Over the course of the same four years, the operational margin grew by 1–13.6 per cent. In order to hold onto this success, Unilever's top priority according to Polman is to gain the trust of citizens, who need to understand the company cares about their world more than anything else.

'We want to help create a world where everyone has enough to eat. Right now, nearly one in eight people on Earth go to bed hungry. Sadly, the majority of these people are farmers or farm workers supplying the very food system that is failing them. Yet there is enough food for everyone. That's an outrage.' The message sounds like one of Paul Polman's but it's coming from Oxfam Novib. The Dutch-British NGO shares his belief that multinationals are going to have to play a decisive role in ending food poverty and make more of an effort than they are currently. They need to start taking responsibility. Oxfam Novib has spent two years setting out how the biggest 10 food companies behave, how they treat these poor farmers, how they treat women, how they treat the environment. How transparent they are. The project is called 'Behind the Brands'. What is going on behind the brands we know so well?

Oxfam Novib maintains a 'critical friendship' with Unilever. The NGO is constantly on its guard, the Dutch arm Novib even more so than the British Oxfam. The workers at Novib meet with even greater scepticism from colleagues at other NGOs, and particularly from their Dutch trade union FNV, when it comes to Unilever's efforts to be a force for good. They certainly don't want to be regarded as bosom buddies with Unilever, like the World Wildlife Fund.

Recently, there have been various discussions with Unilever, which Oxfam still regards as underperforming when it comes to the treatment of women, the use of land and even the issue of transparency. When it comes to its treatment of farmers and use of water, however, the company is more than satisfactory.

All in all, Unilever comes second in the list of 10 with a score of 34 points out of a possible 70. Nestlé is in first place, much to Paul Polman's chagrin.

Rachel Wilshaw, the manager for ethical trade at Oxfam, thinks there is a big gap in the USLP. When it comes to people, Unilever is mostly talking about its own people and hardly at all about the millions of people working in Unilever's supply chain. Nowhere does the plan address the question of whether all these people earn enough to make a living. Miguel Veiga-Pestana agrees with her. Unilever needs to take a broader approach and start looking at things more holistically. He thinks that the USLP is focused too narrowly on climate issues. That isn't enough, it needs to pay more attention to eliminating poverty. As long as there's poverty, the world cannot be made sustainable.

Wilshaw would like to keep working on this with Unilever, she's been collaborating with them for 10 years at this point. The 2005 co-written report on Unilever's impact on poverty in Indonesia was the first time a multinational had dared to open itself to criticism. It had determined that there were 300,000 independent food producers contributing to Unilever's supply chain in that country alone. Polman wants to do more with Oxfam Novib too. So, in 2011, they signed a 'memorandum of understanding' in which they agreed to map the gap between what Unilever wants to achieve in terms of combatting poverty and what is actually being achieved on the basis of one of their markets.

Polman sees this as a logical step. 'The adoption of the UN Framework for Business and Human Rights has led us to rethink the integration of our human and labour rights strategies.'[10]

Working with Gavin Neath and Miguel Veiga-Pestana, Wilshaw looked at Brazil and India. They eventually choose Vietnam. A local think tank had already done some research into Unilever's engagement with socio-economic developments on the ground. The company's turnover there equates to 1 per cent of the country's GDP. The conclusion was clear: Unilever is crucial to the prosperity of communist Vietnam. National manager Marijn van Tiggelen has already followed William Lever's example by taking the initiative to help the country get old-age pension legislation up and running.

In order to avoid a repeat of the issues surrounding the Indonesia research, Oxfam has designed the study and build in a procedure in case disagreements arise over the text. The agreement is that Oxfam will be trusted to write an honest report, which Unilever can critique, and that Oxfam will listen to this critique properly. If there is still conflict, they've agreed that Oxfam will publish the report accompanied by a statement from Unilever.

Wilshaw thinks that when the report is finished Oxfam will need to be very firm. This is the moment to force change. She notices that the people she meets from Unilever seem pretty nervous. And rightly so. The conclusions Oxfam draws don't pull any punches: 'Unilever has made a commitment to social responsibility by adopting the United Nations Guiding Principles of Business and Human Rights. It also has a Code of Business Principles; a Respect, Dignity and Fair Treatment Policy; and a Supplier Code, all publicly stated. Despite this, human and labour rights of workers are conspicuous by their absence from the Unilever Sustainable Living Plan. Unilever management in Vietnam were found to lack the capacity and knowledge to ensure the company's operations comply with international standards, nor they don't have the authority to support suppliers to do so.' Wilshaw hopes that the report will be a clear wake-up call for the multinational. She wants Unilever to acknowledge that there's much to be done.

Unilever and Novib are both pleasantly surprised with the measured reactions from the media. To Wilshaw, this is proof that transparency works. In many write-ups, Unilever is even praised: if this company is being so open about such matters, how bad must things be at their competitors who are still so secretive about them? Paul Polman tells Oxfam that Unilever will do a review of all 180 countries in which it is active, under the banner of 'sustainable living'.

'I have good news, after 144 years Heinz is going back to where it began. It's being put back in private hands.' William Johnson calls the members of his management team with this message in February 2013. The ketchup manufacturer has been bought by the Brazilians from 3G Capital and Warren Buffett. They have put down $23 billion for the company. Buffett and Jorge Lemann, the head of 3G, have been friends for years. The richest man in Brazil had persuaded Buffett they could team up and take over Heinz, and that they could make a lot of money from doing so.

In December, Jorge Lemann had invited Johnson to a lunch. Johnson had assumed Lemann wanted to strengthen ties with Burger King, another of 3G's holdings. Heinz is an important supplier. A month later, Lemann puts his cards on the table. He wants to take over the whole company. Johnson was then invited by Warren Buffett to come and eat a hamburger with him and the prospective new chairman of Heinz, 3G manager Alexandre Behring, in the Hilton Hotel in Omaha. 3G Capital and Warren Buffett will each put in $4 billion cash, Buffett will invest a further $8 billion in preferential shares, for which he will receive a 9 per cent dividend per year. Sixty-four-year-old Johnson, who has been CEO and president of Heinz for 14 years, will receive $212 million to make his early retirement a bit more bearable.[11]

Analysts are flummoxed. They had understood 3G's takeovers of Anheuser-Busch and Burger King. By making deep cuts to what 3G called 'non-strategic costs', they had freed up capital to invest in marketing and acquisitions. At the brewery firm AB InBev, the margin had risen from 23 per cent to 37 per cent within a couple of years. This was largely achieved by demanding a price reduction of 20 per cent from their suppliers.

The concept of 'non-strategic costs' comes up frequently in 3G's philosophy. Jorge Lemann learned it from Bob Fifer, the CEO of the consultancy firm Kaiser Associates. In his book *Double Your Profits: In Six Months or Less*, Fifer explains the difference between strategic costs, which contribute directly to turnover and the improvement of profit margins, and non-strategic costs. 'These latter costs must be rigorously cut, down to the bone, every single year. These non-strategic costs include lots of managers, a large number of staff, buildings, consultants, lawyers, computers, office equipment, et cetera, et cetera. Because we're here to make money, as much money as possible. Profit is the most accurate, comprehensive measure that demonstrates we are truly the best.'[12]

But will this approach work here, analysts wonder. Heinz has been busy cutting costs for the last seven years, and has grown for 30 quarters in a row, allowing the share price to rise 27 per cent in just two years. What's the plan here? If 3G Capital wants to cut even deeper, they run the risk that Heinz won't set aside enough money to invest in renewals. Or will this be the beginning of a completely new, much bigger adventure?

Roel van Neerbos, Europe boss and the man responsible for Heinz ketchup worldwide, gets a call that evening from Paul Polman. His old comrade in arms from Procter & Gamble warns him: look out, you've joined a nest of dangerous bloodsuckers. The contrast could hardly be any greater. Polman tells Van Neerbos that he's just that evening been invited to visit the president of the United States. Barack Obama wants to hear from a selection of captains of industry on the topic of sustainability.

The top managers at Heinz all receive an invitation to give a presentation to the new CEO of Heinz, Bernardo Hees. They are required to lead a discussion of their results over the previous three years. They have to bring along two sides of A4 on which they answer two questions: Who are you and what do you stand for? And: what would you do with this company if you were us? In June they will hear whether they will be allowed to stay.

Van Neerbos has prepared himself well for this performance. Jorge Lemann is sitting beside Bernardo Hees, ready to listen to his vision. In a tub-thumping speech, Van Neerbos proposes that in the case of the Heinz brand, they go back to the roots of the company, to Henry John Heinz, who put the customer first as the most important ambassador of his product. Van Neerbos knows that 3G will come down hard on costs and says he will look at these more closely in future but parting with Heinz's two corporate jets would be a first step.

Lemann suddenly feels like he's being called upon to explain why he came to the meeting on just such a plane. He informs Van Neerbos that the jet doesn't belong to 3G but to him personally. He's so rich that he can buy one of these himself, so he doesn't burden any other shareholders with the costs. Lemann wants to make it clear to Van Neerbos that as an owner of a company you can only get that rich personally if you consistently cut all extraneous costs in your business.

The Americans get the blame. In an interview with the Canadian newspaper *The Globe and Mail*, Polman explains what he means by this: 'In the 1980s, Milton Friedman came out with theory that said the purpose of business is business and created a very narrow definition of shareholder value creation. And people like Chrysler's Lee Iacocca, Coca-Cola's Roberto Goizueta and General Electric's Jack Welch were exemplifying that idea. We now need to go back to what capitalism is supposed to be. If you go back to Adam Smith, his thoughts were that capitalism was intended for the greater good. When our generation grew up after the Second World War, our parents wanted the same kind of thing; they wanted us to go to university and have a better life. Certainly, capitalism has done positive things. But in 2008, we found the way we were doing it – high levels of public and private debt and over-consumerism – is not sustainable. What will happen with the 50 to 60% of youth unemployed in Spain or Greece – or with your children or my children who don't get a job? Capitalism is in crisis and increasingly social cohesion will be the biggest challenge. Unfortunately, the Occupy Wall Street movement represented frustration without solution.'

The journalist wonders how Polman can flood the world with adverts, to the tune of €8 billion per year, and at the same time talk about responsible consumption, even in emerging markets. Polman is annoyed: 'I travel the whole world, and I see over and over that when brands can compete freely, choice is created and consumers are better off. [...] I often hear that if we are consuming so much, why are we selling cars to poor people in Africa, and why should the Chinese drive? That is about the most arrogant argument I've heard. Consumers will self-select companies that provide responsible products and operate responsibly. Consumers want to know how you treat people in the whole value chain, or if the products are sustainably sourced. With the help of technology, consumers can see these things right away, and bad behaviour gets punished more quickly. Certainly, it is Economics 101 at the entry point. If Lipton tea doesn't taste good or is too expensive, you are not going to buy it. But after that, other factors start kicking in – such as the fact we have carbon-neutral tea plantations, and we treat people fairly. We have, for example, 75,000 small-hold tea farmers who work for us. Finally their children can go to school, rather than work in the tea business, and we give the farmers soil-management training. Their yield is 20–40% higher, and we get a sustainable supply of tea.'[13]

Paul Polman is working hard on his homework for the United Nations' High-Level Panel. Princess Maxima, Prime Minister Rutte and around twenty-five heads of big companies, the VNO-NCW trade union and various NGOs gathered at his request in early March 2013 at the Foreign Ministry in The Hague for a round table conference. The CEO of Unilever wants to hear from everyone in the room what they think big business can do to solve the issue of poverty. In various such sessions, scattered all over the world, he will ask around two hundred and fifty companies, responsible for more than $1 trillion in revenue, the same two questions: What objectives would you like to see among the UN's New SDGs, and how should the business world be approached to contribute? Gavin Neath and Miguel Veiga-Pestana hope that this will mean that many other large companies are inspired by the thinking behind the SDGs and their inescapable leading role in implementing them.

One of the delegates in The Hague is Adrian de Groot Ruiz. At 30, the director of the social enterprise True Price is probably the youngest participant. He tells those assembled that the new SDGs can only be realised if companies start looking at the true costs at the level of individual products and start paying that cost in future. From environmental impact to increasing the gap between rich and poor, what are the true costs of their product?

His message mostly leads to some raised eyebrows. De Groot Ruiz listens as the crème de la crème of Dutch business do little more than reel off a list of the good things they're already doing. It's clear they still don't understand what's needed. He empathises with them, this is enormously complicated. Milton Friedman and the Chicago school were warning people as much 45 years ago: in order to bring in factors other than profit, you need completely different information and systems. If you don't make your efforts comparable and measurable, you run the risk of CEOs prioritising their own hobby horses. Doing this properly requires a completely different business model. Actually, it requires a new language, and the people here have yet to learn it. De Groot Ruiz is impressed with the initiative from Feike Sijbesma, the CEO of DSM, to build a team of 40 participants and set up a Dutch SDG charter, combining efforts to see what they can learn from one another to actually meet these targets by 2030.

'How wonderful to be allowed here in this church. As some of you probably know, I once had ambitions of entering the priesthood. But don't worry, I won't be making my first sermon here. I've become a businessman. Even if I did read a piece in the tabloid *Trouw* a few weeks ago calling sustainability "a new religion".'

Paul Polman has been invited by Ernst & Young and chairman of the DSGC, Jan Peter Balkenende, to give the annual Hofstad Lecture in The Hague's Grote Kerk. The audience notices immediately that this CEO isn't a typical suit. He even says as much. Polman is only too pleased to tell people that his suits never cost more than £200 and that he never pays more than £20 for a shirt on principle. But he won't be talking about that today.

Failing governments, conscious consumers, collaborating with NGOs, the necessity of reforming capitalism, the limits to what the planet can tolerate, the need to lift 800 million people out of poverty, the High-Level Panel, the central role for big business, and of course the USLP – each of these are touched on in a heartfelt speech. The audience listens breathlessly. This man inspires his public.

Polman once again underlines his belief that the Netherlands can play a key role. 'And I am also delighted that the Rutte cabinet have combined trade and aid, both crucial to the development of poorer countries, in a holistic way to make a new position of Minister for Foreign Trade and Development Cooperation. This provides the Netherlands with a good example. Let's hope that this coalition between the VVD and the PvdA becomes the second sustainable growth coalition. And I'm very honoured that we have Minister Lilianne Ploumen, who carries both of these heavy responsibilities, is here with us today.'

Ben Knapen's successor listens attentively, nodding her agreement. She thinks Polman's logic is unassailable and believes that he is solving this old 'salesman-pastor' dilemma many business leaders struggle with. She hopes this will work out, because if we don't start dealing with this then in 30 years there will be nothing left, not even Unilever.

Ploumen has good memories of the company, or rather of Van den Bergh & Jurgens. For a moment the PvdA politician's thoughts go back to her father, a catholic dairy farmer from Maastricht. For years she helped him in the farm shop, where he sold a great deal of Blue Band margarine. It was unbelievably popular, most normal people couldn't afford the much more expensive high-grade butter. She can still remember exactly what those tubs of healthy, but more importantly, affordable 'fake butter' felt like to pick up. It gave her a good feeling even back then.

CHAPTER 11

MAKING MONEY CAN
NEVER BE THE GOAL

April–October 2013

Jean-Marc Huët is frustrated. Unilever's CFO is not being given the freedom to do what he wants to do: what he's good at. The former banker would much prefer to focus on strategy and making plans to speed up expansion at this company as he did at his previous firms. He wants to pursue a more proactive takeover strategy. And Unilever has the capacity to do so. There's relatively little debt on Unilever's balance sheet. As far as he's concerned, the firm uses too much of its own relatively expensive equity. Shareholders are demanding a higher dividend each year, debt is cheaper and the interest rates are low. And didn't the multinational promise its shareholders it would have reached €80 billion in revenues by 2020? Aggressive takeovers are needed in order to reach that goal.

Various directors hear Huët warning of the lack of debt on the balance sheet. That has risks attached. Unilever is big and difficult to take over thanks to its complicated NV–PLC structure but there is growing pile of cheap capital around the world, hunting ever more aggressively for a return. A company like Unilever, with lots of costs and overheads, is exactly what they're looking for. The idea that the two activities, food and care, would be worth more separately than they are combined is still doing the rounds. A company like that can attract attention. Private equity firms regularly demonstrate their ability to finance big takeovers by stacking their prey's balance sheet with debts, thereby letting the company pay for its own take over.

Kees Storm is in full agreement with Huët. The chairman of the Audit Committee doesn't think Unilever is using its balance sheet to its best advantage either. That can be solved pretty quickly, of course, by buying up their own shares with borrowed capital; the share price will rise automatically if they do. But the men regard this as a *testimonium paupertatus*, a testament to poverty. In doing it, what you really tell your shareholders is that you have run out of ideas as an entrepreneur. Then you're putting yourself on the bench as management. The company learned that lesson 15 years previously, anyway. Back then the shareholders received a handout of $8 billion, money Unilever could have done with a year later when they embarked on the exorbitant takeover of Bestfoods, which they'd paid for with borrowed funds.

Polman shares their deep distaste for buying up the company's own shares, but otherwise disagrees. Storm and Huët talk about a potential takeover of Colgate-Palmolive, or the French company L'Oréal, companies with a turnover of $17 billion and €23 billion, respectively, that would cost them between €50 and €70 billion. The CEO doesn't regard these as an option. Obviously their operations fit well with Unilever in a strategic sense, and with their ambition to focus on growing in the personal care market. But Polman thinks they are far too expensive. He also thinks they are being led and managed well already. How will Unilever recoup such an enormous investment?

Various colleagues notice that Polman's resistance to large-scale takeovers goes far beyond these calculations and assessments. He really doesn't want them to continue being guided by aims formulated with primarily financial motives in mind. The former Nestlé CFO, who once started out as the financial controller at Procter & Gamble, no longer wants to be ruled by the expectations of financial markets and analysts. He is wholeheartedly convinced that this kind of financial straightjacket eventually leads to ruin.

What Unilever needs to focus on right now is communicating more and more effectively about meeting the targets of the USLP. That's what the focus needs to be, not extortionate, barely justifiable takeovers. The financial results need to pass muster and improve slightly every year but Polman doesn't think that constantly shouting about them from the rooftops fits with the culture of Unilever anymore.

It annoys Polman that many of his colleagues, especially marketers, still don't grasp the fundamental core of his sustainability message. They're lagging behind the rest of the organisation. Marketers of his generation come from the best schools but have been instilled with the belief that they need to talk in a top-down way to their consumers, explaining to them why they should buy their products. They keep on 'pushing' their wares even though it no longer makes sense nowadays.

The consumer doesn't want that anymore, online they are making very clear what they do and don't want. As a marketer, you have to listen to this.

Then you'll see that consumers are increasingly aware of what the impact of their purchases is on their environment and the planet. They're going to realise that their freedom sometimes comes at the cost of others' freedom. This doubting citizen–consumer can help Unilever develop a product that explicitly takes into account this wider context. Polman is in a hurry, he wants to integrate the USLP goals into the marketing and management of Unilever straightaway. He is being asked about this increasingly often by his board, Louise Fresco in particular is concerned.

Huët is asked to start focusing more intensively on the accounting side of his CFO role, by getting started on optimising the IT processes, for example. But the former investment banker isn't particularly interested in this. He enjoyed the period in which he and Numico CEO Jan Bennink were making plans and finally managed to sell Numico successfully to Danone. He wants to work like that with his present CEO. Some of his colleagues suspect that Huët even dreams of succeeding Polman. However, Polman really only has one message for Huët: get back in your cage.

This irritates Storm, as far as he's concerned, you don't ask a man like Huët to work on upgrading your accountancy system. That isn't necessary anyway, it's in great shape and there are more than enough exceptional people working on it already. The Unilever CEO seems to have no desire to team up with his CFO. Storm regularly speaks to Huët about the tight hold Polman keeps on all the reins. They call that hub and spoke management. Polman sits in the middle, directing all the other managers in such a way that none of them know what each other is doing. This places the CEO, who does have all this information, firmly in the middle, but occasionally he obstructs the organisation around him. It also means that the people who report to him aren't part of a team with each other.

Huët is losing enthusiasm for this set-up and making it obvious. This irritates his colleagues. They think he's spoilt, some even call him lazy. Storm wonders how long Huët is going to tough it out here. Polman wonders whether Huët understands what the leadership of *this* Unilever needs to stand for.

Paul Polman feels like he's been chosen. He's on this Earth to make a difference, to take the values instilled in him by his parents and use them to care for the world. From his dream of being a priest, to becoming the CEO of Unilever and all the adventures in between. Serendipity – when he thinks about where he comes from and where he's going, this little word always springs to mind. You're looking for something but you hit upon something else, only for that often to turn out much later to be very useful to realising your ideals. That's why he stumbled across Unilever. He feels favoured and special and is becoming increasingly convinced that he's in a position and an atmosphere very few people share: he's a CEO in the world of the United Nations.

For Polman, the last eighteen months in the service of the United Nations have been the best and most educational of his life. Surrounded by genuinely dedicated people, he has started realising even more clearly what the world needs, and how public and private interests interact with each other. His network has also grown enormously. He'll have to draw on it to help Unilever make the USLP goals a success. He is often reproached for not listening to his colleagues enough but he does listen to *these* people, he has something to learn from them.

Polman is the odd one out in the High-Level Panel. In the experience of the other panel members, CEOs of multinationals tend to be on the other side of the equation, focused mostly on their personal and business interests and making money. Polman is pleased with the level of trust they place in him despite this. Because of their explicit agreement on the need to build bridges with the world of big business, they also listen to him attentively. This gives his sign-off on the formulation of new SDGs a particular weight. A weight he doesn't hesitate to use.

'We transmit our recommendations to you with a feeling of great optimism that a transformation to end poverty through sustainable development is possible within our generation.' After 18 months of research, consultations and four meetings of the panel at the UN in New York, and in Monrovia, London and Bali, the home countries of each of the three chairmen, the High-Level Panel of Eminent Persons presents its findings to Ban Ki-moon.

Combatting poverty and inequality stands at the heart of the report: 'the 1.2 billion poorest people account for only 1% of world consumption while the billion richest consume 72%'. The report underlines the fact that the issue of climate change is going to be absolutely crucial to the future distribution of wealth. 'The stresses of unsustainable production and consumption patterns have become clear, in areas like deforestation, water scarcity, food waste, and high carbon emissions. Losses from natural disasters – including drought, floods, and storms – have increased at an alarming rate. People living in poverty will suffer first and worst from climate change. The cost of taking action now will be much less than the cost of dealing with the consequences later.'

The report states the need for a paradigm shift. Business as usual is no longer an option. It proposes a universal agenda driven by five transformative changes. No more hunger, everyone reaches a living wage. A sustainable development of social, economic and environmental issues is central. A quick switch to sustainable production and consumption in which the innovative potential

of companies is used as effectively as possible and inclusive growth is made possible. Peace and proper governance with honest and accountable governments
are a core requirement. And the most important change: we need to develop
new cooperative relationships that are driven by a spirit of solidarity, cooperation and shared responsibility.[1]

Rob Swartbol is particularly pleased with this last point. This is what it's
all about: cooperation. The SDGs offer all parties clear guidelines for working together going forward. The Dutch 'experiment' has been a success. The
director-general for International Cooperation has received nothing but praise
from all sides regarding Polman's involvement; he has clearly put his stamp
firmly on the project.

Polman and his 'Sherpa' Gavin Neath are also proud of the result. More
than ever they are convinced that the issue of poverty needs to be given top
priority. This conviction poses all kinds of big dilemmas. Especially for a company like Unilever. As the company grows, it needs more raw materials, for
instance palm oil, which is used in almost everything, from a Magnum ice lolly
to a bottle of Dove.

Unilever and palm oil have been dependent on one another for a long time.
The rapidly growing demand for palm oil is one of the top causes of deforestation alongside meat, soya and paper. It's going to be hard, very hard: around
seven million hectares of forest are disappearing each year, the equivalent of
29 football pitches is felled every minute. If deforestation continues at this rate
there will be no trees left within a hundred years. In order to meet the growing
demand for palm oil, two million hectares of new plantations are needed each
year, around half the area of the Netherlands.

Demanding that countries like Indonesia and Malaysia ban logging isn't
an option. An Asian colleague once pointed out to Gavin Neath that the
British also had to cut down their forests before they could build factories.
Can you really blame a poor farmer for wanting to farm two extra hectares
in the knowledge that those extra yields will allow him to keep his children
in school? And it is these small, hard to monitor farmers who are doing the
most damage.

Marc Engel is also unpleasantly preoccupied with this problem. Sadly there
is no alternative to palm oil. The production of, for example, sunflower oil
requires 10 times the land. The director of purchasing also believes that marketers need to increase their effort to sell the importance of sustainable palm
oil to their customers. However, even he realises that this is hard for them. But
Unilever's mission will only have succeeded once consumers across the board
are buying Unilever products on the basis that they contain sustainable palm

oil. It's nice Unilever is receiving so much praise from NGOs but that praise needs to come from the consumers, from the people.

By 2014, Unilever needs to know exactly where all the palm oil it purchases is coming from. Six years after that, all of their palm oil needs to be certified sustainable. This is all set out in the USLP of 2013. Marc Engel has calculated that 20 per cent of palm oil production worldwide needs to be sustainable in order for Unilever's specific requirements to be met. As it stands, it's about 10 per cent. One of the big problems is that the demand for palm oil from quickly expanding consumer markets like India and China is rising rapidly. There is still little interest in certified palm oil there and barely any willingness to pay for it. This year, as a result, around half the sustainably produced palm oil is having to be sold as normal palm oil, without the premium price tag. The willingness of producers to invest in the accreditation process is therefore also low.[2] Engels is pleased that Polman has made progress on that front in cooperation with the Consumer Goods Forum.

Working with Marc Bolland, now the CEO of Marks & Spencer, Polman has taken on the co-chairmanship of the sustainability agenda of this club of multinationals. He represents the manufacturers and Bolland represents the retailers. Various participants have stopped Bolland in the corridors to ask him to make sure Polman doesn't get too much airtime. Paul Bulcke from Nestlé is among those who complain that Polman keeps speaking to them as if they're children, teaching them their lessons. They know what the main points are by now, this is getting counterproductive.

Bolland therefore suggests to Polman that they'll be better off presenting the sustainability agenda together, so that he can drum up support among the retailers too. Bolland subtly interrupts the indefatigably sermonising Polman by asking if he can deliver part of the presentation himself. It works, the talk is a success. The 40 biggest multinationals in the world agree to organise their purchasing in such a way that by 2020 they will no longer be contributing to any further deforestation. Unilever's biggest supplier of palm oil, Wilmar, which controls 40 per cent of the trade, has promised not to cut down any more forests without replacing the trees.

This mission is the reason Cherie Tan joined Unilever two years previously. The political scientist worked for the WWF on making palm oil production sustainable but realised that it was the business world in particular that needed to make a change. The USLP gave her hope. The world's biggest user of palm oil necessarily needs to have ambitions of making the whole industry more sustainable. Tan is now employed helping to make palm oil production by relatively small-scale farmers in Malaysia and Indonesia more sustainable.

In the summer of 2013, Polman and Tan are at the inaugural meeting of the Tropical Forest Alliance, set up the year before. This is a combined effort by companies from the Consumer Goods Forum, a number of governments, including the British and Dutch governments, and NGOs, aiming to put an end to deforestation. The Indonesian president Susilo Bambang Yudhoyono, one of the three chairmen of the UN's High-Level Panel, opened the summit by expressing his personal interest in the issue. Paul Polman refers back to this in his speech and emphasises the importance of cooperation between companies and governments.

Tan sees Polman as a visionary, she feels that he supports her. She likes the fact that the CEO is joining discussions on the world stage and delivering the right message, that's his role. But will he realise that there's a world of difference between these narratives and what's actually happening in the field? Polman has told her on several occasions that she's welcome to email him anytime. But that's difficult for her, it would mean going over her bosses' heads. And that's something you don't do at Unilever, there are risks attached.

Cherie Tan often goes on research trips herself, meeting with local producers and talking to local authorities. This is where change needs to happen. She's pleased with the growing awareness of the issue. But in her experience there is a gap between what national and local governments think and do. Where poverty is strongly in evidence, local governments have a different set of priorities to deal with. These politicians like to win votes by giving the farmers some extra land.

The production of palm oil can only become sustainable if all these small farmers commit to it fully too without losing out. More than anything, this will take large-scale investment in their productivity. Their yield per hectare is too low, sometimes as little as 1.5 tonnes of palm oil. A yield of seven tonnes is more than possible but requires investment. Unilever can help by building relationships with small-scale farmers through cooperatives and, for example, guaranteeing a fixed price over a longer term, so that the farmers are confident they can make the necessary investments in their farms.

But when Tan suggests this at the regional office in Singapore, things hit a roadblock. She doesn't get anywhere. Her colleagues in purchasing don't want to pay over the odds and eventually explain to her that their room to manoeuver is limited by their colleagues on the marketing side of the company. If anything, they want to lower prices in order to head off competitors. In order to keep the margins on track, they need to reduce costs. It's a shame for those small farmers, of course, but this is the reality. After all, Unilever's sales growth has to come mostly from this part of the world.

For Tan, this represents the biggest challenge. She thinks that Unilever needs to make sure that the palm oil they use is no longer seen as a substitutable raw material. Responsibly farmed, truly sustainable palm oil needs to become a proud, iconic aspect of Unilever's products. The marketers need to be motivated to actually start marketing the sustainable nature of the palm oil they're buying. Just like with Lipton, they need to make sure that customers get a good feeling from using Dove because it contains sustainably produced palm oil.

But whenever Tan talks to the marketers, she notices that they mostly want sound bites and are always in a rush. In her view, they're spending much too little time actually learning about the issue. They always refer to the easy example of Ben & Jerry's, but even there Tan thinks they prefer to talk about milk from cuddly cows than about the sugar they use, because that's another ingredient with bad associations, just like palm oil.

Of course, it's far from simple to sell Dove by linking it more explicitly to the issue of deforestation, Tan understands that. Women rubbing on moisturiser would rather think about the promise of better self-esteem than endangered orang-utans. But as a marketer it's only when you really reflect on these things that you come up with real solutions and pave the way for a paradigm shift. This is why Tan thinks they need to put much more energy into co-creating solutions across the different disciplines. Lots of her colleagues are stuck in the old ways of thinking and calculating, trapped in their respective worlds. And they won't leave them voluntarily. The leaders of Unilever have to do a lot more work here if they want a truly sustainable business model.

Peter ter Kulve, the boss of Asia, understands the complaints about marketers coming from various quarters. He is wrestling with this issue too. Himself a dyed in the wool marketer, he can see how the USLP is inspiring young colleagues to work for the company out of personal conviction and their own sense of a calling. That brings lots of energy and creativity with it. But he's also uncertain: How much can the growth of the company be derived from the USLP itself? It works for products like Ben & Jerry's and Lifebuoy, brands that were, as it were, born with a particular purpose. But what about the rest? He isn't convinced. How do you do the same with the US fabric softener Snuggle? Or Domestos, which had always been sold on the basis of its effectiveness in killing bacteria but is now being styled in terms of making a cleaner world. Aren't the competitors doing the same? When it comes down to it, he doesn't even regard Dove as a sustainable brand, it's a brand with a clear purpose but it's one that has nothing to do with sustainability. In his eyes, it's also to some extent spin. As far as he's concerned, the USLP isn't just about sustainability, it's about making consumers feel like better people. In this way Unilever is also contributing to a better society.

His colleague Jan Zijderveld, responsible for revenue and profit in Europe, also notices that marketers find it hard to balance the USLP goals and the need to drive up growth and profit in the short term in their daily practice. Polman is doing great things with the Unilever brand but how do you do the same with the hundreds of brands within Unilever? It only takes the smallest obstacle for frustrations to boil over. How can you make sure that people start believing that Unilever is really making a contribution to a more sustainable economy? Zijderveld has long been convinced that it isn't possible to ask consumers to pay extra for sustainable efforts. They expect companies to take care of those costs.

In *NRC Handelsblad*, Anniek Mauser explains that changing consumer behaviour is by far the most challenging aspect of the USLP: 'We as a company have made enormous strides when it comes to our factories and logistics. But a big part of the environmental impact comes from the farmers and especially from the consumers of our products. They need to start using less water, for example. When it comes to washing detergents and household cleaner, 85% of CO_2 emissions come from the consumers.'

For this reason, Unilever wants to ensure that 200 million people around the world start taking shorter showers. The Dutch and the British spend an average of eight minutes in the shower; this needs to be reduced to five. The company wants to help them by making a shampoo that's quicker to use. As Mauser explains: 'Showering is a nice habit to have. No one sees the negative effects on the climate or the energy bill immediately. But a change in behaviour is urgently needed.' Together with the WWF and Princess Laurentien of the Netherlands's Missing Chapter Foundation, Unilever kick-starts a campaign in Holland called 'Water Savers', a curriculum for primary schools about climate issues. The aim is for children to explain to their parents and siblings why they should take shorter showers. That has to have an impact. After all, this will be the generation that pays the highest price if this behaviour doesn't change now.

Meanwhile, Unilever is doing its best to make the results of the USLP better measurable. The objectives have been translated into attainable goals for each manager. There are more than a hundred key performance indicators (KPIs). The boss of Indonesia is required, for example, to fill in a monthly spreadsheet indicating how many children's hands have been washed, how many people have been educated on how best to brush their teeth, how many girls have received 'Dove training', aimed at building self-confidence, and so on.

Unilever pays the accountants at PwC about €10 million a year to compile and monitor all these data. The accountants look at the pre-agreed definition and assesses on the basis of random sampling whether Unilever is keeping to its own, self-imposed rules. Sustainability development manager Jan Kees Vis spends a couple of days each year in discussions with these accountants about what can and cannot be taken into account when it comes to an area like education and information. Do the Dove commercials they broadcast count towards this, how is that domain measured, what correction factor do you apply?

Eventually, the accountants give a 'declaration of limited certainty' on the USLP figures, which are to be published alongside the profit-and-loss calculation in the annual report. The biggest handicap for the accountants is the lack of generally accepted standards. What Unilever is doing is so new that these don't exist yet. According to the accountants, limited certainly isn't intended to mean much more than: if the figures you've given us are accurate, then these figures are accurate. Financial analysts can't do anything with that, they don't even look at them.

Within Unilever there is constant debate over the extent to which the targets met as part of the USLP should be linked to bonuses. At the moment, around 10 per cent of the bonus depends on the reaching or missing of the USLP targets. Zijderveld thinks it's logical not to make this percentage any higher. You'd soon run the risk of someone having their water-saving programme in good order but not making quite as much profit. That's when the model stops working, as far as he's concerned. You have to be delivering on both sides, the two of them reinforce each other. If consumers start spending less time showering because they've started using your more efficient shampoo then you're onto a winner.

Ter Kulve also finds it difficult to make the KPIs from the USLP concrete. The discussions with colleagues about how to do this are potentially endless. Can you measure how many women are feeling more confident thanks to Dove? And you constantly wonder: Shouldn't you just want to hit these targets anyway, simply because working decently and sustainably is the right thing to do? The fact that the vast majority of the bonus is linked to driving up share price seems self-evident to Ter Kulve too. That's where all value ends up together. When the company is growing, the share price goes up. And you only grow if you're selling more products to more people, and doing so very efficiently.

'He talks – and talks – with the evangelical enthusiasm of a born-again green, intent on saving the world.' The journalist from *The Telegraph* sometimes finds it hard to believe that the person he's trying to interview is the CEO of one of the biggest companies in Europe. 'But there is a sting in the tail. If

Polman is to meet his targets for Unilever, then his customers – all two billion of us – are going to have to join his crusade.'

Unilever buys about eight million tonnes of agricultural products a year. At present, 36 per cent of them are produced sustainably, by 2020 it needs to be 100 per cent. For this reason, Unilever buys as much RSPO-certified palm oil as it can. Gavin Neath is remarkably transparent in an encounter with the same *Telegraph* journalist who interviewed Polman: 'Our dirty secret is that we often don't even know who our suppliers are.' Gail Klintworth agrees: 'That is not good enough, we want 100% traceability.' In order to make that possible, Unilever intends to bid farewell to 80 per cent of its small suppliers. According to Gavin Neath, this 'cleaning house' is necessary in order to reach the right standard in time. But it's a sensitive topic. Unilever has also committed to helping as many small farmers as possible increase their financial security. Klintworth calls it a 'trade off'. She would prefer to talk about Unilever's biggest supplier: the Singaporean firm Wilmar. They have been under fire for the past two years because they are accused of demolishing entire Indonesian villages in order to farm palm oil. Under pressure from the Consumer Goods Forum, Wilmar seems to have decided to cut its losses and promise to start fighting deforestation. 'We've had to make some difficult decisions', Klintworth says.

The journalist is invited to come and visit Unilever's research centre in Port Sunlight. There, 800 researchers develop products that do what they're supposed to do *and* are good for the environment. 'They're not only juggling ingredients to give us the whitest wash, they're also trying to wash white while using less water and less energy to heat that water. With Unilever's products providing the suds for an estimated 125 billion washes worldwide every year, even the smallest tinkering can have a global effect.' Then there's a proud presentation on the success of Lifebuoy soap. Adverts are encouraging 71 million people in Africa and Asia to start washing their hands before they eat. The USLP report claims that 224 million people have been helped to improve their hygienic living conditions since the plan started. Lifebuoy has been enjoying growth in the double figures for two years in a row.

But do investors follow this narrative, the journalist wants to know: 'Polman may sit in his London office thinking 30 years ahead – figuring out how to sustain supplies of raw materials on a crowded planet, and how to be a good corporate citizen – the City boys over the road that he relies on for finance often have time horizons of more like 30 minutes.' Neath acknowledges the issue: 'Investors can't build long-term stresses such as climate change and deforestation into their valuation models for companies they are thinking of investing in. So they ignore them.' Polman continues: 'We have to change the parameters of capitalism. Even after the Second World War companies were still focused on the common good. Then came Milton Friedman and the "me" culture. The end result is that today the richest 400 Americans have more wealth than everyone in India. We have to get back.'[3]

The people gathered at the Four Seasons Hotel in San Francisco view this a little differently. Every June, the top brass at Heinz are invited here with their spouses and pampered in between their meetings. Whether it's the latest iPhone or a nice set of luggage, on their return to their rooms each evening the managers and their partners find a lavish present. The card accompanying it contains warm wishes from William and his wife Susy Johnson.

This year will be the last time. 3G Capital, the new owner of Heinz, will be announcing which of the present management team are allowed to remain. They've gathered once again, with no idea which of their colleagues will be allowed to stay. As a guest speaker tries to capture his audience's attention, they keep a close eye on each other. The mood is strange. The top 12 in the company have been asked to sit in the back row. They're going to be tapped on the shoulder one by one and invited into a small room down the corridor to hear from CEO Bernardo Hees what their fate will be. The guest speaker doesn't have an easy task, as most of the audience's eyes are trained on the door. Who is going to come back? And, more importantly, with what expression on their face?

The first, Michael Mullen, comes back smiling, he's allowed to stay. Hein Schumacher, responsible for China, is the second to go. He started out at Unilever once upon a time but he's been in service at Heinz for 19 years now. He's also allowed to stay. The Dutchman is responsible for Asia-Pacific, around a quarter of Heinz's business. Schumacher is well pleased with the package of terms he's been offered, with the concrete prospect of a final remuneration of around $35 million at the end of five years or so. The new leadership of Heinz has chosen to call the people they want to keep first and thus secure their loyalty. After that it's a bloodbath.

Roel van Neerbos has received so many calls over the past few months from people, including from InBev, with unsettling reports about the tough culture under the Brazilians that he's now hoping he won't be asked to stay on. Van Neerbos knows he won't be going home empty handed if they get rid of him. When Bernardo Hees asks him upon him entering the room whether he's recovered from his jetlag, he knows that it's over. Hees wouldn't waste the 10 minutes allotted to them with this kind of question if he wanted Van Neerbos to take on new responsibilities.

He isn't surprised. Van Neerbos understands by now that the Brazilians are intent on appointing as many obedient managers as possible. A manager who's already in a senior position is harder for them to command. They would rather bump somebody up two levels. After a giant promotion like that, these managers think two things. 'This is brilliant, I'm going to grab this opportunity with both hands.' But also: 'how in god's name am I supposed to pull this off?' They're crapping their pants. And that's exactly where the Brazilians like their subordinates, because then they have free rein to decide what needs to happen and how it should be done. And indeed, they do swiftly appoint dozens of relatively junior Brazilians to relatively high positions. They're putty in their hands.

Of the 35 Heinz managers, 28 are told to pack their things. Only two of the top 12 are allowed to stay on. There are tears, the men go back to their hotel rooms with their partners to process the news. Schumacher has mixed feelings about this turn of events. He's pleased to be allowed to stay on but his whole team is falling apart. He doesn't feel too sorry for his former colleagues, though, each of them is being given severance packages of between $5 and $20 million.

That evening, they all go out for dinner together one last time at the 'Silver Oak' vineyard. This is where William Johnson gets his wines. Many of them had expressed their disapproval over the $212 million their former boss retained from the sale of Heinz. They complain about that again tonight. They all get roaring drunk.

Polman shakes his head pityingly when he reads the reports. Rumours had been flying that Heinz would be losing its independence. The company had approached Unilever asking whether they were interested in acquiring Heinz. They'd looked into it, of course. The necessary analyses had been carried out under the leadership of Jean-Marc Huët. But Polman's conclusion had been clear: not interested, this company has no more room to grow. He thinks it's a shame, Heinz has a wonderful history. But Polman doesn't believe they'll keep going much longer without serious investment in product renewal. And how long are people going to keep using ketchup like that anyway, that stuff's almost 25 per cent sugar.

'Plan A – where companies have been driven by the profit motive alone – is no longer acceptable. As business leaders, we know that what we're proposing will be a challenge, or even an affront, to many of our colleagues and competitors. But we're confident that those who choose to work with us will see that in the long run what's better for the planet and its people is also better for business. The ultimate aim, with support, energy and ideas – and yes, constant, frank criticism – is to get millions of business leaders committed to a better way of doing business.' This is the mission of 'The B-Team' pressure group.

Paul Polman joins big names like Richard Branson, Gro Harlem Brundtland, Mo Ibrahim, Muhammad Yunus, Arianna Huffington, Strive Masiyiwa and Indra Nooyi. He is a highly active member, joining various working groups aiming to promote cooperation between big business, governments and NGOs, and prompt accountants to come up with new ways of measuring environmental impact so that it can be counted as part of existing profit-and-loss calculations. Through the *Huffington Post*, he and other members of the B-Team will regularly put out research and opinion pieces to a world audience.

Polman is also appointed chairman of the WBCSD. The 200 companies that are members of this organisation aim to ensure that the nine billion inhabitants of the world projected for 2050 will be able to live together healthily and well without devouring the world. Peter Bakker, former CEO of TNT, leads the day-to-day running of the organisation. Under the headline 'Accountants Are Going to Save the World', Bakker explains to the *Harvard Business Review* why it is that the rules of accountancy urgently need to change. Accountants need to make sure that all true costs and results are counted in evaluations of companies, not just the financial ones. Polman later sums up this message perfectly: 'As long as a dead tree is valued more than a tree that is alive, we have a big problem.'

The Dutch-British firm is still wrestling with its European results. Now that inflation has more or less died down, there is hardly any scope to raise prices or salaries and keep paying everyone a little more. Costs need to be significantly reduced. Competition on the shop shelves is fierce. As a result of increasing pressure for product promotions and special offers, necessary to retain their market share, their prices go down about 2 per cent.

In the United Kingdom, around 90 per cent of Unilever products are sold for less than standard price. The marketers know that if they skip a single 'buy one get one free offer' they miss their targets for the year. This is their reality, they have to live with it. To Jan Zijderveld, the European boss, this is an energy-sapping game, a fight in which the aims of the USLP basically play no role at all. To keep the margin in decent shape, and pay for all these special offers, costs have to be brought down sharply. And he has no control over some of these costs.

Indirect costs make up about 13 per cent of the total. Half of those are related to market research and development. These are incurred centrally, he can't do anything about them. Zijderveld regularly complains about these expensive people in London, who keep drawing their hefty salaries and travel budgets even though it's not at all clear what all of their contributions are. He calls for redundancies, replacing them locally with young, cheap people who are closer to the market. The people in London see this differently, of course.

He does have some influence over the other 50 per cent of the indirect costs, however. Over the past few years, he's stripped about a third of the European operation's overheads. His colleague Ter Kulve, boss of Benelux until 2011, made a big contribution to this effort. Dozens of jobs were cut. The frustrating thing is that most of their local competitors are much smaller, their indirect costs often work out at less than 8 per cent. So it's still hard to compete. But maybe he can do something about that.

Zijderveld had noticed that the head office in Rotterdam was pretty much empty. There is even a tenant on some of the floors of the building. This meant Unilever's head office was effectively in London. Zijderveld had realised that they were better off either shutting the office in central Rotterdam or filling it up again. He suggests to Polman that they move all the marketers and managers of product categories (ice cream, tea, personal hygiene, etc.) from the 11 European locations and gather them here in one place. This would concern 700 people in total. Doing this would mean combining forces and costs, making the European operation more responsive and effective. Polman had thought it was a good idea.

The only problem was that those category managers didn't report to Zijderveld but to their chief category managers in London. This had caused Zijderveld some sleepless nights but he had persevered, setting up a programme promoting the Netherlands. All colleagues and their families were invited to take a tour of Rotterdam, driven around the Netherlands in tour buses and given information about schools and the housing market. Most of them had come around.

In the end, it was the British who proved the hardest to convince. This was obviously where the dislike of Rotterdam was most deeply rooted. But Polman had been strict, making it clear that even the Brits needed to go to Rotterdam. And so the completely refurbished office found itself brimming with new life.

In October 2013, Paul Polman, Jan Zijderveld and Ahmed Aboutaleb, the mayor of Rotterdam, officially opened the 'European marketing and innovation hub'. In a speech, the potential of this new research centre was uttered in the same breath as the potential of Wageningen University and the Netherlands to act as a catalyst in the big issues related to global food provision. The men can see a bright future ahead. The Dutch 'head office' has been rescued from destruction. For now.

Polman is in a rush, he wants to do more. The collapse of the Rana Plaza building in Bangladesh the previous April in particular had made him realise that Unilever had left something important out of the USLP: the social component isn't represented well enough. When the textiles factory collapsed, it killed 1,134 people, the images were horrific. So long as people have to work under such conditions, the world can never be sustainable.

Inspired both by discussions at the United Nations of the crucial importance of combatting poverty, and by the Oxfam study of working conditions at Unilever in Vietnam, a study is initiated almost three years after the start of the USLP, looking at how Unilever can bring about more sustainable growth under the banner of 'sustainable living'. What barriers need to be removed? The results of this study form the basis of a new ambition within the USLP: improving the living conditions of as many people as possible.

By the end of this year, Unilever will have improved the lives of around 570,000 small farmers. The new USLP states that by 2020 the company will have improved the lives of at least 5.5 million small farmers, retailers and young entrepreneurs. In that year, 100 per cent of the materials they buy will have been produced not only sustainably but by suppliers who respect fundamental human rights. The point of departure for this is the guidance of the United Nations.

Regarding the importance of women, the USLP now states: 'Around the world many women face discrimination and disadvantage, lack access to skills and training, and face roadblocks to their active participation in the economy. At the same time, women form the majority of our consumer base. They are strongly represented in our agricultural supply chains and in distributing our brands to market. We are a large employer and need the best available talent to succeed. By 2020 we will empower 5 million women. To achieve this, we will build a gender-balanced organisation.'

Referring to Rana Plaza, Polman tells *The Guardian*: 'To pay a textile worker in Pakistan 11 cents an hour doesn't make good business sense. We had a lot of cost pressures before I came and the business also wasn't doing that well. Now we pay more and we have greater loyalty, more energy and higher productivity.' Among the top managers, Louise Fresco and Ann Fudge are particularly enthusiastic. They think that the position of women needs to be consolidated inside Unilever too.

Sixty-two-year-old Fudge knows what she's talking about. She is one of the most successful African American business women in business. As an eye witness to the urban riots in the aftermath of the murder of Martin Luther King Jr in 1968, she had decided she needed to seize opportunities, and that she wanted to do something that had never been done by a Black woman before. As a celebrated marketer, she would become head of one of the biggest divisions at Kraft and then chairman and CEO of the advertising firm Young & Rubicam.

Ever since starting as a non-executive director at Unilever in 2009, she has been shocked by the fact that despite all its positive messaging the company is in reality still led almost exclusively by white men. She remarks on this at every meeting: of the 16 top managers who make up the Unilever Leadership Executive (ULE), only two of them are women and only two are people of colour. She tells them that it's crucial, not least to Unilever's ambitions, to bring in more women at the top.

When it comes to diversity, Unilever's board sets a much better example. It's probably the most diverse board of any multinational in the world: seven white men and five women, of whom only one is white. That attracts attention and is regularly called inspirational by the media. That's how things should be.

Not all of Unilever's directors are convinced. Kees Storm thinks there's too little cohesion. A highly diverse group of people like this has little in common, and in his eyes they don't form a proper team: they're fragmented. He's also disappointed with the contribution some of the women are making. They dutifully attend meetings but most of them hardly say anything. This plays right into Polman's hands, Storm realises. This board is easy for him to control. He's got it completely in his pocket.

Polman thinks this is nonsense. He is in full agreement with Ann Fudge. The more women at the top, the better. He tells *The Guardian*: 'It's all about the way we value things. If you look at the female brain, it's differently developed from the male brain; there is a better balance between the left and the right side. So there is more empathy, more purpose, longer-term thinking, more partnership and a sense of equality, a better understanding and listening skills than men. So the skills you need to be more successful in the future probably are more in the female than they are in the male. For that reason you need to be sure that you have a very diverse organisation.'[4]

Fudge likes the fact that Polman speaks so enthusiastically about women's indispensable abilities. She would rather have a passionate CEO who makes a mistake here and there so that the board has to rein them in, than a well-behaved CEO who spends the whole time flying under the radar. In his book *True North*, Bill George quotes Fudge: 'Any of us can figure out ways to drive a business for two years and make a boatload of money and move on. That's not leadership. That's playing a game. Leadership is leaving something lasting.'[5]

Polman reflects on this as he talks to *The Guardian*: 'a good leader, I think, is a good human being in the first place. Too often we are being programmed by the environment around us to behave differently. But I think a true leader is an authentic person, who feels good about who he is. I don't have a problem crying when I need to cry. There's nothing wrong with that and showing that you care because it's the same in any organisation; if you show that you care, others will care for you, 100%.'

CHAPTER 12

THE WORLD'S BIGGEST NGO

November 2013–February 2015

The top brass at Unilever are getting a bit fed up with Polman's tears. They believe these represent genuine emotion, but he does cry rather often. The tears mostly accompany instances of frustration and anger. Anger because he thinks the people around him aren't giving him their best. He can rage at colleagues who he thinks aren't getting the message.

The impatient Polman is being disappointed more and more often. Nothing is going quickly enough. He regularly scolds his managers for keeping too much to the old ways, acting based on systems steered by financial results. He calls on them to show courage, to start working on the basis of their personal calling and to set different priorities. Surely they've created the space for that at this point?

Polman thinks his colleagues in the field need to start working together more intensively; there's room to do more on both fronts. They need to work together, but especially with other interested parties. Change the conversation with suppliers, retailers, competitors, governments and NGOs, don't just talk about price but about the collective effort to educate customers, for example. By doing that you generate free publicity and save on the costs of advertising. Work together online to build the transparency that gives consumers confidence that they are really being listened to.

The CEO understands that the people below him are uncertain. It's still new to them. These are new risks, where is the data that shows this actually works? Really, Polman thinks Unilever managers have two jobs. Of course they have to try and sell as many bottles of Dove or Magnums, that's inevitable. They will have to spend 40 hours per week making enough money. But they also need to spend at least as much time trying to realise the aims of the USLP. Which means trying out unconventional approaches to find new ways of helping to advance the world around them in both social and environmental terms.

Sometimes there is push-back. Polman can demand all he likes that they spend more time on future-proofing their brands; most of the category managers, marketers and salesman will likely only remain in post three or four years. That limits their horizons. Why should they trouble themselves investing in things that will only bear fruit once they are long gone? They need to meet their financial targets, that's what they're actually being judged on.

Shortly before Christmas, Polman gives an interview to *NRC Handelsblad* in which he explains once again how he does what he does. 'People who don't have any choice, that's who I'm fighting for.' He explains that he sees himself as a responsible entrepreneur whose duty it is to fix the system, just like William Lever a hundred years before him, because governments aren't doing their job. 'It was needed then and it's needed now. Since the crisis, and even before it, we've had an economic system from which too small a group of people have profited. Look at the US and Europe, the disparity in incomes is getting bigger and bigger. The American economy is growing but the middle and lower classes are worse off than they were ten years ago. That's a huge problem. When you look at the enormous rates of youth unemployment in southern Europe, then you see you've got a society that isn't working. The problems in Africa and the Middle East aren't caused by religion, they're caused by poverty. We've got a collective responsibility to solve them. As a company, we're trying to help the Netherlands. I talk to politicians like Lilianne Ploumen, I talk to Prime Minister Mark Rutte. Not a single week passes without me talking to someone from an NGO on the phone. In the past that was unthinkable. If Greenpeace called, or Oxfam, or UNICEF, you wouldn't have answered the phone. Now those are our partners.'

Over the course of 2013, Unilever once again performed better than the market average, with growth of 4.3 per cent, the margin has improved and risen to 14.1 per cent. In the annual report, Polman writes: 'Over the last five years, we have established a simple framework for driving long-term success – to grow ahead of our markets, expand our margin and deliver strong cash flow. We achieved this again in 2013, despite further investments in advertising and promotion to strengthen the business.' When it comes to the success stories of the USLP, Polman points to the brands Lifebuoy, Knorr, Pureit and Domestos, just as he has in previous years.

The numbers are healthy, so investors are boosting Unilever's share price. This comforts Polman; as long as the share price is going up, he doesn't have to concern himself with his shareholders. He has zero desire to do so. The financial world is still showing barely any interest in the progress of the USLP. Even during the latest meeting with analysts, none of them asked him about it.

But that August, the analysts start taking an interest after all. They're concerned by a dip in growth in the first half of 2014. Unilever is on course for a halving of its growth rate, to 2 per cent. 'The slowest growth the company has seen for years shows no signs of improving', reports the analyst from J.P. Morgan. 'We get the impression that investors are waiting for more substantial and swifter action to be taken', the analyst from Merrill Lynch complains. 'We're detecting an increasing focus on profitability to compensate for declining growth in revenues, but in this Unilever is no different from its competition.'

A chorus of analysts suggests that it's time for Unilever to bid farewell to its margarines division, which has been in a declining market for years. An estimated return of €5 billion could be put to good use in a takeover to expand the quickly growing personal care division. In response, Polman points out the consistently huge margins on margarine, which are necessary for paying their dividend. He believes you need to ask yourself the question: Is there someone who could run this more effectively than I can? Because if that isn't the case, you'll sell without getting enough for it. That wouldn't be good.

Voices in the financial sector are also increasingly advising Polman to take a closer look at the possibility of taking over Colgate-Palmolive or Reckitt Benckiser, the maker of brands like Dettol, Clearasil and Gaviscon. Polman doesn't see this as a logical move. 'Many people are focused on what they know of companies in the developed world, but there are many new companies that are coming along. We don't see Procter & Gamble as our toughest competitor. People still have this framework – that you compete with these three [global] companies – it's just not true anymore. Most of our competitors in the emerging markets are regional players.'[1]

Inside Unilever, pressure is mounting from various quarters to start mostly letting go of the strategy of the last fifteen years, which made decision making more and more centralised. Some marketers think that after years spent being 'hopelessly local', Unilever has become 'hopelessly global'. The result being that it can't react quickly enough to the ever-growing competition from small, local competitors.

Polman thinks that it will help if he takes on Harish Manwani's role himself. The COO is retiring at the end of 2014. Polman thinks Manwani is a good executive director but he's also a critic. The Indian has gathered his own club of people around him over the past few years. This layer of people, the 'global marketing executive', has become too powerful and in Polman's view is frustrating the necessary incorporation and integration of the product categories into the regions. The board is quickly convinced by Polman's diagnosis. This will mean removing a whole management layer, which allows the company to speed up the operation.

The fact that as a result 19 people are directly reporting to him is a non-issue to Polman. At that level, people no longer need to be told what to do, they know what to do and how to do it. That's their responsibility, after all, and they're paid handsomely for it for that matter. Once you're in a position like that, you no longer need to look for guidance from your boss the whole time. Ugh, he hated people doing that.

However, there's little support for this move across the organisation. The COO role is a heavy, full-time responsibility and requires that you be easy to contact at all times. The Unilever managers liked the split in leadership, the division of labour. Manwani had a good grip on what was happening in the company. A good COO needs to be on top of things, it's a demanding job. You can't just do it on the side. In order to do the job properly, you also need to be in the office a lot. Polman barely shows his face there. Manwani doesn't think it makes sense to get rid of his role either. His being in charge of the sales side of the company is what allows Polman to dedicate himself to building up momentum outside the company. This is going to be a lot to take on. Some people are worried that the CEO is starting to suffer from delusions of grandeur.

Kees Kruythoff agrees with Polman that the matrix is not being managed to its best advantage. The categories need to be given more influence on strategy, this is needed to bed the USLP into the various regions properly; each requires a bespoke approach. But on the other hand, he's concerned. All roads now lead to Polman and that's a problem. Because he refuses to form teams, the CEO is now the only one with oversight. All information, all power, lies with him. The people who make up the ULE, now also reporting to Polman, aren't a proper team either. They are the leaders of the eight geographical regions and the four product categories, plus seven staffers. Polman is going to start having to spend a lot of time on these eight markets to prevent a power vacuum from forming.

Just like Kees Kruythoff, Jan Zijderveld hopes to one day succeed Polman as CEO. After his stints as head of Asia and Europe, he thinks it would have been logical for him to get Manwani's job. Does Polman realise fully that being COO means having to come back to the company? That he's largely going to have to leave behind the new world he enjoys so much, the halls full of the warm applause of governments and NGOs?

Polman has no intention of doing that, however. In various speeches and interviews, he claims that thanks to its fulfilment of its 'doing well by doing good' adage, Unilever is now effectively the biggest NGO in the world. He tells the German *WirtschaftsWoche* financial paper: 'I'd much rather be remembered as someone who left the world a slightly better place. That's much better than leaders who have focused on improving profitability or increasing Dove's market share by a couple of percent.' The journalists ask whether his board or the analysts agree with him on that. Polman reacts irritably: 'You'll have to ask them that. And I've long since stopped reading anything analysts write. They think in financial quarters, we think in the long term.'

His interviewers express their surprise: 'We can't shake the feeling that we're sitting talking to the messiah among the world's board chairmen. Wouldn't you have been better off going into politics, working for the United Nations or an influential NGO?' 'Unilever is one of the biggest NGOs in the world', Polman replies. 'We aren't a state-owned enterprise. We have more women working for us and spend more on small loans in our value chain that any other NGO. The biggest difference is that we don't need to ask anyone else for money.'[2]

These kinds of pronouncements alarm Ann Fudge. The Google news alerts on her phone tell her whenever Polman is in the news, having told some glittering story about ending poverty somewhere in the world. She often thinks that she'd rather hear that he'd told someone about Unilever's strategy, the sale of new products or them breaking into new markets. Fudge values Polman's passion enormously but he's beginning to go too far. What does he mean Unilever doesn't need to go asking anyone for money? If shareholders stop investing their money in Unilever, it'll soon be curtains for this 'NGO'. And for Paul Polman.

She's not the only worrying. Fellow directors Paul Walsh and Kees Storm are particularly concerned. Will financial markets, investors and banks understand this kind of remarks? It's their money Unilever is putting into this, they're the ones running the risks. If the CEO starts behaving like the head of a non-profit organisation, is their money really still safe there?

Storm, the chairman of the Audit Committee, thinks that Polman is a magnificent leader but worries about the way he seems to be slowly but surely disappearing into another world. At each board meeting, Polman spends a good portion of the morning regaling them with his adventures at the United Nations, his concerns about deforestation and persisting poverty, and his deep conviction that companies like Unilever need to take the lead in transforming the economy. Storm finds these speeches inspiring too but he believes a company first and foremost needs to focus on results. The CEO needs to direct Unilever, that's what they're paying him for.

The one time his use of time comes up explicitly, Polman explains that he's able to combine everything splendidly. He thinks that all of the Unilever top brass should be able to manage such a combination. He confirms that he spends about 20–25 hours per week on his work for the United Nations and similar outfits but emphasises that he often works more than hundred hours per week. He easily spends 70–80 hours a week on Unilever, is someone trying to suggest that there's something lacking with the company? Or that he's not doing his best?

Louise Fresco notices that Polman is getting more and more impatient. And that he wants to go faster than the board. She sees that he wholeheartedly enjoys the warm reception he gets at the UN and from NGOs. He's celebrated there. Perhaps it's only logical that he thinks he can change the world single-handed. But can he? She can see that this is leading to serious conflict with Jean-Marc Huët. The CFO is sceptical about this.

Some board members think that their rather shy and retiring chairman Michael Treschow is giving 'his' CEO too much licence. They urge him to express their concerns to Paul Polman too. They know that there's not much else they can do. The company's results are still in good shape. This CEO is being praised pretty much wherever he goes. To some extent, Polman has become untouchable for the board. He's above them.

Treschow shares their concerns. Doesn't Polman seem too busy outside the company being this kind of environmental Jesus? Even he sometimes gets the impression that Polman styles himself more as a world leader than the sober CEO of a large company. The Swede warns him regularly: be careful, not everyone understands what you're doing, they don't care about the agenda of NGOs and this is confusing to them.

Obviously, Polman is working his socks off, but Treschow does wonder whether he's using his time properly. When the CEO complains that those under him don't take the initiative enough, Treschow challenges him, saying that this timid atmosphere is his doing. He's spoilt them over the years by constantly telling them what to do. That makes people wait for their boss's word on things and stops them from thinking for themselves.

Treschow doesn't think that Polman is a particularly good team player either, he wants to take on too much himself. He warns Polman now and again, telling him that he needs to put others forward and let them take the lead. But the chairman also knows that this is the nature of the beast: you can't change it just because you want to.

Treschow resolves to start asking Polman in their weekly telephone calls how his potential successors are getting on. How are they shaping up? This isn't always comfortable but doing so means he forces the CEO to start contemplating his own end, as it were. Being regularly confronted with the fact that he is also only there on a temporary contract will hopefully help Polman to keep both feet on the ground.

Nico Roozen, director of Solidaridad, is on his guard. His initial enthusiasm about Polman is giving way to doubt. He is increasingly coming to the conclusion that the CEO is extremely present in his area – the ongoing conversation about sustainability – but Unilever is mostly absent. The agreement that the company would actually start investing in making its manufacturing processes more sustainable seems to him to be bearing disappointingly little fruit. Polman's strong public image may be making enthusiastic governments and NGOs put their money into projects but Roozen thinks that Unilever should be doing more itself. That's what they promised, after all.

Sixty-year-old Roozen warns Polman that he needs to stop acting so much like a politician. As far as he's concerned, Polman is much too preoccupied with broadcasting from all kinds of podia filled with important people. He understands where he's coming from, in the public domain Polman is adored, of course he enjoys that more than boring shareholders' meetings. Roozen isn't calling Polman's integrity into question, but he's worried about his addiction to these appearances. It's high time that he starts putting his vision into practice at Unilever and making the changes to the organisation necessary to do that. When he tells the CEO of Unilever this, he reacts coldly. Polman tells him that all this requires more time, that Unilever shouldn't get too far ahead of the curve. Otherwise he'll run the risk of losing his audience and winding up stuck between the interests of various stakeholders.

A critical analysis in *The Economist* questions whether Unilever's shareholders are going to give it the time to realise the goals of the USLP. 'Its recent annual results disappointed the markets and the share price recently dropped below what it had been a year earlier.' An executive from Unilever tells the magazine that a serious crisis might be what's required in order to induce the markets to start valuing Unilever's sustainability efforts, something that sends the worldwide food prices skyrocketing, for example.[3]

Here and there, Polman inspires other leaders of the business world. Hein Schumacher has seen this happening year after year at Kraft Heinz. He realises that he actually fully agrees with Polman's position and accepts an invitation to become CFO of Royal FrieslandCampina, a cooperative, maker of dairy brands like Chocomel and Yazoo. Schumacher is disappointed in Kraft Heinz, he thinks they invest too little in product renewal, meaning that even their revenues are feeling the pinch. The only thing they care about is increasing the profit margin, they're completely obsessed with it. Schumacher had also been angered by the consultants from Accenture, who are hired in like butchers with sharp knives to keep on looking for further cuts to make without giving a thought to the business. The growing number of young Brazilian colleagues with a lot of power and relatively little experience doesn't help either. More than anything, though, Schumacher is tired, really tired. He himself has had to do terrible things over the past year and fire an enormous number of people.

Kraft Heinz still holds a place in his heart. The philosophy is a good one, as far as he's concerned. It's brilliant and inspiring, it changed him as a person. It's good that clear objectives are agreed with all the managers. Everyone is given six of them. Each meeting starts with the question: How are your targets looking? And everyone helps each other to hit them, not out of friendship, that's the death of meritocracy, but out of a shared focus on the bottom line. This creates a tremendous team spirit. He thinks it's good for people who are capable and work hard to be rewarded accordingly.

Schumacher even finds the thinking behind 'zero-based budgeting (ZBB)' refreshing in principle. It makes sense. Why would you give up what you were due in order to balance the previous year's budget? Follow that up thoroughly, ask questions. And working that way also frees up money for big investments. If they needed to, Kraft Heinz could splash out $4.5 million on a 10-second ad during the Super Bowl.

As far as he's concerned, there's only one big drawback to Kraft Heinz's model: their enormous profits should be invested in making the company, and the world in which the multinational operates, more sustainable. If they did that, Kraft Heinz would make themselves unbeatable, in the long term as well as the short term. They could do this precisely because they only have a handful of shareholders monitoring the company and their share price isn't overly dominated by the moods of the market.

But they, the owners, aren't doing this. All the money is disappearing into 3G Capital and Warren Buffett's pockets. They don't give a hoot about sustainability, poverty or climate issues. That's a matter for governments, they say. Schumacher fears that the Brazilians don't even understand the concept of sustainability. They live in a volatile world of uncertainty and inflation. They don't know how to operate without maintaining buffers. It's a survival mechanism. They aren't familiar with macroeconomic security in the same way the Europeans are. The job offer from FrieslandCampina had been a gift. Its vision of cooperation with farmers spoke to him. It immediately felt right, they're paying attention to what's important.

Mark Rutte is in no doubt: 'its companies and universities, not government, that are creating solutions for today's problems and for the future'. The

Dutch prime minister is giving a short speech during a conference in New York, organised by Unilever in autumn 2014 under the title Transformative Change for a Better Future. 'Business is leading the way, and not only from noble motives. To quote our host Paul Polman in his speech to the UN: it is not just about philanthropy or altruism. It makes business sense'.

The prime minister goes on: 'Sustainability is becoming mainstream. Consumers demand it. They want products made in a responsible way. And they stand up to companies who don't meet high standards. Sustainable innovations create income and jobs. So there's a future to be won and money to be made. In short, the Sustainable Development Goals can't be achieved without the private sector. Without the University of Wageningen's smart solutions. Without Unilever's Sustainable Living Plan.'

Gail Klintworth does have doubts. She is starting to be more and more irritated by Polman. She thinks calling Unilever a big NGO is flat out stupid. The chief sustainability officer thinks it almost sounds neocolonial. She tells him as much. She thinks he's wonderfully successful at creating awareness but now needs to make sure he doesn't start behaving too much like a Gandhi figure; people are going to start thinking that all this is temporary, that it lives and dies with him. Because a new boss is about to come along who'll want something different. She thinks Polman should be modest, so that the people he wins to his cause also get some time in the spotlight. She's warned Polman a couple of times already: it isn't about you, it can't all be about one person.

She also thinks that Polman is much too concerned with what the Davos crowd thinks. They're an elite that believes even more globalisation will present the solutions. Klintworth doesn't believe in that at all. A sustainable future has more to do with local initiatives, bottom-up, than with rich, powerful elites who think they can organise a better world from atop their 'global panels'. The advantages of scale previously only available to big business are now available to everyone. She admonishes Polman to spend more time on his own business, rather than going to all these Davos-type meetings. He needs to be talking less and listening more to what *Unilever* needs. But she's afraid he won't listen to her, to do that this CEO first needs to have a long conversation with his own ego.

Really, Klintworth mostly feels disappointed. If she had to give Unilever a mark out of 10 for the extent to which it has managed to operate more sustainably, she'd give it a seven. That's all well and good but the company could have done much better. She doesn't think Unilever is taking enough risks, it could have bought up far more small, truly sustainable companies like Ben & Jerry's. It should have had a little more patience when it came to improving the margin, thus making more space for big investments in R&D for products aimed at sustainability. Unilever regards itself as a radical force for renewal but how radical is it actually? It's still mostly just a bureaucratic company in which savings immediately disappear straight into the profit–loss calculation rather than being invested in the innovations they desperately need.

For their part, some of Klintworth's colleagues are wondering what exactly *she* has managed to achieve. She's a member of staff too, and, like everyone else in the company, is wrestling with the 'say-do-gap', the gap between thinking things and doing things. This staff is mostly made up of people who are frustrated because they have absolutely no executive power. They just have to keep on hoping the people responsible for revenue and profit will listen to them. And they often have zero inclination to listen to people like Klintworth, who are at one remove from the business.

On balance, Klintworth is proud that this commitment to 100 per cent traceable, sustainable palm oil is going to become a reality in a couple of years' time. But in the meantime she's become convinced that this won't mean an end to deforestation. Three-quarters of all palm oil goes to Indian and Chinese companies and they aren't showing any serious interest in the issue. She and Polman agree on this point. Deforestation is only going to stop once the whole system is on the brink. And that's only going to happen if the financial sector finally starts to take into account seriously the long-term risks of an unsustainable future.

After 28 years at Unilever, Gail Klintworth throws in the towel. The South African financial services giant Old Mutual has offered her a position looking into their sustainability. She tells Polman that although she has to leave, she'll remain his disciple in the world of high finance. She hopes that from there she'll be able to keep helping companies like Unilever to do more.

Miguel Veiga-Pestana is disappointed too. Polman's fine words are not being put into practice sufficiently. Both inside and outside Unilever they aren't winning enough support. One of his explanations for this is the lack of recognition of others' efforts. You have to listen and give others a voice. Paul Polman has become much too dominant. He sucks up all the oxygen in every room he enters, leaving too little for others to realise their potential. That lack of recognition turns them off, whether they're colleagues or competitors.

Veiga-Pestana has often pushed Polman to tell the organisers of the umpteenth 'global panel' on sustainability that they should invite another CEO. But he can see that Polman can't say no. He's become addicted to the limelight and to his sermons. Yet somehow Veiga-Pestana also understands why Polman can't give it up. Hadn't it been his childhood dream to become a priest? Things like that run deep. And Paul Polman is only human too.

For a while it worked well but now it's no longer effective. Veiga-Pestana notices that his colleagues are getting tired of it, just like he is. It's just like church, really. Some priest stands there declaring God's word and explaining top-down how the world works. This man mostly seems hell-bent on making his audience feel guilty about their own shortcomings. The audience listens and respects the priest but is happy to go outside again and get back to the real world, where it's all about 'market and struggle' after all.

Almost five years ago, Veiga-Pestana had set out his purpose on paper under Nick Craig's guidance. He had written that he wanted to become the head of sustainability at Unilever. But Klintworth's job is split into two parts and both of those roles go to other people. Veiga-Pestana decides to go and work for an actual NGO. He becomes director of communications at the Bill & Melinda Gates Foundation.

Kees Kruythoff, still the man in charge of the US operation, can understand these frustrations. Unilever has simply got far too many staff. They're all clever, ambitious people focused primarily on maintaining their own position. That leads to complication and lots of political wrangling. He notices that much of this wrangling tends to originate from Keith Weed. His colleague and friend Peter ter Kulve, the Asia boss, shares this concern. They see Weed as a smooth political operator: good at managing relationships but primarily focused on consolidating his own position. Both of them wonder why Unilever even has a chief marketing officer, a function without any concrete responsibilities. They understand that Polman made this appointment in 2010 in order to underline the fact that Unilever needed to focus more on marketing than on finance. But in doing so their boss created further complexity. Because actual responsibility for marketing operations is shared between the category managers and the brand managers in the regions and in the countries.

Keith Weed is tasked with making sure all the digital information they have about their customers is compiled and translated into usable information colleagues working in the markets can use to their advantage. By buying media centrally, he can ensure that Unilever, still the second biggest advertiser in the world, doesn't pay too much to big advertising companies or global players like Facebook or Google.

Weed, often clad in loud suit jackets, speaks passionately in interviews about the changing preferences of consumers and how Unilever tries to respond to them. He talks about the importance of using digital resources to get to know these consumers as well as possible. In an interview with the London Business School, under the title 'Managing Brands', Weed talks at length about the development of the Unilever brand. It used to be completely unknown, but thanks to the rise of the internet it had to start to take on a clear form; consumers increasingly wanted to know who was manufacturing their favourite products.

'That little U appears on more bits of packaging that any other logo.' Weed touches on the term 'purpose' as he explains that it's at the heart of the brand. But as the head of marketing goes on it seems like he has more interest in how this purpose comes across in adverts than in the purpose itself. He doesn't even mention the USLP. Even Polman is increasingly wondering whether Keith Weed isn't actually most focused on promoting himself. On the other hand, Weed is an incredibly hard worker, which Polman likes.

Meanwhile, Kruythoff is beavering away in the United States. He believes in the USLP heart and soul. Those around him are whispering that he might even be Polman's successor. They think 47-year-old Kruythoff is his favourite. And Polman did once exclaim that Kruythoff had the USLP in his DNA.

Working on the DNA of 'his' brands, Kruythoff asks himself three questions. Is there a clear 'functional advantage'? This is where it all began: a cleaning product like Cif needs to be good at cleaning. Since the 1980s, the 'emotional advantage' has been added to the mix. The adverts show gleaming taps in which you can see the reflection of the housewife as she does the cleaning. She needs to feel good about her efforts. Since the USLP, marketing and advertising needs to make the third pillar: 'social advantage'. Teaming up with third parties to tidy up neighbourhoods and cities, for example, should make the consumer to feel good about the wider responsibility being taken by the Cif brand. Kruythoff calls this dramatising the emotional advantage. That's the big challenge now. Just like Polman, Kruythoff can talk about this for hours, with great passion.

The Dutchman is proud of the success of Hellmann's mayonnaise, by far the biggest and relatively quickest growing mayonnaise, with annual revenues of $600 million in the United States. Hellmann's needs to be the tastiest (functional advantage) and, thanks to the proper, sustainable ingredients, should no longer be associated with junk food (emotional advantage). The mayonnaise contains eggs from free-range chickens, and from 2017 all of the soya used in the mayonnaise must come from sustainable, American farms. That last criteria turned out to be a tricky one to achieve. Back in 2011, there was still no agreed standard for sustainable soya, so Unilever once again teamed up with the World Wildlife Fund to find one, just as it had 20 years previously for sustainable fishing. Farmers who want to be considered for certification have to install software to monitor how much water they use, how much CO_2 they emit, etc. On the basis of this comparison, the farmers who do better than the standard are given a certificate.[4]

Kruythoff is proud of the third step. How do you make sure that mayonnaise is perceived as benefitting society? Hellmann's has taken on the task of helping Americans to throw away less food. The total amount of food thrown away worldwide adds up to one in three calories, an average of dozens of kilos per person, per year. Americans especially don't give this a second thought. By offering them recipes explaining how to make nice meals out of the leftovers of their often excessive Thanksgiving dinners over the days after the holiday, Hellmann's wants to show them what they can do themselves to combat the problem.

Hellmann's is growing quickly. The brand isn't included in the same division as spreads, particularly margarines, which is now being partitioned. It's been Dutchmen like Kruythoff, Zijderveld and Ter Kulve who have pleaded with Polman regularly over the past few years to give Unilever's Dutch roots another chance. But Polman's patience has run out. The division, which makes up 7 per cent of turnover, is being separated from the rest of Unilever. Now analysts can see Unilever's figures both with and without the frustrating, years-long decline of these spreads. Investors react enthusiastically to the news. The Unilever share price rockets. These analysts conclude that by doing this, he has brought the sale of the 142-year-old margarine division a step closer. Some of them go even further and conclude that parcelling off this division is the next step in bidding farewell to what was once the heart of the company: food. Still responsible for 35 per cent of revenue in 2008, this side of the business now contributes no more than 24 per cent.

'If my father could see me now, shaking hands with heads of state. He'd laugh his head off.' In a candid interview for *Happily Ever After: A Storybook for Adults* in November 2014, Polman is invited to tell nine- to twelve-year-old children about his greatest dilemma. He tells them:

> It's lonely being a CEO. After all, I'm the face, I have to make lots of decisions. I do a lot of things on my own. I am a big believer in solving problems, that you can do something, that it's possible. Not everyone goes along with that. I do too much on my own, bite off more than I can chew. So it's impossible for me not to disappoint people. Maybe I need to work with other people more.
>
> The biggest problem I face? I'm impatient, I want to do everything. And there's lots *to* do. Things aren't going well in the world. I now have influence over climate change, I feel responsible. I find it hard to say no. I only have 24 hours but I've got 48 hours of commitments. It's a shame people have to sleep, sleeping takes time. And to be completely honest, I'm

a bad listener. That comes from the fact that I know I am doing the right thing. I'm very strongly values-driven. I'm a man on a mission, a man in a hurry. It's difficult to say no to that.

People find working for me difficult but they also know I'm not doing it all for myself. That helps them to accept my impatience, my anger. I can be really tough on people, they call me the bulldozer. I quickly fly off the handle with people who don't give me my way. Really viciously. When I look at myself in those moments I'm reminded of my father and how he was when I didn't finish everything on my plate. That made him furious. And it's stayed with me, you know? Plates must be emptied, whether it's my plate or my children's plates.

The most difficult thing in life is realising that it isn't about you. For a long time, you're self-obsessed. But it's really all about other people. I always want to be myself and be able to show the same face to everyone, to my colleagues, to my shareholders, and to my wife. Otherwise it's too tiring. So this is what I do, and it makes me feel 100% free. I'm a free agent, that's been the case my whole life. I don't belong to a specific club, I've never golfed. While studying in Groningen I was a member of two different fraternities. I was the only one who was.

I didn't need to take on all this work just to make money. I don't have a contract at Unilever. I never put my signature to anything. The board as some kind of employer monitoring me? No thanks. I don't even regard this as work, I'm a volunteer. That applies to the people around me too. It's all so fleeting. The moment I'm not a CEO anymore, they will stop calling, three quarters of my Rolodex will have disappeared. I don't look back on principal. It doesn't get you anywhere. But sometimes, just sometimes, I think: if only I'd become a doctor. Yes, really! Maybe I can still do it, once I'm done here.

When he hears that a friend said that if he'd become a priest, he'd be pope by now, his eyes get misty. For a moment he can't speak. 'Yes, well, I can't know that of course. But I do see him, the pope. We're in touch.'

Paul Polman summarises his dilemma for the children with: 'How do you listen to other people properly if you're 100% sure about your personal belief?' One of the children, 11-year-old Karo, gives him advice: 'Why do you think that the world is going to end if you can't sort everything out in one day? That's dangerous. Because the quicker you work, the worse the end product. You need to work quickly but thoroughly.' Kiki, also 11, says: 'Why should you disappoint someone if it's not necessary. As the captain of my hockey team I have a responsibility, particularly to listen. You don't always need to be friendly as a leader, but you do need to take everyone into account. So think about the tone in which you say things.' And nine-year-old Bedirhan says: 'You really need to realise that you *can* listen. If you don't think you can listen properly then you're not going to listen properly.'[5]

When Unilever's spokespeople are called by journalists wanting to know whether their CEO really didn't sign any kind of contract, they are blown away. They weren't involved in this interview in any way. And of course he signed a proper contract regarding his working conditions, it's a legal require- ment. They're becoming more and more concerned about this CEO who's acting completely independently and telling his own version of events.

Kees Storm thinks the Unilever board, and Paul Polman particularly, need to do far more to make sure they're hearing opposing views. It's happening too little as it stands. In an ordinary meeting of 10–12 people you can eas- ily sit back in your chair, nodding along and agreeing. You hear a little from one director, a little from another, the time passes quickly enough. He thinks Polman is far too dominant. That isn't good, not for the CEO and not for the board. It's important to create moments in which they actually test each other's mettle. That takes time. Over the past few years he's suggested in vain during each of the Unilever board's internal evaluations that they take a couple of days each year to get down to brass tacks and see what they all really think. He's experienced the enormous advantages of doing this as the chairman of the board of AB InBev. Just last December that outfit, including the CEO, all went to visit Jim Collins for three days. The author of books like *Build to Last* and *Good to Great* no longer likes to travel so they had to go and seek him out in Boulder, Colorado.

Four Brazilians, four Belgians and four independent directors including Storm spend three days sitting at the feet of the guru. Even the three founders of 3G Capital, Jorge Lemann, Carlos Alberto da Veiga Sicupira and Marcel Herrmann Telles, almost always join them. On Saturday Lemann takes his private jet to go and pick up Warren Buffett from Omaha, Nebraska. The programme is the same each time. There are three central questions: What has gone well, what hasn't gone well and what are we going to do? They keep dividing and redividing into little groups in the same room and spend three days chewing over these questions together. There's so much time that nobody can avoid having to give their opinion. Collins does nothing more than ask questions and summarise their answers: he turns out to be very good at distill- ing the essence of what they say and keeping the conversation flowing. The 2007 meeting is graven into Storm's memory. Collins asked the group what it was they actually wanted to achieve. The answer was: we want to be a key player in the beer industry. In response, Collins had gaped in feigned astonishment and asked why they hadn't bought out a big player like SABMiller or Anheuser-Busch. A couple of months later InBev had decided to opt for the latter. And in summer 2008 they'd put their $52 billion on the table.

These are the sort of ventures Unilever's Jean-Marc Huët has been given no scope for at all over the past few years. By the beginning of 2015, the relationship between the CEO and CFO has seriously deteriorated, they don't see eye to eye anymore. Polman has come to the conclusion that Huët is mostly just lazy. He might say clever things but he isn't doing anything.

Kees Storm doesn't agree with Polman on this but he's coming to the final months of his tenure. Chairman Michael Treschow agrees with Polman, as does Ann Fudge and some of the other members of the ULE, the top 12. As Treschow sees it, Huët isn't creating the platform Unilever needs and he's spending too much time complaining about Paul not being a team player and not listening to him.

Louise Fresco thinks it's a crying shame that things are going wrong between the two executive directors. She sees it as predominantly a clash between two very different personalities, one extroverted, the other introverted. Huët is reserved and internal looking, he refuses to give Polman the reassurance he needs as CEO. She believes he does share the same dedication to sustainability, however. It would have been good if Treschow had shut the two of them up in a room for couple of days, so the two of them could have asked each other why they were working for Unilever, that way they might have discovered that they wanted the same things, and that they even complemented one another. She would have liked to organise this meeting of minds herself, come to that, but really you need the chairman's authority to do that kind of thing.

Polman doesn't think this would have helped. He is completely washed his hands of Huët. He's convinced Huët sees the USLP as so much softy nonsense. The former banker has remained a true finance man. He thinks the best thing Huët can do is leave. Polman is angry with himself. He didn't do his homework properly five years ago. This is the big risk, he thinks, of hiring someone born with a silver spoon in their mouth.

CHAPTER 13

MORE PRIEST THAN CEO

March–December 2015

Ann Fudge is really angry now. Polman is being irresponsible. Once again, he's turned down the raise proposed by the board. It's the sixth time he's done this. Polman the man might well feel that he earns enough already but this isn't about what he thinks. He's the CEO of a publicly listed company. He needs to realise that investors and analysts are comparing his salary to that of other CEOs in their peer group. That salary needs to make sense to *them* and increase as he meets his targets. This progression reflects a CEO's success. His remuneration is published in the annual report, it's the most eye-catching part of the entire Unilever pay structure. All Unilever's employees, from the top of the company to the bottom, want to see the potential for them to earn more. That alone is reason enough to tie the boss's salary clearly to the results. Not to mention that they'll eventually start looking for his successor and they won't understand why the salary is below the going rate either. What's going on here?

Her fellow director Paul Walsh, chairman of the Compensation Committee, agrees completely with Fudge's analysis. He wants no part of this. In the 2014 annual report, he refers to the report from 2011. Even back then, he'd been proposing increasing Polman's base salary after consulting with concerned shareholders: an increase of 6 per cent, to €1.2 million. Polman had refused. And continued to refuse during the intervening years. Walsh writes: 'At that time the Committee stated that it would look to make further increases, as appropriate, to address this over the next few years. Since then, largely at the CEO and CFO's own insistence, we have consistently awarded less of a salary increase than we believed was merited by the performance of the Executive Directors.' He doesn't understand Polman's attitude at all. 'Having held their salaries steady for longer than intended and in view of the sustained track record of performance delivery, the Committee recommended, and the Boards approved, salary increases for the CEO and CFO with effect from January 2015. In making these recommendations the Committee considered the strong performance of Unilever and alignment, both to increases in pay for the broader employee population and externally.' Once again, the board was turned down flat. 'The CEO and CFO have turned down the salary increases recommended by the Committee for 2015.'

Paul Walsh and Paul Polman; the two men don't see eye to eye. At all. Colleagues describe 60-year-old Walsh as a street fighter. A bruiser. The son of a plumber and a stay-at-home mother, Walsh had once dreamed of being a fighter pilot. His eyesight wasn't good enough so he'd ended up in business. He'd spent 12 years as the boss of Diageo, makers of brands like Johnnie Walker and Guinness. After he was appointed there, he'd sold off the entire food division and thrown himself into the task of renewing and marketing their biggest drinks brands. Diageo had bought more than twenty-five companies with him at the helm. By the time he quit, two years ago, they'd quadrupled their share price and Diageo's value had increased from £20 to £50 billion in the last three years of his leadership alone. He himself had been taking home £15 million a year, almost twice the amount Polman is earning now. When he left Diageo, *The Guardian* wrote, 'Finding anyone to criticise Paul Walsh is hard.'

They weren't entirely right. Polman isn't a fan, he thinks Walsh is a terrible person: a director with the wrong set of values. While he suspects some other directors of harbouring a certain distaste for the philosophy behind the USLP, with Walsh he knows this is the case because he tells him as much directly. Walsh thinks the USLP is nonsense. From Polman's point of view, this means that continuing to work with him is impossible. He's managed to persuade the board that it would be best if Walsh didn't complete his contract, set to finish in 2018. The long-standing darling of the British stock exchange leaves in style, slamming every door behind him as he goes. Nobody outside the company is allowed to get wind of this, however.

Ann Fudge takes over from Walsh as the chairmen of the Compensation Committee. The American never ceases to be amazed by the way intelligent men like these end up losing their heads when they encounter conflict. The way two Pauls lash out at each other is like two rutting stags. There's zero willingness to listen.

Fudge will handle things differently, she's found her own way to calm Polman down. It's often difficult to make any kind of point during meetings. Tempers tend to run high and Polman often allows his passion to run away with him. Fudge knows that men like Paul Polman find it hard to listen to one another in these situations. They're solely focused on the outcome of the fight to be proven right. They're competing to see who the winner is.

Fudge doesn't allow herself to be sucked into these kinds of fights. Whenever tempers run high like that, she makes it clear that she's not backing down, then waits for a quieter moment to make her point properly. Often, that quieter moment comes when she's sharing a car with the CEO on the way to a meeting. Then she has his ear and there's no competition from any of the men. Polman listens to her then. Of course, this doesn't always mean he'll take what she says on board.

Polman, meanwhile, thinks he earns more than enough money. He doesn't think increasing his basic salary sends the right message either. As far as he's concerned, his and his colleagues' remuneration should only increase when the share price is going up. Isn't driving up the share price what the shareholder's interested in too?! If you don't believe those two things go together, you don't belong at Unilever. Over the long term, they're all going to share in the company's success.

Polman takes home €2 million more in 2014 than 2013 anyway, mind you. The vast majority of his €9.5 million remuneration package is variable, almost €6 million is paid as a result of targets he's met or exceeded during the year. In terms of things like cash flow and turnover, Unilever has grown more than 25 per cent over the past three years.

He's required to invest at least 25 per cent of his pre-tax bonus in Unilever shares; all Unilever CEOs are required to have at least four times their annual salary invested in the company. Polman goes above and beyond, he's taken on a tidy 200,000 shares over the past year, partially through his bonus and partially by buying them directly. At this point, he owns 755,487 shares, two-thirds of them in the Dutch NV and the rest in the British *PLC*. On paper, these shares are now worth around €23 million.

Ten years ago when he left P&G, Polman had already decided he didn't need any more money. He thinks it's stupid to leave a huge fortune to his children, they need to go and make their own money, so he gives a lot of what he earns to good causes. He estimates that he donates around €1 million a year to the Kilimanjaro Blind Trust. He and his wife Kim sit on the board of the foundation with Erik Weihenmayer, the man who he climbed Kilimanjaro with 10 years previously. Over the years, they've helped thousands of blind, mostly destitute children.

Polman has no shortage of good causes. One of them is his large extended family. When appropriate, he chips in to help his nieces and nephews get a good education. He also pays for all the family's travel when they meet up somewhere overseas. After all, it was he who decided not to live in the Netherlands.

In May 2015, he tells the *Washington Post* that he's ashamed of how much money he makes, 'People at our level shouldn't be motivated by salary. If you would pay me double, I'm not going to work twice as much, because I'm already probably maximising my time available. I've often said that even if I didn't get paid, I would still do the job. I'm still ashamed when the topic comes up. I always feel embarrassed, to be honest. The board is trying to change the compensation and move it up, and we have steadfastly refused to do that – not for heroic reasons, but I think there has to be some sanity. The board believes this is affecting my behaviour, they tend to think if CEO's don't get a salary increase, or if they don't earn a lot of money, they are not being seen as good-performing CEOs.'

Polman worries about the way these comparisons lead to leapfrogging: 'That is really what has happened over the last decade or two. You have to break that. You don't have to just go with the waves. I've always felt, as a philosophy in life, it's better to make the dust than eat the dust. If you are fortunate enough to be in our position, you probably belong to the 2% of the world population that is well educated, financially independent, can do what they want, can live and work where they want. If you belong to that 2%, then it is your duty to put yourself to the service to the other 98.'

'Less than 30% of people are happy at work nowadays, which is a frightening statistic given the time that we spend there. And often that is because the values that you permeate at home with your family are not the same as the ones at work. That's sad, because it means you either have to wear a mask or you have to be a good actor, and that's going to catch up with you at one point in time.'

He goes on to take aim at bankers' bonuses: 'We have 175,000 people who are directly on our payroll. Our total salary bill, everybody included (myself as well), is less than the bonuses that were just paid to the financial industry in London. And I'm just talking the bonuses. The financial industry talks about not being able to attract talent, and how they're worried about all the restrictions on that compensation. What they really should be worried about is communicating and lifting the purpose for that industry. If that purpose is strong enough, you'll be able to attract the right people. We're looking ourselves to strengthen and continuously work at that. But, for example, if you work at an insurance company that sells products you wouldn't even sell to your wife or your mother, how happy would you feel to work there? It's going to eat you up over time.'[1]

These kinds of declarations make no sense to people in high finance. Why on earth is the boss of Unilever ashamed of his income? Why on earth would he do his job for free? Shareholders invest in Unilever expecting to make a good return. If the boss then starts behaving like he's in charge of a government ministry or a charity rather than a company, and explicitly says he doesn't see making money as a priority, is it still a good investment? If someone isn't interesting in making money for himself, how can he still be interested in doing his best for the people who've invested their money in him? Ann Fudge almost falls off her chair when she reads the *Washington Post* interview. She calls Polman out for his reckless behaviour, this isn't good for Unilever. He promises her it won't happen again.

Fudge and her fellow directors are starting to realise that they're never going to manage to corral Polman back into the traditional CEO role. The adulation he's getting within, but especially outside the company, has become too great for that. This means they're particularly pleased with Jean-Marc Huët's successor as CFO, Graeme Pitkethly, who gives them more detail about how things are going. The new CFO not only makes a good impression on them but manages to build a good working relationship with John Rishton, the head of the Audit Committee. The two of them give the board more insight into how things are actually going, which reassures them greatly. The board has also agreed that once they've announced a successor to Treschow next year, Polman will give up the reins to a successor in 2017.

The results for 2014 are disappointing. The underlying turnover growth is 2.9 per cent, the lowest in 10 years. Declining sales in emerging markets are particularly concerning to analysts; those are the engine of Unilever's growth. Unilever is still beating its competitors but the era of quick growth seems to be over. Even more worryingly: Polman has declared himself to be less optimistic for the current year. The growth engine is struggling. Sales in emerging markets were still growing by 12 per cent in 2011, they're expecting no more than 1–2 per cent this year.

Analysts are suddenly wondering what this means for all the CEO's big ambitions, especially as those are mostly related to the USLP. The firm had promised to halve the environmental footprint of its whole supply chain by 2020. They've made great strides in terms of sustainable sourcing, almost 50 per cent of the agricultural produce they purchase now comes from sustainable growers, three times as much as in 2010. Their own greenhouse gas emissions are down 40 per cent, water consumption is down 31 per cent. But this seems to have been the last of the low-hanging fruit.

Looking at the whole supply chain, these figures look a lot different: greenhouse gas emissions per consumer have risen by 4 per cent since 2010 and total water consumption is only down 2 per cent. Analysts are worried. Is this CEO going to incur even more costs in order to speed up his USLP agenda?[2] What will investors do then? Is there still scope for a further increase in share price? It was €18 when Polman arrived over six years ago and now its €41.

They laugh as all three of them admit that they used to be altar servers. Lilianne Ploumen, the Dutch minister for overseas trade and development, Paul Polman and the former Mexican president Felipe Calderón Hinojosa are sharing a taxi to the Vatican. They're on their way to meet Pope Francis, a selection of cardinals, representatives of various governments and businesspeople to discuss climate change and how it relates the economic growth necessary to help put an end to global poverty.

The meeting, organised by the Dutch government, the World Resource Institute and The New Climate Economy, comes ahead of the pope's encyclical *Laudato Si'*, due to be published in a couple of weeks' time. Ploumen is struck by the fact that you're not allowed to take any photos during a meeting with the pontiff. Photos are taken for you to buy afterwards. These people, at least, seem to have a clear understanding of how to make money.

Kitty van der Heijden is a key figure behind the event. She's the European director at the World Resource Institute and has been on the Unilever Netherlands board since 2014. She's also good friends with Prince Jaime de Bourbon de Parme, the Dutch ambassador to the Holy See in Vatican City. Van der Heijden is no Catholic herself, but she's pragmatic. She's convinced that the world only has 10 or 15 years left to get to grips with big issues like climate change and the pope, a moral leader to over 1.2 billion followers worldwide, can help accelerate this process. On her advice, Polman has brought a rosary with him for the pope to bless. His mum will be delighted with it.

The participants are pleased to see that Christ's representative on Earth is concerned about the levels of poverty persisting worldwide and interested in the impact of climate change on this issue. But they also notice that the word 'economy' is nowhere in evidence in the pope's message, let alone no mention of the business world.

Can you make money by addressing poverty? Can making the world a better place be profitable? This is a difficult proposition to square with the gospel. Jesus's message in the Bible is unmistakeable: 'No man can serve two masters: for either he will hate the one, and love the other; or else he will hold to the one, and despise the other, ye cannot serve God and mammon.'[3]

Polman doesn't see any tension between the two. Christ kicked the money lenders out of the temple, sure, but that's because they didn't belong there. You can't turn a temple into a den of thieves. But Christ didn't mean that earning money was a bad thing, so long as you use it to do good. As a former altar boy, Polman still believes in God but he wouldn't say he was a practising Catholic. Organised religion uses fear to demand good behaviour: you're going to heaven or you're going to hell. He doesn't believe in that sort of thing. All it does is paralyse people, it doesn't do any good.

Polman admires Pope Francis, he's obviously a man who wants to effect change. He also understands that as an Argentinian, the pope is used to being surrounded by poor people. It's no wonder he's so focused on combatting poverty and it's equally understandable that this experience has coloured his perception of business. If Polman himself had become a priest, he'd probably have been much more left-wing himself. The pope doesn't fully understand the untapped potential of private companies to help the world and Polman is going to be the one to explain it to him.

The CEO of Unilever is satisfied when he reads the Laudato Si' several weeks later. He recognises his messages and reads: 'Never have we so hurt and mistreated our common home as we have in the last two hundred years. Yet we are called to be instruments of God our Father, so that our planet might be what he desired when he created it and correspond with his plan for peace, beauty and fullness. The problem is that we still lack the culture needed to confront this crisis. [...] The exploitation of the planet has already exceeded acceptable limits and we still have not solved the problem of poverty [...] we need to reject a magical conception of the market, which would suggest that problems can be solved simply by an increase in the profits of companies or individuals. Is it realistic to hope that those who are obsessed with maximising profits will stop to reflect on the environmental damage which they will leave behind for future generations? Where profits alone count, there can be no thinking about the rhythms of nature, its phases of decay and regeneration, or the complexity of ecosystems which may be gravely upset by human intervention. [...] We lack leadership capable of striking out on new paths and meeting the needs of the present with concern for all and without prejudice towards coming generations. [...] Politics and business have been slow to react in a way commensurate with the urgency of the challenges facing our world. Although the post-industrial period may well be remembered as one of the most irresponsible in history, nonetheless there is reason to hope that humanity at the dawn of the twenty-first century will be remembered for having generously shouldered its grave responsibilities.'[4]

The pope hopes his message will help inspire the world leaders, who will meet in Paris in a couple of months to discuss the climate issues, to reach an agreement. He also hopes his public stance will help them speed up the ratification of the UN Sustainable Development Goals. Paul Polman hopes so too.

It's his dream that in 2016 these goals will form the basis for unambiguous, global rules of play that will put an end to poverty and curb global warming.

'Of course we are not going to realise our USLP goals for 2020. I knew that from the start. And I am not ashamed to make this confession, if you make a plan with a 10 year horizon, many things will change in between. The ambitious goals are meant to change our way of thinking.' He goes on to say that Unilever doesn't only work for its shareholders, and CEOs can't be slaves to their investors.

It's summer 2015, and the journalist from *Forbes Magazine* is rather alarmed by these statements. He asks Polman whether good intentions can't sometimes lead to bad results. He replies: 'My biggest doubt is, when you have to make a decision based on a sense of purpose or values – Do you have the right values? What gives you the right to believe that what you're doing is right? That is where I have my biggest doubts, always because it should not be about yourself. And sometimes even your own convictions are wrong. So my biggest doubts are, as we are pushing all these things, is it my own agenda or is it something that is needed for the company long term? And that's always a very fine line, because we are all products of things that have influenced us and given us a certain perspective across our whole life. So your doubt is more towards yourself – is it arrogance? Is it ego? Those are the worst things that creep into a person. And then it blurs decision making. Often it leads to the wrong decisions.' Polman prefers to look ahead: 'We're doing a lot on climate change and calling for prices on carbon and trying to get the COP 21 [the upcoming Conference of the Parties to the 1992 United Nations Framework Convention on Climate Change] in Paris to be successful, working a lot with these governments. That requires courage, because sometimes you don't have all these answers and there's a high level of scepticism as a result. And there's probably a lot of vested interests that will work against you. So you have to find a way to enrol, to change, to make them part of it, or not, but to create a majority to move things forward.'[5]

Polman is optimistic. The United Nations Sustainable Development Goals are going to come into effect in 2016 and, with a bit of luck, the governments meeting in Paris at the end of the year will manage to reach agreements on combatting global warming. Half of all the greenhouse gases ever produced through human actions were emitted over the last thirty years. It's clear to him that the current system isn't going to solve the climate problem or raise 800 million people out of poverty, let alone offer the next four billion people born on Earth the prosperity that is their inalienable right. More urgently still, the United Nations is warning that there will be between 200 million and 1 billion climate refugees by 2050 if the world gets any hotter.[6] All these displaced people will be looking for food, water and a way to make a living. If, for example, Bangladesh were to end up under water, 10 million people would have to relocate.[7] And that's just one country.

Quite aside from the tremendous human cost of this suffering, the financial cost for the whole world would be astronomical. If we manage to limit the increase in temperature to 1.5 degrees Celsius rather than 2 degrees, then the world economy will be $20 trillion better off.[8] An increase of 3.7 degrees could lead to inconceivable damages, around $551 trillion. By way of comparison, in 2017 the entire world's financial assets were estimated by Credit Suisse to be $280 trillion.

With those kinds of figures in mind, Polman is convinced that the world is going to wake up to the challenges they face. It has to. And imagine if they manage to make global agreements to tax greenhouse gas emissions, things like CO_2. This is exactly the type of measure that Unilever has been waiting for to help level the field. Their USLP would place them ahead of the curve and they'd start making headway again.

Polman uses these kind of predictions to buoy up his board and get them on side, not that this is all that difficult anymore. Most of the eleven non-executive directors currently on the Unilever board were appointed by him, a fact he sees as only logical. You need a board that gets on well with the CEO and he has no desire to waste time managing 'his' board. Bringing on Feike Sijbesma on as a non-executive at the end of the previous year had been a good decision for that reason. Polman has gotten to know the CEO of DSM well in recent years, not least from their time spent teaming up to create the DSGC. Both of them share the same values and have since become good friends.

DSM is about five years ahead of Unilever in terms of sustainability. Sijbesma's predecessor Peter Elverding had been spreading the message 'people, planet, profit' all the way back in 2000. Sijbesma had come in and made the chemical concern, which sells raw materials to other companies keen to produce 'healthy food' or source good materials (for example for carpets), even more sustainable. Inspired in part by Elverding's vision, Sijbesma decided where he stood 17 years ago. As a trained as a microbiologist, he was firm in his Darwinian belief that only the ones that adapt the best survive. He soon became highly successful within DSM. For a while, he was very pleased with himself but after the arrival of his first son he was confronted with his own mortality. One day his children would ask him what he had achieved, he then wanted to be able to give them a better answer than 'I increased sales and profits at DSM'.

When Sijbesma was invited to take over as CEO at DSM in 2007, he told the board he wanted to do two things: he wanted to lead the company to success *and* make the world a better place. The board members had demanded that he focused on making money; if that went well then he could turn to his other commitment. But Sijbesma refused to choose between them, instead announcing his intention to help 30 million people improve their nutrition, a number far exceeding the one million people they had previously pledged to provide with better food. For a short while he had been convinced he was going to be the shortest-serving CEO in Dutch history, but as it turned out, his leadership at DSM meant they were able to prove that both commitments – making money and doing good – could go together. Sijbesma is convinced that his philosophy will be common practice in 10 years' time. He and Paul Polman are often mentioned in the same breath by the media.

Sijbesma also hopes that the Paris Agreement will immediately make a difference and prompt countries to start addressing climate change more urgently. On a UN trip to Bangladesh back in 2011, he'd had an experience that had changed his life and revealed this urgency to him. A homeless woman had suddenly tried to press a baby into his arms with the words 'you know'. He had no idea what to do and asked his interpreter what this woman meant. In the exchange that followed, it became clear that the woman wanted him to take her baby with him so that it could have a chance for a better life; it would likely die if it stayed here. Her words, 'you know', were her way of saying that he, as a member of the elite from the wealthy West, must understand her plea.

He regularly looks back on that moment in which the fact that someone on Earth dies of starvation every five seconds became more than a statistic to him, when famine gained a human face. Ever since, Sijbesma has been acutely aware of the fact that these poverty-stricken people have no voice at the table and are at the mercy of the rich elite. This elite is about to gather in Paris, and their job is to ensure that this woman no longer has to live with such heartbreaking worries.

Polman isn't the only one frustrated by shareholders calling for quicker results. Sijbesma has to deal with this regularly too. 'A while back, I was sitting around a table with a couple of shareholders who thought we were spending too much time on sustainability and were worried this might harm our results. The first thing I did was ask them whether they had kids and whether they were worried about climate change and the future of energy supply. Of course, they said they were. So then I asked whose job it is to solve those problems. Governments can't do it alone, they have to get re-elected all the time, so I asked them whether they didn't agree that we as a company had a duty to do something. They said it was someone else's job to step in and do something about it. Complete nonsense, of course, we all need to take responsibility for what's happening. Otherwise we're screwed. They shrugged it off and closed by telling me they hoped their message had been clear, that they were interested in profits and returns, nothing else. I fundamentally disagree with this position. I truly believe that as a company with have a bigger role to play.'[9]

Shareholders need to stop coming to him complaining that it's all too complicated and they prefer to keep things simple. Like Polman, Sijbesma thinks the shareholders are the ones who need to change their attitude the most. But there is a big difference. While Polman is convinced that the current system needs to change and he should be the one to lead the charge, Sijbesma thinks they need to put all their efforts into pushing the limits of the existing rules, and that it isn't a CEO's job to try and play a new game. In doing so, you run the risk of being sidelined.

Sijbesma thinks that Polman is being praised so effusively that he's started believing his own hype and lost touch with reality. A CEO needs to be in tune with the real world and the realities of doing business, it's a boundary Sijbesma constantly tries to keep an eye on himself. It's not easy when everyone is cheering you on, the temptation is strong, but shareholders don't hire CEOs for their world-shaking visions for sustainability. Perceptions can sour at a moment's notice. Polman is running a real risk by allowing himself to be seen as anything other than the leader of a company and that risk is growing by the day.

It's obvious to Sijbesma that the rest of the board is uneasy too but there's no mechanism for reining in the CEO on this score. The share price is healthy, employee satisfaction is at a record high and as non-executive directors, even in a one-tier board, they have to base their assumptions on the information from the directors involved in the daily running of the company. If management says things are going well then it's hard to pierce the veil. The executive directors are saying that the promised growth is going to come and they're saying it with conviction.

Sijbesma is realising that reaching targets like those set out in the USLP is a good deal more complicated for a company like Unilever with a huge supply chain and so many well-known consumer brands, than it is for DSM. Integrating sustainability is going to take a massive amount of work.

His fellow director Louise Fresco is completely on the same page: Unilever is a long way from managing to integrate the USLP in its supply chain, even in terms of sourcing raw materials. Sustainable palm oil continues to frustrate them. The CEO is going to have to push much harder and put much more pressure on certain people for this saga to reach a satisfactory end.

Lilianne Ploumen knows both Polman and Sijbesma very well. Six months ago at a tête-á-tête during the World Economic Forum, the two of them had horrified the Dutch minister for Overseas trade and Development by expressing their fears for their own positions. As they discussed the news of a recent surprise takeover of a large company, the CEOs had told her that their position was far from safe either. Sadly, they had explained that the moment their shareholders stop being on board with their sustainability plans, they'll be out on their ear. Ploumen was shocked. She never would have suspected that these bosses saw the behaviour of their shareholders as a risk. Even these big shots, great mean capable of winning anyone to their cause, don't see themselves as invincible.

Ploumen has been working closely with Unilever for almost two years at this point. Polman has proven to be a trustworthy partner and they've made around twenty joint appearances at various summits and public events. All this is very new for her. She's a Worker's Party (PvDA) MP with years of experience working for the Dutch aid organisation Cordaid; back then she saw working with private companies as a step too far. It simply wasn't done. Since then, however, she's become convinced that you need key players from the business world if you want to change things. She realises that when it comes to something like raising the wages of low-income tea pickers, its companies like Unilever that make it happen.

The minister also needs people like Polman to put pressure on the rest of the business world. Businessmen only listen to the biggest bully in the playground and Polman is the most successful one of all. The fact they'll only listen to a man like him is fine by her. She can tell a lot of them are jealous of Polman and would love for an organisation like Oxfam Novib to pat them on the head and tell them they're doing well. Or at least doing better than they were to start with. The tell-all report Oxfam put out on Unilever's human rights record in Vietnam proved to Ploumen that openness builds trust. Polman's logic is pretty much unassailable: if we don't solve these problems now, there will be nothing left in 30 years' time, not even Unilever. She thinks he's a genuine guy, authentic in his quest to save the world. The fact that he's a tough customer at the negotiation table doesn't do any harm either. He doesn't budge under pressure and he doesn't compromise when it comes to making good on his promises. Every Unilever operation she visits overseas is obviously hard at work implementing the USLP, she hears about it everywhere she goes. Ploumen is keen to hold the company up to the rest of the business world as an example; its success is proof that there's another way.

Foreign NGOs often criticise her close relationship with Unilever. They think the way the firm targets low-income customers is irresponsible. It markets its cheap, small packages of things like washing powder too aggressively, and without thinking about the huge environmental damage caused by all those little packets. Ploumen can see the other side, too: it's only natural for mothers to want their children to go to school clean and with clean clothes. To her, this is all about the bottom of the pyramid. Meeting people's basic needs is how you create prosperity and how you make money. Unilever is focusing on where it all begins, and doing it well.

When Unilever moots the possibility of formalising their relationship with the government, Ploumen agrees to give it a try. For the first time in history, the Dutch government agrees to enter a strategic partnership with a multinational company. They make joint resolutions on issues including deforestation and sustainability in the tea industry. Unilever will even exchange staff with Den Haag in a series of secondments designed to allow the two organisations to learn from one another. Ploumen sees this as a blue print for future partnerships with private companies and hopes others will be inspired by it. Even so, she doesn't yet dare bring this idea to the DSGC chaired by Jan Peter Balkenende. She doesn't think that the coalition's members are quite on the same level as Unilever and Polman; their appreciation of the situation is still developing.

In September 2015, Paul Polman receives the United Nations 'Champion of the Earth' Award, the UN's highest honour for people active in global sustainability. He wins the 'Entrepreneurial Vision' category and the judges praise his 'personal commitment' and 'bold leadership', saying 'as Unilever CEO, he is demonstrating the need for long-term corporate thinking that accounts for social and environmental concerns'.

In his acceptance speech, Polman dedicates his award to all the people 'who couldn't make it here tonight because they're either too hungry, didn't make it past the age of five, or didn't have a chance like all of us to go to school and participate in the workforce'.

'The pope was talking about many things and one of the things he was talking about was the moral framework that we have to put in place. The SDG are probably the only chance we have to have a global moral framework.' Polman quotes the astrophysicist Hubert Reeves: 'man is the most insane species. He worships an invisible god and destroys a visible nature, not realising that the physically nature he destroys is the same god he's worshipping.'

'We have a unique opportunity to address one of the major challenges in about eight weeks' time at the COP21 in Paris. Business increasingly understands that there is no business case in enduring poverty. Business also increasingly understands that they cannot be a bystander anymore in a system that gives them life in the first place. A thousand companies signed the call from the World Bank to put a price on carbon, we have 400 companies that have an internal price on carbon. Momentum is building.'

Polman refers to Viktor Frankl and the importance of a 'Statue of Responsibility'. 'Unilever has the liberty to operate in all the countries of the world – reaching 190 countries a 2 billion consumers a day – but by doing so we should also be aware of our responsibility, a simple responsibility to irreversibly eradicate poverty in a more sustainable and equitable way. Any system where too many people still feel that they are not participating or are excluded, which is still the case today, will ultimately rebel against itself and we see that more and more. It's a great celebration here tonight but I hope that we can all come back here in 15 years and simply say: "we did it."'[10]

Inspired by the birth of his first grandchild, Polman writes an open letter to her in the year 2030, when she'll be 15: 'You were born in 2015, born in 2015 – a year that I hope comes to be seen as a turning point in history. Above all, I hope that we live in a world that is more equitable, safe and peaceful. This is a world in which business thrives, working within our planetary boundaries, not against.'[11]

Polman is in his element. He loves working with government ministers and NGOs and sees it as the best use of his time. He finds as time goes on that people he meets struggle to believe him when he says he's also the CEO of Unilever. He takes their surprised looks as a compliment.

Unilever director Louise Fresco has mixed feelings when he tells her about this. She thinks it's risky for Polman to focus so much on these people's opinions. They shouldn't be his most important sounding board. It seems like he's becoming a man with two faces and losing himself in the process. On the one hand, he's a celebrated activist, trying to save the world, on the other he's a tough, calculating CEO, hectoring his employees to cut costs. It seems like he's constantly having to change hats and it's eroding the trust people have in him. To them, he seems almost schizophrenic, and Fresco is afraid he's not spending enough time reconciling these two messages. It's hard for him to take the necessary step back, he's too emotionally involved to be pragmatic.

Keeping everyone on side is a huge balancing act. When Polman does something like call Unilever a giant NGO, he makes new friends in the activist world but alienates his business allies. When he insists they raise their share price, that side is encouraged but the other side grows suspicious. He's being torn in two trying to win the trust of two worlds that don't trust one other. Worse still, the incentives he's offering them are currently hypothetical; even he says they'll only reap the rewards of working together in 10 or 20 years' time, once they've learned to speak the same language. The only he's already speaking.

Polman is still being lauded by NGOs, universities and governments wherever he goes and he's even managed to inspire a handful of competitors to invest more urgently in sustainable projects. Customers seem to be responding positively to Unilever's sustainability campaign, or at any rate the brands the company has flagged internally as their most sustainable are selling faster than the rest. The big challenge when it comes to persuading people remains the world of finance. Those making the calculations there aren't so easily sold on delayed gratification or anything that can't easily be reduced to numbers. For them it's all about the bottom line. The moment Polman announced he was going to stop publishing his quarterly figures, he became the object of intense suspicion.

Larry Fink and Leen Meijaard exchange glances. What is this all about? A couple of days ago, Fink, the founder and CEO of BlackRock, the largest asset management company in the world with a portfolio of around $5 trillion, had asked his Dutch colleague whether he knew Paul Polman. Meijaard, head of BlackRock Europe, Middle East and Africa since 2002, had told him that he's seen him speak a couple of times and thinks he's a courageous guy, even if his aims seem a little pie in the sky. Interviews in which Polman claims he would be willing to be CEO of Unilever for free sound all well and good, the public likes it, but pronouncements like that make finance people suspicious. He also seems to be getting more radical in his views as he goes along.

In October 2015, the three men meet in New York at Polman's invitation. The Unilever CEO wants to talk to Fink about increasing investment in the so-called circular economy. Around $4.5 trillion of BlackRock's $5 trillion portfolio is tied directly to global share indexes so the size of Unilever means that they are de facto shareholders. Their interest in Unilever works out at about 6 per cent, between $7 and $8 billion; they're effectively their biggest shareholder.

Fink and Meijaard feel like they're being lectured. Polman explains the need for a circular economy in passionate terms, telling them what needs to happen to make one a reality and what BlackRock's role should be. It's a strange meeting. Meijaard notices that Polman doesn't ask a single question. Fink listens silently, that's his skill. Looking and listening closely when it comes to a potential investment is how you reduce risk. The 63-year-old billionaire is sitting back and trying to decide what he's dealing with.

Once Polman leaves, they turn to each other. Fink thinks the Unilever CEO has started believing his own hype; drunk his own Kool-Aid. And that's dangerous: if he's not willing to listen to us then he probably isn't willing to listen to the people close to him either.

Fink agrees with Polman when it comes to the fundamentals: public companies need to start thinking more long term and stop letting themselves be ruled by the whims of opportunistic shareholders. This is the message he tries to get across ever year in his annual letter to the CEOs of the 500 biggest companies. In that year's letter, he writes: '[there is] acute pressure, growing with every quarter, for companies to meet short-term financial goals at the expense of building long-term value. In the face of these pressures, more and more corporate leaders have responded with actions that can deliver immediate returns to shareholders. In 2014, dividends and buybacks in the U.S. alone totalled more than $900 billion, according to Standard & Poor's – the highest level on record. Corporate leaders [must] engage with a company's long-term providers of capital, resist the pressure of short-term shareholders to extract value from the company if it would compromise value creation for long-term owners and, most importantly, clearly and effectively articulate their strategy for sustainable long-term growth.' Fink sees this as a dangerous development, promising support for companies that buck the trend.[12]

Meijaard respects Fink's decision to speak out and his skill as a marketer. This positive message sets BlackRock apart from its nearest competitors Vanguard and State, which are nowhere near adopting such a position. The letter is good for their image, although its impact on those it addresses is necessarily limited. Since BlackRock invests in the whole share index, it can't withdraw its investment from any of the companies listed there. So long as a company is in the index, it's in BlackRock's portfolio and its CEO doesn't have anything to fear. When you invest in the index, you invest in everyone in it, regardless of whether you approve of them.

Sad as it is, Leen Meijaard doesn't think financial markets will ever pay much attention to such intangible things as ethics and morality. There's only one real solution and that's making the costs of unsustainable impacts more concrete so that they can be included in financial calculations. He can see tentative moves in this direction coming from the oil industry. If you can calculate that global warming means that some oil will have to be left in the ground, then accountants should include this information in their valuation of oil companies. Then investors will weigh this up while deciding whether or not to invest in a company like Shell, for example, and those decisions will steer the company in the right direction. It's going to take a while for these sorts of calculations to have any effect though, they don't carry any weight at the moment. If Unilever wants to increase its efforts in the short term, it's going to have to find an investor willing to take it off the market and make it a private company.

BlackRock aren't the only investors raising their eyebrows about Unilever's ambitions. Erik van Houwelingen, chairman of the investment the Dutch civil service pension fund ABP, shares his concerns with Herman Bots, the executive director of investment policy at their daughter company APG, which administrates their portfolio. The two men agree that the shine has gone off the Polman project. They don't doubt his vision or his integrity but they question whether he's still making a business case for sustainability. If Unilever is doing so well, why aren't they talking more about the numbers?

They get in touch with the top management to warn them that Polman's narrative is starting to sound a bit one sided. The company is starting to lose touch with short-term realities. They need to be careful. That could make Unilever vulnerable. A friend in need is a friend indeed, especially on the stock market. Van Houwelingen and Bots worry that if Unilever gets into difficulty, they might find they don't have any left.

Polman doesn't appreciate these kinds of warnings. Don't people realise he's appealing to investors on moral grounds, asking them to commit to Unilever for the long haul and help them realise the crucial USLP objectives? Van Houwelingen has zero interest in this approach or in saving the world. ABP, with its €344 billion portfolio and duty to provide pensions to 2.8 million people, might have an obvious commitment to the long term but daily share prices rule those decisions too.

Every month, they calculate their pension coverage ratio, a comparison of the fund's assets and the pensions they have committed to paying out. The lower the interest rate, the more money a pension fund has to hold in reserve in order to ensure that their assets cover their future costs. This monthly calculation means they have to be constantly on guard, they can't put themselves at the mercy of a CEO, no matter how good his plans sound. Their systems don't allow for long-term investment. The fund managers are also usually only around for a year or two and their contract is tied to very specific returns' targets. The low interest rates of the past few years have made their jobs very difficult.

Amid all this, ABP is trying to get ahead of the curve on sustainability and has instructed its executor APG to go in search of sustainable investments. They decide to invest a cool €700 million in Unilever, which means that Herman Bots is following the company's fortunes very closely. To him, Unilever isn't an obvious candidate for sustainability. With its ice creams, deodorants and washing powders, Bots certainly doesn't see it as sustainable in terms of its products; calling Dove ice cream sustainable is nothing short of ridiculous. He did once ask Polman how sustainable it was to sell ice creams to already obese Americans. The CEO had been visibly annoyed and accused Bots of missing the point. After a bit more prodding, he'd explained that if Unilever didn't sell the ice creams, another, less sustainable competitor would. It's a question of damage limitation. However, despite his reservations in some areas, Bots has great respect for Unilever's leading role in making the palm oil industry more sustainable. That had been a disaster waiting to happen.

As one of Unilever's top 20 investors, Bots attends a meeting every year with board chairman Michael Treschow. This year, he expresses his concern about recent media reports that Unilever's Indian tea plantations are using child labour. He asks Treschow how he intends to prevent this in future, explaining that it's not just Unilever's reputation that stands to suffer from such revelations. Investors like ABP are trying to create a message of sustainability through their investment portfolio and this scandal will blow back on them too.

It was the BBC that revealed the malpractice on plantations belonging to Unilever suppliers, having been inspired by Unilever's claim to have succeeded in making 100 per cent of its Lipton tea sustainable and meeting all of the Rainforest Alliance's requirements. The investigators discovered abuses ranging from poor hygiene to child labour.

Unilever immediately promises to take the accusations seriously: 'We need to do more to raise standards.' The terrible images of poor sanitary facilities are seen all over the world, Unilever is in the dog house. The Dutch newspaper *Het Financieele Dagblad* is damning: 'These revelations must have been very unpleasant for Polman and his colleagues. A cynic might say that Unilever is nothing more than a marketing company selling the idea of sustainability. This doesn't do justice to the efforts the company is making but this is the price of acting like Bono. The U2 singer presented himself as a hero trying to save the world and was criticised all the more heavily when it turned out he was dodging tax.'[13]

Thirty-six hours in advance of publication, the journalists reached out to Unilever for Polman's comment. But ever since *Het Financieele Dagblad* had responded sceptically to a 2012 interview in which he set out his sustainability ambitions, Polman has refused to speak to the paper. The public relations department tells the journalists that Polman is in China and unavailable for comment. But to the surprise of these same PR officers, Polman does respond, on the Dutch food industry and health news site foodlog.nl.

On the site, journalist Niels Willems writes, 'Fallibility leads to secrecy and denials unless you have the courage to keep putting it all on the table. Then the recognition of one's own shortcomings becomes a source of inspiration to keep working passionately on improving oneself. If that's how it is for people, why can't it be the same for companies?' Steven Schepers from Oxfam advises Unilever to confront the scandal honestly: 'When it comes to communication there is one golden rule: if all else fails, try telling the truth.'

Writing from his hotel room in Beijing at 2.30 am, Polman seems to take this message on board: 'I agree with you both completely, the ultimate test is to be completely transparent and show whether something is working. That's why we publish our USLP goals and have independent third-parties monitor them.' The blog page immediately fills with commentators, many of them simply can't believe that it's the CEO of Unilever posting. Many applaud him for it but the criticism is overwhelming. Unilever is compared to the Dutch Rabobank: 'The top brass set sustainability goals, the lower orders tinker with Libor.' Polman is called on to admit the blunder publicly. He should show vulnerability. The next evening, the CEO pops up again: '*Het Financieele Dagblad* admitted today in a telephone conversation that their reporting was unfair, but refuse to print a correction. We only had 24 hours to respond. I support a free press, I support activism, I believe in the right to free speech but somehow I feel we allow certain people to follow their own set of rules. This means that a lots of people who want to help, want to make a difference – and I believe that there are lots of companies who want make a change – increasingly feel the need to distance themselves from the whole project. As a father and a concerned citizen, who also happens to be the CEO of Unilever, this worries me. This is nothing to do with the company.' He continues: '*Het Financieele Dagblad* is completely in the wrong here. They rely on the primacy of shareholders and in doing so they're setting back the clock. This isn't about my, this is about my children and grandchildren. I'm going to bed now but I call on you all to continue the discussions and make sure that you keep on being part of the change we need. And yes, hold us accountable exactly as you do others. And yes, we will make mistakes now and again, for which I am ultimately responsible, for which I offer my apologies and from which I, I hope, am learning.'

Wouter Keuning, one of the editors concerned, says that *Het Financieele Dagblad* stands squarely behind what was published and hasn't told Unilever or any other party that what they printed was 'unfair', during a phone conversation or otherwise. Keuning has been in the room with Polman at various press conferences over the years and noticed that he's not good at fielding critical questions. He has regularly heard him complain that analysts and journalists are stupid and that Dutch journalists are the stupidest of all. He seems to think it's when he goes home to the Netherlands that he gets the most narrow-minded, petty questions, often about things that journalists abroad no longer need explaining to them.

Keuning is completely on board with Polman's mission but thinks that Polman himself is mostly just a good marketer, one who has understood how to attract customers with this narrative and make money from good people. He sees how differently Polman is treated from other CEOs, hence the Bono remark. In a conference call, he calls Polman out and challenges his narrative. With the pace of growth as it is, wouldn't he need to stay on as CEO of Unilever until 2047 to meet his €80 billion target? Polman has his own question for Keuning: Are you really from the *Financieele Dagblad*, aren't the people there supposed to be able to do maths?

An outraged commentator in the paper's comments section has their own perspective: 'So long as Polman's heart is in the right place – and does anyone really doubt that it is? – we should be calling the whole marketing model and its myopic focus on consumption and growth into question, not fretting over Unilever's sincerity. Enough blethering, there's work to do!'

The Dutch paper *De Telegraaf* offers its own criticism of the Lipton scandal. The new editor-in-chief, Paul Jansen, is invited to Rotterdam to meet Polman. He wants to know why the paper prints such harsh pieces on Unilever, is it to do with wanting to sell more papers? He doesn't wait for Jansen's reply but launches into Unilever's grand mission. He talks about the United Nations and climate issues, explaining how hard it is to teach people to turn off the tap while they're brushing his teach.

Jansen impresses upon Polman how good he thinks it is that Unilever is trying to make the world more sustainable but adds that it is the duty of journalists to hold their claims of 'doing good' up to scrutiny. If sustainability is the heart of Unilever's marketing message and how they hope to make money, journalists have to find out whether Unilever is sticking to its claims. This helps their readers, Unilever's customers and shareholders, to decide whether to buy products from Unilever or to invest in its shares. Surely he understands that?

Polman is angry. He can't understand why journalists fail to see that this kind of approach is getting in the way of his mission to rid the world of poverty. How are they against that? Surely, as a newspaper, they support this kind of aim? With that, he's back on his hobby horse. Jansen wonders how it is that a man like Polman, CEO of an enormous company, is so evidently incapable of having a discussion, asking questions and waiting for the answers. He notices that the four PR officers there haven't dared say a word the entire time. They seem terrified.

Polman's troubled relationship with the media keeps deteriorating. The impatient CEO had already lost his temper publicly at a press conference a few months earlier. As he was telling those assembled about Unilever's investment in skincare products he'd gone on to claim that journalists still weren't doing enough to help promote Unilever's sustainability agenda. One journalist had shouted out that maybe Polman should go buy some of his own skincare products to rub into his own apparently very thin skin.[14]

Unilever's CEO is starting to feel the pressure. He's been at this for seven years. The only way to shut critics down is to prove that what he's proposing is possible.

Sue Garrard is hard at work trying to do just that. The communications specialist had swapped her position at the British Department of Work and Pensions for a spot at Unilever in 2012, believing she could have a greater impact in the private sector. It was the USLP that captured her imagination. In 2014, she had taken over responsibility for all communications surrounding the plan, including many of the tasks Gail Klintworth had been in charge of before she left. Garrard had immediately done her own study of the state of play and quickly came to the conclusion that even if the USLP was a flagship project for the company, it had yet to translate into real-terms growth for the business. With the exception of a couple of small brands like Lifebuoy and Ben & Jerry's, customers barely associate any of Unilever's brands with 'doing good' and very few brands are driven by a purpose recognisable to the consumer.

Garrard's research alarms many of colleagues but a few had come to the same conclusion on their own already. Karen Hamilton, one of the originators of the USLP, has been feeling let down by Unilever's marketers for some time now. At a conference she says: 'The biggest challenge to our on-going shift to become more sustainable is our marketers. We do regular staff surveys to check our progress around sustainability and marketing is 20 percentage points behind the rest of our business when it comes to embracing these changes.'[15]

The trouble is that lots of her colleagues don't know where to begin. They need to be building up a broader range of skills in order to unite growth and sustainability under the same umbrella. In order to get the message across, they need to be doing research and collecting data. Business as usual isn't enough. For example, if they can find the scientific research to prove that children who start brushing their teeth at a young age don't lose any of their adult teeth by the time they're 10, they can take that data to NGOs and governments and collaborate on a campaign promoting the sustainable advantages of good oral health at different phases of life. However, these kinds of projects are a lot of work. Each country has its own set of priorities and advertising regulations that will determine the precise form of such a campaign and it is local marketers who have to get to grips with them.

Sue Garrard's task is clear: there's no point talking to investors about the USLP, they don't understand it. They aren't particularly interested in it either. When you talk to them, all they want is proof that it is working. Unilever doesn't have that yet so the company needs to make sure it delivers concrete proof as soon as possible. This will show investors that brands that are actually sustainable make more money than brands that aren't, even in the short term.

It occurs to Garrard that part of the problem is Polman's failure to explain his policy to people inside the company. For all his inspiring speeches to the UN, his visits to Unilever operations around the world are dominated by sales results and cost savings, often with a CEO who isn't in the best mood. Whether he's actually irritable or just visibly impatient, Polman isn't inclined to answer questions from puzzled colleagues. Surely they can see what needs to happen? They have a unique chance to help Unilever prove that a new, sustainable business model is possible and show that businesses can make good money from doing good. Why don't they just get on with it?! What is he paying them for?!

Looking for someone to replace board chairman Michael Treschow has also hit a snag. This task has been given to Feike Sijbesma. A while ago, Polman asked the chair of the Nominations Committee to start looking for Treschow's replacement a while ago. Sijbesma brought in Russell Reynolds and MWM consulting to help in the search but so far they've had no joy. They were the ones that helped to find Sijbesma.

Unilever's previous arrangement with executive search firm Egon Zehnder has broken down completely thanks to a conflict of interest. Polman had become annoyed with the firm after their advisors, whom he pays through the nose to carry out regular performance assessments on his manager, had tried to headhunt some of those very same managers for rival firms only shortly afterwards. It seemed to him that Egon Zehnder was trying to have their cake and eat it, behaviour that went against his sense of fair play. An exclusive arrangement, in which Unilever retained the firm on the promise of eight to ten big recruitment contracts per year, ended in a massive row. Polman's insistence on a clause barring Egon Zehnder from headhunting Unilever employees had horrified Egon Zehnder's partners in India and Brazil, who pointed to the money they would lose as a result of the deal. Former Unilever people were highly prized among rival firms and they feared losing their competitive edge. Worse still, Polman had made this exclusivity arrangement with 85-year-old Egon Zehnder, the company's founder, who had been semi-retired for years and refused to get involved in solving the dispute. He passed the buck to the partners, and the two men who had first got into business with Unilever, David Kidd and Joost van Heyningen Nanninga, had to go and face Polman. He gave them both barrels, making it clear that he had no intention of working with the company ever again.

After consulting with Polman and Sijbesma the consultants at Russell Reynolds started by making a list of 5,000 CEOs before reducing it to 300 who had just retired or were about to retire. They then went through that list one by one, arriving at a list of 20 possible candidates to replace Treschow. Louise Fresco notices that there's only one woman on the list but her own priority is to try and find a candidate from Asia. This is their fastest growing region, after all. Her colleagues are less convinced, believing that Unilever's Western roots and cultural values mean a Westerner would be a better fit. Russell Reynolds is dealing with a lengthy list of criteria, it needs a chairman with good industry knowledge and experience running at least a couple of companies, Polman also wants them to be fairly young, and neither Dutch nor British. Every candidate they come up with turns them down after their initial couple of conversations. And time is growing short now.

Marijn Dekkers isn't on the first list they make. It had been announced back in 2014 that Dekkers, the CEO of German chemicals company Bayer, would have his contract extended by two years, to 2016. The brevity of the extension had surprised people, Dekkers was only 57 so why would he be leaving? Dekkers told *Het Financieele Dagblad*: 'I've been a CEO for 17 years or so at this point, a job comparable to elite sports in terms of the physical and mental demands it places on you. Once I take over somewhere, I'm the lynchpin of the whole operation. People are there to see me. I'm always fully present, I can't sit back and start zoning out thinking about whether or not I'm going to play tennis that evening. I've had enough of being that person.' The end of 2016 is too late for him to be considered for Unilever chairman, the job requires someone available three days per week.

But Dekkers has decided to leave Bayer early. He's dead set against the planned $63 billion takeover of the American agro-biotech giant Monsanto, makers of genetically modified seeds and pesticides. As a trained chemist, Dekkers isn't convinced that their approach is the right one, getting chemicals and plants to talk to one another is technologically very tricky. He's also increasingly turned off by the clashes he anticipates between the German and American business models. He was the CEO of the American firm Thermo Fisher Scientific for eight years, a publically listed company with a $10 billion annual turnover specialising in medical diagnostics. Those eight years had been spent sprinting from quarter to quarter, obsessing over numbers; it had been a terrible experience.

It had been Johannes von Schmettow from Egon Zehnder who had placed Dekkers at Beyer so it was only natural that he was among the first to hear about his departure. Dekkers had told him that he'd like to become board chairman in a company with robust accountability so Schmettow showed him a list of possibilities, including Unilever. Dekkers had been immediately interested. The status of the company was a major selling point but the prospect of returning to the Netherlands was another factor. Dekkers had grown up there and wanted to spend more time 'back home'.

Unilever struck him as an interesting company. Business is always about the bottom line, about earning money, but Dekkers believes this can be done in more and less meaningful ways. Unilever's focus is hygiene and nutrition, which is a big plus, they're products people can understand and really need. Joost van Heyningen Nanninga discretely passes on news of Dekkers's interest to Feike Sijbesma.

Eventually, Marijn Dekkers is one of two candidates put forward by Russell Reynolds. On first consideration, the board finds a few details that speak against Dekkers as chairman: he's Dutch, like Treschow he doesn't have much hands-on experience of fast-moving consumer goods and he's hardly a spring chicken at 57. But then Dekkers meets with Polman one Saturday morning, at Heathrow of all places, and the two Dutchmen hit it off straight away. Polman thinks that Dekkers seems like a good man and a safe pair of hands. Dekkers suspects that the fact they were both brought up Catholic didn't hurt either.

Egon Zehnder opts not to send a bill for its help with the tip. The executive searchers know that they'll be rewarded in a different way.

Following his success in helping the UN come up with the SDGs, Polman is enthusiastically invited to take part in preparations for the Paris Climate Conference. His partners at the UN are totally bowled over by how effective he has been in getting big businesses involved with developing the goals. He sent out hundreds of letters to CEOs of large companies asking them to show their support and the reaction had been universally positive. The United Nations had never seen such a thing and they would love the same kind of support for the Paris congress too.

Governments and NGOs trust Polman and he's the only CEO to work closely with host and chairman of the conference, Laurent Fabius, the French foreign secretary. He estimates that 75 per cent of the companies in attendance to show their support are there at Unilever's invitation or because he spurred them on to join in, that's 1,500 companies in total. Their representatives are present at every panel, participate in subcommittees and announce ambitious plans to help combat climate change.

Unilever is the only company to have been given permission to set up a stand during the conferences. Ben & Jerry's are allowed to hand out samples of their ice cream 'Save Our Swirled', developed specially for the occasion. The brand has collected over three hundred thousand signatures over the past few months, calling for world leaders to make a binding agreement on climate change. 'Our stance on climate change and our ice cream is one in the same: if it's melted, it's ruined! It's a climate change message you can't ignore.'

No matter how much Unilever celebrates Ben & Jerry's, the brand remains remarkably hostile towards its parent company. Every other ice cream brand, from Cornetto to Magnum, clearly names Unilever as its distributor in its advertising, Ben & Jerry's is the only one that doesn't. Their packaging always carries a photo of the two founders laughing together but you have to look closely to see the tiny, almost invisible Unilever logo.

As the moment comes to close the conference, Laurent Fabius is visibly moved: 'It's only a little hammer, but I think it can achieve great things.' The hall erupts in a standing ovation that goes on for minutes. Twenty-three years after the first Earth Summit in Rio de Janeiro and at the close of the hottest year on record, 195 countries are committing to reducing their CO_2 emissions. Global warming needs to be kept below 2 degrees Celsius for the rest of this century, 1.5 degrees if possible. The agreement deadline had been pushed back a couple of hours at the last minute by the Americans because the Obama administration, fearing pushback from the Republican Party who have the majority in congress, needed to change the wording. The text originally stated that developed countries 'shall' reduce emissions throughout their economies but changing it to 'should' means that the agreement can be adopted by the American government without a reading in congress. Going forward, all 195 countries will meet every five years to check whether revisions are needed to the accords, which are based on the self-designed, voluntary climate plans submitted by each country. Poor countries will receive $100 billion per year to help them hold up their end of the bargain.[16]

This support is sorely needed. While Paris is going on, the Rainforest Action Network is criticising Unilever for not doing its best to promote sustainable palm oil. 'Unilever is considered by many as the first company to recognise their Conflict Palm Oil problem after international campaigns exposed the link between rainforest destruction in Indonesia and Dove personal care products. In 2008, Unilever agreed to support an immediate moratorium on the destruction of forests for palm oil and the company has been a leading advocate in talking about the need to break the link between palm oil and deforestation ever since.' The reason for the criticism is that Unilever has been buying palm oil certified under the Green Palm initiative, which the Rainforest Action Network sees as insufficiently sustainable. There is a roaring trade in these kinds of certification schemes but it's far from clear that Green Palm or any of the others like it actually denote palm oil that has been produced sustainably.

'Unilever has failed to cut problematic suppliers from its supply chain', the activist organisation declares in its progress report on the industry. Their findings even suggest that companies like Mars and Nestlé are outperforming Unilever on palm oil. The same can't be said for Kraft Heinz, which has only just joined the RSPO. 'They have not taken any meaningful steps to deal with their Conflict Palm Oil problem. H.J. Heinz Company, once recognized as a leading company through its reduction of the use of palm oil and its sourcing of traceable and RSPO certified palm oil, is now lagging behind its peers.'[17]

Marc Engel can see where the Rainforest Action Network is coming from. He gets demoralised with it all himself from time to time. Unilever have been plugging away at this issue for 15 years now and deforestation is still continuing apace. Certification schemes are also becoming less meaningful, they're becoming too cheap and accessible. Engel, the recently appointed director of sourcing and a member of the ULE or top 13, wants to start installing software in each of the windmills used to press palm oil on Sumatra. By using blockchain technology he hopes to gather information about the quality of the product. That kind of oversight should help improve production standards, especially among small-scale farmers.

With financial support from the IDH, which Engel sits on the board of, Unilever is going to start helping small farmers move to areas of forest that have been restored and where they can increase their yield using the best methods available. Engel wants to bring in the same strategy for tea production, not least because it will improve the lot of poor farmers and increase their income. He's proud that Unilever pays its in-house tea pickers a minimum of $2 per day but he also knows that for every one of the pickers paid directly by Unilever, there's another eight earning less than $2.

At the end of 2015, Unilever is the first company in the world to publish a human rights report. The report talks about a 'decent pay framework' which lays out how Unilever manages to pay its own workers a living wage. Unilever is trying to go further and extend this framework to all its suppliers and contractors, an enormous task for a company with 76,000 suppliers in 190 countries, 'each of them with its own cultural norms, social and economic challenges, varying levels of the rule of law and divergent views of what it means to respect human rights'. They're talking about millions of people. Polman therefore points to the importance of the partnerships Unilever has with Oxfam and Solidaridad. They'll have to start working even harder together in order to find 'systemic and sustainable solutions'.[18]

CHAPTER 14

TOO FAR AHEAD OF HIS TROOPS

January 2016–January 2017

From shareholder meetings to honorary doctorate ceremonies and from key-note addresses to everyday speeches, Kim Polman accompanies her husband wherever she can, just so long as the cellist doesn't have to perform herself. If she is there, she usually sits in the front row, listening attentively as he delivers his speech. She knows her presence there makes him feel safe.

Kim Polman believes in and supports her husband's mission like no other. The American musician has been an environmental activist for decades and is convinced that the current system of capitalism, focused on short-term results, needs to be replaced as quickly as possible. In the foreword to her book *Imaginal Cells*, she writes: 'Our generation has the potentially calamitous honour of wit-nessing the birth of a new era, the Anthropocene. It is an era defined by man's irreversible impacts on the world, by changes to the climate, worsening threats to eco-systems, a rapid rise in extinction rates and burgeoning levels of pollu-tion.'[1] Kim Polman insists that the much-needed change will be based on the 'Golden Rule': treat others and the planet as you yourself want to be treated. This altruistic precept has formed the basis of the most successful religions and cultures for the last three thousand years and is, according to her, the most important guiding principle of human interaction.

The Unilever directors are impressed with the loyalty of the CEO's part-ner, now 63 years old. In Louise Fresco's experience, Kim Polman is the first to defend the non-materialist dimension of their shared vision. For Polman, three years his wife's junior, Kim is the voice of truth.

He needs this voice right now. Paul Polman still often feels misunderstood and life as a CEO in the world of the United Nations is confusing. He no longer really regards himself as a businessman. The fact that he is a CEO, and that Unilever 'touches' around two billion people with its products every day, means that he can lead the world in the right direction. If he hadn't been given the room to do that, to hitch his wagon to Unilever, then he would have left after five years. Being CEO wouldn't have been enough on its own, he may even have found it boring. Thankfully, he's now seeing more and more leaders like him emerge, people who think holistically and are open to cooperation.

Just like her husband, Kim Polman is convinced that this totally new type of leader is what the world needs. She would like to see men like Donald Trump, Vladimir Putin and Recep Tayyip Erdogan go off and play their game of human monopoly together on some distant mountain, so that world leaders who *do* have a desire to build bridges can get down to working on mankind's collective future. Women are increasingly going to take over the leadership role, if only because they have a better understanding of concepts like community and sustainability. During the many Unilever board meetings she has attended she often noted that it was the women who were asking the best questions.

Kim Polman has resolved to go in search of this new type of leader, spiritual kinsmen operating in similar circles who dare to take the initiative in the way she does, contributing to what she calls 'a worldwide transformation so fundamental that it's hard to imagine'. Fundamental and inescapable. Her key to picturing this profound and startling change is the image of the caterpillar and its inevitable transformation into a butterfly. After a period of ravenous consumption, comparable to the years leading up to the global financial crisis, the caterpillar builds a chrysalis. Inside it, the caterpillar dissolves into a biological melting pot, in which only a few dormant 'imaginal cells' team up to slowly but surely resist and defeat the caterpillar's immune system. This creates space for more of these cells, which start concentrating and connecting until they reach a tipping point and are able to start building a beautiful butterfly. For Kim Polman, this butterfly represents the new, decent, sustainable system the world needs.[2]

She and Stephen Vasconcellos-Sharpe, the man behind the magazine *Salt*, which focuses on driving 'meaningful change', compiled a list of 25 of these innovative thinkers: from Desmond Tutu and Al Gore to Nobel Laureate and microfinance pioneer Muhammad Yunus and former UN Development Programme administrator Mark Malloch Brown, and from *Big Issue* founder Antony Jenkins to WBCSD president Peter Bakker to Paul Polman. They asked them to join forces by each contributing a personal essay to their book *Imaginal Cells: Visions of Transformation*.

Her husband is enthusiastic, he knows most of these people. Polman also hopes that 2016 will be the year they reach that tipping point. With the launch of the UN's Sustainable Development Goals and the ambitious climate agreement reached in Paris, the world can now get to work on agreements that apply to everyone. These agreements and the resulting collaborations are designed to rid the world of poverty and make the global economy more sustainable. Working with Mark Malloch Brown, former deputy secretary general of the UN, the indefatigable Polman also launches the Business & Sustainable Development Commission in Davos that January. This forum will spend the next two years doing all it can to get big business, governments and NGOs working in the same direction. The men have calculated that around $2.4 trillion (2,400 billion) are needed each year in order to reach the UN sustainability goals by 2030. According to them, however, this isn't necessarily a problem, given the fact that around $290 trillion is currently sloshing around in the financial sector, a figure increasing by 5 per cent year on year. They conclude that this money will only flow in the right direction if there is a globally accepted standard that enables businesses to report on their efforts to realise the UN's sustainability goals.

Dame Ellen MacArthur also causes a stir at Davos that year. Back in 2005 when she was breaking the world record for solo circumnavigating the world, she started to worry about the sustainability of the economic system. She realised the importance of recycling plastics. At the World Economic Forum, 39-year-old MacArthur presents research findings suggesting that the production of plastic has increased 20-fold over the past fifty years, to a height of 311 million tonnes in 2014. Eighty million of those tonnes go into packaging. MacArthur predicts that over the next thirty years there will be a further quadrupling of plastic production. This will have serious consequences for the environment. As it stands, a lorry load of plastic is dumped into the world's oceans every 60 seconds, by 2050 this will have increased to four lorry loads. She summarises this horrific prediction in an image that shocks the whole world: in 2050 there will be more plastic by weight in our oceans than there are fish.

And it's crystal clear where all this plastic packaging is coming from. Volunteer groups are cleaning plastic waste from beaches all over the world, particularly in Asia. Since most of the discarded items carry a clear brand or manufacturing label, the groups make lists of the biggest polluters: Unilever, Procter & Gamble and Nestlé are all firmly in the top 10 list. Polman calls the report a milestone and rolls up his sleeves: we need to give up single use plastics. The company announces that by 2025 Unilever will only use plastic that can be recycled and ensures that 25 per cent of the plastic it uses is recycled plastic. In the press release, the company proudly announces that it has managed to reduce the amount of pollution from Unilever products by 31 per cent per consumer.

Nevertheless, Unilever clearly still has a long way to go when it comes to plastic. Only 2 per cent of plastic is reused globally. Unilever falls short of even this figure. The company currently produces around two hundred billion units of product each year; packaging these requires around two million tonnes of packaging materials. Eighty per cent of those materials contain plastics. They use between 600,000 and 7,000,000 tonnes of plastic per year. In total, less than 1 per cent of the plastic Unilever uses is recycled plastic. To Marc Engel, the head of sourcing, this is nothing short of disgraceful.

The man poised to take over as the new chairman of Unilever's board is in complete agreement with Engel. As a trained chemist, Marijn Dekkers worked with plastics for years, he met his wife in that field. The two of them even have a selection of patents to their names, such as the one they applied for in 1992 on a method for recycling plastics. No one has ever done anything with it.

A couple of hours after Bayer announces that Werner Baumann, the chief architect of the Monsanto deal, is to be their new CEO, Unilever announces that Marijn Dekkers will succeed Michael Treschow as their new board chairman. When Treschow reflects on his time as chairman, he's proud of the leading role Unilever and Polman have taken on. But he has his concerns too. Treschow thinks that a CEO must recognise his own limitations and exercise self-control, Polman obviously hasn't managed to do that as well as he should. Of course, when you're getting so much praise from outside the company it's hard to hear or act on criticism from closer to home. Over the past few years, colleagues have mostly complained to Treschow of Polman's absence. Whatever the reality of the situation, he's barely ever in the office now. Treschow understands why Polman gets tired of this constant reproach; he's always in touch, keeps a close eye on everything going on and answers his emails within twenty-four hours. They know where to find him so why are they complaining?

In Treschow's opinion, this habit of answering his team's questions one on one is one of Polman's biggest weaknesses. No matter how well he performs for a big audience, he isn't good at playing the role of an engaged team leader. You can't make up for that by answering an email promptly. When it comes down to it, there isn't really any team to speak of, which is a crying shame. The ULE is made up of smart, dedicated people, they deserve more space to tell their story, to share their ambitions. He should spend more time listening to *them*.

Polman may say that he's listening but he doesn't follow-through. He responds to their questions, giving step-by-step instructions for what he thinks they should be doing. In order to give them real freedom to operate, he needs to give them his undivided attention, build up a rapport and actually listen to them. Treschow doesn't think Polman has the first idea of how to go about this and his tremendous impatience doesn't help matters either. He constantly gives off the impression that he thinks everyone else is stupid. To Treschow, the fact that Polman is himself so knowledgeable and often more informed than those around him is also somehow tragic. It means he doesn't feel the need to listen to other people. He needs to watch out, though. A CEO doesn't get colleagues on board by telling them what to do. People only cooperate when they feel they are truly being heard.

Various members of the ULE are worried about exactly this issue. Even Kees Kruythoff, a long-standing member of the executive, thinks that Polman always gets his own way. He has others report to him individually, never creating any collaborative relationships. The CEO works alone.

The ULE isn't a team at all. Many of its members complain about this. And the ULE certainly isn't Polman's team. He's always somehow above it and therefore not a part of it. He dismisses all suggestions that they should spend more time together and work on building team spirit. He has neither the time nor the inclination for such things. And he doesn't see it as necessary. Hasn't he made it clear what needs to happen? Is there anyone here who *doesn't* want to see an end to world poverty?

A number of colleagues view the fact that Polman's message of trust and connection doesn't carry over into his own relationships with the people around him as highly problematic. His refusal to listen to anyone is starting to annoy them. Being on the side of right doesn't mean never having to discuss things with people. In fact, exchanging ideas is a requirement when you're building or managing a team. It's how you show that you can't do it alone, that everyone is important and that it's a shared endeavour. This simply isn't getting through to Polman.

Jan Zijderveld is struck by the fact that no one is allowed to talk to the media. There's a ban on communications from anyone other than Polman, enforced by Sue Garrard. Zijderveld wonders why this is: Why doesn't Polman trust anyone else to speak publicly? Does this really serve Unilever, given that Polman's relationship with the press isn't exactly cordial?

Anniek Mauser is butting heads with Sue Garrard on exactly this issue. Unilever's vision is still being particularly well received by NGOs in the Benelux countries, a trend Mauser largely attributes to the company's close relationships with various stakeholders there. She works to maintain a transparent relationship with the media, even if she too is irritated by their penchant for sensationalist stories. It's a shame they take this approach, it makes the public numb and disengaged. Mauser truly believes Unilever's sustainable agriculture programme is much better than that of most other brands but this receives barely any attention in the press.

For a long time, she was forced to work with marketers who barely incorporated the message or necessity of sustainability into their approach. This is changing now. She delivers a whole plethora of training courses in which she emphasises the same points: make sure the consumer understands sustainability, make sure it's accessible to them, make sure it's attractive to them, make sure it provides emotional as well as financial benefits and make sure it becomes a habit. Finally, marketers are beginning to get the message. Mauser thinks that the Dutch are ahead of the curve in this respect, Polman is an inspirational figurehead to them. She wants to bring the same lessons to London but Garrard isn't letting her make any headway.

Garrard, responsible for communications about the USLP in the London office, is much less enthusiastic about how things are going. Polman seems to be working on the assumption that the necessary change will take place simply because he's in the right. He isn't concerning himself in the least with how that's supposed to happen in practice. Sure, he can process huge volumes of information and use it to deliver a rousing speech, but Garrard is becoming increasingly impatient with a boss who's too proud to see what's going on right under his nose. Realising his glorious vision is proving very difficult in reality.

In her view, the big sticking point is that everyone is still working very much in his or her own silo. Motivated by bonuses and raises awarded on the basis of individual results, they remain each other's competitors. Garrard keeps on making the case for a shared target that will eventually lead to more interesting and better results. Just like Gail Klintworth before her, she's also annoyed that people, particularly men, are still using every excuse in the book to get out of working collaboratively. They actually seem to dislike developing sustainable models. It comes as no surprise to her that many of Unilever's female employees *are* hard at work on this. Apparently they aren't as troubled by their egos.

For Garrard, the growing disparity between the promises Polman is making to the rest of the world and the demands he's making inside Unilever is becoming schizophrenic. Internally, he mostly talks about the need to grow and to make cost savings. She also doesn't think he's spending enough time with the people working under him on finding concrete ways to implement his sustainable message for each brand. She decides to take the initiative and set out which characteristics of their products have historically been regarded as sustainable, in the hope that these features will form the basis of the growth plans for each product. If it works, this will provide proof of their claim that products that do good can perform better. She starts by doing this for 40 of their key brands.

While various colleagues of Polman's are getting restless, most of them remain in awe of him. They think that the fact he's hard at work on the business and on their results despite all his work outside the company to keep the 'flywheel' spinning is impressive. They need his support on that front. They don't doubt the usefulness of what they do. Providing good quality food and hygiene at a good price is at the core of the company, people need those things. Beyond that it's all just marketing, sales and communication. Of course they want those 800 million hungry people to get a better income too, so that they can start buying their products. Unilever profits from this as well. The message of the USLP has helped the company to plug itself into present-day concerns but Unilever is still a company, the CEO shouldn't start acting too much like a world leader. If he does, he'll end up losing touch with his staff, like a general too far ahead of his troops.

Jan Zijderveld increasingly suspects that leading Unilever has become boring to Polman. He respects his CEO's enormous dedication to solving the problems facing the world and his preference for focusing solely on that. But whenever Zijderveld asks Polman to spend more time closer to home, he tells him that his staff should be running the company, without complaining, and they are being paid handsomely to do just that. Then he returns to the importance of the USLP. He doesn't want to hear about any reservations, such as their concerns about the food division's shrinking margins or encroaching, often local competitors. If they do bring these things up, he's hurt and berates them for letting him down. Their best needs to get better.

If you don't get behind the plan, it won't work. Peter ter Kulve has lost count of how often he's heard Polman say that. It strikes him that Polman barely ever has time for them. His diary is packed, meetings can never last more than twenty to thirty minutes. Very occasionally they do find the time and use it to enjoy themselves. Both men are from Twente, which creates a bond between them. Both of them have a sense of humour about themselves. But when it comes to his mission, Polman is always deadly serious. If he thinks you're getting in the way of his mission, he becomes enraged.

Ter Kulve, the man in charge of South-East Asian operations, set up a book club with his good friend and Asia expert Hans Vriens in Singapore. One of the members is Dwight Hutchins, managing director of Accenture for the region and a specialist in advice on ZBB.

Accenture is Kraft Heinz's main supplier in this field. Their policy is return to the same question every year regarding expenses: Are these costs necessary and is the money available being spent properly? They have long since given up the principle common to bureaucratic organisations of setting aside the previous year's budget for the next financial year. When Ter Kulve suggests to colleagues in London that they adopt the same strategy, they turn him down flat: this isn't a good fit for Unilever, we focus on the consumer, on growth and on the USLP, not on the obvious, simplistic issue of cost savings. They refuse to give Ter Kulve any funds but he ploughs on regardless. He asks Hutchins whether Accenture could try out its ZZB technique on Unilever's Thailand operations. That would mean combing over eight hundred thousand cost units and deciding whether or not each one is a strategic cost. In lieu of a fee, Accenture will be allowed to pocket a third of the savings it makes.

The results are astonishing. Ter Kulve suddenly sees how much money an organisation like Unilever spends on nonsense, simply because a budget has been allocated to it. It seems people barely think about costs at all. Marketing can have 20,000 displays made almost without a thought, even though the sales executives only need 8,000 of them. All in all, they manage to reduce between 10 per cent and 15 per cent of costs through this exercise. When Ter Kulve reports this to CFO Graeme Pitkethly, asking for permission to extend ZZB to the whole of Asia, the CFO springs into action. He wants to do this for the whole of Unilever.

Paul Polman signs off but doesn't want the plan to draw too much attention, otherwise it will seem like Unilever is allowing itself to be driven by financial targets after all. They'll let people know about it once the results are in. Polman prefers to keep talking about the USLP goals, which he sees as a 'reflection of the SDGs'. In particular, he hopes that they'll soon arrive at an international standard that gives the results achieved through the USLP a measurable weight in the eyes of the 'spreadsheet monkeys'.

When are accountants finally going to start working in earnest on a standard for 'integrated reporting'? When are they going to take the baton from Peter Bakker and start engaging with the promise that they can save the world? Polman is desperate for this to start happening. Whether he's speaking to people at Ernst & Young, KPMG, PwC or Deloitte, he notices that the bean counters are loathe to engage with him on this issue no matter how he brings it up.

Louise Fresco, chair of the Unilever board's Corporate Responsibility Committee, is similarly disappointed by this. As far as she's concerned, the annual 'declaration of limited assurance' the accountants at PwC stamp on the USLP results don't mean very much at all. They are paid a considerable amount of money but contribute little in terms of added value. She doesn't think that PwC are supporting them in their search for a more serious audit, comparable to the ones they carry out for financial results.

Robert van der Laan agrees with Fresco. For six years he's been trying to put integrated reporting on the map. The PwC partner, himself a tax specialist by training, was deeply touched by the book *One Report*, which he read in 2010. In it, scholars Robert Eccles and Michael Krzus make a heartfelt plea for integrated reporting. Because PwC's 'sustainability activities' fall to the accountants, he's attached to them as managing partner. His young sustainability specialists are surprised to find themselves being led by a tax expert but this is outweighed by their delight at being led directly by one of the partners, maybe this means people at PwC are finally starting to take them seriously.

For the first two years, things went well. Internally, Van der Laan's message came to be known as 'a spearhead for the future'. There was room to invest. But then Van der Laan was forced to start focusing on turnover and ensure this activity would contribute to the PwC's results. This isn't going well. Worse still, his colleagues on the accountancy side are still focused on finding ways to perfect the financial reporting processes, they don't seem to know the first thing about integrated reporting. In fact, they're terrified of it. They worry it will mean them suddenly having to start telling their clients to look more closely at their CO_2 emissions because they're going to start monitoring them. That would mean telling those clients they haven't been doing it right this entire time. The client is the one paying and as long as they aren't concerned about environmental metrics, the accountants are loath to bother them about them.

Van der Laan can understand that well enough. He's spoken with various company boards over the past few years to alert them to their environmental responsibilities and their climbing CO_2 emissions. He was mostly met with glazed expressions from the other side of the table. He realised that these people manage their companies on the basis of concrete figures concerning revenue, margin and cost. As long as an increase in CO_2 emissions doesn't cost them much money, they won't take it into account. A tough, worldwide tax on CO_2 emissions would be an enormous help on that front.

Van der Laan feels like Don Quixote, fighting against a dominant system. He also empathises with Polman: he has to overcome this kind of resistance on a daily basis. It takes a lot of energy and courage to go up against the system.

Pushing this agenda at PwC is also proving impossible. Accountants are used to giving a declaration of reasonable assurance that gives 90–95 per cent security, which counts as a positive declaration. The relatively intangible nature of Van der Laan's work means it's still only getting a declaration of 'limited assurance', which amounts to no more than 60 per cent certainty.

Does that fit into their business model? Partners go home with between 400K and 700K a year, this is only covered if they can assume an hourly rate of at least €300 per hour. Currently, clients are unwilling to pay that for the services provided by Van der Laan and his team.

After six years at PwC, he throws in the towel. He no longer believes that accountants can save the world, they simply aren't capable of it. It requires a completely new logic that stands in opposition to the one they're used to. Accountants are followers, not leaders. They follow their clients and would never dare to bite the hand that feeds them. Van der Laan shares Polman's belief that the world is at a tipping point, and that a more radical system is required. But at a certain point they have to face up to the fact that the old logic isn't going to get them there.

Paul Hurks worries that getting the message across is going to require painful crises. The director of international affairs for the Dutch Chartered Accountants Organisation (NBA) is the secretary of the working group ESG Assurance. For two years now, NBA has organised this platform for members to make tentative suggestions about how to give the vague 'limited assurance' category more weight and modernise their approach. Hurks is disappointed too. They're not getting anywhere. A recent attempt to include more non-financial information in the finals of accountancy training programmes was a bust. He discovered that the current generation of lecturers and professors has zero desire to change, they want to teach what they have always taught in the way they have always taught it; they regard integrating reporting as a fad. This means the next generation will follow in the old guard's footsteps. The situation is so dire that they've even had to cancel NBA courses on integrated reporting due to lack of interest. Not enough people signed up.

The SDGs may be a nice banner to follow but they aren't written in clear business language. To Hurks, this is a big problem. In reality, integrated reporting isn't just about what companies have done already but about the future. It concerns not only the company but the whole supply chain and not only the investors but NGOs, governments and consumers. These are all things that scare your average accountant silly.

In Hurks's view, laws are ethics made concrete through experience. This is why he's so enthusiastic about Unilever. It's where the first bits of this experience are being gathered. The new USLP evaluation asks accountants to lend credibility to the information provided to them by the company. This entails a gradual shift from financial to non-financial information, and from always looking backwards to cautiously looking ahead. He hopes this will be replicated elsewhere one day. That would gradually allow new laws to be created.

Hurks is pleased to see the new European guideline requiring the biggest companies to give a clear indication of their environmental impact in their annual reports. It's a small step but it's a start.

Slowly but surely, Unilever's tone is changing after six years of the USLP. They're taking stock. By the end of 2015 they had reached 482 million people in their quest to help a billion people to improve their health and wellness, 337 million of whom were part of Lifebuoy's handwashing campaign. The proportion of sustainably sourced agricultural products has risen slightly, to 60 per cent, and improved eco-efficiency means they've saved €600 million in costs. This is a pittance compared to the yearly purchasing bill, which runs to tens of billions.

The text of the USLP report is almost sombre in places, it's clear that they aren't managing to get the whole supply chain on board with their aims. Consumers especially need to start doing much more. There needs to be more cooperation. 'In an uncertain and volatile world, we cannot achieve our vision unless we find new ways to operate that do not just take from society and the environment.'

As Garrard and others have predicted, Unilever needs to stand resolutely by its own sustainability principles. Halving the environmental impact of the whole supply chain by 2020 is not going to happen. Now the company is talking about its mission to be 'carbon positive' by 2030. Even that is a big ask, the predicted halving of greenhouse gases by 2020 has so far turned out to be an increase of 6 per cent.[3]

Going forward, Unilever is going to start making a distinction between 'sustainable living brands' and the rest. The definition is strict: 'Such a brand must not only have a clear purpose that contributes to a social or environmental concern. The product itself must also contribute to one or more of the targets we have set in the USLP. In 2016, we analysed our top brands using this methodology. Our analysis revealed that in 2015 Sustainable Living brands grew even faster than they did in 2014. They also delivered nearly half our growth and grew significantly faster – in fact 30% faster – than the rest of the business.' The five biggest brands – Dove, Surf, Knorr, Hellmann's and Lipton – fall under this category.

Here and there they do come up with good examples. By switching to smaller spray cans, Dove deodorants have reduced their carbon footprint by 25 per cent, cutting down on packaging, materials and transportation costs. Allowing people to communicate online with farmers in South America who grow sustainable tomatoes for Unilever has created a new sense of engagement, leading to an increase of 10 per cent to Hellmann's market share.

In an effort to show how the breadth of Unilever's efforts, a 30-page document outlines their progress in meeting dozens of targets: trans fats have been removed, the sugar content of ready-to-drink tea products in the Benelux countries has been reduced by 10 per cent since 2010 and all ice creams aimed at children now contain fewer than 110 kcal. Promises are repeated. For example: in 2020 up to 75 per cent of the Unilever products will meet salt levels which will help consumers not exceed the recommended five grams of salt per day. 'In cooperation we have enabled 800,000 women to access initiatives aiming at developing their skills' and will 'empower 5 million women by 2020'.

This is one of the topics that comes up in the interview Sebastian Polman, Polman's youngest son, conducts with his father as part of a series of conversations published by the *Huffington Post*. He wants to know which of the 17 development goals his father really believes can change the world. His father doesn't hesitate: 'One of the biggest possibilities that we have globally is to give equal rights to men and women. If we would just invest not more but the same in women and girls as we invest in men then the world economy could be bigger by about 28 trillion in the next twenty years alone.' Sonny is also keen to hear what his father would be doing if he wasn't a CEO. Polman replies, 'Well it's not important to be CEO because that's a title you can give to anybody. It's important to be in a job where you can be who you are and develop to your full potential.' When asked whether companies are capable of changing of their own accord, of learning to do the right thing, his father says: 'They should keep up with, and ideally be ahead of, the standards society demands. I think the best thing about the internet nowadays is the transparency that it gives. Everybody can find out how everybody behaves. Not many places to hide anymore.'

But transparency alone isn't enough, consumers need to understand a sustainable approach properly too. These small deodorant sprays are turning out not to be a success. 'They were an ideal Polman product: good for the consumer and friendlier to the planet', writes the *Financial Times*. The idea was that by 2015, 80 per cent of their consumers would have switched over to the new cans. Only a third of them followed the plan, so Unilever ended up putting the bigger canisters back on the shelves. Pitkethly tells the newspaper about a big town hall meeting during which young colleagues had expressed their disappointment about that decision. The CFO had explained to them 'that if Unilever wanted to convince the world of the virtues of sustainability it had to be a competitive company. What Unilever needed was "a sharpening and redoubling of our resolve to go back, compete, re-establish the strength of our business and find other ways to convince the consumer."' The *Financial Times* summarises it thus: 'In this deodorant-shaped battle between profit and saving the planet, saving the planet had to wait.' The journalists want to talk to Paul Polman about the company's results, the increase in revenues of 4.1 per cent, the increased margins and dividends but Polman wants to talk about something else: 'In the last 16 years, we've had 15 of the hottest years, one after the other – the first three months of this year again beating new records. We have already passed 1 degree and Mother Nature, unfortunately, is increasingly starting to send us the bill.'

The interviewers once again bring up his salary. Polman repeats his claim that he'd do it for free. The journalists describe how he allows a tense silence to form after giving this answer, waiting to see how they react to this remark. He imagines a possible headline: 'His Salary Doesn't Motivate Him', elaborating: 'Then you get people in the financial industry saying: you are not motivated by your incentive system. And then you guys write a follow-up article. That's how we ruin the thing in my opinion, the whole time. That's why I'm never so keen on having all these interviews, because it's the cynical side that gets the attention in the headlines and the rest, people don't want to read.' His challenge pays off. The piece is published under the title: 'Can Unilever's Paul Polman change the way we do business?'[4]

Marijn Dekkers admires Paul Polman's unstinting dedication. The new board chairman sees a lot of himself in the CEO. They were both raised in catholic communities in the Netherlands, they both married American women and they've both stayed married. Both of them have also spent much of their career working for American companies. Dekkers also thinks that the world needs to make the shift to a form of capitalism that focuses on long-term goals. But this can only happen gradually. The major investors are judged on quarterly results so it's only logical for you to judge yourself by the same measure. If Polman is in favour of revolution, Dekkers is in favour of evolution.

They've got a long road ahead of them but a couple of clear priorities. As a CEO of a company, Dekkers believes you have two tasks: to make money and to obey the law. Lots of CEOs do exactly that and have no energy left over to pursue the things that are important but not necessary for doing business. The fastidious Polman sets a good example in that respect. His work ethic inspires the board chairman. The last time he was out cycling along the Rhine with his wife and wanted to spit out his chewing gum, he had realised he had three choices: throw it on the grass; throw it in a waste bin, knowing that a council worker would then have to scrape it off the inside; or wrap it in a leaf and then throw it in a bin. In that moment he couldn't help but think of Polman. He would always go for option three, so he had done the same.

Looking at Unilever, Dekkers can see that it needn't cost much to do good, treat people well, use less water and be more careful with energy. Relatively little effort can yield big rewards. It might cost you a couple of hundred million a year but what is that compared to the billions a company like Unilever makes?

The news is a bombshell to people all over Europe. Almost 52 per cent of Brits have voted to leave the European Union. Many leaders in the business world, including Paul Polman, are deeply concerned. He had previously told *The Guardian* that Britain was stronger in 'an efficient trading bloc in Europe', saying, 'it's better to sit at the table to drive the changes than not be invited to the table'. This is a step in the wrong direction. How can the majority of Brits possible think that they're better off outside such a powerful bloc? The top brass at Unilever are worried about the consequences for the company and how attractive London will be in the future.

Polman asks Peter ter Kulve to come over to England and take on the role of chief transformation officer. This new function will see him combine his ongoing roll-out of ZBB with work on the now Connected4Growth (C4G) programme. He's the logical man for the job. For years, Ter Kulve has been frustrated by the lack of collaboration between the global marketing team, the category managers and the local marketers in the field. The first group see themselves as the poets of the company and constantly claim to be coming up with amazing ideas which their local colleagues simply don't manage to sell because they lack discipline in execution. For their part, the local marketers accuse their colleagues in the centre of having no idea what's going on in the regions. For example, they don't know about the big cultural differences between Muslims in Indonesia and Muslims in Malaysia. Now that local brands are expanding more quickly, it's essential for Unilever to formulate a solution to this disconnect.

Through the C4G, Ter Kulve aims to do them both a service, mostly by giving marketers in the larger markets capacity to make local adjustments to strategy. If these adjustments turn out to be successful, they can be kicked up the chain to the central marketing team. The teams created through the C4G will be able to react more quickly to changes in all these markets. It's crucial that the local managers don't keep the innovations to themselves in order to make their own success greater by comparison. Ter Kulve rearranges things so that all marketers in the same branch have to report to a global category.

It works and leads to dramatic savings. In forming the cross-hierarchical teams they discover that around 15 per cent of the management has become superfluous. Ter Kulve is pleased, fewer people means less talk and more action. They should have done this four years ago.

Marc Engel agrees with Ter Kulve, this should have happened a couple of years sooner. As prosperity in emerging markets grows, so does the pressure from local competitors. He believes Unilever is struggling to take the next step towards the USLP targets on the sourcing side. They're doing everything they can to nudge the somewhat reserved bean counters out of their comfort zone. Engel is pleased with the impact of a rather challenging meeting he arranged between 150 of their purchasers in Turkey. At that meeting they'd literally learned to sing from the same hymn sheet; an Australian singing coach, Corinne Gibbons, had explained to the rather nervous group of executives that it's important to face the fears in our lives. Facing your fears can be liberating.

Let me guess, none of you think you can sing, said Gibbons. But that's rubbish, everyone can sing. Singing is like laughing; is there anyone hear who can't laugh? And remember, this isn't a competition, if we start thinking about who can sing best, it's going to go wrong. Imagine if all the birds in the forest compared their voices to one another, it'd be pretty quiet.

The purchasers spent three hours singing together. Gibbons had prepared a special song for the occasion: 'You can walk alone, but we can also walk together [...] partnerships of value, are the envy of all. I believe, I believe, in what we can achieve.'

Heidi Knight had enjoyed the event, building something together that's bigger than your own interests is what it's all about. It's the whole reason she came to Unilever from Nokia four years previously. Knight is one of the 60 sourcing managers. She's responsible for the sourcing of marketing materials in Singapore. She sees the way Polman's mighty vision is clashing with the company's sourcing team. The people here are still hyper-focused on cutting costs.

Knight had looked on unenthusiastically as Chief Procurement Officer Dhaval Buch appointed a series of whip-smart Indian colleagues to his team, men who spend all their time obsessively poring over the numbers. The USLP is neither here or there to them. She sympathises with her colleague Cherie Tan, who is working hard to make palm oil production more sustainable but is largely ignored by her colleagues in sourcing.

Knight believes that getting good results in terms of both business and sustainability only works if you're completely invested and therefore willing to work your ass off. One of her colleagues is tasked with purchasing paper in markets where they don't even have a word for recycling. The only way he manages to do it is by putting in heaps of overtime.

In September 2016, Unilever proudly announces its acquisition of the American cleaning product company Seventh Generation. The company has an annual turnover of $200 million. 'We know that plant-based products can provide the efficacy you are looking for, and that products designed from renewable plant-based ingredients bring us closer to a sustainable world than ingredients made from petroleum. We see the environment as a top priority and champion sustainable products. We believe that waste, is well [...] a waste. It's why we use recycled materials to design our packaging, and why we design recyclable packaging in turn. We have a lot of beliefs, but the biggest one is that we have a responsibility to this generation and the next seven.' Kees Kruythoff explains: 'Adding Seventh Generation to Unilever's portfolio of purpose-driven brands like Ben & Jerry's and Dove demonstrates our continued commitment to the Unilever Sustainable Living Plan.'

When the company's founder, Jeffrey Hollender, tells Kruythoff that this is the best day of his life, Kruythoff is touched. Hollender has been trying to get damaging chemicals out of the detergents industry for decades and now, with Unilever's support, they can really start to make some headway. This is what Kruythoff wants too. He thinks Unilever's portfolio needs to change much more quickly so that the company can shed the brands that don't fit and buy up outfits like the one Hollender founded. These brands are often set up by true entrepreneurs, people with deep convictions who are trying to make the world a better place. He thinks it's a shame Polman isn't moving more quickly in this direction.

Paul Polman is in New York at the first board meeting of yet another new initiative: FCLTGlobal. Focusing Capital on the Long Term is bankrolled by BlackRock chairman and CEO Larry Fink, who has taken on the role of strategic advisor to the initiative. Paul Polman is joined on the board by Else Bos, CEO of the big Dutch pension provider PGGM.

FCLT is the brainchild of Dominic Barton, the head of McKinsey management consultancy. The Uganda-born Canadian had garnered attention five years earlier with an article warning the business community against falling back into old habits and returning to 'business-as-usual' only a couple of years on from the financial crisis. He pointed out that public faith in the business world as a force for good had slumped to 21 per cent. After speaking to more than four hundred business leaders, he called on them to return to thinking about big issues in a long-term way.[5] As a result, Barton was invited by former McKinsey director Mickey Huibregtsen to deliver the 2013 Citizenship Lecture in Utrecht. Even back then, he was singing Unilever's praises: 'consider what Paul Polman, CEO of Unilever, has been trying to do since 2010. He set out on a pretty outrageous mission: to double revenues while cutting Unilever's carbon footprint in half. The company's successful work on sustainable agriculture suggests Polman's aspiration may not be so far-fetched.'[6]

After delivering his lecture, Barton had been on his guard. He knew that he was already considered almost a socialist by Wall Street. And a couple of McKinsey's important clients are among those voices. So be it, thinks Barton. McKinsey's latest research shows that 87 per cent of CEOs now feel under pressure, particularly from investors, to get results within two years, 8 per cent more than in 2013.

FCLTGlobal is intended as a platform that will encourage companies and investors alike to embrace the long term. CEO Sarah Williamson is convinced that people make irrational decisions in the short term that aren't in their best interest in the long term. She sees this as a combined result of bad instincts, bad habits and the inability to look at developments over the longer term. The American wants to use FCLT to call on asset managers, wealthy investors and companies to join forces and overcome the mutual distrust that she believes is stopping them from going forward. They need to stop pointing the finger and blaming each other for preventing change. Williamson wants to dispense with terms like 'stakeholders' and abbreviations like 'ESG' too while they're at it. These reek of additional expense and will immediately make anyone in the US business community stop listening.

This minefield is creating headaches for Feike Sijbesma closer to home too. Whenever the CEO of chemical and nutrition company DSM speaks with the board members of pension funds they quickly agree with him that this long-term view has to be central. Of course. But when he talks to the managers of the funds, the people in charge of implementing investment policy, they tell him emphatically that their horizon is 12–18 months max. As far as the CEO of DSM is concerned, this is the problem, these people should learn to work differently.

In October 2016, Feike Sijbesma gives a speech to fund managers of pension provider APG he previously tested on PGGM pension fund managers in spring 2014. Sijbesma is a gifted speaker, just like Polman. He riles up his public, telling them that they're the most important people in the world. He can see that the whole hall is watching him with blank expressions. Sijbesma explains: you're the ones steering the whole world because money makes the world go around and you preside over an enormous pile of money. With that comes great responsibility.

He tells them that by his reckoning their pension funds need to be able to dish out an average of about €900 every month to each (future) participant in the pension scheme. Their current portfolio management strategy, focused on a short-term coverage ratio, means that on average they are in a position to raise that figure by a maximum of €100. Any more would be practically impossible, wouldn't it? The audience nods its agreement. Sijbesma continues: but what is that €100 worth if, for example, it turns out that the short-term orientated companies you invest in turn out to have polluted the world and destroyed the climate to such an extent that the Earth gets 4 degrees hotter. The United Nations have calculated that if this were to happen, hundreds of millions of refugees would flee in this direction. In that case, governments would likely be forced to raise taxes by much more than €100 per month in order to be able to fund the response. Will you really think you've done such a good job then? The fund managers shake their heads sadly. No, of course not, but they aren't the ones responsible for the system in which they operate. They tell Sijbesma to go and have a word with governments and watchdogs like the De Nederlandsche Bank, the Dutch central bank. They make the rules, it is their system they have to operate in.

Sijbesma believes that companies and their shareholders need to get to grips with this issue together rather than waiting for politicians. Polman agrees entirely, he's had the same experience with pension funds. He also thinks they need to be making more effort to approach their task – securing decent pensions – in a more holistic way. But doing that requires courage.

Marcel Jeucken thinks that this courage is entirely lacking at present. The director of 'responsible investment' at PGGM originally chose to study economics because he wanted to do something about the growing inequality across the world. Jeucken is pleased with the strides that PGGM, handling the investments for the Dutch pension fund PFZW (Pension Fund for Care and Well-Being), has been making over the past ten years, and particularly since Else Bos took over as CEO. Yet he's also afraid that those known internally as the 'realists' will win out over the so-called idealists.

As he sees it, the crisis of 2008 put two into motion two distinct developments. On the one hand, there's a growing demand for sustainable investment policy, which means that more people like him are being taken on by companies. On the other hand, everyone was so startled by the crisis that they've also taken on a host of additional 'risk managers'. These managers are totally focused on monitoring and avoiding risks and are allowed to question all decisions made by individual portfolio managers. They often have the power to veto decisions outright. These risk managers base their assessments on tried and tested models that use historical data. There's hardly any such data available on something like climate risk, they can't factor it in so they quickly conclude that it's not important enough to take into account.

Jeucken thinks that pension funds need to start doing something about that. This is where the power lies so that's where they need to find the courage to ensure that short-term losses (and risks) are accepted for the sake of long-term objectives. But for that you need to have people who create space for a degree of idealism. Jeucken finds himself wondering whether any of these people exist in the rather old, conservative management boards of pension funds. The simple fact is that these boards aren't getting any younger, despite efforts to the contrary. He also observes that the pension fund regulator De Nederlandsche Bank is often less than impressed with the quality of these boards too, and tacks on additional demands on compliance officers and risk managers in order to compensate. That compounds the problem by making the latter even more cautious.

The same mealy-mouthed phrases seem to come up in all of these discussions about the extent of pension funds' responsibility for big social and climate issues: we want to but it is our fiduciary duty to provide good pensions in terms of money. We need to secure a decent pension for all of our members. Many of the big players, particularly American ones, think that all non-financial factors lie outside their remit; they aren't part of this financial duty of care.

The governor of the Bank of England, Mark Carney, once called this problem 'how to break the tragedy of the horizon'. 'Why isn't more being done to address it? We don't need an army of actuaries to tell us that the catastrophic impacts of climate change will be felt beyond the traditional horizons of most actors – imposing a cost on future generations that the current generation has no direct incentive to fix. The horizon for monetary policy extends out to 2–3 years. For financial stability it is a bit longer, but typically only to the outer boundaries of the credit cycle – about a decade. In other words, once climate change becomes a defining issue for financial stability, it may already be too late.'[7] His colleague Klaas Knot, the president of the Dutch central bank, is also deeply concerned. How can the dynamics of the financial markets be changed so that the consequences of big, unavoidable developments can be anticipated in good time? His bank has recently had to start asking pension funds to what extent their investment policy takes into account environmental, climactic, human rights and social issues. And it's obvious they simply aren't doing so. The bottom line always wins the argument. Their point of departure is what is known as hypothetical liquidation: will this venture be able to pay all of its investors if it goes belly up now.

Jean Frijns, the man who drafted the first of the Tabaksblat Code changes back in 2008 and a dyed in the wool pension funds manager, is unwilling to compromise on this point. He has seen first-hand the way pension funds have increasingly come to be dominated by bureaucracy and short mandates over the past few decades. And remember this is an industry worth €1.3 trillion in the Netherlands alone. He's naturally encouraged by the new governance code recently drawn up by former PwC governance expert Jaap van Manen, which calls on the management of big businesses to focus explicitly on creating long-term value and place the interests of all stakeholders at the heart of what they do. But as far as Frijns is concerned, it's the job of governments to enforce this through legislation. They need to work closely with each other to do so. He hopes that after Brexit France and Germany in particular will be able to revitalise this approach across Europe, where the proximity between business and stakeholders has historically been a central part of the doing business. That could help to square the circle.

Oliver Hart would beg to differ. For him, it's the wishes of the members of pension schemes who provide the key to long-term thinking. The Harvard economist and Nobel Prize winner is convinced that pension scheme members want the fund to work for them on two fronts: they want a good return and they want the money set aside for their retirement to 'do the right thing', thinking of things like the climate and how it might affect their children and grandchildren. Hart calls the latter the desire for a 'warm glow'. It is not easy to combine the two wishes. They simply don't trust the business world enough when it comes to providing that feel-good factor. For that reason, they tend to ask their pension funds to provide them with the maximum possible financial return in order to retain enough assets to contribute to good causes themselves. In essence, holding onto as much money as they can in hopes of securing that good feeling for themselves as individuals.

As far as Hart sees it, this is far from ideal. He thinks that pension funds should be making use of online information technology to ask their members which key sustainability issues they think are the most important. They should then translate that mandate into a corresponding investment strategy. From then on, their investors can make sure that the company they're investing in is providing them with both things: a decent return and a warm glow.[8]

In the meanwhile, Paul Polman is beginning to worry that his new board chairman isn't fully committed to this 'warm glow', the great cause. Bringing him up to speed is taking him longer than he thought. Marijn Dekkers obviously isn't a man with sustainable thinking hardwired into his DNA. Polman often gets the feeling that Dekkers isn't on the same wavelength.

For his part, the board chairman isn't one to conceal his irritation if he thinks they're spending too much time talking about the USLP: he wants to earn money first, then do good. When asked to explain why he takes this position, Dekkers uses his three daughters as an example. When they were younger, they all wanted to stay out late all the time but he asked to see their report cards first. They were only allowed out if they were making good grades – a B+ at the very least.

Paul Polman is starting to feel the pressure. This is clear to Unilever's biggest analysts when they gather to hear him speak during their annual meeting in Port Sunlight in November 2016. Polman always needs to psych himself up for this meeting with a room full of people who've come to talk about margins and sales growth but sit there glassy eyed whenever the topic of the USLP comes up. He decides to focus his presentation on the numbers as much as he can, mostly talking about what's been achieved. Personal care sales have risen from €12 to €20 billion over eight years, the profit margin has improved by 1.7 per cent over the past three years to over 15 per cent. This isn't an impressive figure by the standards of the analysts, a specialist personal care company like L'Oréal is cruising at over 20 per cent and they aren't the only ones. The analysts regard so small a margin as acceptable when a company is growing quicker than its competitors, but when growth slows down, they start to worry.

Looking ahead, Polman is concerned too: 'The market of food is changing incredibly rapidly, changing faster than I have seen in my modest 35 years in the industry.' Turning to the spreads division he says: 'This business is becoming smaller by definition. Putting it into a separate unit has actually been the right decision. From a cash flow point of view it continues to be an attractive business for us but at the same time we will continue to look at other options. If the moment comes where we think that value can be better created outside, we owe it to anybody to pursue that option but we simply haven't found it yet.'

A number of colleagues remark on how timid and cautious their CEO seems. He's obviously in his 'under-promise, over-deliver' mode, with emphasis on the under-promise element. We'll share our results once they're actually there.

Why isn't he talking about the huge investment Unilever has made in brands and processes over the last few years, or telling them what wonderful results they can expect from it. Why isn't he pushing the C4G's ZBB initiative? This is what investors are waiting for, and their trust in Unilever seems to have taken a slight knock over the past few months. In the space of two months the share price, and therefore the company, lost 15 per cent of its value. The share price is back below €37.

On the stage at Port Sunlight, Polman only really comes alive when he starts talking about the USLP: 'It's also important that we talk about the basic philosophy of how we do business and that is captured in our USLP. You've seen some of that today but again increasingly if you open the newspapers on a daily basis. I hope it is increasingly relevant to most if not all of you that running your business in a responsible way for multiple stakeholders is increasingly important. We have to find a system that guarantees the future of mankind and that takes future generations into account that doesn't create a further burden on the world but provides solutions to solve some of these problems and makes it a more inclusive growth model. Otherwise you'll get a lot more results like you've seen here in the UK with Brexit or the recent results of the US elections.'

Graeme Pitkethly is also unsettled. Donald Trump, who was elected US president two weeks previously, has given rise to fresh enthusiasm for isolation-ist economics with his 'America First' message. With Brexit, this is the second time in a relatively short period that a country has explicitly spoken out against further globalisation of the world's economy. He can see that Polman is at a loss here too. What's going on? Neither of them have a ready answer.

The CFO gets on well with the CEO. The Scot much prefers the direct, confrontational approach of his Dutch colleagues to the English approach of not saying what one means. He's happy to be away from all the intrigue.

When Pitkethly hears Dekkers and Polman talking, he thinks that he lies somewhere in between them. He once summed up his purpose in life as 'bringing people together, doing your best and winning with a smile on your face'. For him, the consumer comes first. But if he had to choose between 'making money by doing the right thing' and 'doing the right thing by earn-ing money', he'd choose the latter. If you're not making enough money, you may as well not exist. The CFO also thinks that Polman has lost the plot over the past few years, spending too much time playing the evangelist. Unilever isn't the biggest NGO in the world, that's nonsense. Pitkethly knows full well that Polman only makes such declarations to provoke a discussion but he needs to keep in mind that he's first and foremost the CEO of a publicly listed multinational.

'Unilever forced to do without the tailwind of low interest rates', says the *Het Financieele Dagblad* headline. A whole series of analysts are pointing out that companies like Unilever have had it fairly easy of the past few years. The inter-est rate was so low that a fund that kept on loyally raising its dividend year on year could be certain of a fantastic return. After Trump's election, those inter-est rates had started to climb slightly and government loans once again became an interesting prospect. This does much to explain Unilever's rapid drop in share price over the past few months. The company will once again have to start attracting investors on the basis of revenue growth and improved profit margins. If they don't manage that, it will be a tough road ahead of them.[9]

At the end of January 2017, Unilever announces that turnover in 2016 amounted to €52.7 billion, a reduction of 1 per cent on 2015. Corrected for currency changes, turnover actually did grow by 3.7 per cent but that's also a reduction on the year before. Investors are particularly alarmed by the fourth quarter results: 'In the markets in which we operate sales growth was flat.'

That even applies to emerging markets, the ones Unilever was supposed to derive its growth from over the past few years. Polman tells people to expect the tough market conditions that dogged the business at the end of the year to continue throughout the first half of 2017. Analysts line up to declare the results and projections 'disappointing'. The share price immediately drops 4.4 per cent. Jane Davie, assets manager at Fidelity, tells *Het Financieele Dagblad* that Unilever's valuation has dropped so sharply that it's now hit rock bottom. The value of Unilever is now 12.5 times the expected company result, the average for the sector is around 15 times. Unilever is cheap.

Obviously, Paul Polman is disappointed too. The Brexit result and the election of Donald Trump are signs that the world is going in the wrong direction. Suspicion and self-interest are stymying the ambitions of the Paris Climate Agreement and the UN's Sustainable Development Goals. Year 2016 had not brought what he had hoped.

Nevertheless, he is keeping his nerve. He makes this clear in his presentation of 'Better Business, Better World', the first report from the Business & Sustainable Development Commission of which he is co-founder. This organisation is intended to assist companies in building the SDGs into their strategy. The commission enthusiastically declares that implementing the SDGs is going to create at least $12 trillion in business opportunities. It will create 380 million jobs. 'If a critical mass of companies joins us in doing this now, together we will become an unstoppable force. If they don't, the costs and uncertainty of unsustainable development could swell until there is no viable world in which to do business. Business as usual is not an option: choosing to "kick the can down the road" over the next four years will put impossible environmental and social strains on a stuttering global economy.'[10]

'In recent months we've had the Brexit vote in Britain and the Trump phenomenon in the US, with large segments of both populations revealing that they feel excluded and disillusioned. Both events have been coupled with a concern about the direction of our modern world today; a worry many share about an economic system that isn't quite functioning for us anymore, that caters for the few and not the many.' This is how Paul Polman opens his essay in *Imaginal Cells*, the book by Kim Polman and Stephen Vasconcellos-Sharpe. They combine the launch of the collection with the establishment of a new foundation called Reboot the Future, intended to spread the message behind *Imaginal Cells*. Paul is proud of his wife. He puts a stack of books on his desk to hand out to visitors.

PART 3

Doing Well and Doing Good, 2017–2019

CHAPTER 15

'RESCUED' BY WARREN BUFFETT

11 February–7 March 2017

After Burgmans and Fitzgerald announced their 'Path to Growth' plan back in 1998, he'd briefly toyed with the idea of ploughing money into Unilever shares. But Warren Buffet had decided to put that money into shares in Gillette. That had paid off. When Procter & Gamble sold off the razor manufacturer seven years later, he'd turned a profit of $4.4 billion.

And it was still paying off. During his tenure as a director at Gillette, he'd got to know Jorge Paulo Lemann. In 1998, when the Brazilian billionaire told him he planned to sell his Banco de Investimentos Garantia, Buffet had asked him why. After all, that bank was his baby. Lemann's answer sealed their friendship. He told him he had no desire to wind up as the head of a big bank and would rather do what Buffett did. 'You have better control of your time, you have a better sense of humor, and you are much richer.' Warren Buffet regards the fact that the two men only joined forces in 2013, during the takeover of Heinz, as one of the greatest mistakes of his life. They should have teamed up much sooner. He and Lemann are on exactly the same wavelength.[1]

Buffett and Lemann are dreaming big. Buffet regards his investment vehicle Berkshire Hathaway as his big painting, a piece of art that's never quite perfect but should be improved a little each year. Lemann fantasises of using 3G Capital to build a management model that becomes the benchmark for all successful companies in the twenty-first century.[2] Just like Paul Polman, Jorge Paulo Lemann and Warren Buffett dream of their own immortality.

When asked about his strategy, Jorge Lemann insists that he's basically a clever copycat. Over the last forty years he's been inspired by the success of big American firms and banks like General Electric, Walmart and Goldman Sachs. The two billionaires target their investment at big, globally successful consumer goods brands like Heinz, Kraft, Burger King and Budweiser which make the owner of brands like Dove, Magnum and Lipton an obvious next target. They're all brands the two men regard as more or less immortal. If managed properly they'll keep earning their owners a lot of money for many years to come.

In the run-up to their bid for Unilever they agreed that it would be a friendly takeover. Eighty-six-year-old Buffett doesn't believe in takeovers at the expense of the present management team, and anyway, a welcome acquisition delivers better results more quickly. This is why, as a rule, he always opens proceedings by asking whether the board of the company he's targeting would like to hear his offer. If their answer is a decided 'no', then he breaks off pursuit. Anything else would make it a hostile takeover in his view. His Brazilian partners see things a little differently. This 'no' from the other team could be a strategic move to tempt them into making a higher offer. 'No' can be the beginning of a productive negotiation.

In Unilever's case, they've agreed that if their scout Alexandre Behring feels that his meeting with Paul Polman went well, this means it can't be a hostile takeover. That will indicate that they can work together to find a way to get on the same page. Behring is dispatched to test the water. In due course, the chairman at Kraft Heinz had come back to Lemann and Buffett; he hadn't heard a hard 'no'. His second meeting with the Unilever CEO on 10 February had also been a friendly affair so he had left Paul Polman with an outline of their offer.

The CEO of Unilever experiences things very differently. Polman feels like he's two-nil behind. Kraft Heinz had months to prepare for such an onslaught. Unilever has a couple of weeks at most to get its defence in order. He hears on the grapevine that Kraft Heinz has gone so far as to hire someone to do a background check on him. They'll approach people who know him, pretending that there's a new, prestigious position in the offing for him and asking them to answer a couple of questions about his character: What are his strengths and weaknesses as CEO?

Even more importantly, and more ominously, Kraft Heinz has built an excellent war chest. Polman hears that Jamie Dimon, CEO of JP Morgan Chase, has announced that his bank will underwrite the financing of the takeover. Polman asks his CFO Graeme Pitkethly to dispatch their team of advising bankers and make sure that Unilever has an answer ready for each new development. He warns his financial director; whatever you hear, bear in mind that most bankers want this deal to go ahead. A deal that goes through always serves them better than a deal that fails.

By this time, Unilever has secured the services of around forty bankers from Morgan Stanley, Centerview, UBS and Deutsche Bank to advise them on the situation. They have been chosen as much for their knowledge of their counterparts working for Kraft Heinz, who are mostly being advised by bankers from Lazard, as for their maths skills. They view the whole thing as an elaborate game of chess. The player that best sizes up their opponent will come out on top.

Most bankers, almost all of them men, know each other well. They have come across one another repeatedly at various negotiation tables over the years. A firm like 3G Capital is their favourite type of client. The Brazilians have brought them all some massive deals over the past few years. Four years ago they splashed out over $23 billion for Heinz and two years later they paid around $45 billion to take over Kraft. Last year AB InBev paid out the princely sum of $104 billion for SABMiller. All this is good for business. It's not unusual for each of the bankers involved to walk away from a deal like that with between 1 per cent and 2 per cent of the total transaction in their pocket. Collectively, they've made tens of millions from these Brazilians' ambitions.

A whole host of legal specialists and PR advisors are now on retainer alongside the bankers. Polman takes their advice with a pinch of salt too: these people spend most of their time telling you everything that isn't allowed and everything you shouldn't do. If you listen to them too closely, you constantly pump the brakes, when this sort of situation requires exactly the opposite. You need to be proactive, even if there are risks attached.

While the CFO is working hands-on to deal with this looming takeover – with calculations, scenarios and preventative measures – Polman is doing what he sees as his job: making sure that the context in which this takeover is supposed to take place changes so much that it's completely illogical to go through with the deal. In order to do that, he needs to activate his network, Unilever's network, at exactly the right time, to alert the world to what's happening and ask as many influential figures as possible to express their disapproval. Public opinion has to be mobilised. The more emphatic their negative reaction, the more hostile the climate becomes.

The team of bankers and advisors led by Pitkethly quickly come to a couple of conclusions. Kraft Heinz's timing is impeccable. The dollar is stronger against the euro or the British pound, thanks to Brexit. Their share price is at an all-time high, while Unilever's share price has taken a beating in the last few months and currently stands 13 per cent lower.

The advisors underline what they regard as Unilever's problematic finances. The company is in relatively little debt. They can understand why: big companies want to be in a good position to pursue big acquisitions and being able to borrow large sums quickly means keeping debts in check. This potential financial firepower is important for Unilever especially. The NV–*PLC* structure makes paying for acquisitions with shares basically impossible: their shares are in two different places.

By taking on less debt, companies like Unilever, Nestlé and Procter & Gamble also ensure they receive a so-called A-rating. That declares that lending money to them is a safe bet and that they only need to pay a low interest rate on what they borrow. But while a debt–asset ratio of 1.8 is suitable for a company dealing only in personal hygiene products, companies in the food industry take on twice as much debt. It seems like Unilever has forgotten how deeply involved it still is in food.

The big disadvantage of having so little debt immediately becomes apparent. The Buffett–Lemann offer of €134 billion is 60 per cent cash, with the balance to be paid in shares to Kraft Heinz. They can borrow the vast majority of the approximately €80 billion they need to make the deal because Unilever's balance is so low. Their banks are giving them permission to shift the balance of the debt–asset ratio from 1.8 to between 7 and 8 and thereby take on around €65 billion in new debt on behalf of the company, and put them on Unilever's balance sheet. In other words: they only need to bring about €15 billion to the table themselves in order to buy one of the biggest companies in the world.

The four billionaires are more than capable of raising such a sum. Together they are worth more than $150 billion on paper. Since the vast majority of this wealth is tied up in other investments, Unilever's advisors anticipate that Buffett will be the one bringing most of the money to the table. He could probably manage to extend a loan of $20 billion. They suspect that Kraft Heinz intends to use the takeover to start a completely fresh venture, combining the takeover of all suitable food products by Kraft Heinz with an expansion into the personal and domestic hygiene market. The advisors reckon that a new colossus of that type could make enormous cuts to its costs, not only in its terms of its own manufacturing processes but in terms of negotiating with retailers, including the supermarket chains that sell the majority of the products to billions of consumers. Their calculations suggest that the four men behind the Unilever bid make a profit of 30 per cent on what would be an investment of approximately €150 billion. That would mean them walking away with a total of around €50 billion within only a couple of years.

Reflecting on this news makes Polman sick to his stomach. Unilever is being abused in order to make a couple of already stinking rich billionaires that much richer. And this totally unwanted takeover, which would destroy his life's work, would mostly be financed by Unilever itself. It's also clear that they're in a position to raise their current offer of €47 per share to as much as

€56. Now he's really scared. That would mean a premium of 35–40 per cent or more on the current share price. Unilever's shareholders would eagerly accept an offer like that, destroying 'his' Unilever forever.

He's sleeping less than two hours a night. Every now and then he gets in touch with his wife. Kim Polman is worried. She is well aware that this is the fight of his life, but he needs to take care. Her husband has the tendency to shoulder the weight of the work. The couple have agreed that if Kraft Heinz comes out on top, they'll use the €200 million Alexandre Behring offered Paul Polman to invest in good causes. Kim will spend the week concentrating on sending her husband good thoughts from their house in Geneva, trying to send him the strength to do what is needed. It's do or die now.

For the umpteenth time in these few short weeks, the Unilever board is summoned to a meeting with Polman. It's essential for the CEO to know for certain that he still has their support. After all, they're the ones who have to make the most important decisions. He's been reassured that they've given him the freedom to act as he sees fit during the crisis. As they listen to Polman speak, directors like Louise Fresco, Feike Sijbesma and Ann Fudge can't help but think of Graeme Pitkethly's predecessor Jean-Marc Huët now and again. Didn't Huët warn them back in 2012 about the lack of attention being paid to shareholders' interests? Hadn't he pointed out the lack of debt on their books? That is what has suddenly made Unilever affordable to Kraft Heinz.

In various messages to Behring and Buffett on behalf of the Unilever board, Paul Polman explains that they aren't interested in their scheme. He receives no reply. This makes the Unilever team even more worried. Aren't they listening to these letters, aren't they having any impact? Why aren't they responding? Apparently this isn't going to be a standard negotiation and Kraft Heinz is serious about pursuing this course. Polman doesn't think there's any point talking to the Brazilians but perhaps Warren Buffett will listen.

Meanwhile, the market is responding poorly to the disappointing quarterly figures Kraft Heinz publishes on Thursday, 16 February. Their share price falls 5.5 per cent. The Kraft Heinz board is locked in a meeting discussing what they should do. The decline in their own share price will make the takeover of Unilever a good deal more expensive. They need time to get to grips with exactly what the financial consequences of this dip will be. How much scope do they now have to come back with a much higher offer? Their big fear is that their previous offer will become public knowledge. They now need to make every effort to stop this news from leaking for as long as they can.[3]

A couple of dozen miles up the road, the Unilever board is discussing the advantages of just such a leak, and the sooner the better. If the news comes out tomorrow and Kraft Heinz is put on the spot, they'll only have the weekend to figure out whether they can come up with a much higher offer despite the lower share price. That isn't much time to decide whether to cough up a sum that will soon add up to tens of billions of euros.

With the offer made public, Unilever will also have freedom to work with third parties and build its defence, particularly by putting pressure on Warren Buffet. Effectively, they'd be forcing Kraft Heinz to assess the scope for raising their offer by a considerable amount within only two days. At this point, around fifty bankers and advisors are aware of the bid, so it wouldn't be all that surprising for the news to get out. Louise Fresco thinks this is a smart move. They'll use it to their full advantage.

In fact, the news is already doing the rounds. In the Netherlands, Kees van der Waaij sees the secretary leave the meeting out of the corner of his eye. What could be going on? The Unilever lifer has been chairman of the Dutch daughter company for four years. That Unilever subsidiary has its own board. Even though the spreads division isn't part of the Dutch company, its anticipated sale is firmly on their agenda. They see Polman's internal announcement that the Dutch 'DNA' of Unilever is going to be sold after all as a real embarrassment. This sale will have very real consequences for Unilever's image in the Netherlands. Van der Waaij's executive board acts as a sounding board for the workers' council of the spreads division. They're concerned about working conditions, what will a new owner do with them?

During the lunch break, the obviously stressed secretary tells Van der Waaij that an offer is likely to be made on the whole of Unilever. He explains that he left the meeting so abruptly because he'd had a message telling him that Unilever's share price was acting erratically. For a moment, Van der Waaij is speechless. In the over forty-one years he has worked for Unilever it has never even occurred to him that Unilever – his Unilever – could fall prey to a takeover. With its size and power, Unilever had always been the hunter. This isn't possible.

It's driving Bryce Elder mad. The rumours that something is about to happen are getting stronger by the minute. He wants to publish. The British freelance journalist has spent days working on the spectacular story of how Kraft Heinz wants to make a bid for Unilever. He and a couple of colleagues have interviewed dozens of sources over the past few days, including from the two companies and a whole list of banks. He's convinced that the story is on the level but his colleagues at the *Financial Times*'s Alphaville news service are being cautious. This is big. If you're publishing something like this as fact, you have to be 100 per cent certain. There's no hard proof. Not yet. It almost seems like the key players are stringing them along.

As such, they've reached the decision to publish the news today, Friday, 17 February, at 11 a.m., as a rumour on the *Markets Live* chat. Elder is under time pressure. He knows for sure that he's racing against big competitors like Bloomberg and Reuters. He wants this scoop. The only thing stopping him is that he can't get in touch with Paul Murphy, the editor-in-chief. Something is wrong with the IT system, it's down. As he wrestles with the connection, he keeps an eye on his child, who's got the day off and is lying on the sofa watching *Finding Nemo*.

Twenty minutes later, the two men are in touch over online chat. Elder tells Murphy that Unilever has been approached, people are dropping the names 3G Capital and Warren Buffett. Murphy wants to know how credible this is: 'You can't just put these kinds of reports out there.' Elder emphasises the fact that this is a rumour, spread by people whose tips tend to be on the money. Since Wednesday that week there have been a striking number of transactions on options speculating on an increase to both Unilever and Kraft Heinz's share prices. He tells Murphy that he's made enough phone calls over the last twenty-four hours to be confident publishing this news, 'we're not really doing anything more than spreading a rumour from a small clique to a larger public'.

Other news services, including Bloomberg, immediately get in on the conversation. The men watch Unilever's share price on their little screens. It's gone up over 10 per cent in the last half an hour.

Kraft Heinz is infuriated. They are convinced that Unilever leaked the news in order to force just such a change. Because now the British regulator requires that Kraft Heinz make a statement: put up or shut up. Forty-five minutes later, Kraft Heinz explains in a press release that it made 'a comprehensive proposal to Unilever about combining the two groups to create a leading consumer goods company with a mission of long-term growth and sustainable living'. They also inform the public that Unilever declined their invitation to negotiate but that Kraft Heinz continued to 'look forward to working to reach agreement on the terms of a transaction'. Kraft Heinz emphasises that no formal offer is yet on the table and it feels honour-bound to clarify its position by 17 March.

Unilever responds immediately. On the advice of a couple of their bankers, communications director Sue Garrard turns down the offer in uncharacteristically strong terms. The company claims to see zero financial or strategic advantage for its own shareholders in the deal. The company sees the offer, with a premium of around 18 per cent, as a fundamental undervaluation of Unilever's worth. 'Unilever does not see the basis for any further discussions and recommend that shareholders take no action.'

During his weekly meeting with the press that Friday afternoon, Dutch prime minister Mark Rutte does his best to keep out of it. Naturally, he's shocked. It feels personal for him too. He spent years working for this company, it's where he learned his most important lessons about leadership before going into politics. But he needs more information to go on before he says anything. The dyed in the wool liberal is on his guard: the powers of supply and demand need to have free rein in a free market. Vince Cable, the British chancellor, tells reporters that there are no legal powers to prevent such a deal but asks the competition authority to take a close look at the merger.

Polman feels let down by these meagre responses from politicians. But he notes that his efforts *are* having an effect in other areas. He's pleased to see the quick, unambiguous rejection of the plan from trade unions, particularly the British ones. He's also glad of the petition that's been set up on YouGov protesting the potential takeover, it already has almost 100,000 signatures. The former American vice-president and climate activist Al Gore offers his assistance. Polman is also buoyed by a call from Bono, the frontman and activist from U2, who tells him he's ready and willing to write a protest song. Polman regards Bono as a good friend, they see each other almost every year at the World Economic Forum in Davos.

The Unilever share price closes 13.4 per cent higher on Friday afternoon. The market doesn't seem to be very taken with the offer. Various shareholders come forward, saying that the offer is much too low. In doing so, they co-sign the message coming from Unilever leadership. The bankers advising the company insist that they now need to do everything they can to prevent Kraft Heinz from coming back on Monday with a higher offer. Once that's on the table, investors, particularly hedge funds, will sign up for the merger en masse, in the hope of selling their shares to the obviously hungry Kraft Heinz within the next couple of weeks for as high a price as possible. The British Takeover Code – much hated by Polman for effectively sidelining the sitting management – requires that the acquiring and selling parties are seen to reach an agreement within twenty-eight days. The advisors show the Unilever board research demonstrating that only one in four takeover targets survives the abrupt share price hike as independent companies.

Patrick Cescau, the former CEO of Unilever, is not happy about it. He thinks it's great that Polman has managed to take his ambition a step further. While Polman has spent years talking about 'doing well by doing good', Cescau had focused on 'doing well and then doing good'. For a while Cescau was angry, the media spent years after he'd left going on about the mess Polman supposedly inherited when he became boss in 2009 and how he'd supposedly gone on to transform the company, even though that was nonsense. He, Patrick Cescau, had been the one who transformed Unilever. Between 2005 and 2009 he'd cleared away rubble and tidied up the company, clearing the way, as it were, for his successors until recently so successful adventures.

He sees Kraft Heinz's offer as proof that Polman has got ahead of himself. In the eyes of the Frenchman, the battle with high finance, constantly in search of quick returns, can never be won if you don't work even harder, keep improving the margins and cut the fat when and where you need to. Because outfits like Kraft Heinz won't hesitate to do it for you. They aren't interested in shared values. There is only one value: their wallet. And if they have to destroy a wonderful company like Unilever in order to line it, they will do just that. Cescau sees what a big test this is for Unilever too, it's a fight for survival, life and death. The company, and its CEO, will live or die by the outcome.

For a moment, his thoughts turn automatically to their shared escape from the Taj Mahal Hotel in Mumbai more than eight years ago. They spend hours huddled in the dark with the top brass from the Indian daughter company Hindustan Lever and their respective partners, hoping and praying that they wouldn't be found by the Islamic terrorists who were murdering dozens of people all around them. They'd been incredibly lucky back then.

Harish Manwani, the man who had organised this unfortunate leaving party for Cescau, is very concerned right now too. The Indian thinks that Kraft Heinz started eyeing Unilever ever more hungrily as they started talking more and more constantly about the fight against poverty and climate change and too little about the good financial results they were managing to get. This only increased after his stint as COO came to an end in 2014. In his view, Polman has paid too little attention to the shareholders, not managing to make clear to them how good they've got it already and how good they're going to have it further down the line.

Polman also receives a call from Niall FitzGerald. The Irishman has often helped him out with advice over the past few years. They're both on the board at the Leverhulme Trust, the foundation funded by a bequest from Lord Leverhulme and PLC shareholder to the tune of over 6 per cent. The return is used to distribute around £100 million to good causes in healthcare each year. William Lever would turn over in his grave if his brainchild, his legacy, were to fall into the hands of an outfit like Kraft Heinz. FitzGerald asks Polman whether he can do anything to help and offers to call Warren Buffett the next day. The two men know each other well, for 20 years at this point.

Marijn Dekkers is convinced that Unilever will get into difficulty if the Brazilians raise their takeover bid to 35 per cent. The Unilever board is increasingly coming to the realisation that Warren Buffett is the Achilles's heel of the whole venture. Convincing him not to pursue it is the only chance Unilever has to fend off the attack. And they'll have to do it within forty-eight hours, before the markets open again. Buffett will have to be the one to call off the deal.

Not everyone at Unilever is hoping for such an outcome. Here and there, a few people are even hoping that this takeover will go ahead. There are still those across the company who have never truly understood or believed in the whole USLP idea. A company is just a company and companies aren't brought into the world in order to improve it. But there's another issue. They've read about how the top 30 at Heinz were let go with a settlement of $5–$20 million after the takeover by 3G Capital. Polman is fuming when he hears this could be an incentive. The first person who as much as dares to suggest that accepting Kraft Heinz's offer might not be such a crazy idea from a personal point of view will be fired on the spot. He regards this as high treason.

Polman is also angry about the media reports he keeps happening across. They say it's logical for the highly profitable Kraft Heinz to be making an offer and that there's evidence of underperformance at Unilever. Polman has noticed before that the media never holds back if it sees a fight in the offing. They just love summing up the whole situation into a drama featuring winners and losers. They're always up for conflict, because conflict sells. Bankers, lawyers, shareholders, media, parties on all sides who want to see a fight and a deal: Unilever is surrounded by them. To Polman this is a tragedy, but it's undeniable, they all stand to profit.

A number of bankers, who've been busy poring over on the deal for days now, wonder privately whether Polman wasn't too friendly in the meetings with Behring. They could well imagine that his keeping his composure and reacting reasonably might have confused the Brazilian. He might start thinking: we're getting on well, we'll reach a deal eventually.

The bankers think the people at Kraft Heinz are playing the game very cleverly. They've called Unilever's advisors every so often over the past few days to ask whether they can help with anything. That's obviously out of the question, so the answer is always: be off with you, we've turned down your offer. But on the Unilever side, they believe that these people from 3G Capital are doing it so they can tell Warren Buffett hand on heart that they're trying: do you see, we're in constant discussion with them, this is anything but a hostile takeover. Polman blames the bankers from Lazard, Kraft Heinz's advisors. They seem intent on suggesting that their opponent is willing to negotiate.

He regards this as completely underhanded, there is absolutely no space to negotiate.

However, the bankers wouldn't call Kraft Heinz's preparations completely optimal either. For example, they seem to have been unaware that the Dutch prime minister Mark Rutte once worked for Unilever and has been kept informed about the ins and outs of his former employer's situation over the weekend. Will they take the political climate in the Netherlands or the United Kingdom at all?

Through his network of contacts, Polman hears on Saturday, 18 February that Kraft Heinz has hired the PR company Finsbury to optimise communications around the deal. Finsbury is a daughter company of WPP, one of Unilever's main advertising companies. Polman hits the roof and sends a furious email to Sir Martin Sorrell, the founder and CEO of WPP. If Sorrell wants to keep his relationship with Unilever, the second biggest advertiser in the world, then he needs to make sure that Finsbury withdraw from this contract. Sorrell chooses the bird in the hand; Finsbury quit as Kraft Heinz's advisor within a couple of hours. They have to go looking for another advisor right in the heat of battle.

That morning, Warren Buffett's phone rings off the hook. Various close acquaintances, including Al Gore and Niall FitzGerald, deliver the same message: give it up, this is getting hostile. This will cost you your reputation.

The call from Michael Klein makes a particularly big impression. Polman knows this banker from his role as a director at Dow Chemical. When that company was in trouble, Michael Klein, then at Citibank had negotiated a loan of $3 billion from Buffett. This loan had more than paid off for Buffett and Klein and Buffett regard each other as friends. Polman asked Klein to call Buffett on his behalf. The American investor absolutely doesn't want to talk to Polman directly, let alone get into a negotiation. If it were to go wrong, he'd be directly involved in a hostile takeover attempt and perhaps even a failure. This is unthinkable.

When Buffett hears Klein insist in the same tone as the others that this is going to end up being a hostile takeover, he starts to reconsider. The American billionaire starts to think that he might have given his friends at 3G Capital too much freedom to do it their way. This certainly isn't how he does business. Buffett resolves to get in touch with his friend Jorge Paulo Lemann.

Polman did not sleep a wink. What are his attackers going to do? Are the ones on the other side of the Atlantic awake yet? This deal has to be aborted sometime this Sunday afternoon, morning in America.

When Kraft Heinz tells them that Sunday afternoon that the deal is off the table, the relief at Unilever is enormous. In an ultra-brief joint announcement, The Kraft Heinz Company says that it has agreed to withdraw its proposal to combine the two companies. 'Unilever and Kraft Heinz hold each other in high regard. Kraft Heinz has the utmost respect for the culture, strategy and leadership of Unilever.'

Inside Unilever everyone believes that this is down to Buffett, he withdrew from the deal. Without guarantees from him, the banks would withdraw their promised loans. The Brazilians are rich, but they're not rich enough to put down €135 billion on their own.

A sigh of relief echoes around the Dutch-British company. They've managed to fend off a couple of billionaires with extremely deep pockets just in time. But everyone also knows that this is just the calm before the storm. According to British law, their assailants are allowed to make another attempt in six months' time. And now that Kraft Heinz has demonstrated how quickly value can be squeezed out of Unilever, the shareholders are also going to be expecting something. Unilever has until August to show what it's worth. Doing so is the only way to keep Kraft Heinz from the door.

A tremor is passing through the company. What is all this going to mean? The Unilever share price has continued to rise. Investors will be expecting the price to remain high and to increase. It has to. The higher the share price, the more expensive Unilever becomes and the smaller the chance that the Brazilians will dare to make another attempt. It's not pleasant but in order to do this, Unilever is going to have to read from Kraft Heinz's playbook. Polman is going to have to convince his shareholders to invest further. Unilever is also going to have to take on debt in order to buy shares itself. It's unavoidable now.

Unilever's board members mostly feel relieved. The company has passed through the eye of a needle. They think Polman and Pitkethly have done outstanding work and see the whole affair as a kind of blessing in disguise. Their house had not been in order, they will have to work hard in order to avoid a repeat. But after this wake-up call, both Unilever and Paul Polman have both of their feet firmly back on the ground. Huët's warnings have been followed by a serious yellow card by Kraft Heinz. One more infraction and it will be red, then they're out.

Polman agrees. Unilever needs to become much more efficient in order both to become more sustainable and to earn enough money for its shareholders. This attack has shown him what drastic action needs to be taken against the consensus culture inside the company. The firm is a lumbering beast, it needs to take action more quickly.

It's also clear that the protection implied by the dual structure of the NV and the PLC has stopped working. With Brexit in the background, might this be the moment to bid farewell after all these decades of discussions and manoeuvring. Making Unilever into a single company with a single head office would not only prevent Unilever from being taken over, it would increase their fire power to increase in size whenever the possibility of a big takeover arose.

People responsible for implementing the USLP targets are the first to express concern. This restructuring will put even more pressure on results, costs will have to come down and margins will have to go up. Some outside the company share these misgivings. What would focusing on the share price over the coming period mean for cooperation with NGOs? How will the firm bring these two quickly diverging paths back together? Unilever announces that it will publish a plan on 6 April making clear how it intends to speed up its search for means to create further shareholder value.

'It's concerning.' In an open letter to the opinion page of *De Volkskrant*, two big Dutch pension funds, PMT and PME, call on Unilever to stay true to itself: 'As far as we are concerned, the fact that Unilever now wants to increase profitability as quickly as possible can't mean the firm abandoning its long term trajectory. We're convinced that companies who keep one eye on sustainable long-term development end up achieving more financially too.' They warn Unilever: 'Even though we're already committed shareholders, we are increasingly shifting over to a very conscious selection of companies in which to invest. When deciding where to invest, we explicitly take into account the way they respond to risks and opportunities related to the environment and to society. A strong short-term focus from investors and companies can stand in the way of real economic activity as the basis for sustainable growth and economic development.'

The pension fund ABP also warns Unilever behind the scenes: don't make any rash decisions, don't go down the Kraft Heinz path too quickly and don't start cutting costs willy-nilly. At pension provider PGGM, owner of around €500 million in Unilever shares, an internal discussion erupts. Their Unilever shares are scattered in seven different portfolios. In several areas, the rise in share price has meant they've reached their stated share price aim. To the portfolio manager, this is a clear sign that they should sell. Others argue that this would send the wrong message, PGGM wants to lead the way when it comes to sustainability goals. Director Else Bos, a close acquaintance of Paul Polman, wants to take a clear position in the public debate and support Unilever. However, she and the other PGGM directors can't reach an agreement between themselves and so are keeping quiet.

Kraft Heinz's big blunder is dominating the headlines. Warren Buffett tells news broadcaster CNBC that he had received a number of phone calls that made clear to him that the takeover wasn't welcome. 'Alex Behring, Jorge Paulo and I agreed on making a friendly offer on Unilever if they were open to it. If it's unwelcome, there is no offer.' He explains what he believes went wrong. 'Behring went to London and met with their CEO and brought up the idea of possibly making an offer late in the conversation. And he didn't get a "yes", didn't get a "no", he got a perfectly polite conversation and came back and said that he hadn't been thrown out. And the CEO, actually, Greg Abel of Berkshire has known him twenty years and we heard nothing but good reports of him, we felt fine about it.'

Buffett tells the reporter that they went ahead and set out a rough sketch of their proposal on paper. 'He went to see him again maybe two weeks later and he had a letter that was the outline of a deal, which he thought, if he got a neutral response, he would give the letter [to Polman], and if he got a negative feeling, he would not. And he went over and felt he got a neutral response and therefore gave the letter.'

But maybe Behring wasn't clear on the type of person he was dealing, wonders the reporter. Buffett loves a metaphor and grins as he shares an adage about the difference between a diplomat and a lady: 'When a diplomat says "yes", he means "maybe", when he says "maybe", he means "no", if he says "no", he's no diplomat. If a lady says "no", she means "maybe", if she says "maybe", she means "yes", and if she says "yes", she's no lady. So he probably got a "maybe" and didn't know whether it was coming from a diplomat or a lady, essentially.'

The journalist from CNBC remains unconvinced. She asks again whether the deal was really never intended as a hostile offer. Buffett reaffirms that this definitely wasn't the case but admits he can't exclude the possibility that it was interpreted as unfriendly by the other side. He immediately goes on to defend Behring's eagerness. 'When people say "we don't like this price", that's usually a maybe.' According to Buffett, this was Polman's response in the first meeting but not in the second. Was it a case of the Unilever CEO being overly polite, the interviewer wants to know, was that the problem? Buffett: 'It can be, it can be polite, it can be differences in culture even in the way people express themselves. Alex's second language is English. I've seen misunderstandings before, that's one reason I like to do it the way I do it: I just go in and say if you want me to make an offer, I will, and if you don't want me to, forget it. But there's usually much more of a dance back and forth than that. And part of that's what subtle law is […] but in any event, within an hour we got across to them that we were not making a friendly offer, so we'd go away.'

Polman appreciates Buffett naming Greg Abel. He and Abel worked together 20 years ago on the board of the Newcastle Initiative. They'd both worked pro bono on investing in and developing the economic infrastructure of Newcastle. Abel saw him in action there, saw how selflessly he'd committed himself to a good cause. He sees this as yet another wonderful example of serendipity in action. For years, he's tried to contribute to building a better world via a whole range of organisations. Polman comes to the conclusion that, to a certain extent, his network saved Unilever.

That said, he is annoyed by what he regards as the American's nonsensical explanation of what happened. He finds the diplomat–lady comparison downright sexist. And in what way was he too polite, when did he ever say that he didn't like the price? As far as he remembered, he'd made it very clear from the start that he saw no prospect for a deal. Why didn't they respond to the letters Unilever sent? That way they could have avoided this whole affair. If they'd done their homework on Unilever just a little bit, they could have anticipated this resistance.

Polman is convinced that the Brazilians would never have called off the bid of their own accord, they've never done such a thing before. He also suspects that Buffett had failed to keep his house in order. He had given the Brazilians his blessing, then kept out of it, allowing them to ignore Polman's clear rejection. It was only on Saturday, when he started getting approached by all kinds of acquaintances that the penny dropped for the American. This battle could cost him, the 'Oracle of Omaha' his wonderful image as the 'kindest investor of the century', right in the autumn of his life. He couldn't allow that to happen, of course.

Polman realises something else. What exactly is it that makes Buffett a successor investor? Unilever's returns over the past eight years have been a good deal higher than Buffett's. He also thinks that Unilever has done more to make Buffett's ideals a reality that Buffet has. Many of his investments have yielded absolutely no real value for society.

The Unilever board reaches the same conclusion: Warren Buffett was the one who pulled the rug out from under this deal. Unilever has managed to drive a wedge between the Brazilians and the American.

Former Unilever chairman Antony Burgmans is following the news as it emerges. He sympathises with Polman. Burgmans is also being kept on his toes this week, as chairman of AkzoNobel. Their competitor, the American paint manufacturer PPH, wants to take over the whole of AkzoNobel for €21 billion. Burgmans is completely against it. Aggressive shareholders are breathing down his neck wanting to cash out, they have no interest in what might happen to AkzoNobel after this kind of takeover. Their greed is threatening to destroy AkzoNobel. He won't let that happen. Burgmans has already been in touch with the Dutch minister of economic affairs Henk Kamp, who told him that a takeover of this kind would be against the interests of the country.

Worries about Unilever and AkzoNobel prompt Dutch politicians to show their patriotic pride ahead of the general election on 15 March. In an interview on Radio 1 on the politics show *Kamerbreed* (Across the Chamber), Finance Minister Jeroen Dijsselbloem, from the centre-left PvdA (Worker's Party), says: 'Unilever needs to devise a defence mechanism in order to ward off a takeover by vultures and hyenas poised to take over your company.' He calls for legislation to hinder the takeover of strategically important firms. He sees some call for having foreign takeovers vetted by a government commission, as the Americans do. That commission would investigate whether or not such a takeover was in the interests of the Netherlands.

The moment the deal fell through, the CEO and chairman of Unilever immediately set about explaining themselves to their shareholders. On 7 March, they welcome Unilever's key Dutch investors to Rotterdam head office. Polman seems overwrought. He doesn't look good; he's a bit red, bloated. Throughout the whole presentation, Erwin Dut gets the impression that the people at Unilever are in panic mode. And really, Polman only has one clear message for him and his fellow investors: buy our shares. Buy them now, make sure that our share price increases, and that Kraft Heinz find someone else to fantasise about instead of coming back to us. The portfolio manager of Kempen Capital Management has been invited to have lunch with Paul Polman and Marijn Dekkers along with two other fund managers. Together he reckons that they represent €2 billion in Unilever shares. The main course is sushi but nobody pays it much attention.

During the lunch, which lasts two hours, Polman gives a presentation. The first part focuses once again on everything they've achieved. A range of slides shows how much better Unilever has performed than its competitors, both in terms of revenue growth by volume and in terms of generating cash. The second part of the presentation is an attack on Kraft Heinz's 'buy, squeeze, repeat' model. Polman explains that the Americans are solely focused on price and volume – what they can have the consumer pay, what the consumer is willing to accept. The other side of the equation – suppliers – are squeezed dry. This is a way to make a lot of money, a portion of which goes to back into the company in order to service debt but then largely flows into the pockets of the owners. According to Polman, they barely invest at all in either existing or new brands or markets. The last slide sets out the way Kraft Heinz's value is set to shrink over the long term.

The CEO rages against Kraft Heinz and against the American system that seems to have declared such businesses sacrosanct. But he also bares his own bosom. He thinks he could have broadcast the value Unilever has created for shareholders over the last few years and his ambitions to increase this value even more in the future more effectively. He had known for a while that Unilever's margin could increase from 16 per cent to 20 per cent, but he hadn't wanted to express this belief publicly. He's a conservative guy, after all, people from Twente don't believe in counting their chickens before they hatch. He promises his shareholders: we're going to see even better returns, I just haven't been explaining this very well.

Polman acknowledges that his focus on the sustainable long term has led the organisation to sleep on its short-term results. He recognises that many investors are attracted by more short-term returns and that he needs to address their priorities too. He also admits that he hasn't managed Unilever's books as well as he could have. His guests hear the rage in his voice as he tells them that Kraft Heinz would largely have been able to fund the takeover with Unilever's own money. So now Unilever is going to borrow heavily in order to prevent that from happening in the future. Dut suspects that they might be in a position to consider a couple of big takeovers for once. He immediately thinks of Colgate – that would be a perfect fit. But he's not the only one who thinks so, their share price has jumped over the last few weeks.

A couple of weeks ago, Polman would never have thought he'd find himself having to consider buying up Unilever shares, but now he has to make allowances. For years, he had been loath to even consider it, he regarded it as the lowest of the low. He always suspects CEOs who announce they are going to purchase shares of wanting to drive up the value of their own shares as quickly as possible. Anyone who buys shares in order to inflate the share price is a bad businessman in his eyes, someone who doesn't know how to invest his capital in the things the world needs. And this poor world needs so many things.

His guests notice that Polman's brainchild, the USLP, doesn't come up this afternoon. They don't so much as hear the word 'sustainable'. Polman is speaking the language of the financial investor.

Dekkers is very much pleased with this change. Over the past few days, he's told Polman repeatedly not to mention the USLP and to instead focus on the shareholders and earning money. The former boss of Bayer tells an anecdote from his time there. At Bayer, it takes 10 years to develop a new medicine, but the one-quarter in which you manage to get your medicine to market ahead of your competitor is the one that makes the difference. That leads to twice the market share, because you've been able to visit doctors and market the product a couple of months earlier. So we can spend as much time on a wonderful long-term plan as we like, beating the competitor in the short term is still essential.

Polman repeats his call to the shareholders to buy up Unilever shares. The three guests are impressed and promise to take the matter to their respective colleagues and shareholders.

After lunch comes the turn of Herman Bots, the portfolio manager of APG. An investor the size of this Dutch pensions giant can have a one-to-one with the Unilever leadership. Bots can also see that Polman is out of his comfort zone. He receives the same presentation as the others and tells Polman that APG has faith in Unilever; Bots hopes that Unilever won't go to too many extremes when it comes to responding to the takeover threat. Polman is visibly annoyed: If you've got so much faith and wish to support me then why don't you have more shares? Bots promises to look into the matter too.

Polman is being driven to distraction. He thinks the people he's talking to are pots calling the kettle black. Pension funds should work on the basis of a 25- to 30-year horizon but are ruled by fund managers that only look one or two years ahead at most. They've been one of the biggest disappointments over the past few years. He wonders whether these Dutch pension funds, who are all talk in terms of sustainability, have any idea what's at stake. And if they do understand, then how come only 8 per cent of Unilever's shares are in Dutch hands? He senses that they aren't making the effort to see what he, what Unilever, is trying to achieve. He thinks they're taking the path of least resistance and feels completely unsupported by them.

But he's under no illusions when it comes to anyone else, either. Even investors who've declared their love for Unilever for years and complemented their sustainable approach won't hesitate in August if Kraft Heinz comes knocking at Unilever's door again. If it means them being able to make a 30–35 per cent return on their investment at a single stroke, they'll sell. They'll say that they have to, that it's their fiduciary duty; after all, they have to ensure people have good pensions. And they would promise to reinvest their profit in new sustainable companies. But they'll sell their Unilever shares to a company like Kraft Heinz of all things, a company that has nothing to do with sustainability. He can't rely on these shareholders.

CHAPTER 16

A MAYOR IN WARTIME

March–April 2017

Marijn Dekkers believes this is the right time to adjust their course. Unilever can't allow itself to become an easy target. The board chairman warns Paul Polman. Over the past few years the Unilever CEO has behaved like a boxer who's only ever on the offensive. But a good boxer needs to be able to defend himself too. He needs to start doing that now. Dekkers repeats his message during every meeting he has with the day-to-day leadership of Unilever: a high share price is the best defence against an unwanted takeover. At the beginning of his first annual report in 2016, he declares their intention 'to accelerate delivery of value for the benefit of our shareholders'.

The shareholders are ready and waiting. The Brazilian-American fantasy about the tens of billions of euros they would've generated by combining Unilever with Kraft Heinz has also fired the imaginations of the shareholders of the Dutch-British multinational. As is always the case on the stock market, this optimism quickly translates into a 30 per cent increase in the Unilever share price, to over €47 per share. The company is now worth €150 billion, €35 billion more than two weeks ago.

If Unilever wants to stop Kraft Heinz from making another attempt in August, it needs to ensure that the company has become unaffordable by then. A rumoured target of over €50 per share is doing the rounds internally. It's unlikely that Kraft Heinz or any other party for that matter would be able to put up over €200 billion, including a takeover bonus, for Unilever.

It's a bizarre paradox for many of Unilever's managers. The threat of this absolutely unwanted, get-rich-quick takeover by an outfit like Kraft Heinz has made them a good deal richer on paper in a very short time. The same applies to Paul Polman. The shares he owns, now a total of 1.13 million, have increased in value by around €14 million.

The fact that Polman doesn't give the financial results priority is no longer important. If he wants to keep Unilever on target to meet his precious USLP targets then he'll have to put them on the back burner for now. Worse still, Polman is going to have to do exactly what he so emphatically refused to do during his abolition of published quarterly results. Now the whims of analysts and shareholders are setting his agenda for him. He has to start listening to people he regards as only half human, people who simply cannot understand that earning money is a means, and can never be an end in itself. He'll do it, but only for the time being.

Louise Fresco can see that Polman is feeling threatened. She senses how much his self-assurance has been thrown off by what has happened. But like the rest of the board, she is in no doubt: Unilever has to take advantage of this opportunity and Paul Polman has to lead the way. He is the CEO tasked with saving his vision. In order to preserve his legacy, he needs to change tack and show people that he can still be the tough, business-like expert ready to clean house. Ann Fudge agrees with this assessment. This is exactly the kind of moment in which it becomes clear that the company isn't in working order. She compares it with surviving a life-threatening illness, from then on you start doing things differently. She thinks it's only right for Polman to face this challenge, since he's the one responsible for the situation that has developed. This is a moment of enormous clarity, they need to use this moment to their best advantage and Paul Polman has to be the one to do it. The plan had been for him to retire later in the year but that is no longer an option.

The way ahead is clear. Kraft Heinz believed it could cut a third of Unilever's costs, so now they need to get to work to do the same. The entire organisation quickly realises that this will mean deep cuts to budgets. Everywhere. The C4G programme announced the previous year will have to be implemented more quickly. They will have to look at Unilever's balance sheet and be prepared to buy billions of euros in shares. The sale of spreads will now have to go ahead quickly. Various directors are surprised that their CEO is suddenly wholeheartedly back at the helm of the company. Marijn Dekkers is impressed. Polman catches his drift immediately, Dekkers is paying him a compliment.

Polman doesn't understand why they are so surprised. If something happens that he doesn't like, or that doesn't suit his plans, he never spends any time wondering about why it's happened to him. He doesn't think like a victim, he focuses on asking questions like what it means, what he can do about it and what he can learn from it. He's always worked like that. All this set back demands is that he and the people around him start working even harder so that they can achieve the required results and thereby eventually meet their sustainability targets. That isn't opportunism, that's logic. He wants to change the system, a system that is much bigger than Unilever. That's his priority. For him, everything is secondary to that goal. The fact that he now needs to do all kinds of things he would prefer not to is part of that priority too. Doing them doesn't mean having to violate his own values. Sometimes you need to be pragmatic, the ends justify the means.

However, Polman does also believe that Unilever needs help from governments to defend against aggressive parties like Kraft Heinz. They need to ensure that companies aimed at a sustainable future are given sufficient time to make that transition. In the *Financial Times*, he criticises the British takeover code, which gives prey to little time to arm itself against the aggressor. 'We're not talking about protection; we are saying that when you have a situation like this, with a national champion, there should be a level playing field.' Polman refers to the fact that the board of an English company focuses primarily on the interests of shareholders, while in the Netherlands they also take a close look at the interests of other stakeholders. The Unilever CEO calls on Prime Minister Theresa May to look into the matter thoroughly.[1] Commentators in the British media immediately begin to speculate about whether Polman is hinting that he wants to move Unilever head office to the Netherlands.

Shortly before she became prime minister in 2016, May had indicated that she had some sympathy with the idea. Notably, she'd taken Kraft as a prime example, after the company broke its promise to keep open factories and guarantee jobs at the UK following its takeover of another world champion, the chocolate-maker Cadbury's, in 2010. She had stated that employees, local communities and the whole country had a vested interest in such matters that needed to be taken into account going forward.

She'd been criticised roundly for those remarks. The British chancellor, Philip Hammond, had warned against any measures, arguing that the country had to avoid frustrating foreign investment streams, particularly after Brexit. He'd also warned of the dangers of taking the 'Danone route', a reference to the French government that tried to block the takeover of Danone by the American firm Pepsi. Two months ago, Prime Minister May had gone back on her earlier words. As far as she is now concerned, any measures would be aimed solely at companies that are important to the critical, internal infrastructure of the UK.[2]

'Hostile takeovers are the dark side of capitalism', says Jeroen van der Veer, who was elected non-executive board member at Unilever in 2011 and has since been appointed chairman of the board at ING bank and Philips, on Radio 1. The former Shell head honcho is reacting to the news about Unilever and the still threatened takeover of AkzoNobel by the American firm PPG. He's worried: 'You don't want globalisation to mean that we start selling off our big companies here in the Netherlands.'

Van der Veer warns of the American focus on shareholder value, profit and short-term returns. 'A company also has a social function, think about jobs and collaborations with universities. Americans mostly just want to make a quick buck.' As he sees it, this boils down to a question of culture. In Europe we're already struggling to take into account the long-term effects on things like the climate, Americans have a tendency to only want to solve problems as and when they arise. Van der Veer thinks that the government should resist hostile takeovers. 'Ten years ago we wouldn't have wanted complex protection structures but the whole global political situation and globalisation have started to change my mind. Companies need at least six months to weigh up their options. That allows you to avoid rash, panicked decision-making when faced with a hostile offer.'

His old friend Antony Burgmans knows what Van der Veer means only too well. The chairman of AkzoNobel is doing all he can to keep the wolf from the door. The American paint manufacturer PPG is proving considerably more determined than Kraft Heinz. A second, higher offer of €22.4 billion has since been rejected by AkzoNobel's board. Activist shareholders think that AkzoNobel should allow itself to be bought. Elliot International, a fund with a 3.25 per cent interest, is pushing increasingly hard for that to happen. But AkzoNobel declared that the proposal represented a 'significant undervaluation' with 'considerable risks and uncertainties'. 'It is not in the interest of the shareholders or in the interest of other stakeholders such as clients and employees. It endangers AkzoNobel's global efforts on behalf of sustainability, communities and R&D organisations.'

In short, the management of AkzoNobel wants to take their own action to make their shareholders happier. Where Unilever is talking about selling of its margarine activities, AkzoNobel is pursuing the accelerated sale of its chemicals divisions, a sector of the company that provides a third of their total annual turnover.

Burgmans is feeling intimidated. A representative of Elliott International has informed him that he'll be richly rewarded if he cooperates but that they'll make life very hard for him if he doesn't. To Burgmans, there's only one explanation for their aggression: unchecked greed. And a total disinterest in the consequences of that greed for other stakeholders. Burgmans is concerned about the welfare of AkzoNobel's CEO, Ton Buchner. He questions whether he can withstand this enormous pressure. He agrees with Van der Veer that legislation is needed to protect companies like AkzoNobel and Unilever from these kinds of situations.

After the Dutch elections on 15 March, which once again see the centre-right, liberal VVD win the most votes, negotiations begin to see which parties will enter into a coalition to form the new government. Hans de Boer, the chairman of the Dutch employers union VNO-NCW, sends an urgent letter to the woman leading the negotiations, Edith Schippers, urging the government to 'strengthen the legal basis' so that companies are better able to defend themselves from unwanted offers. 'Our country can't be a passive bystander to a process of asset stripping that is leading to the structural impoverishment of the Netherlands.' De Boer thinks that there needs to be an 'adequate response time for hostile takeovers or in cases in which an activist shareholder is acting in conflict with the long-term strategy of the business'.[3] A copy of his letter is sent to Jeroen Dijsselbloem and Henk Kamp, the outgoing ministers of Finance and Economic Affairs. Rients Abma, the director of Eumedion, an umbrella organisation for institutional investors, is immediately ill at ease. He is on the same page as the British prime minister. 'We only see a role for government where there is a threat to national security or public order.' Abma fears legislation that offers the management of publicly traded companies so much protection that they no longer feel the corrective effects of the market and are lulled into a false sense of security.

In *Het Financieele Dagblad*, Hans de Boer expands on his plea for government measures: 'The Netherlands has a couple of global players like Unilever. They attract and stimulate business. They also make access to foreign markets easier for other companies. Around two million jobs rely on Unilever. Those jobs are twice as well paid as others. So these big firms have a multiplier-effect on the whole economy. We want to keep it that way. Why don't want to seem opportunistic, but we're dealing with a very real problem here. We are seeing that the world is no longer a level playing field. The Americans or the Chinese come here to take over the establishment but at the same time, they keep their borders closed to business. There's no reciprocity. While we're playing hockey, they storm onto the field playing rugby.' Unilever non-executive board member and DSM CEO Feike Sijbesma offers his own two cents on the matter. In the same paper, he issues a stark warning: 80 per cent of all R&D being undertaken in the Netherlands is paid for by six to eight big companies: AkzoNobel, ASML, DSM, Philips, Shell and Unilever.

Unilever wants to show everyone that it's now primed and ready. On 6 April, the company presents its promised list of dramatic measures intended to improve the bottom line and give shareholders much-needed trust in the future. In other words: measures designed to compensate for the pain they're feeling in their wallets thanks to the failure of Kraft Heinz's takeover bid. The first thing readers notice is the total absence of the USLP. There is absolutely no mention of Unilever's big sustainability mission. Various commentators detect the guiding hand of Marijn Dekkers.

The ambitions set out in the list suddenly sound very traditional and concrete. The margin will grow from 16.4 per cent to 20 per cent over the next three or so years. The plans for C4G, for which Chief Transformation Officer Peter ter Kulve had set aside 18 months, will be completed in six months. Ter Kulve is pleased with this turn of events. Unilever doesn't have all the time in the world, it needs to show these results now and communicate with shareholders about them very explicitly.

Over the coming three and a half years, they will make structural savings of €4–€6 billion. A third of that needs to come from their own overheads, the rest will be made up with tougher sourcing strategy. They've set aside €3.5 billion for the restructuring. In order to save on costs, the tea and ice cream (refreshments) division will merge with the food division. The dividend will increase by 12 per cent. Unilever is also going to borrow €5 billion and immediately return it to the shareholders by buying shares.

Feike Sijbesma is pleased that Paul Polman intends to repair all that he has neglected over the past couple of years. They're all good, logical decisions because whichever way you slice it, if the shareholders jump ship, you're done. To him, the CEO of DSM, that's a given. Shareholders set the rules of the game.

Polman sees this mass purchase of shares as a form of financial manipulation. Many of his colleagues understand his aversion, it does somehow seem like a sign you're throwing in the towel. Kees Kruythoff, responsible for the US operation, thinks it's high time. In his view, Polman has been rather cautious, conservative even. If you don't want to embark on any big takeovers, you have to give the money back to the shareholders by buying shares. In the United States, this happens on a grand scale, it's what the financial markets dictate. And now it's what needed. In total, this will mean a cool €11–€12 billion flowing back to the shareholders, mind you, because they're also going to get the profit from the sale of the margarine division. Polman hates it, this isn't how you create value for all your other stakeholders, and it definitely isn't inclusive. But needs must.

Unilever's decision to bid farewell to its margarine division is another part of the plan. This sale is a bitter moment for many at the company, the spreads are still operating with a margin above the dreamed of 20 per cent

Unilever is now aiming for. Based on an estimated turnover in excess of €2 billion, analysts assume an operating profit of €420 million. In this sector, sales frequently reach a price of 15 times the operating profit. Unilever should be able to make between €6 and €7 billion. *Het Financieele Dagblad* reports that the company is currently valued at around €1.4 billion and should therefore provide a decent net profit.

Even though it's been expected ever since the division was separated from the company in 2015, the news that Dutch brands like Becel, Calvé and Blue Band are going to be sold sends shockwaves through the Netherlands. The head office of Unilever Benelux on the Nassaukade in Rotterdam is going to have to be physically separated from the over hundred-year-old factory there. This is the site of over one hundred and forty years of Unilever history. To veteran employees this is scarcely imaginable. Floris Maljers, chairman of the NV from 1984 to 1994, calls the sale a disgrace. Nobody can run this business better than Unilever. If anyone claims they can, there's something wrong with their figures.

Rogier Smeets thinks that Unilever has been milking this division dry for a long time. The enormous pile of money they've made despite the decline in turnover has mostly been invested in expanding their personal hygiene activities in Asia. He understands, that's how a multinational works, but at a certain point you begin to pay the price for it. Your prospects for growth vanish and those with real talent no longer want to have a career with you.

Smeets is one of the exceptions. Since the summer of 2016, this 36-year-old high flyer has been responsible for Benelux and Southern Europe, and been a member of the team directing the spreads division. Ever since then, he's been working on the assumption that he might be coming to the end of his time at Unilever. On 5 April, he was on his way to the airport when his boss called to tell him to turn back. There's an announcement coming the next day and he'll have to be the one to explain it to his staff of 450 in Rotterdam.

Even though Smeets has known that a sale was in the offing, the decision to sell so abruptly still comes as a surprise. Smeets and his boss Nicolas Liabeuf think it's a crying shame. If their team had been given another two years, they could have shown just how perfectly spreads fit with Unilever's sustainability ambitions, and even how they could contribute to increased turnover. Since being freed from the Unilever matrix the year before, they've been able to cut through a lot of time-wasting red tape. In doing so, they've halved the time it takes to get a new product to market, reducing it to a couple of months. Smeets has also become increasingly convinced that – in the spirit of the USLP – sustainable, plant-based margarines might eventually win out over real butter, derived 100 per cent from animals. Obviously, he heard about the enquiries Unilever made to companies like Kraft Heinz at the end of 2016 about whether they'd be interested in buying the margarine division, but back then they could still have decided not to go ahead. Sadly, Kraft Heinz's offer has accelerated the sale. There's no going back now.

If you pay that little attention to an operation for so many years, they deserve the chance to make a recovery. Conny Braams, the director of Unilever Benelux, thinks that the decision to sell now feels almost unjust. It doesn't help that Unilever has outsourced the spreads division's entire supply chain. Back in the day, the company used to make its own oils. Over the past several quarters, Braams has been asked to present the results of the Benelux with and without the figures for spreads. She understands that Unilever's mission to increase turnover from €40 to €80 billion is being frustrated by the declining turnover of the spreads division. But the division, which is still growing in the Netherlands, puts the 'Uni' in Unilever. Doesn't that count for something? She thinks it's terrible that the entire profit from the sale is going to be used to mollify the shareholders. This has nothing to do with the USLP targets. She gets the distinct impression that the top management is desperate to make some big, exaggerated statement to show people that they're a strong leadership. As she stands before her staff in Rotterdam, explaining the sale, she doesn't hold back, expressing her own doubts about the decision. She understands it with her head but not with her heart.

For now, Smeets and Braams will remain colleagues. They decide to process their grief together. They take their management teams to the pub and stay there until the wee hours. In between the many beers, they speculate intensely. Smeets agrees with various external analysts, he wouldn't be surprised if today's announcement marked the beginning of the break-up of the whole foods division. Maybe that's the reason that the merger of the NV and the *PLC*, suddenly regarded as so important for streamlining their strategic portfolio, has to happen now.

The announcement that Unilever intends to give up either its British or Dutch citizenship after almost ninety years is the biggest news. There needs to be one head office with one legal structure: 'We think it's important to increase the possibility for future changes in the portfolio. Our legal structure with two head offices adds complexity.' Unilever wants to go over to having one set of shares, all shareholders should have the same voting rights.

Even though they're not saying so, the timing of this decision seems to be based on the announcement that the UK will be leaving the European Union and on Paul Polman's inevitable departure within the foreseeable future. He's decided to address the issue of unification, which each of his predecessors handed on like a political hot potato, once and for all. The company needs to be steered into calmer waters.

Every detail will have to be examined carefully but Polman already has a good idea of the course they must pursue. Brexit is going to cause a lot of trouble. It's better for a multinational like Unilever to be a relatively small fish in the big European pond, than to be a big fish in the small, uncertainty-ridden British pond. Better the robust euro than the floundering pound. In the not too distant future, the world is going to be made up of a handful of massive trading blocs, a large company like Unilever needs to be inside one of those blocs. He sees more scope for Brussels effecting change in the world than he does for post-Brexit London. What's more, when it comes to making the economy more sustainable, Unilever gets a friendlier welcome in Brussels than it does from their British counterparts.

Even though he often thinks of the Netherlands as little more than a small, narrow-minded country, Polman also believes that the Dutch model of corporate governance, in which the shareholders are considered no more important than other stakeholders, is a better fit for Unilever. He also knows that Brits will be reluctant to transfer to Rotterdam, the moves brought about by the European Marketing and Innovation Hub four years ago made that abundantly clear. He also needs to make sure that people don't jump to the conclusion that this move is simply a coup cooked up by himself and Dekkers, two Dutchmen. His argument must win the day. His fellow directors think it's brave of the CEO to take on this mammoth task; whatever happens, part of the company will be deeply disappointed.

After the news comes out, the Dutch head office in another part of Rotterdam is immediately abuzz with excitement. Of course a head office in the Netherlands is a better fit for the kind of Unilever Polman has been leading over the past few years, but do they really have a shot at making it happen? Conny Braams is sad to note that the team charged with examining the pros and cons of unification has barely any Dutch members. The Brits have taken over the whole affair. This is going to be an uphill battle.

Dutch NV board chairman and Unilever veteran Kees van der Waaij thinks the same thing. The Unilever lifer has spent decades working alongside his British colleagues and you never know whether they're going to do what they've told you they will. Shell didn't quite manage to pull it off either. Their head office is in The Hague but they've remained a PLC. He's optimistic, even so. He hardly has any choice but to place his hopes in unification, he believes that a British PLC based in London would effectively put an end to the sustainability agenda.

Angelique Laskewitz has agreed with Paul Polman that she will be allowed to ask the first three questions at the Unilever NV shareholders' meeting in Rotterdam. As the director of the Dutch Association of Investors for Sustainable Development, Laskewitz is trying to make sustainable investing mainstream. Unilever is on her Advisory Board. Polman hopes that the questions he has agreed in advance with Laskewitz will set the right tone for the meeting. He'd have loved to invite her to the meeting of the PLC in London; he could really do with these questions of hers there.

During the meeting at the end of April, Laskewitz asks the less than half-full room in the World Trade Centre in Rotterdam why it is that Unilever isn't managing to spell out its contribution to the United Nation's SDGs much more explicitly. Laughing, Polman points to the pin that's been fixed to his lapel for the last two years, with a colourful visualisation of the 17 SDGs. He takes the opportunity to share that Unilever has now helped 600 million people to improve their hygienic living conditions. The pledge to provide job prospects for 5.5 million people has so far translated into better jobs and wages for 1.6 million people. Polman's tone is strident: 'It's my aim for every company to declare what it has achieved in terms of sustainability each and every year. If you as a company can't do that, what are you even doing here?'

One shareholder wants to know what exactly went wrong, why did Unilever need this wake-up call from Kraft Heinz in the first place? Chairman Marijn Dekkers chooses his words carefully: 'What they managed to pull off there is unbelievable, they raised their margin by 10 per cent in 18 months. We don't think that you can deliver long term results just by cutting your costs. We are using the bid as an opportunity to hold the whole company up to the light and see where we can accelerate. We are seeing great opportunities to answer this challenge in our own, evolutionary way. And we also have to be honest: Kraft Heinz's offer shows us just how much the world has changed.'

Polman doesn't mince his words when it comes to their American competitor. 'It was an opportunistic offer, but one with a limited lifespan. And rightly so, because Kraft Heinz's way of working does not lead to a sustainable result. I may as well tell you, I've thrown away their ketchup that I had in my fridge and you won't see it in there ever again.'

The next day, during the shareholder meeting of the British PLC in London, Polman permits himself to make a joke as he takes the stage from Dekkers, who opened the meeting. 'I was quickly looking; when Marijn announced the 12 per cent dividend increase, we had four people applauding and when Marijn talked about our long-term strategies and values, we had two people applauding. So that's a message to me that we still have some work to do.' He goes on to say that the company intends to make the best of the still turbulent economic climate: 'as Churchill said: never let a crisis go to waste'.

Polman still has his reservations about the chairman of the board. Dekkers still doesn't seem entirely convinced by Polman's sustainability agenda, and that's going to have to go back to being their priority fairly soon. It's the core of what they do. He trusts that once he's led Dekkers to water 10 times, he'll eventually start drinking. The CEO gets fired up once questions about Unilever's efforts on sustainability start to come up: 'The availability of food is a big problem. This is mostly a result of the fact that women, who contribute more than 50% of agricultural production, only own 10% of the land. Much more needs to happen. It's unbelievably that 800 million people still go to bed hungry, not knowing whether they'll wake up the next day, while in the rest of the world 30 to 40% of the calories produced are thrown away.'

Marijn Dekkers gestures to Polman to start wrapping up his talk but the CEO has warmed to his subject: 'In Rwanda, 20,000 pickers work on our tea plantation. By paying them extra, we help a total of around 80,000 people to improve their living conditions. We are investing in training, teaching them to be more efficient in their use of water, but we're also helping them to send their children to school. Take it from me, we're introducing our USLP thinking throughout our supply chain. Anyone who wants to be a Unilever supplier has to cooperate.'

Polman is pushing this project despite the necessity to start cutting costs harshly. Unilever is investing around €30 million in what he terms the model plantation in Rwanda. They've built a factory there on 300 hectares of land for around 8,000 farmers. He's convinced that his personal contribution to the United Nations SDGs has enabled Unilever to win the trust of the Rwandan government. This is where they will produce their highest quality tea.

Marc Engel, the director of sourcing and production, has calculated that it will probably take between ten and fifteen years for this investment to pay off. There isn't a single other commercial company, let alone a publicly listed company, that is working with these kinds of investment horizons. Engel thinks it's wonderful that Polman is ploughing ahead with this despite the fact that Unilever's margin now needs to be improved at an accelerated pace. He's still doing all he can to make sure that all the tea Unilever uses is produced sustainably by 2020, including the 75 per cent that they buy in from other growers.

Unilever is trying to raise the income of poor farmers at an increasing number of locations around the world. But how do you raise their salaries? If you increase the yield per hectare then you'll drive the already low tea prices down even further and create even more pressure on the already pitiable incomes people are making. The key will be to improve the quality of the tea to such an extent that Unilever can ask a *higher* price for it from the consumer. In order to make this happen, Unilever needs to create, or buy, specialist tea brands. This is why it's currently busy taking over the exclusive Tazo brand from Starbucks. And meanwhile, in Rwanda, tea production needs to switch over to these high quality, so-called category-5 teas. Unilever pays its pickers more than $2 per day for these teas, the same as on the Kericho coffee plantation in Kenya. There's a lot of resistance from local plantations that sometimes pay their tea workers as little as half that amount.

One thousand two hundred miles further south, in Malawi, Unilever has been working with IDH for two years to secure a living wage for around 60,000 tea pickers by 2020. IDH director Joost Oorthuizen estimates that their income needs to increase by 300 per cent in order to achieve this. Of the 12 plantations in the country, two are leading the way, so Unilever tries to do its business with them. In exchange for higher wages, they need to supply higher quality tea. Jan Kees Vis is finding this task a tall order, because what exactly constitutes a living wage? It doesn't help that the owners of the other 10 plantations have zero desire to increase wages and are therefore determined to obstruct Unilever's plans.

Marc Engel hopes that these for him self-evident but to the consumer still invisible developments will be accelerated by technology such as blockchain. Five years ago, neither the marketers at Unilever nor the majority of consumers really spared a thought for these extremely poor tea pickers. He hopes that soon a consumer enjoying a cup of Unilever tea will be able to scan a code on the back of the box and see exactly who it was that picked their tea leaves. They could then express their thanks, or take the initiative to send a few pence extra to that person with the touch of a button. That way, the consumer enjoys the feel-good factor and can contribute directly to combatting poverty.

Dutch pension funds ABP and PFZW and other big institutional investors like Kempen & Co think this is a stirring vision. But they're also proceeding with caution. Polman's long-term logic isn't something you can simply adopt into another organisation's investment policy. Naturally, they've taken Polman's appeal on board and bought up more of Unilever's shares. That's pretty much self-explanatory from their point of view. The threat from Kraft Heinz means Unilever will need to quickly redirect its effort towards a swift improvement of the results. That will translate into a higher share price, they can see as much already. This is the logic that dominates their approach to business. They make no bones about that.

As individuals, as 'real people', they loved Polman's message, they wish the world would live up to such as an example. Yet, just as Polman predicted, as investors they will have to sell their shares if Kraft Heinz comes back in August with a 30 per cent increase in their offer. Their hands are tied, they say.

The two biggest pension funds in the Netherlands, ABP and PFZW, have tentatively been improving the sustainability of their investments for almost ten years at this point. Most of their directors have enthusiastically embraced the UN's 17 new sustainability goals. These could end up becoming the yardstick that will lead to new rules of play, and mean that new risk–reward estimates can be standardised. But there's still a long way to go.

Erik van Houwelingen, the chairman of ABP's investments committee, sees this as a change of course that the pension fund should embark on slowly, taking its time. Van Houwelingen wants to get the investment managers at APG, the firm that puts ABP's investment policy into practice, on board too and that isn't going well so far. These managers are trained to make decisions on the basis of current price setting and market developments. Thinking decades ahead, thinking holistically and inclusively, considering things like development, poverty and climate collapse, they simply don't have the training for that. It's a completely new language to them, with many risks that aren't yet understood by most people. There horizon simply doesn't stretch more than a year or two ahead and, even worse, they are often only in their jobs for a couple of years. They have a limited mandate. Mostly, these managers think in terms of the bottom line, questioning whether a share is still worth the price attached to it. They need to learn to think beyond financial value and take all kinds of other values into account. But you can't take a fish out of water and tell it to breath, thinks van Houwelingen.

Felix Lanters, responsible for the share portfolio at PGGM, is wrestling with the same issue. Particularly frustrating for him is the fact that the public perceives PFZW, the pension fund for which PGGM manages investments, as part of the government, and its fund as public money. The money actually belongs to the members, people who have often spent decades putting money aside for their pension. They set the rules and are absolutely clear on their priorities: the financial aim, the return on their money, has to come first. PGGM, which provides pensions for people in the care industry, has actually been working with a message of sustainability for years. It's common sense to realise that the degree to which you enjoy your retirement is partially determined by the context in which you hope to spend the money. Who wants to have to wear a face mask because pollution has got out of hand? But when push comes to shove, the company's investments in a clean environment can't come at the expense of the expected return; every questionnaire the members are asked to fill in reinforces this message. Lanters can understand why, a nurse's pension is hardly a gold mine. He sees his task mostly as keeping an eye on the risks associated with non-sustainable investment. Lanters examines to what extent companies that fly the flag for environmental, social, governance also show an improvement in terms of the risk–reward ratio. Sadly, this hasn't been the case so far.

Polman's refrigerator doesn't remain ketchup-less for long. The takeover of the American firm Sir Kensington, makers of responsibly sourced ketchup, mustard and mayonnaise, means that Unilever now sells its own ketchup. The first takeover after the successful battle with Kraft Heinz is charged with symbolism. Kees Kruythoff points out that their big competitor mostly churns out junk food. This is the logical response to that. Founders Mark Ramadan and Scott Norton sound like Ben Cohen and Jerry Greenfield did back when they opened their first ice cream factory. The New York entrepreneurs see food as a dialogue, an opportunity to bring people closer together. That's why they wanted to make a ketchup that was healthy and honest, made using natural, healthy ingredients. They're delighted to have been bought out by Unilever, claiming, 'it's hard really getting the ear of the grocery store buyers and category managers who are the gatekeepers to the American people and their stomachs'. Unilever intends to help these entrepreneurs take over the world with their organic ketchup.

For a while, the possibility of moving head office to Singapore is on the table but in the end the board decides this would be a bridge too far. Unilever is still a European company in terms of culture, the single head office will either be in Rotterdam or in London. The pros and cons of each of the two cities are still being assessed. Every meeting sees an addition to the colour-coded list: the big red mark next to London is Brexit, the big red mark next to Rotterdam is dividend tax. Twelve years after the Dutch tax inspectorate made an agreement with Shell and then secretary of state Joop Wijn predicted that this tax would eventually go the way of the dodo, it's still stubbornly clinging on. It's the British investors in particular who will have to start handing over 15 per cent of their dividend in tax if they were to exchange their PLC shares for shares in the new Dutch NV. Most investors can write off the dividend tax but since the United Kingdom doesn't have any equivalent tax, the British investors aren't able to do the same. The Brits in London head office wring their hands and insist that so long as this tax exists, Unilever can't become a Dutch NV.

Scrapping the dividend tax has been on the agenda of the Dutch employers' union VNO-NCW for 15 years at this point, but it has never been given top priority. Nobody has ever even tried lobbying for it to be added to an election manifesto.

Shortly after the 2016 general election, the chair of VNO-NCW, Hans Boer, invited the victors to his office. He told them that he has gathered during his trade missions that Brexit, this dreadful, costly mistake that also stands to cost the Netherlands money, offers new opportunities too. A number of big, international banks have told him explicitly that they would like to move their operations to the Netherlands. There's only one thing holding them back: the cap of 20 per cent of annual salary on bankers' bonuses agreed under Minister of Finance Jeroen Dijsselbloem. De Boer suggests that the Netherlands starts working on the basis of the 100 per cent cap agreed in Brussels. This topic needs to be given top priority in the formation of the new cabinet and comes at the top of his wish list, which he has dubbed the 'Brexit package'. In second place is a drastic reduction in corporation tax needed to make the financial climate more hospitable for business. De Boer is convinced that the Brits are going to have to reduce their corporation tax, already low at 19 per cent, even further as a result of Brexit. Scrapping the dividend tax is his third suggestion. When he brings this up, some of the politicians at the meeting exchange confused looks. What's that one again?

The big red mark on Unilever's pro and cons list will have an effect on this front too. A big team of lawyers and other advisors is currently hard at work in the London office mapping the implications of the two scenarios: London or Rotterdam. Dekkers emphasises the need for precision. Unilever doesn't suddenly want to find itself with a tax bill of billions of euros. They need to meet with representatives of both countries to negotiate on the tax implications.

Paul Polman also goes to see Hans de Boer. He tells him that he's tremendously worried about Brexit and hopes that Unilever head office can come to the Netherlands. He tells him how much he misses the Dutch stakeholder model. But he's also clear that they'll only pull it off if at least 75 per cent of the British shareholders vote for the move. And they'll never do that if the dividend tax hasn't been scrapped. De Boer knows that Paul Polman is lobbying actively on this, he's told Mark Rutte exactly the same story.

The chairman of VNO-NCW promises the Unilever CEO, who, after all, is one of his most important members that he'll do his best to help. He tells him that men in the very same type of suits they are currently wearing oversaw the demise of ABN AMRO Bank 12 years previously. The takeover and destruction of the bank, and its huge international network, are still being felt in the Dutch business world all these years later.

If it was up to De Boer, the government would pull out all the stops to avoid a repeat of that upset. Unilever and Shell have to be protected and have to remain Dutch. De Boer gets in touch with the Shell CEO Ben van Beurden personally to tell him the same thing. Paul Polman is reassured, things are going in the right direction.

CHAPTER 17

FOR SALE: DUTCH DNA, MILKED DRY

May–December 2017

It would be a marvellous twist of fate if he somehow ended up being appointed the board chairman of his great-grandfather Sam van den Bergh's life's work. Jean-Marc Huët has been brought in by the investment group Blackstone in order to advise on an offer on Unilever's margarine arm, which was founded almost one hundred and fifty years ago by his great-great-grandfather Simon van den Bergh in the small Dutch town of Oss. Blackstone people have even been talking about the possibility of restoring the company's original name 'Van den Bergh'.

Blackstone is a major player in the world of private equity. The same is true of the other names going around as potential buyers: CD&R and Bain Capital, KKR and Apollo, all outfits everyone assumes are capable of coming up with the €6–€7 billion Unilever's daughter company is expected to fetch. All parties interested in buying the spreads business must take part in an auction. Ahead of the first round of bidding, Unilever has given them the same presentation on the background and results of the division. After the first bid, the highest bidders are invited to take part in the next round. These parties receive more detailed information allowing them to refine their offer. From the very beginning, Unilever has made only one demand: the buyer must commit to this Unilever subsidiary's sustainability ambitions.

Under the leadership of Marc Bolland, now a partner at Blackstone, several million dollars are allocated for a detailed investigation into the worldwide spreads business. The investigation focuses on three central questions. Revenues have been dropping by 5–7 per cent per year, can this decrease be halved? How do we get future customers interested in margarine again and what will it cost to awaken this interest? How difficult will it be to separate this daughter company from the rest of Unilever? The division may well already be separate on paper, but it's still an integral part of the parent company. What are the risks, what could go wrong there? The former CFO of Unilever is helping Blackstone to answer these questions alongside former Unilever COO Harish Manwani, who is also linked to Blackstone out of Singapore.

Bolland wonders how much scope still exists for a sandwich spread with margarine now that customers in Europe and the United States seem to vacillate between a croissant with real butter and super-healthy muesli washed down with a glass of water. Bolland and Huët sense opportunities too, not least when it comes to margarine's plant-based, sustainable nature. They fantasise about how the company might be able to work in consultation with the University of Wageningen to become a world leader in the field of food technology. But they also see limitations. They'll need to invest an enormous amount, there's a lot of overdue maintenance to take care of and the management of the Unilever division would need replacing. It isn't made up of the best people.

Many Unilever employees, particularly the Dutch ones, don't like the fact that other people are harbouring such fantasies. Why hasn't Unilever thought of any of this over the past ten years? Admittedly, the falling revenues had kept on frustrating the rest of the company's efforts to grow. The last big setback had been the Ukrainian boycott of butter exports to Russia. After Russia had invaded Ukraine, business had slumped and butter had flooded the European market. The price had dropped so sharply that 'real butter' had become just as cheap as margarine.

Colleagues in Rotterdam accuse Polman of having never taken the trouble to truly understand the business, relying instead on his background in hygiene at Procter & Gamble. The last big, expensive innovation in spreads had been back in 2000. The cholesterol-lowering spread Flora ProActiv, good for your heart and blood vessels, had gone on to be a major hit. Margarine is healthier than real butter, at least since trans fats were removed from it 20 years ago. And perhaps even more importantly: it's plant based, meaning that it's also better for the planet. This is exactly what Unilever needs to capitalise on.

A variety of commentators are also baffled by this, observing that basically all plant-based substitutes seem to be enjoying a boom, apart from margarine. And that is exactly the kind of sustainable, healthy and cruelty-free product people are looking for. Why isn't anyone explaining this more clearly? 'My real hope is that health-food companies like The Vegetarian Butcher will start buying Unilever margarine and imbuing the stuff with a new, vegan image. This is a potential growth market,' says microbiologist and food expert Rosanne Hertzberger in her column in the Dutch broadsheet *NRC Handelsblad*.

Her statement encapsulates exactly what Rogier Smeets hopes to do. He even plans to start investing in vegetarian meat substitutes, and in a vegan version of Magnum. They made the first Flora products entirely plant based back in the summer of 2016. Those products are selling significantly better than the rest, even though most people have no idea that the stuff is entirely plant based. This is a pattern. If they can make a big audience aware that margarine is cheaper, healthier *and* better for the environment, then they can buck the downward trend. But you have to be willing to invest.

According to Smeets, the reason this wasn't possible for so long was because Polman simply isn't all that interested in Unilever's food operations. When Smeets had success with the introduction of frozen ready meals in the United States under the brand of the restaurant chain P.F. Chang's, with sales of over $100 million in the first year, Polman's response had been lukewarm. The CEO believed that Unilever should be building on its own, scalable brands, brands with global appeal. Food products tied to local eating habits are much harder to produce than personal and household hygiene products, even at the best of times.

Smeets and some of his fellow directors think that Unilever is missing the boat in terms of foods. The multinational has failed to make any impression in the fresh meals market, shops now do all of this in house, via their own brands. The sale of spreads pushes the Unilever food category even further back into the so-called middle aisles, where the non-perishable, factory-packed tins and packets of processed food reside. Fewer and fewer people are interested in buying such products.

Do you like your sandwiches? Is it a good meatball with a tasty gravy? You grow up with I Can't Believe It's Not Butter, you bake with Stork and Flora ProActiv protects your heart and arteries. Generations of Unilever marketers grew up believing that the company helped the housewife to overcome the various hurdles she encounters every day. They still manage to sell the so-called boring margarine with considerable margins thanks to 'psychological compartmentalisation' and clever adverts. In order to justify those margins, researchers have been constantly at work to develop and refine the products. Health had emerged alongside price and flavour as one of the most important factors.

As a result of the abrupt increase in patients with heart and circulatory conditions after the Second World War, hospitals had asked Unilever to make a margarine that didn't raise cholesterol. The first version of Flora was available in pharmacies all the way back in the 1960s. Expanding on this health claim led to consistent revenue increases. For decades, Unilever's margarine business grew, especially in the United States and Europe. Until the early 1980s, this Unilever subsidiary was probably the most profitable company in the whole of the Netherlands.

The history of Unilever's Dutch DNA begins in 1866. The French emperor Napoleon III was looking for a *beurre économique* in order to feed his people and his soldiers. Real butter is nourishing but expensive and it goes rancid quickly. The emperor offered a reward: Who will offer me a healthy, cheap alternative? The chemist Hippolyte Mège-Mouriés spends three years experimenting with churning melted kidney fat and minced udders into a butter substitute. Its pearly gleam leads him to christen the substance margarine, from the Greek *margarites*, meaning pearl.[1]

His invention is nutritious and cheap but the inventor is too late. Napoleon III has been overthrown in the meantime and no one is interesting in the patent he's taken out on his invention. This changes when a businessman of his acquaintance offers a little of this margarine to the butter dealer Antoon Jurgens from Oss. He looks at it, tastes it and is immediately enthusiastic. He sees a gap in the market.

In spring of 1871 Jurgens visits Mège-Mouriés in his little factory in the French town of Poissy and offers him his congratulations. The flattered Frenchman reportedly answered, 'Jesus was such a genius that he could turn water into wine, but I can turn fat into butter.' Jurgens promises the Frenchman an annual fee of 10,000 Francs on the condition that he kept the procedure secret.

A couple of months later the first margarine factory in the world is up and running in Oss. Jurgens's son, Jan, is so proud of the discovery that he invites his biggest local rival, the butter dealer Simon van den Bergh, to come and taste it. His son Sam would later say that Jurgens had been going around bragging about his 'fantastic profits' for a while at that point. Reason enough for Van den Bergh senior to also set out for France in order 'to gain there all desirable insights concerning the new product'. It's possible that Jurgens's yearly payment had lapsed by that time because Mège-Mouriés certainly didn't keep his secret, showing this Dutchman how he made his margarine too.[2]

Patent law didn't yet exist in the Netherlands back then so the Frenchman's patent was not protected under the law. A year after Jurgens started his factory in Oss, another financed by Van den Bergh began producing this artificial butter too. It was the beginning of a feud between the Catholic Jurgens family and the Jewish Van den Bergh family.

In the meantime, rising prosperity in England meant that there was a growing demand for imported butter and eggs. And so, in 1886, 35-year-old

William Lever crossed the Channel in search of new butter suppliers for his father's grocery wholesale business. Lever even went to visit Antoon Jurgens in person a couple of times. But after the enterprising Brit suggested that they supply the margarine in packages rather than in vats, Jurgens begins to smell a rat: 'We need to keep a close eye on this man and his new-fangled ideas, you mark my works.' A few years later, in 1884, Lever set up his own soap brand, Sunlight, and would remain focused on selling this soap until well into the next century.[3]

In 1891, the Van den Bergh family moved into a new factory on the Nassaukade in Rotterdam. Catholic-dominated Oss has become too unwelcoming and now that imports are becoming more important, being close to the busy and expanding port will also be useful. In Zwijndrecht, Van den Bergh had built a factory to produce Stuiverzeep (penny soap) which was sold in cardboard packaging just like Sunlight, which has since become popular in England. Making and selling soap is relatively simple for a margarine manufacturer. It's made from almost exactly the same raw materials and makes its way to the customer along a similar route. In order to simplify the financing of his plans, Simon's son Sam founds a British corporation that allows him access to the London financial market.

In the Netherlands, margarine is still being sold unbranded, scraped out of barrels and sold by the pound wrapped in greaseproof paper. Inspired once again by modern, British businessmen like William Lever, Van den Bergh decides to give his products a brand name: Zeeuws Meisje (Zeeland Maid) and later Vitello, aimed at the German market. Back in Oss, the Jurgens family followed these developments with deep suspicion.

In 1888, Antoon's grandson Anton took over the company after the untimely death of his father Jan. He decides to follow Van den Bergh's lead by attracting investors to help finance more factories and establish offices overseas. Jurgens and Van den Bergh cross paths everywhere they go. In order to avoid the import duties their forced to pay every time they cross a national border, they each set up margarine factories in Germany, France and England.

Over the next twenty-five years, the two rivals continuously try to one-up each other by claiming to have developed a better margarine. On 14 May 1906 Jurgens claims: 'Yet if you were now to taste each sample, we'd snatch some of the feather from our esteemed competitor's overstuffed caps. We are pleased to announce that our pilot testing has confirmed that the culture we are now working with is the correct one and that it will create much better margarine than the one currently on sale from the Jew.'[4]

By this time, both men are making serious money. In 1905 alone, Van den Bergh makes a profit of £220,000 (roughly €30 million in today's money), with 16 per cent returned as a dividend to the family.[5] Sam van den Bergh regards himself as a progressive liberal but it will take him until 1919 to recognise the trade union movement as a credible partner in dialogue. The fact that his workers are in seven days a week, working a total of around 70 hours, leads to heated debates with his wife. Rebecca Willing is a committed social democrat, an ethical thinker with a sensitivity to issues of rights.[6]

Every so often, Sam van den Bergh and Anton Jurgens experiment with working together. Each of them knows that combining forces, particularly for things like purchasing raw materials, could be highly advantageous. As part of their search for new, plant-based sources of fat, they decide to team up and invest in palm oil plantations in the German colony of Cameroon. The venture is a failure. In 1908, they agree to combine and share their profits and losses from producing margarine, with 60 per cent going to the Van den Bergh and 40 per cent to the smaller partner, Jurgens. Whatever they make on the sales of their own products, they keep themselves. Throughout all this, they remain on guard. 'We know them well enough to know that usually only make promises for the sake of the cause, to keep someone on side for that moment, which is why we don't rely too much on Sam's word', says Anton Jurgens on 9 March 1908, shortly after putting his signature to this agreement. In 1913, with each Dutch person then eating around five kilos of margarine a year, they realise that their firms have become pretty much equally profitable, with an annual profit of two million guilders (€50 million today) and decide to work on a 50–50 basis from then on. After the First World War, they both set up their own palm oil plantations in the Dutch East Indies, with fleets of steam ships to transport the palm kernels and palm oil to Europe.[7]

Sam van den Bergh realises that an even greater combining of forces will lead to even better results, particularly through savings on raw materials, manufacture and advertising expenditure. Jurgens is by now slightly bigger than Van den Bergh in the Netherlands, with the latter even seeing a drop in sales. Starting in 1923 Van den Bergh tries to break their hold on the domestic market by introducing the brand Blue Band (now known as Stork in the UK), 'a margarine of higher quality, intended for a higher class of people'.

Sam van den Bergh decides to follow the British model and invest heavily in a new phenomenon: visual advertising. Before he places his advert with the hand-drawn portrait of the 'Blue Band girl' in leading newspapers, he asks his biggest buyers for their opinion. The claim 'freshly churned, stands up to any comparison with butter. Blue Band is much more affordable,' prompts a furious backlash from the dairy industry.[8] Nevertheless, the consumer is quickly sold on the idea. Jurgens watches Van den Bergh's market share grow.

In 1927, the two families shock the business world with the announcement that they are going to merge. The fight has literally gone out of them. The immediate cause of their decision was the latest big bust-up about the distribution of profits according to the agreement of 1913. Van den Bergh is demanding £200,000 from Jurgens, Jurgens is demanding £300,000 from Van den Bergh: the two fighting cocks disagree on practically every point. Paul Rijkens, Van den Bergh's agent, calls it 'the most grotesque dispute ever to have arisen in the Dutch business community', saying that 'the legal costs are into the millions'. While the matter is going through arbitration in London, the two sworn enemies are still trying to steal market share from one another in the Netherlands. The members of the board on both sides have become convinced that the chance of one company gaining overall supremacy is slim and that the destruction of both parties looked much more likely, in fact practically inevitable. A blanket merger is the only way out of the impasse.[9]

Anton Jurgens is the one who finally suggests the merger. A flabbergasted Sam van den Bergh asks Rijkens what he thinks he should do. Rijkens, the son of a margarine manufacturer who sold his business to Van den Bergh, suggests that he keeps an open mind and sees what they are proposing. On 24 September 1927, the agreement is signed by 10 members of each of the families. Van den Bergh has stipulated that neither of the families be allowed to run the show. Two external candidates, the British aristocrat Vere Brabazon Ponsonby and the Dutch politician Rudolf Johan Hendrik Patijn, a member of the same party as Sam van den Bergh, become the chairman and vice chairman of the Margarine Union (Margarine Unie). The rest of the board is made up of five members of each family. This marks the beginning of a balancing act that will grip the company for decades to come.

Dutch newspapers dub the deal 'The Peace of Oss'. The parties have also agreed that Sam van den Bergh, now 64, will give up his responsibilities at the end of 1928; he has no desire to run a company if he himself cannot make all the decisions.

The first big saving of one million guilders per year (the equivalent of €18 million today) is quickly achieved by transferring production from the Jurgens margarine factory in Oss to the Van den Bergh factory in Rotterdam. Anton Jurgens, three years younger than Sam van den Bergh, is also losing interest. This isn't his company anymore. In 1929, he agrees to a merger with the financially troubled Lever Brothers. His family are told to put up and shut up. When Paul Rijkens comes to the Van den Bergh family with the news, a huge debate erupts. Sam van Bergh, the retired paterfamilias, puts an end to it with the words: 'Gentlemen, you've all got the wrong end of the stick. For the Van den Bergh family as shareholders, this is a fantastic deal. Rijkens is right, you have to say yes. This is going to be the deal of the century.'[10]

On 2 September 1929, the Margarine Union and Lever Brothers merge to form Unilever. The Dutch NV and the British PLC remain distinct entities for tax reasons. Organising the merger, which sees two mother corporations with around two dozen daughter companies forced to work together, falls to the 32-member strong board. This is led by a Special Committee, with one British and one Dutch director and a third man charged with keeping the peace between them. It is decided that 57 per cent of the dividend will go to the Dutch NV, which is still the larger of the two. In 1933, 66-year-old Anton Jurgens steps down, he just can't get used to not being able to make any decisions anymore and has grown impatient with the arrogant attitude of Lever's British employees.

Eighty-four years later, almost nothing has remained the same, except the NV, the PLC, Dutch directness and British arrogance. No Brit working at London head office can imagine all the big decisions being made in Rotterdam.

At the beginning of May 2017, Polman calls Henk Kamp, the outgoing minister of economic affairs, to tell him what conditions Unilever would require in order to become a Rotterdam-based Dutch NV. The ministry has already proclaimed that 'proactive intervention from the Dutch government is desirable for the maintenance and expansion of Unilever's operations in the Netherlands.' Polman thinks that Kamp is a brave man.

In a letter to the Dutch parliament at the end of May, the minister calls for a longer period to consider takeovers because 'the risk exists in the case of some takeovers that the focus on the long term will be overshadowed in favour of profit in the short term'. The well-known Dutch businessmen Jan Hommen, Peter Wakkie and Jeroen van der Veer each react enthusiastically in *NRC Handelsblad*: 'It's of crucial importance that a corporation that has been taken over continues to promote the interests of all the stakeholders in that business as well as possible and that the takeover is focused on long-term continuity. The means to achieve this are rarely if ever offered. This is what stopped ABN AMRO from escaping a hostile takeover in 2007. When it comes to takeovers, emotions sometimes tend to get the best of us and winning can become an end in itself. While feelings don't actually help the whole process of takeovers at all. Not for the party acquiring or the party being acquired. They require what you call "slow thinking". Big decisions of a crucial, strategic nature require carefully considered processes and sufficient time,' so say the influential Dutch businessmen. All this is music to the ears of Paul Polman.

On the day Kamp sends his letter to parliament, the Unilever CEO is busy telling *The Guardian* how much more liberal the takeover legislation is in the United Kingdom than in the United States or the Netherlands. He warns: 'You have to have a discussion of why these differences are there, and whether you are putting yourself in a good position or a bad position, especially at the time of Brexit and many other things.' He once again criticises the Takeover Code: 'A 28-day timetable is not long enough for defending companies to audit detailed cost-savings.' He repeats his suggestion of how this could be improved: give shareholders who have been investing for a longer time more of a say. He points out that Unilever has 10,000 direct employees in the UK but almost another 200,000 working indirectly in supply chains. Then there are the 80,000 Unilever pensioners in the UK. 'So the importance of a company like this is not a national test of security, but a national test of what sort of economy we want. I think more and more people are starting to discover that the economy needs to work for more people and needs to be more inclusive. Do you want short-term forces – that work for a few people, and make a few more billionaires – to be the dominant force? Or do you want the system to work for the billions that need to be served? It's a fundamental choice.' He says he could easily manufacture a higher share price at Unilever by cutting jobs, factories and research. It would be five years before the market noticed the underinvestment: 'Graveyards are full of companies that have been cutting costs but ultimately not fulfilled their purpose to do anything useful for society.'[11] Polman calls on governments to take a stand against the violence of these results-orientated shareholders such as hedge funds. When it comes to the matter of his own departure he says: I won't be abandoning ship before she's in a safe harbour.

But the abolition of the dividend tax in The Hague is far from a foregone conclusion. Civil servants inside the Ministry of Finance think it's a bad idea. Jan IJzerman, the director of Direct Taxation, explains to his Secretary of State Eric Wiebes that Dutch multinationals with a large number of portfolio shareholders in the United Kingdom are the only ones negatively affected by the tax. He calls scrapping it, 'a big, generic measure for a specific problem,' whose biggest effect will be to create a €1.4 billion euro gap in state finances. 'The majority of this loss will be in favour of foreign governments. Maintaining the attractiveness of the Dutch fiscal climate to corporations in a responsible way would be better served – from a long-term perspective – by a reduction in corporation tax. The conclusion that scrapping it is essential for the corporate climate is simply unsupportable.'[12]

IJzerman does allude to the fact that abolishing the tax would decrease the chance of Unilever or Shell moving their headquarters overseas. But he doesn't believe there are any guarantees there either. 'It's largely a political issue.' Since the cost of scrapping the tax would be borne by the business community you could also say that it would make the climate for investment less attractive.

On 13 June, Polman speaks to Eric Wiebes, who had applied to Unilever but eventually went to work for Shell after graduating university. IJzerman warns the secretary of state in advance: 'the question of whether scrapping the dividend tax is a good idea is likely to come up. Tell him that this issue is a matter for the coalition negotiation.' He tells Polman that this has already been agreed with the civil servants from the Ministry of General Affairs and the Ministry of Economic Affairs. 'The civil service side of Economic Affairs does say that they would like to get rid of the dividend tax.'[13] IJzerman repeats his objections to a scrap.

That same afternoon, at the Ministry of Economic Affairs, Polman receives a promising commitment from Minister Henk Kamp: 'The cabinet will draw up a "bid book" for Unilever, aimed at helping to bring that head office to the Netherlands.' This scheme is christened 'Project Smile'. Kamp calls Rutte to report back.[14] Polman has made it clear to both men that there is zero prospect of a Dutch head office for as long as the dividend tax is still in place.

Regardless of the outcome, this is still a great day for Polman. It's the first time that the top 200 have gathered in the Rotterdam head office for the annual CEO-Forum since the battle with Kraft Heinz. After a day of presentations and ambitions, just as Polman is making moves to leave the stage, Harry Brouwer, the CEO of food solutions, decides to stand up. Brouwer is one of the only two Bestfoods veterans who still works for Unilever. The marketing expert had been turned down by Unilever in the 1980s, they'd thought he was too touchy-feely, too open. Brouwer loves the company but hates the often so cold corporate environment. Polman is the only CEO he's actually felt a connection to in all that time.

How is it possible that no one today has taken a moment to recognise the brilliant way that Polman has managed to keep them together, allowing them to still be sitting here together and to keep on doing their important, wonderful work? This hasn't been so much as mentioned. Not a goddamn word. Well, he's going to mention it, he has to mention it right now.

Brouwer tells those assembled that it's amazing that they're still even sitting there together. That they have Polman and his team to thank for that. His words strike a chord. His colleagues rise as one and start applauding; it's an ovation that goes on for minutes. Polman stands on the stage looking rather uncomfortable and asks his CFO Graeme Pitkethly to come up and join him. He doesn't want to, the Scot thinks this applause is going to the right person already.

Members of parliament also implicitly applaud Polman later that month. They're debating Kamp's letter and the 'takeovers of Unilever and AkzoNobel'. Most of them express their concern. GroenLinks MP Tom van der Lee almost sounds like Polman: 'I think that if we as legislators create opportunities for protection, we need to ask for something in return. We want managers to do business responsibly and sustainably. If they prove their company is doing this, they have a right to protection in line with that behaviour. I respect Unilever but recognise that the threat of a takeover has precipitated a strategic change of course that I would have preferred not to see. I hope that everyone comes to their senses and makes sensible choices for the future.' The CDA, PvdA, PVV and GroenLinks put forward two motions calling on the government to ensure that 'companies are offered sufficient instruments to make the right decisions in resisting hostile or unwanted takeovers'.

This is no good to Unilever now. Preventing Kraft Heinz from coming back again in two months' time requires showing that they have good results. And they have. The clean-up on costs is having an effect, the margin has improved to 17.8 per cent, almost 2 per cent higher than this time a year ago and that in turn is driving up profits, so far by 22 per cent to €3.3 billion. The promised €6 billion in savings by 2019 already stands at €1 billion only a couple of months in. Savings on marketing, for example by showing the same TV adverts for longer, already amount to €300 million. Overheads have gone by €200 million, partly because of a 30 per cent reduction in the number of flights taken by staff.

However, 50 per cent of all these savings are coming from suppliers. Director of sourcing, Dhaval Buch, is playing a leading role on that front. Under his leadership Unilever has been buying around €35 billion in raw materials and services each year. His message to suppliers is always the same: we don't want to be taken over by a company like Kraft Heinz and you should not want that either. Because when we suffer, you suffer. So let's just be happy that hasn't happened. In his meetings with suppliers, the Indian follows this message up with a harsh truth: we're now facing a new reality. Let's try to work together to make sure this doesn't happen in the future either. If you want to remain our supplier of choice, you have to drop your prices by 10 per cent.

Marc Engel, Buch's boss, is well aware that this message is severe but he's also completely convinced that there's no longer any alternative. They're in this together. He'll find a way to thank the suppliers who cooperate later.

Graeme Pitkethly is completely uncompromising when it comes to this process. But the Unilever CFO is also currently working on a framework intended to help companies to capture the effects of climate change using financial metrics. Pitkethly is the vice-chairman of the Task Force on Climate-Related Financial Disclosures. Established by the influential international Financial Stability Board, this task force has constructed a system that can map out the financial risks of climate change in a consistent fashion. FSB chairman Mark Carney, who expressed his huge concerns about this issue two years previously in a speech entitled 'Breaking the Tragedy of the Horizon', wants investors and bankers to help incorporate these new risks into their models. He knows that there's still a long way to go. 'We know climate change creates a potentially huge cost for the future generations, but we don't currently have an incentive to fix it. The horizon for monetary policy extends out of two to three years. For financial stability it is a bit longer – about a decade. So once climate change becomes a defining issue for financial stability, it may already be too late.' By making these risks more transparent, companies can discover what they need to do in order to meet with what's ahead. As Pitkethly says: 'It is, for sure, just a matter of time before most investors – as well as consumers and future employees – actively ask for this information from companies. As further evidence of the direction of travel, more than 1,200 companies have committed to implement a price on carbon. And 400 investors with $25 trillion of assets under management are participating in the Investor Platform for Climate Action.'[15]

To Antony Burgmans, the as yet insufficient efforts to make the paint industry more sustainable are an important reason to keep obstructing the American firm PPG's plans to take over AkzoNobel. After the chemicals company turned down three unwanted takeover offers from PPG, the activist shareholder Elliott Internal had tried to force negotiations with AkzoNobel via the Enterprise Chamber of the Amsterdam Court of Appeal. They had also demanded that Antony Burgmans step down. At the beginning of June, PPG finally threw in the towel after these demands were rejected by the courts. The entire process took far too long. A couple of weeks after PPG's withdrawal, AkzoNobel announces that their CEO Ton Büchner is stepping down on health grounds. The whole thing had been too much for him.

Paul Polman is enraged when he reads this. To him this is further proof that activist shareholders are devoid of all human feeling and driven solely by greed. Never mind semi-human, they're barely a quarter. They calculate their own value solely on the basis of their net worth. It's all the same to them what effect they have on the people at companies like AkzoNobel.

He's relieved that Kraft Heinz didn't get back in touch in August, and he finds it bizarre that for many people this way of doing business represents proof of an efficient free market rather than the opposite. Polman wonders once again whether politicians fully grasp what's going on here. Do they realise that our future and our children's futures are being endangered by people like this? Changing laws won't be enough to prevent this kind of behaviour. It's a deeper issue. There is a deep crisis of ethics when it comes to doing business.

Burgmans agrees entirely with Polman. He is following the news of the potential move to Rotterdam very closely. He looked into whether the company would be better off with a single head office himself 12 years ago. Dividend tax had been a massive obstacle even back then. With Brexit looming, he thinks Rotterdam is a logical choice for Unilever. The company mustn't end up trapped on some isolated island. He doesn't think that the fact that many Brits can't imagine Unilever's head office going somewhere that isn't a real metropolis is a particularly good argument against the move. Nestlé's head office is in the Swiss backwater of Vevey and that company seems to be doing pretty well.

Burgmans also thinks the time has come for more legislation. It's needed to restore faith in business. It also presents an opportunity for Dutch businesses, which are ahead of the pack when it comes to sustainability. But it will also require CEOs to learn to communicate more effectively when it comes to the positive contribution these businesses make to society.[16] If they could make these results measurable, express them in euros, then all the better.

That's still proving difficult. In the journal *Economisch-Statische Berichten* (Economic Statistical Reporting), director of True Price Adrian de Groot Ruiz and Professor of Banking and Finance Dirk Schoenmaker make forward an attempt to it. Using a 'social cost-benefit analysis', they calculate what the true costs of a takeover of AkzoNobel by PPG would have been. They estimate the effective cost in terms of job losses, higher prices for customers and increased CO_2 emission and arrive at a negative value of −€6 billion. A calculation of this type carried out by the Enterprise Chamber of the Amsterdam Court of Appeal could, they argue, form the basis for the government to veto these sorts of takeovers going forward, or force guarantees designed to prevent such societal damage, which they term 'market failure'.[17]

The formation of a new coalition cabinet in the Netherlands is taking a long time. Finally, in September, they make a breakthrough. In the negotiations, the CDA and the Christian Union (ChristenUnie) are given the flat tax they've been calling for. In order to prevent this system of only two tax bands from increasing the gap between rich and poor, the liberal-democratic D66 party demands an accelerated cap on the mortgage interest deductions and is supported in this by the Christian Union. Coalition negotiator Gerrit Zalm (VVD), who gave up his position as CEO of ABN AMRO a few months earlier, supports the three parties. But this kind of quick reduction in mortgage interest deductions has traditionally been a big problem for the VVD in terms of support. As they sit at the negotiation table, prospective prime minister Mark Rutte is visibly upset by their suggestion. He thinks his party will be seriously damaged by this move. Rutte wants compensation in the form of a measure to improve the economic climate for corporations. The rest of them are fully on board, they haven't liked what's been going on with Unilever and AkzoNobel either.

Rutte suggests that they either go along with the VNO-NCW's suggestion of scrapping the bonus cap for bankers or get rid of the dividend tax. This last idea comes completely out of the blue for his fellow negotiators. They know all about the cap on bankers' bonuses, getting rid of it is risky in terms of public opinion. The negotiators from D66, Alexander Pechtold and Wouter Koolmees, call it a political suicide. Some at the negotiation table suspect that Rutte is relying on just such a reaction.

The negotiating politicians then hear arguments from various sides to clarify their position on abolishing the dividend tax. Rutte emphasises the risk of the Netherlands becoming a nation of subsidiaries, like Belgium. Civil service reports show that there's a decent chance that the Dutch state will lose the 11,000 cases currently underway against them in the European Court of Justice in Strasbourg over so-called double taxation. The plaintiffs claim that the tax is in contravention of the EU's principle of equivalence: some investors have to pay the tax while others don't.

Hans de Boer once again explains how half of all small and medium companies' exports 'surf' on the back of the big players. His great enthusiasm helps to sway them towards abolition, as does a visit from Rotterdam mayor Ahmed Aboutaleb, who underlines the importance of Unilever to the Rotterdam region.

At this point politicians and business leaders have been dancing around this issue for 12 years. Former CDA secretary of state Joop Wijn's misgivings were followed by interim action by the PvdA minister of finance Wouter Bos, who offered Dutch businesses that wanted to protect themselves from unwanted private equity takeovers a helping hand in 2007 by exempting them from paying dividend tax on purchases of their own shares.

At Rutte's request, Wiebes has written an internal VVD memo on the advantages of scrapping the dividend tax. In doing so, the secretary of state

for finance has made a clear departure from the advice of his civil service colleagues. The prime minister uses the text in his informal, bilateral discussions
with other parties. It makes a strong impression, as it says: 'The Netherlands
are home to fourteen corporate offices of *Fortune* 500 companies, a figure which
has not grown in many years. Worse still: this number is under increasing
pressure. The tax on dividends is increasingly starting to pinch. If we keep
doing nothing then the Netherlands is only going to be attractive to operating companies. If we do nothing then there is a very real risk that existing
listed companies like Unilever (this year), Shell (possibly within the coming
government) and AkzoNobel will leave the Netherlands and the AEX-index
will continue to shrink. We're facing a loss of tax revenue. Provided they are
backed up by swift consultations then Unilever and Shell will still be able to
opt for the Netherlands when choosing their single nationality.' Wiebes calls
for the scrapping of the dividend tax. According to him, the costs of doing so,
now around €1.4 billion, will be repaid by the business community operating
in the Netherlands via corporation tax. Wiebes also warns: 'Even if we don't
change anything, we can expect a considerable erosion to revenue. The potential departure of the two biggest limited companies would reduce tax revenue
to €850 million even on its own.'

Sybrand van Haersma Buma, the CDA chief whip, sees this as a nightmare
scenario. He doesn't want it on his conscience, these companies are too important to the Netherlands. Paul Polman and Johan de Koning, the Unilever government liaison officers, have told him that the Unilever board will vote to
move its head office to the Netherlands by the end of the year if the dividend
tax is scrapped. He knows that De Koning was a CDA parliamentary staffer
back in 2000, which creates a sense of kinship. Van Haersma Buma quickly
opts to support Rutte and De Boer's proposal. We need to do everything we
possibly can to stop Unilever from leaving.

The other coalition negotiators and prospective cabinet members are also
on board, they think that this measure will go down well with the public, it's
one they can explain fairly easily. All they want to do now is get down to the
business of running the country, so they agree to scrap dividend tax. They
brace themselves for criticism from the opposition, expecting them to target
the proposed increase of the low VAT rate, from 6 per cent to 9 per cent.

Things don't turn out as they expect. Bart Snels, the specialist for finance
and the economy for the GroenLinks party, almost falls off his chair when he
reads the coalition's programme. This measure, set to cost €1.4 billion per year,
wasn't in any of the coalition members' manifestos. He is immediately certain
that the Ministry of Finance won't be happy with it. They already worked out

that it would only help a handful of Unilever's foreign shareholders, with the rest disappearing into foreign treasuries. This is highly controversial. He goes to see his chief whip Jesse Klaver with the news. In the parliamentary debate with the coalition negotiator Gerrit Zalm, Klaver is confrontational, demanding to know which lobbies sent what letters asking for the sudden scrapping of dividend tax. This stinks of voter deception. He doesn't get a clear answer. Klaver can smell blood.

On 3 November 2017 the only Dutchman in the recently published *Harvard Business Review* list of the top 100 best CEOs starts his morning in Wageningen. Polman has been invited to break ground on the construction of a food innovation centre. The ceremony is disrupted by 200 workers from the Unox sausage factory in Oss. Unilever is set to sell the factory to Zwanenberg Food Group. Output is too low and wages are too high. By handing over production to Zwanenberg, Unilever hopes to continue making the sausages in an affordable and sustainable way. The suggestion to keep production in-house and buy out Zwanenberg instead was taken off the table a while ago. Zwanenberg produces many private-label sausages used by supermarkets and as a leading premium brand manufacturer, Unilever can't buy such an operation.

The Unox employees have gone on strike because they disagree with the significantly worse working conditions Zwanenberg offers. Polman explains to them why Unilever is selling the factory: 'Despite your hard work, Unox was no longer viable. You might well say: we need to make people in the Netherlands eat more smoked sausage but nowadays everyone does their shopping at Aldi and Lidl. The brand is under pressure.'

Unilever has invited around forty representatives of governments and NGOs to come and speak with Polman in Amsterdam that afternoon. Anniek Mauser is pleased that she's finally managed to get her contacts and her boss around the same table. She's spent a great deal of time preparing and is disappointed to discover that Polman has not spent much time looking what she's sent. She does understand why though; the CEO's schedule is brutal.

Polman dives right in. This is his audience, this is where he's on form. Over the course of an hour he runs them through his favourite topics, his USLP success and growing concerns from the future. The SDGs and the Paris Climate Agreement put in an appearance, as do increasing deforestation and the growing CO_2 emissions. 'We've already got 120 million refugees as a result of climate change. We need to see a tariff on CO_2 emissions as soon as possible. Normally we would trust in our democracy, our governments but those institutions were built after the Second World War to meet the needs of that era. They don't have any answer for the big issues of this time, those require a global agreement.'

He gives an example: 'The Port of Rotterdam is the biggest in terms of the transport of non-sustainable palm oil. I often say to Rutte: do something about it. But the problem of government is that to them 2030 is too far away, they can't work towards that kind of date.'

'Perhaps the most important thing is that the people are scared. My wife comes from the American Midwest, people there fear for their jobs and they're afraid of new technology. They are vulnerable, with an average pension of $17,000. Getting social cohesion back on track is an enormous challenge.'

The audience responds positively. Some of them are concerned, however. Heske Verburg from Solidaridad is noticing growing tensions within Unilever. She has productive meetings with the people working on sustainability but the minute she starts talking to their colleagues in purchasing the atmosphere is completely different. All they are interested in is whether they are meeting the agreed quotas for certified products. They see answering the question of whether those quotas have really done anything to help poor farmers as completely beyond their remit. It's clear: the promised 20 per cent improvement in profit margin will have to happen here.

When asked whether Unilever can still stand by its pledges to help those poor farmers now that the financial goals have become so much more stringent, Polman becomes visibly annoyed: 'We don't have to consider that question too long: we've created 2.5 million jobs for small farmers over the years.'

'My biggest problem is the financial markets. If we don't start making sure that they start focusing more on long-term issues then we won't solve anything. An investment of $3 to $4 trillion per year is needed. That's a lot of money but eventually it will create between $12 trillion and $22 trillion in value. There's a lot of lazy, passive money. And sadly pension funds aren't really doing anything to help. I'm finding myself wondering more and more how exactly they reward their fund managers. I'm convinced that everything can be resolved. What we need most is time. But try explaining that to some finance guy.'

That evening, Polman is invited to give a speech to the annual Unilever-sponsored summit at the Amsterdam Concert Hall (Concertgebouw). This year his new friends, the leaders of each of the coalition parties, are also invited. Only the CDA leader Van Haersma Buma accepts the invitation. But Polman says nothing in his speech about the brave politicians swimming against the tide in an effort to scrap the dividend tax. They are working hard on Unilever's behalf amid an increasingly damaging debate about the dividend tax but all Polman talks about is saving the world.

Whenever Polman's name comes up, the leader of the opposition Jesse Klaver recalls how much he would had liked going to have visited the Unilever CEO after his appointment as leader of GroenLinks. Klaver was keen to familiarise himself with the sustainability agenda of interesting companies like TNT, DSM and Unilever. Contacts like that are always worth saving for a rainy day. Only Feike Sijbesma from DSM had invited the party leader to a meeting; GroenLinks only had five seats in parliament back then. Both Tex Gunning and Paul Polman had informed Klaver that such a meeting didn't fit with their priorities.

The GroenLinks leader is convinced that at the very least, the decision to get rid of the dividend tax is premature. A much better idea would be to wait and see what happens with Brexit; after that Unilever and Shell might come over here of their own accord. Emotions are running so high in the UK right now that there are no guarantees that scrapping this tax will get them over the line anyway. When he tells Rutte this, the prime minister seems touchy. He tries to persuade Klaver that it's precisely the abolition of the dividend tax that will determine where or not Unilever relocates to Rotterdam. Klaver isn't so sure. He gathers from the British newspapers that the UK isn't about to let the manufacturer of that beloved, terrible, typically British substance Marmite leave without a fight.

The third cabinet led by Marc Rutte is making sustainability in the economy its flagship policy. The Netherlands has some catching up to do, it's a long way behind the targets set by the Paris Climate Agreement. Wiebes becomes the new cabinet's Minister of Economic Affairs *and* Climate.

His civil servants present him with an improved version of the bid book designed to persuade Unilever's management to move to the Netherlands. Unilever employs over 3,100 people, including 1,800 at head office. The company has 4,200 suppliers with a combined turnover of a cool €1 billion. The company spends €120 million on R&D each year in the Netherlands. Last year, it decided to invest €70 million in the global food R&D centre on the campus of Wageningen University.

'Please find enclosed the Dutch government's contribution to Unilever's unification study.' On 15 November, a civil servant from the Ministry of Economic Affairs sends the bid book, containing the first official commitment on scrapping the dividend tax, to Unilever. On the same day, there is a parliamentary debate on the question. The opposition asks the government to share all memos related to the topic and indicate which information has been used to reach this decision. Prime Minister Rutte says that as far as he knows no memo on the dividend tax ever crossed his desk.

Klaver is now 100 per cent sure that Rutte is lying. He was involved in the first 100 days of the coalition negotiations in the spring and knows full well that stacks of civil service memos were produced for decisions concerning as little as €50 million, reports laying out all the pros and cons of what was being proposed. When Minister Wiebes says that he also can't remember which documents did and didn't play a role in the decision, suspicions in the chamber quickly grow. What is going on here?

We're talking about a sum of €1.4 billion, which could be used to address big issues in the care system or education. The opposition ignores the fact that this comparison does not hold water because the business community is supposed to cover the deficit by paying more corporate income tax. On the contrary, immediately the suggestion is made that this is a case of multinationals in backroom meetings trying to get the government to do their dirty work.

Out of nowhere, Rutte makes the scrapping of the dividend tax personal. During the debate he says: 'To my core, I am wholeheartedly convinced that getting rid of the dividend tax is necessary to bring new multinationals to the Netherlands and keep our Dutch multinationals here.' This statement implies a deep connection with the interests of Unilever and Shell. Commentators note archly that Rutte worked in Unilever's HR department back in the 1990s. Was that when this love for Unilever took such deep root?

Opposition increases when civil service documents obtained through freedom of information requests show that there was considerable disagreement between the Ministry of Finance and the Ministry of Economic Affairs on the matter. To Jesse Klaver, this is irrefutable proof that there was no overwhelming argument for getting rid of the dividend tax. It wasn't that straightforward.

The GroenLinks party leader might be able to use the good relationship he has managed to build with Feike Sijbesma to get to the bottom of why Unilever coming to the Netherlands is a good idea, what exactly is the thinking behind this and could it reflect an approach to sustainability that fits with that of GroenLinks? But he doesn't reach out. Klaver doesn't even realise that Sijbesma is on Unilever's board, the body making the decision. The reason he doesn't make the connection is probably because of the way he was brushed off two years earlier when he wanted to introduce himself to Polman.

The CEO of Unilever hasn't been in touch with Klaver either. He can't understand why Unilever isn't being welcomed in the Netherlands with open arms. In the meantime, the British media is sneering about the Netherlands' 'lofty ideals'. Surely *their* Unilever isn't going to move headquarters to Rotterdam? That can't be! Rotterdam instead of London, the AEX instead of the FTSE-100? They can't even picture it.

A lot of civil servants and a handful of politicians in The Hague can picture it quite well. They've been busy working on what it might look like for months. The only thing they seem not to have considered is that the decision isn't down to the Unilever board. They can want whatever they like, it's the PLC shareholders who have to vote for its dissolution, and it will take a majority of 75 per cent.

And the end of November, Unilever announces that it won't be making any decisions before the end of the year. Polman tells the *Financial Times*: 'I'm advocating to postpone decisions because it's a moving playing field – with political turbulence out there. The emotions of the moment are really the issue.' In response to the suggestion that former Unilever employee Mark Rutte is actively trying to bring the head office to the Netherlands, Polman is eager to emphasise that 'the British government has woken up' too.[18]

Sybrand van Haersma Buma is angry. This the second time Unilever has postponed the decision. In November, they'd said it would be settled by December, now they're talking about early 2018. Annoyance increases exponentially with every delay. Gert-Jan Segers, his coalition colleague from the Christian Union, has already said publically that he finds the scrapping of the dividend tax a very tough pill to swallow. D66 politicians are hiding behind the argument that 'an agreement is an agreement'.

Hans de Boer, Mark Rutte and Sybrand Buma are the three musketeers left, the only ones fighting to defend the resolution. The CDA leader has come to realise that he'll need to go way beyond his usual pain threshold to keep his own parliamentary party on board with the proposal. The longer they have to wait for Unilever's decision, the greater the pain and the political fallout will be. And that's not the only thing that disturbs him. He's also desperately lacking ammunition. Why aren't they being given much more information about the importance of Unilever to the Dutch economy? And why isn't Unilever – why isn't Paul Polman – expressing their love for the Netherlands much more emphatically in the media? That would make his job much easier.

He doesn't get Polman. He constantly gets the feeling that he sees the Netherlands as just some piddling little country and isn't bothering to get to grips with how things work here. He's told Polman more than once that most Dutch people don't hold him in particularly high regard because he makes €10 million a year. He needs to justify that to them more clearly. But Buma doesn't get the impression that his message is getting across. Polman reacts with the attitude of a citizen of the world, far removed from little old Holland, along the lines of: that's just how it is in the real world, in the grand world of Unilever.

Polman's salary is the last thing on the minds of the forty or so financial analysts who have gathered at the Unilever head office in New Jersey at the end of November to hear from the top of the company. As usual, they ask about plans to grow revenue and increase the margin. At the end of the presentations Polman flies completely off the handle when someone asks him whether Unilever wouldn't be better off investing more in revenue growth rather than worrying so much about improving the margin.

'We invest €7.5 billion a year in advertising, that's enough to grow our brands', he says. We are not doing anything on the volume side differently because we are promising you the margin', Polman said. 'The margin is entirely coming from what something that you should demand, but nobody is demanding, which is very amazing to me. You've been telling us the margins were low for the first five years, and I've been telling you we have made investments to be able to get this company back on track and where it belongs to be. Here you are all saying "I want shareholder value, I want to drive it," and you're pissing it away by not even asking us to give it. To me, that's incomprehensible. Last year, I told you that these investments were starting to pay off, that the margin would go up from 14 per cent to 18 per cent. But now you're suddenly saying: maybe we shouldn't go up to 18 per cent, because then we're not investing enough in increasing revenue. But that means you don't get it at all, this is the *pay-out*, the return, on the investments you let us make previously. If you don't want it then why on earth did you let us get away with it in the first place?'[19]

It seems like Polman wants to take revenge for the previous year's meeting, where his message was met with scepticism and the Unilever share price went down. That had ended up being the prelude to the hostile approach from Kraft Heinz. He waves his arms wildly: 'Oh, oh, oh, and you're all sitting here with the same old refrain: give us shareholder value. But you don't seem to understand the first thing about it. If we build a factory, then we invest and it takes five years for us to start making money off it. But then when revenue goes up, and that's the result of the investment that we've put in over all these years. That's the proof that we have become a stronger company.'

He shakes his head at the sheer stupidity of all this: 'I'm a Dutchman, maybe we need more level-headed Scots and Dutchman in your world.' Polman closes the session still angry.

Maybe that would be his last end-of-year meeting with analysts. Polman had confirmed a couple of weeks earlier that the search for his successor had begun, directed by Egon Zehnder. The executive recruitment agency so despised by Polman has been hired again after all, at the explicit request of Marijn Dekkers. Egon Zehnder always tries to have a search such as this done and dusted within six months. But Polman tells the *Financial Times* that he doesn't plan to step down until the end of 2018.

The paper tries to sum up Polman's legacy ahead of time, describing him as a 'self-styled long-termist' who warned of the dangers of climate change and claimed that more value is generated for shareholders by buying up small, sustainable brands and making them bigger. But Kraft Heinz forced him down another path. Because 'the US company's private equity backers at 3G Capital, who have set new standards of profitability in the consumer goods industry'.[20]

This scepticism is the exact thing making Polman start to long for a head office in the Netherlands more and more. But in the 'Low Countries', suspicion of him is growing and ramping up the debate about the abolition of dividend tax even further. Who is it setting the new government's agenda: The voters, or a couple of multinationals in back rooms?

On 14 December, Unilever, Shell and a handful of professors are invited to a round table discussion on dividend tax with members of the Dutch parliament. A couple of weeks earlier, *De Telegraaf* had run with the headline that 'nine out of ten economists see no value in scrapping'.

His wife warned him not to go because there was no way it could end well. But Kees van der Waaij thinks he has to be there. The chair of Dutch Unilever believes in Polman's vision, it *has* to work. If the company becomes a PLC then their sustainability vision is over, it's gone. He wants to remain optimistic.

Van der Waaij talks to Polman twice in the run up to the roundtable. He insists on having these conversations in Dutch, after all, this is what they'll be speaking when they meet with MPs. Polman grudgingly agrees. He doesn't think that his Dutch is good enough anymore to be able to communicate as well as he'd like. He constantly worries about this when he has to speak publicly in his homeland, isn't his use of language too weak?

Conny Braams is more than happy for Van der Waaij to go in her place to the meeting, it's a no-brainer. He's steeped in the material, having worked on it since 2005 back when Burgmans was in charge. Marjan van Loon, her counterpart at Dutch Shell, has had to put a huge amount of time and effort into preparation in order to get to grips with the issue properly. Braams is being spared that now. The director of Benelux is still questioning whether they're going to manage to bring head office to Rotterdam. And she understands the Dutch politicians' reproaches. Sadly it just isn't possible for the company to declare Unilever's love for the Netherlands, the UK is an important Unilever market and a much larger one. They sell too many ice creams and detergents there to risk burning any bridges.

There is very little enthusiasm for the Netherlands among Unilever management. Which Brits wants to trade London for Rotterdam? The few Dutch legal experts who were involved in the committees looking into the PLC–NV issue seem to have been pushed out. In Rotterdam, there's a rumour that the ULE feels like it's being bypassed, that Polman and Pitkethly have had several frank exchanges of words.

How is bringing over the single Unilever head office in the interest of the Netherlands? This is the central question of the roundtable discussion with the MPs. The Central Planning Bureau has declared that they can foresee no positive effect in terms of employment opportunities. Various professors have more nuanced criticisms. Harry Garretsen, professor of International Economy in Groningen, thinks that scrapping the tax is nothing short of a bad idea: 'The dividend tax is of no real significance to the corporate climate in the Netherlands, corporation tax is more important on that score.' All this is oil on an ever-growing fire. In the court of public opinion, the words 'dividend tax' have become synonymous with a gift to Shell and Unilever or 'the most expensive jobs programme of all time'.

The fact that Rutte and Polman are in touch with each other is a truth only discussed unofficially. 'Unilever talks to many governments and can't do anything to compromise on the confidentiality of another party', Van der Waaij states when he's asked about possible contact. But the MPs want total clarity. 'Who is in charge in the Netherlands? In giving no answer, you're fuelling populism', sneers Jesse Klaver. When they ask him when he last spoke to Rutte, Van der Waaij has a clever answer ready: the last time I spoke to him officially was 14 years ago when he still worked for Unilever.

Unilever workers in the Rotterdam office are stuck on an emotional roller coaster. On the one hand, there is a growing hope that the Dutch-British company could become a Dutch company. A rumour is going around that the company intends to go much further than Shell when it comes to restructuring. Choosing Rotterdam wouldn't just mean moving the physical head office, the whole company would become an NV too. That would be a big turn up for the books for those a few doors down already looking at how they're going to separate off their margarine operations.

A day after the roundtable discussion, Unilever announces that it has sold its spreads division for €6.83 billion to the investment company Kohlberg Kravis Roberts & Co. They haven't reached any specific agreements on the retention of the 2,290 employees, including the 400 jobs based in Rotterdam. However, KKR has been forced to promise that the company will only buy sustainable palm oil by the year 2019.

In the press release, Polman keeps it factual: 'After a long history in Unilever we decided that the future of the Spreads business would lie outside the Group. The announcement today marks a further step in reshaping and sharpening our portfolio for long term growth. The consideration recognises the market leading brands and the improved momentum we have achieved. I am confident that under KKR's ownership, the Spreads business with its iconic brands will be able to fulfil its full potential as well as societal responsibilities.'

Huët's dream is over. In the end, Blackstone teamed up with another investment firm (CVC) but they had bowed out after the second round. When they heard that KKR had ended up on 15 per cent over their offer, it was clear. Huët is certain that for a price that high, the next step would be nothing but a hatchet job. In order to make back the investment on time, he would have had to preside over nothing short of the dismantling of his great grandfather's work.

After 125 years, the production of Flora and Blue Band in Rotterdam is to be separated from the Unilever offices and handed over to the American venture capitalists. Rogier Smeets trusts in the process. Unilever's ugly duckling has been heading in the right direction for a while now. Even though he still feels attached to Unilever, he's decided to stick with spreads and see what KKR has to offer. He thinks that they realise how quickly and radically the marketplace is changing, and that plant-based margarine is becoming the norm. All off KKR's investments have been going in that direction since 2008, they're committed to having a positive effect on people and the planet.

Lots of the old hands are much less at ease about it all. KKR can promise all they like, what will happen if they decide to sell the whole thing around six years in, as these kinds of outfits are wont to do? Analysts calculate enthusiastically that KKR can squeeze a lot of money out of their operation. Former Unilever director Anthony Ruys reckons that the University of Marketing has given way to the University of Cost-Cutting under KKR. That's something Unilever has never been much good at.

In *De Volkskrant*, PvDA senator Erik Jurgens, the 'distant descendent of one of the founders', airs his disapproval of the Unilever leadership. 'The administrators are obvious lacking any appreciation of the company's history. Selling to a venture capitalist because you've lost your own stomach for new ventures: let KKR get on with it then. From now on, Unilever is a "Lever" without the "Unie": without the union. Until one day they sell off the soap too. Then it'll be called KKR.'

CHAPTER 18

'ROTTERDOOM': MISSION IMPOSSIBLE

January–September 2018

The Brits have never really been able to grasp it, either emotionally or intellectually. They don't quite understand what all those Dutch types mean when they say Unilever has another headquarters in Rotterdam. And whenever those same Dutchmen observe that at 55 per cent the Dutch NV is actually the bigger of the company's two pillars, they just look at them pityingly. As if that has anything to do with anything! This is where everything happens, in their language, on their home turf; the history of Lever is afforded much greater prominence than that of the recently sold Van den Bergh & Jurgens. For years now, Unilever's growth has been coming from their personal and home care products. And the magnificent Blackfriars House office backs right onto the Thames. Other headquarters? What are you talking about?

The Dutch have felt dominated by the Brits for decades. That feeling comes to the surface at the oddest moments, like when British colleagues get a couple of beers inside them at a company outing and start belting out the jingles of their biggest brands. The Dutch wouldn't be so quick to do the same. For the past ten years, the Dutch-British issues have been pushed firmly onto the backburner; Unilever management had become much more international, most of the growth has been coming from Asia. That was another of Polman's contributions, he was a Dutchman who scarcely felt Dutch, and didn't *seem* Dutch at all.

However, now that unification is at the top of the agenda and they're being asked to choose, the old tension is back with a vengeance. Ever since the Dutch government announced they would be scrapping dividend tax, the Brits have no longer been so certain that they'll get their own way after all. There's been talk of an impending Dutch coup in the corridors of London head office for some time. Because the big red mark against London – Brexit – isn't going anywhere. The UK's departure from the EU, which promises to be such a disadvantage for Unilever, is now unavoidable.

No Brit wants to move from London to 'Rotterdoom'. The thought of Polman saddling them with this move right as he's retiring and will never have to live there himself drives them crazy. Even those who report to him directly are having kittens. This irritates the CEO. Obviously, Polman had expected the Brits, including those around him, to push for London. Even so, he has no time for what he sees as a stupid, nationalistic attitude; it is unjustifiable.

Although they do make some good points too. The way AkzoNobel was able to show PPG the door was proof to many in London that the Netherlands supports and protects everyone, from employees to environmental interests. The system works in the interest of all stakeholders except one: the shareholders. Nevertheless, Unilever is a global player and unification is the best thing for the company. In Polman's eyes, that's what it has to come down to, not this Rotterdam–London issue.

Unilever's directors echo their CEO in insisting that this decision has to come down to the pros and cons, and be made in the interest of all parties involved, emotions mustn't be allowed to play a role. Many others find this position naïve. Everyone at this nearly 90-year-old Dutch-British multinational knows that nationality *does* matter, particularly at crucial times like this. What's more, their board, probably the most diverse in the world at this point, is made up of a Dane, two Chinese, an Italian, an Austrian, a Zimbabwean, two Americans, two Brits and three Dutchmen. Two of them call the shots.

The issue stays on the board's agenda for months. Each time they meet, the red and green marks are explored one by one and adjusted for significance. The accessibility of airports, the education system, the housing market, infrastructure, the R&D environment, history, the tax structure for head offices, everything is discussed several times. The directors mostly regard the problem as a bitter pill, their job now is to find a way to swallow it.

New information and developments arise constantly, meaning that the coloured dots shift and change in size. However, one topic is never addressed explicitly during all these meetings: the fact that as an NV in Rotterdam, Unilever will be better protected from aggressive shareholders. They can't simply put that on an agenda. To do so would mean the directors no longer act in accordance with their primary objective, enshrined in British law: to serve the owners of the company, the shareholders, as well as they can. Even so, Rotterdam keeps coming out slightly on top in their analysis, although this analysis relies on the dividend tax being scrapped. That is an absolute necessity.

They carefully map out the voting behaviour of the PLC's bigger sharehold-ers. A number of index funds, which have to invest in Unilever because they invest in the FTSE-100 index, aren't going to like it if the company becomes a Dutch NV. If that happens, the chances of Unilever being allowed to remain in the FTSE-100 are vanishingly small. Those funds would then be forced to sell their shares and for a less than favourable price. The board is working on the assumption that 16 per cent of the PLC shareholders will probably vote against a Rotterdam head office for this reason. They are certain that 72 per cent of the shareholders will vote in favour but the remaining 12 per cent are an unknown quantity.

Polman is irritated by an enormous structural flaw that exists in Unilever's governance. The investors in the Dutch NV make up 55 per cent of the votes, they are all in favour. If the 32 per cent of positive votes from British investors across the whole company are added to that, it means that in reality almost 90 per cent of all shareholders are already in favour of the proposal. The flaw means that a minority of just over 10 per cent of all Unilever shareholders can veto the board's decision concerning the location of headquarters. One more good reason to put an end to these bizarre arrangements.

The board is setting course for a Rotterdam-based NV. A group of 20–30 advisors and legal experts are tasked with steering them towards that outcome. They share their latest insights and updates on negotiations twice a week.

The *Financial Times*'s influential 'Lex' column has a good sense of the mood and diagnoses the move as a result of Unilever having been 'rattled by a take-over approach emblematic of modern Anglo-Saxon capitalism', and that 'it would be easier for Unilever to take the moral high ground from the Low Countries. Laws there permit bid defences that are prohibited in the UK.'[1]

The handful of Dutch colleagues who know that the Rotterdam option is being explored in more detail are wandering around with big smiles on their faces. Jan Zijderveld is one of them. He knows that the Brits have insisted on the impossibility of a Rotterdam head office because of the dividend tax in the Netherlands. They had been swept aside at a single stroke once it became clear that Polman had managed to arrange for the Dutch government to remove that particular barrier. The Brits no longer have a leg to stand on.

He can still hardly believe it, having experienced the force of the British resistance to Rotterdam first-hand. Only a couple of years ago, Rotterdam had been dead in the water in terms of management influence. Zijderveld was the only member of the ULE who still regularly spent time there. Moving their European operations there four years earlier had allowed him to bring life back to the office in the heart of the city's business quarter. Now there was this: the biggest prize. This Unilever lifer, boss of European operations for seven years at this point, regards it as a breathtaking victory over the often cunning but ever unreliable Brits, Brits who are always in the majority at head office and balk at any meeting in the 'backwater' of Rotterdam. Well, now they'll have to attend.

As it happens, Zijderveld won't be there with them. He would have liked to have become the next CEO of Unilever but he doesn't see any prospect of that. Zijderveld has become convinced that Unilever needs to become a home for local, sustainable brands. He doesn't see Polman's global message as a sensible option to pursue going forward. For his part, Polman thinks that Zijderveld isn't invested enough in the USLP. Zijderveld takes over as CEO of the huge, troubled cosmetics company Avon. Hanneke Faber, chief e-commerce and innovation officer at high street retailing giant Ahold, takes over from him as Europe boss.

Faber is another person with an unusual background. She had once been the Dutch national diving champion and studied business and journalism in the United States. Her grandmother was horrified when Hanneke told her that she would be going to work for Procter & Gamble in 1993: 'But darling, you went to university, why are you signing up to sell washing powder?' Her father Mient Jan Faber, the face of the Dutch peace movement in the 1970s and 1980s, can't make head nor tail of his daughter's decision either.[2]

Her former colleague Paul Polman had called asking her to come to Unilever and find new ways for them to communicate with the consumer directly. Over the past year, online sales have grown by 80 per cent to €1.7 billion. Faber is a fan of Polman and fascinated by the USLP. Once she's on the inside, she quickly comes to the conclusion that the USLP is not being implemented by middle management, at the level of the brands. How can you make a concrete connection between a cleaning brand like Cif and the shared effort to build a better world? That's where she has to concentrate her energies, this link has to be made much clearer. In the spirit of her father, she resolves to give each brand its own specific mission.

Paul Polman wants to be reassured that his legacy will be left in good hands. Since Marijn Dekkers wants the 2019 financial year to belong entirely to the new CEO, they've agreed that he will hand over the reins at the end of this year. For the sake of his legacy, it would be good to announce this now but that would immediately transform him into a lame duck at the company. An old anecdote about how this had happened to Niall FitzGerald still does the rounds. An email with 'N wants x' had always been enough to get things done but the moment he'd announced his departure these emails changed to, 'N. would like to know what we're doing about x'.

Polman has zero desire for such a change, he wants to remain effective for as long as he can. As long as nobody knows when he's leaving, he can place his own stamp on the search for his successor and make sure that it's someone who will elevate his vision even further.

In the meanwhile, he's also busy trying to work out what his role will look like after he leaves Unilever. Polman has accepted an invitation from UN secretary general António Guterres to become the vice-chairman of the United Nations Global Compact. For Polman, this is where the United Nations' agenda and the business world as he sees it come together. It also fits well with his new role as the chairman of the ICC. This agenda will allow him to keep pushing forwards, with the whole world as his stage. If it were up to Polman, the person he'd be speaking to from Unilever in the future, his successor, would be someone already at the company. Only a candidate from his own stable will prove that his message has taken root.

But who? Most Unilever observers think that Alan Jope stands the best chance. The 52-year-old Scot is a lifer and the personal care division has grown considerably over the past few years under his leadership. The board identifies four internal candidates: Amanda Sourry, Kees Kruythoff, Nitin Paranjpe and Alan Jope. Polman decides to put all of them to the test by seconding them to another role for a short time. The Brit Sourry takes over from Dutchman Kruythoff in the United States, Kruythoff takes over from the Indian Paranjpe in the home care division and Paranjpe takes over the foods division from Amanda Sourry. Polman and Dekkers want to see if they're capable of grasping and tackling new sets of issues at speed.

The only one to remain in his current position is Alan Jope. The Scot didn't apply to be a candidate for CEO. He has seen how hard Polman works. He doesn't want that for himself, there's more to life than work. Jope wants to be a good father and husband and maintain his friendships, that's what living is all about. To him, the 60 hours a week he puts in at Unilever are more than enough. He and four friends have made plans to ride around the world on their motorbikes, they head out on tour twice a year for at least a couple of weeks. He's about to head off for Mexico, Guatemala and Honduras, and a trip to Columbia, Ecuador and Peru is scheduled for six months' time. A number of people have warned them that travelling in these countries isn't without risk but this sense of danger is what energises Jope. He is hungry for the kinds of adventure in which it's not entirely certain you'll make it back. Jope is well aware that the Unilever board doesn't approve of this.

There's something else holding him back too. A friend once explained to him that being a CEO is actually a degenerative illness. If you're successful, you get all the credit and think the whole thing hinges on you. In the end, you start believing your own hype, and that's when you stop listening to anyone else. You automatically start behaving more and more poorly, with all the dramatic results of such a shift. Why on earth would he go down that path?

Nevertheless, they keep on pressing him. Marijn Dekkers is particularly invested. Jope is his favourite. He must realise that he's made for greater things? Himself once a skilled tennis player, Dekkers is fascinated by the story of multiple Grand Slam-winner Björn Borg, who gave up tennis at the age of only 26. He'd never been able to understand it. With a good coach, Borg could have gone on to achieve so much more. Jope allows himself to be persuaded to work with a coach and look more closely at whether being CEO really isn't for him. Maybe it could be after all.

Alan Jope goes on a short trip with executive coach Sander Tideman. In order to avoid a conflict of interest, Egon Zehnder hires in coaches via the American company Mobius Executive Leadership now and again, to test the suitability of particular people for particular jobs. Tideman is well acquainted with Unilever, having helped Patrick Cescau to set the Unilever top 100 on a different path 12 years earlier, back when the power of the national managers needed breaking.

The former China-based ABN AMRO banker has spent the last few years setting up research projects into the hallmarks of sustainable leadership at various Dutch universities. He also organises annual leadership retreats, mainly to Bhutan, to help managers who aren't very in touch with themselves to gain insight into their personal motivations. In doing so, Tideman aims to access and harness their full potential, transforming them into leaders who can contribute to a sustainable economy. This meditation teacher and disciple of Buddhism is tasked with helping Jope to reach clarity during their trip, to articulate what it is he wants and what's important to him.

Marijn Dekkers can rest easy. Jope has decided to put himself forward as a candidate after all. He's set out his purpose once again. In 2010, he had been dissatisfied with how things were going. He'd almost immediately forgotten the purpose he came up with during the Unilever Leadership Development Program sessions. Now he concludes that he hadn't been ready to find it back then, now he is. He wants to lead the great adventure known as Unilever. That is his new goal.

Regardless of who they actually appoint, Polman thinks it's important for the whole of Unilever's top management to take a clear position on the future of his most important baby, the USLP. He wants them all to have the solid, secure feeling about it that he has. They need that in order to be able to keep building on the plan. He has asked Valerie Keller from Ernst & Young's Beacon Institute to interview the 11 members of the ULE and the managers immediately below them intensively on the subject. She needs to help them articulate their personal meaning, their purpose, in clear terms and tell her how they intend to contribute to a new and improved USLP.

Polman is deeply impressed by Keller. She has done research in partnership with Said Business School and the *Harvard Business Review* into the degree to which CEOs see themselves as successful. That research revealed that only 34 per cent is satisfied with the results of their work, 84 per cent of CEOs worldwide believe that they could be much more successful if their efforts were integrated with their personal purpose. Keller talks about a 'secret sauce'. She now sells this 'secret sauce' via Ernst & Young with the promise that 'purpose-led transformation promotes productivity and profitability'. Keller always asks the same question: What is the reason for your working life; does it serve humanity? She warns them that this doesn't mean immediately setting the bar too high. Your purpose could also be satisfied customers or happy employees. It doesn't immediately need to mean that you want to solve the issue of poverty in Africa, even if that would be a good fit too, of course.[3]

Polman admires the way Keller interviews people. She starts by asking his interviewees what they hope their children, friends and colleagues will say about them at their funeral. It's immediately obvious what the interview is going to be about: Have you been a good person; what have you contributed to the world? Once they've articulated this, the participants are asked to translate that vision into the here and now. Really, Keller is revisiting the process Polman set in motion eight years earlier with the Unilever Leadership Development Program. This has clearly faded into the background here and there.

The Unilever CEO knows that this is a decision that will weigh heavily on his shoulders for the rest of his life. At the beginning of March, he announces that the multinational's head office will move to the Netherlands. And that's not all: the British company will be transformed into a Dutch NV.

Under his leadership, Unilever as a Dutch-British company will cease to exist, after 89 years in operation. The CEO of Unilever will pilot 'his' Unilever into a safe harbour by the end of this year. That's how it feels anyway. And it's good timing, because then the captain himself can leave with peace in his heart at the end of December.

In Rotterdam, they can barely believe their ears. The excitement is enormous but there's no sense of them openly celebrating. Kees van der Waaij gets a call from Polman, the two of them have agreed that they won't shout the news from the rooftops. The United Kingdom is still extremely important to Unilever, the main challenge now is helping the Brits to process this set back. It's important that they play down the move to Rotterdam when they talk about it. It's just a head office; it's only going to affect a handful of jobs; two of the three divisions are remaining in England; all of the 7,200 jobs there are being protected; they'll still be spending £1 billion in the UK on R&D every year. At the end of the day, this unification is necessary in order to be able to complete big takeovers more quickly in the future, or to sell off big chunks of Unilever, even if they've currently no plans in that direction.

The board is in total agreement. But Polman has never asked the 11 members of the ULE what they think of it all. The entire topic has never been discussed with senior managers who run Unilever on a day-to-day basis. In effect, the board is giving them the task and it's their job to carry it out. It's obvious that not all of them are happy with that. And the managers who report to them aren't either. Some people are concerned that this might become an issue.

In interviews, Polman and Dekkers do their best not to tread on anyone's toes. They explain that the decision to move to the Netherlands has nothing to do either with Brexit or with the Dutch government scrapping dividend tax. It's a completely separate issue. 'With our 55% shareholder base in the NV we need to make the decision for the Netherlands. We are committed to both the UK and the Netherlands.'[4]

Nobody is buying this explanation, but everyone understands the sensitivity of the situation. Polman has met to discuss the issue with British prime minister Theresa May on several occasions, including her in the decision-making process. If a British government expresses a negative view of the decision, it could prove a real stumbling block for getting a PLC shareholder vote by the end of October. In the end, the May government keeps out of it, not least because of their shared interest in emphasising that Unilever's decision has nothing to do with Brexit, which is supported by the majority of the British public. Prime Minister Rutte is also reticent, not wanting to give the impression that scrapping the dividend tax is anything to do with Unilever.

The Dutch opposition parties are reacting fiercely to the scrap and scornfully demand to know why it is they're dishing out €1.4 billion per year if this doesn't really affect anyone. Rutte is being accused of allowing himself to be taken in by a couple of big multinationals. They'll keep on doing everything they can to scupper the plan.

Now that it's coming down to it, CDA-leader Van Haersma Buma is satisfied with the decision to scrap the tax. He's often spoken to Rutte about the plan, usually after the latest round of furious criticism, when the two men needed to reassure each other of its viability. In moments like that, they'd imagined sitting in front of a parliamentary inquiry, being asked why they'd done nothing to prevent Unilever, Shell and AkzoNobel from leaving the Netherlands. They'd have to say that they had caved to public opinion. That would have been weak. Luckily, they've stuck to their guns.

But the CDA-leader is worried even so: he's now reading for the first time that 75 per cent of Unilever *plc*'s shareholders still need to vote in favour in October for the plan to go ahead. That comes as a surprise, no one has told him this before. He has always worked on the assumption that the Unilever management knew what it was doing and that there was no risk. It will all come out in the wash, although even then there will hardly be reason to celebrate. The political damage has been bigger than they could afford and isn't going to be repaired by Unilever moving to Rotterdam.

Antony Burgmans thinks that it's sensible of Polman to present the whole matter as an insignificant, mostly legal issue, so that he can keep the emotions in check a little bit. He knows better than anyone how much pain this decision is causing the British contingent and Unilever desperately needs those people on side in the future too. Polman needs to respect the Brits' feelings and keep in mind the fact that many of those employees are also firm believers in the stakeholder model they're now pursuing.

In his view, Unilever is only being forced to resolve this thorny issue now because of Brexit and the narrowly avoided takeover from Kraft-Heinz. He sees the Netherlands as the logical choice. The Dutch model of governance suits them much better than the hard, shareholder-focused British model. He's thought as much for years. Brexit also brings many additional risks with it. Will foreign employees still be able to relocate to London easily, for example?

In the British media, emotion is king. The link to Brexit is being made very explicitly there. The papers point out that the two top bosses, Polman and Dekkers – both Dutchmen mind you – are in talks with another former Dutch Unilever employee, Prime Minister Rutte. It's only natural they've managed to wangle themselves a good deal. Rajesh Agrawal, the deputy major of London, calls on the British government to act fast to reach a deal that will ensure London keeps its place as the centre of European business. 'The best way to do this is for London and the UK to remain part of the single market and customs union', he tells *The Guardian*.[5]

The *Financial Times* quotes boxer Mike Tyson: 'everyone has a plan until they get punched in the mouth'. This punch came from Kraft Heinz and now

Polman has a new plan: Unilever will be safer from takeovers as a Dutch company.[6]

Mere days after the decision is announced, one of Unilever's top 10 investors, Columbia Threadneedle Investments, comes out saying that the company has done too little to explain why it needs to move to Rotterdam. Leaving the FTSE index comes as a particular blow. A second major shareholder announces that it will probably vote against the move.[7]

The *Financial Times* immediately starts calling all the big shareholders in the PLC and reports in April that 'Unilever faces mounting investor unrest over UK exit'. Three of the top 20 shareholders are apparently considering voting against the proposal. The paper promises to keep reporting on the growing dissatisfaction. The percentage of no-voters is climbing. It doesn't help that 'boxer' Paul Polman is slowly but surely slipping back into his old fighting stance.

In New York, at a meeting of the Chief Executives for Corporate Purpose organisation set up by film actor Paul Newman, Polman doesn't mince his words as he complains about the way the financial markets are getting in the way his plans. 'We had to make some practical compromises [...] which I frankly would not have done. We did a €5 billion share buyback to satisfy some others. We were well on track to do that but I would never have put the margin [of 20%] out there. I come from a part of the Netherlands that we deliver. We just deliver and let the numbers talk, but unfortunately that's not possible for the majority of how the financial markets still operate.' He doesn't mention Kraft Heinz or Warren Buffett by name but he describes the takeover attempt of a year previously as 'a clash between people who think about billions of people in the world and some people that think about a few billionaires'.

He asks the room, filled with portfolio managers with a collective responsibility for around $25 trillion in investments why they constantly question Unilever's environmental and social commitments but don't ask companies 'why [they] have the courage to destroy [...] this wonderful planet'. Polman is angry: 'I don't get it. If business cannot show what positive impact it has, why should the citizens of the world let business be around?' The analysts don't escape his ire either: 'In over a decade of earnings calls, none of them have asked me a single question about climate change, diversity or human rights.'[8]

Polman is stuck between a rock and a hard place. They have to make savings *and* the scope for Unilever to make a positive contribution to the world is also seriously limited. And so he denies a request for support from the organisation IBFD CapaBuild. This respected charity helps developing countries to build up knowledge and expertise around fiscal issues, so that they can build their capacity to generate tax income. Turning them down is painful. They've spent months working with enthusiastic tax specialists from companies like Unilever, Shell and DSM trying to get this initiative off the ground. The Dutch Ministry of Foreign Affairs intends to give the foundation a €500,000 subsidy over three years, but only on the condition that the companies match the funding. Former PwC tax specialist Paul de Haan, one of the leaders of CapaBuild, had suggested that they each chip in €150,000. The request was lowered to €75,000, or €25,000 per year. But to his great astonishment, Unilever had backed out. Providing expertise was one thing but there was no way they could actually hand over money. There was no budget for it. And then the fact that Unilever of all companies, the company doing the most to promote the interests of these kinds of initiatives, had dropped out had started to give the other companies cold feet.

De Haan tried to get Polman on board as a personal supporter. Training tax officials in developing countries creates more stable governments, thereby allowing business to flourish. That benefits Unilever too, surely? This should be one of his priorities. Polman tells him that he thinks it's an important initiative but he doesn't want to overrule the decision his people have made. The Unilever CEO also wonders why the private sector is being asked to foot such a large chunk of the bill.

Paul Polman may have few friends in the financial world but he remains the darling of NGOs and governments. In the last few years alone, he has been given the Climate Visionary Award, the Ordre National de la Légion d'honneur, the UN Champion of the Earth Award and the Oslo Business for Peace Award. Now Polman is in the Stevenskerk in Nijmegen being awarded the Treaties of Nijmegen Medal. This biannual prize is awarded to 'key international figures committed to European development'.

Members of his family, including his 90-year-old mother, are there in the church to see him get his award. Thea Polman is being congratulated by everyone but she would prefer not to talk about Paul, this whole day is about Paul. She is proud of all six of her children, they're all doing wonderful things. She even gets cross with her son for a moment when she hears that he has asked one of his colleagues to step out and get him a fried kroket sandwich. It's one of the few things he always wants when he's in the Netherlands. His mother doesn't think this is something you should ask a colleague for, if he wants one, he should go get it himself. She's not the only frugal woman in the CEO's life. On noticing that Polman's wife Kim is visibly cold, one of his Unilever colleagues asks whether she should nip into town and buy her a scarf. Kim declares this a terrible waste of money, she'll ask her sister-in-law to bring one along when she comes.

While he was preparing for the ceremony, Professor of Philosophy and 'Thinker of the Fatherland' René ten Bos was summoned to see Han van Krieken, the chancellor of Radboud University in Nijmegen, which awards the prize. They'd had a lively exchange of views about Polman. Nijmegen has been selected European Green Capital 2018 by the European Commission; is it really seemly to award this prize to the boss of a massive polluter like Unilever, a manufacturer of fast-moving consumer goods? Van Krieken warns Ten Bos: this is supposed to be a celebration! This isn't the time for some pig-headed lecturer to stand up and starting insulting the recipient. Ten Bos tells the chancellor he has no intention of singing Polman's praises himself. Sigrid Kaag, the minister for foreign trade and development, will likely be the one to give that speech.

The philosopher wants to get people thinking and warn them away from this new 'sustainability' cult. He's already spoken to Paul Polman in advance. The philosopher thinks that the CEO is wrestling with what Ten Bos calls 'the problem of the pure soul'. He doesn't believe in this himself: there are no pure souls, everyone in this toxic world is contaminated.

As he addressed the packed Stevenskerk, he says: 'We're all grains of sand contributing to a worldwide crisis. Even if maybe we don't call it a crisis. Regardless, wherever there's a crisis comes management and then there comes the idea that everything can be solved properly, because that management thinks that partial solutions will automatically lead to a solution to the whole problem, as if that gap between the grain and the pile of sand doesn't exist. People these days call that "sustainable development".

I am against placing trust in these solutions: as if we are somehow going to make sure they result in the right climate. We need to think through our dis-turbed relationship with the world much better. We don't rule over that world. We aren't stewards. We aren't caretakers. We are together on that world with other animate and inanimate things. Nothing more and nothing less. This is a basic ecological insight […]. An interesting paradox arises: as a species we are responsible for what we call nature or the environment but we're not above it. That is the lesson of ecology. We need to start thinking about responsibility without us claiming any moral superiority. In that respect we would do well to free the concept of "sustainability" from its age-old connection to steward-ship, guilt, care and other catholic residues.'[9] The audience doesn't applaud too loudly, they realise that the professor is criticising the guest of honour pretty pointedly.

Ten Bos is proven right. Dutch minister of Foreign Trade and Development Cooperation Sigrid Kaag doesn't hesitate in praising the Unilever CEO to the heavens. 'Hopeless, desperate and in need of heroes, those are a few of the feelings I have when I look at the situation the world faces. But thankfully there are people like Paul Polman who can dispel a sombre thought like that in a single tweet.' The minister sums up the state of play: 'Last year, a shameful 82% of all new wealth generated went to the richest 1% of the world's population. We are exceeding the limits of biodiversity and land. We are laying the world to waste, our world, the one that has to feed and provide a home for our children. The realisation that it's five minutes to midnight is broadly felt. It's at the forefront of governments' minds, just as it is for NGOs and, increasingly, companies. Because what is our wealth worth if the clothes we wear are made under poor working conditions by children who can't read or write? If behind the luxury chocolates we eat stand coca farmers who aren't receiving a fair price and can hardly keep their head above water? If forests are being chopped down on a massive scale just to plant palm oil plantations to produce our home care products? Combatting extreme poverty means addressing a number of underlying causes. Things like hunger, health, education, clean water, hygiene, fair wages, equality, nature and the environment, sustainability. A keyword in all that is "partnership". By taking responsibility as a society, we can tackle and even prevent abuses in the supply chain from raw material to final product. But for that to happen, a basic requirement is cooperation.' The minister jokingly suggests they switch over from the celebrated *polder* model of Dutch democracy, to the 'Polman model'. Rounding off the event, she puts a few more feathers in Polman's cap: 'For you, sustainability is not so much a pressing concern as it is a source of opportunity. As long as there are people like you, the world isn't in despair, the future isn't without heroes and I'm not at a loss.' Shortly after her speech she tweets: 'Combining sustainability with inclusive growth, that's what the Polman model means. Congratulations on the Treaties of Nijmegen Medal.'

That evening, Polman and Ten Bos are seated together at dinner. Polman was born in Enschede, Ten Bos not far away, so they have quite a lot in common. Polman's mother, sitting opposite the philosopher, reminds him of his own mother. She also always used to say that only one thing was worse than being busy, and that's not being busy. The CEO explains that he was raised with a workers' ethos, working hard is the only way you can achieve anything in this world. He compliments Ten Bos on his elegant argument. The philosopher wants to know why he liked it, but has to be satisfied with friendly non-answers. Somehow, he understands why. This isn't the time, it's a day of celebration.

Encouraged by all the recognition he's receiving, Polman uses his speeches to expound ever more emphatically on the shortcomings of high finance. He complains about the lack of loyalty shown by his big shareholders. They should adopt a holistic approach and resist the temptations of short-termism. Sue Garrard sees flaws in his logic. To her, it's self-evident that the pension funds will sell their interest in Unilever if they can get something like a 30 per cent premium on it. They have to, it's the role of shareholders to keep the management sharp, if they can suddenly make a 30 per cent profit on their investment, then something is obviously wrong with the company. The buyer can clearly see something the current management is missing.

Sue Garrard is one of the very few people at head office to tell Polman that she thinks moving their head office to Rotterdam is a really bad idea. She is getting clear signals that many investors don't understand the decision. Garrard had also been remarkably frank in her interview with Valerie Keller. As she was outlining her USLP ambitions, she had explained that she had been working with a small team for some time on closing the gaps she believes Polman is leaving.

Her immediate boss, Keith Weed, fires her. Some of the members of the ULE understand the decision: Why did Garrard think it necessarily to criticise Polman so openly? That was disloyal. Garrard had also fiercely criticised Weed, who she saw as lacking a proper understanding of sustainability.

Others think Polman should have intervened. They don't understand this abrupt dismissal. Garrard had handled communications concerning the attack from Kraft Heinz extremely well. Unilever is here facing considerable opposition, having to pull out all the stops to get the key PLC shareholders onside in order to win approval for unification, and the most important general has been kicked off the battlefield. They regard this as a grave strategic error. Polman doesn't see this as a logical argument. The moment someone stops respecting his values, he can't help himself, he comes down on them like a tonne of bricks. And unification is just one blow in a much bigger war, one which is about nothing more or less than saving the world.

Garrard isn't the only woman to leave Unilever disillusioned. Director of Purchasing Heidi Knight spent over six months in Singapore trying desperately to force her suppliers to agree to a price cut of 10 per cent as she had been tasked. Their shared plans to spend the next three to five years investing in making the chain more sustainable had come under enormous pressure as a result. Suppliers asked her why they had to accept such a rough deal. They want to know exactly how important the USLP is to Unilever. Knight can't explain, she takes voluntary redundancy instead. Her boss at Unilever, Karin Hagen-Gierer, had already left back at the end of 2017.

Cherie Tan is disappointed too. She's worried by all these women leaving the Singapore office. It's women who understand the USLP the best. The men she speaks to over on the purchasing side, under Dhaval Buch, mostly think in terms of measurable outcomes. Ever since 'Kraft Heinz' these have suddenly become much more important again and she can feel the culture shifting. The people who had their doubts about Polman's message before the crisis are now taking the opportunity to ditch it. Tan thinks that the philosophy of the USLP still hasn't gotten through to enough of the organisation for them to offer any real resistance now. Everything is getting increasingly shaky, and implementing the USLP was never exactly easy to begin with.

Tan has spent five years moving local palm oil producers towards a more sustainable approach. If you want someone to work with you on sustainability then it's a case of building trust and long-term relationships. The tough cost-cutting measures now being imposed on them are getting in the way of that process. She doesn't think Unilever is doing enough to actually implement sustainability in any case. The company is too fragmented. On top of that, the various job roles all have differing priorities. There's a lot of talk about sustainability, but not enough is being done.

She has gone along to the same Unilever meetings year in, year out, hearing the same story each time. It's taking more energy than it's worth now. She has to keep putting in more and more effort in order to convince the people around her that it's all going to work out. Now when she's somewhere trying to explain for the umpteenth time that there's still scope to make progress despite the cuts, she no longer believes her own words. Cherie Tan also decides to leave, turning her back on her great love after five years.

Marc Engel, Dhaval Buch's boss, is disturbed by these developments in Singapore. It's clear that Buch has less of an affinity for sustainability than some. He's also gathered a whole team of slick Indian managers around him who have the tendency to focus on costs, and on meetings the KPIs. The threat from Kraft-Heinz has given them additional ammunition on that front. But this is driving away the people who have been focused on realising their sustainability goals. This process has to be put into reverse. Luckily, Buch is set to retire soon.

Polman is pleased to receive messages from his contacts that suggest all is not well at Kraft Heinz. One article claims that employee satisfaction has plummeted to an all-time low at their former aggressor. In the next, analysts claim that the magic formula has lost its power. Sales have been in decline for seven consecutive quarters, the share price is now down 30 per cent. Warren Buffet, still in possession of a 27 per cent share, has had enough. In April 2018, he announces he will be leaving Kraft Heinz's board. The 87-year-old claims he's fed up with all the travelling.

To Polman, these developments prove that the Unilever model is superior to Kraft Heinz's. They can no longer risk it being destroyed. The Dutch prime minister agrees. Mark Rutte needs to pull out all the stops to keep the door open for Unilever to become a Dutch NV. Emotions run high during a debate in the Dutch parliament, the Tweede Kamer. GroenLinks leader Jesse Klaver presents proof that the prime minister has kept MPs in the dark. He thinks that Rutte should step down and enters a vote of no confidence on behalf of almost all the opposition MPs. The motion is defeated when put to a vote.

At a shareholder meeting of the PLC in London that May, Marijn Dekkers thanks Polman for the 'magnificent implementation' of their plans over the past year. Sales have gone up 3.5 per cent, with Asia once again providing the strongest growth. The margin has been improved thanks largely to cost-cutting measures, to 17.5 per cent. Their sustainable brands grew 46 per cent quicker than the rest and contributed 70 per cent of sales growth. Polman adds: 'the deeper their purpose, the faster these brands actually grow. This is proving our model works. In the process it is crucial to be as transparent as possible. Transparency delivers businesses the most important quality to build on: trust.'

The discussion turns for a moment to the relocation to the Netherlands. Another shareholder expresses his chagrin: 'you aren't saying it out loud but our country has decided to turn its back on the rest of the world, there are only 65 million customers here, it's logical for you to leave'. Another shareholder wants a guarantee that he won't suddenly be forced to pay dividend tax. Pitkethly is cautious: 'We're still talking about the PLC's place within the new structure. It's absolutely not our intention for you to be left in a disadvantageous position relative to shareholders in the NV.'

The fact that the planned raise to his salary, or rather, his successor's salary, receives so much attention and criticism drives Polman mad. The board had indicated last year that these remuneration packages had to be brought into line with the rest of the market in order to attract a suitable replacement. A remarkable number of shareholders disagree. Only 64 per cent of investors vote in favour of raising the CEO's basic salary by 5 per cent, while allowing them to raise the bonus cap by 23 per cent. But in order to receive such a bonus, the new CEO will have to put much more of their own money into Unilever shares and perform quite a bit better over the long term than Polman has.

On one level, Polman can understand their resistance. His income went up sharply during 2017, to more than €11 million, his successor will be able to take home €14 million. When a shareholder calls him out on it, he once again puts his hand on his heart and says, 'I'm ashamed of my salary. I would do it for free, I really would.' The next day, during a shareholder meeting of the Rotterdam NV, 27 per cent of shareholders vote against the raise.

Rients Abma, director of Eumedion, an umbrella organisation for Dutch investors, and spokesperson for the big, institutional investors, wants to know why such a salary increase is necessary: Dutch pensioners have been facing a flat rate of return for years. The proposed transition package of many millions designed to attract some theoretical outsider CEO is galling to them. That, at least, has to be taken off the table. Abma is horrified that Unilever isn't taking Eumedion's suggestions seriously. He is simply told that there's insufficient support for such a decision on the PLC side. All while his British colleagues are telling him that *they* are being told there's insufficient support on the NV side.

Abma hopes that Unilever will take these narrow votes as a wake-up call. It's high time they stop fobbing off shareholders and sit up and listen to them properly. Especially when it comes to unification. But Abma isn't sure they'll actually do it. He finds it strange that Unilever didn't ask its shareholders in advance what their preference was: London or Rotterdam. And he doesn't understand the decision to move to the Netherlands. For its part, Eumedion would rather see a reduction in corporation tax than the end of dividend tax. Abma estimates that only 17 per cent of investors in the PLC are Brits, only a limited number of them will face any real difficulties from the dividend tax. Accommodating this handful of investors is simply costing the Dutch treasury too much money.

He doesn't understand why Unilever hasn't opted for a public offer, then the new NV could buy shares off the NV and the PLC. If you offer the Brits a premium then they'll go along with your plans. The people at Unilever think this is a crazy suggestion: we're *one* company, we can't start paying a premium to one group of shareholders and not the other.

Paul Frentop and Jacques Schraven meet with Marijn Dekkers at Schiphol. The two directors of the Stichting Administratiekantoor Unilever – an organisation for Unilever investors – want to know what lies ahead of them. This independent voting trust foundation, one of many such Dutch foundations known as STAKs, administers the shares in Unilever NV for which it has agreed to take on legal ownership and exercises the voting rights attached to these shares whenever the shareholder, who retains financial ownership of the shares, hasn't declared their intention to vote themselves. In order to take legal control of the shares, the STAK issues certificates of trust, officially relinquishing rights to dividends, which go to the shareholder. Having issued such certificates for around 74 per cent of all shares in Unilever NV, Stichting Administratiekantoor Unilever is an important voice in all decision-making processes. The company's move to Rotterdam in the form of a new NV spells the end of this organisation.

Frentop in particular has been critical of Polman and his USLP over the past few years. He thinks it's all well and good for the Unilever CEO to mobilise tonnes of public money in order to operate more sustainably but he worries about the amount of money Unilever itself is investing in sustainability. He's never received an official answer to any of his concerns, but he's been told off the record that this will be a negligible sum. Frentop is relieved at this. Unilever is operating in a competitive world; they'd be swept off the map if they starting pumping serious amounts of money directly into it.

The men cross-examine Dekkers on the motivation behind going ahead with unification. What are the benefits to their certificate holders, why is this all so unclear from the documentation? They find Dekkers's argumentation lacking and want to know whether there's a Plan B. It turns out that there isn't. According to Dekkers, there's no way there can be. There's only one possible plan, you take it to the masses, talk with authority and give your best guess on what the consequences might be. He reassures Schraven and Frentop: at the top estimate, only 15 per cent are going to vote against the proposal.

Dekkers also wants to win over the British investors and explains in interviews that they've no need to fear the dominance of preferential shareholders in the Dutch NV. Unilever has spent €437 million buying back the preferential shares, 0.5 per cent of the total but with a voting right of 17 per cent, from the insurers ASR and NN. He explains that their voting trust foundation Stichting Administratiekantoor Unilever will be wound down in exactly the same way. Not long from now, it really will be one vote for each share.

During her visit to Kempen & Co in Amsterdam that June, Sarah Williamson tries to persuade Dutch investors and companies that it's in their shared interest to enter into a long-term relationship with one another. Williamson, the CEO of Focusing Capital on the Long Term (FCLTGlobal), notices that Polman's word carries the most weight.

The American somehow feels sorry for the passionate Polman. He is much too evangelical, scaring off investors who don't want to feel responsible for all the misery in the world and are just in search of returns. Most investors, certainly the Americans and the algorithms that guide their investment strategies, will never understand Polman. Let alone follow him. But maybe it helps if you have the same culture and the same language, as they do here in the Netherlands. Williamson gets the feeling that something important is happening in this little corner of the world. Maybe it will yield a 'Dutch model', something the rest of the world can learn from. FCLT wants to help to build it. But she does have some doubts. These big Dutch investors are only placing 3–5 per cent of their capital into Dutch companies. The people she's speaking to at Kempen probably only hold about 1.5 per cent of Unilever shares. That's much too little.

Jaap van Dam, PGGM's director of strategy, didn't think the meeting was particularly exciting. But Polman is right: even PGGM will go along with the sale of Unilever shares if Kraft Heinz comes knocking again later in the year. They won't pass up a premium of 30 per cent, no matter who the buyer is. It's unthinkable that PGGM would accept the possibility of a lower pension in exchange for a better world, not least because there are so many different possible answers to the question of what exactly this better world might look like.

Van Dam hopes that by 2030 pension funds will be in a position to invest a third of their capital in real, long-term commitments with companies. In his view, the number of companies in which pension funds invest would have to be reduced drastically in order for that to happen. Only then can you build a proper relationship with those companies and ignore the manic-depressive financial markets. It's going to be a long road, you need a different language, different ways of calculating and a completely different type of employee to make it a reality. The space for this to happen will have to be created by the boards of pension funds over the years to come. Sadly, they're lacking exactly the kind of leadership Polman had been calling for so passionately that afternoon.

In the meantime, the summer sees growing opposition to the Rotterdam move in the City of London. People are openly criticising Unilever's poor communication. Andy Griffiths, the director of the Investors' Forum, states that Unilever is willing to talk but not actually willing to listen. His organisation represents the combined interests of 23 key investors in the PLC. The departure from the FTSE is going to hit them especially hard. Griffiths says that Unilever is incapable of making clear to investors what the benefits of a relocation to Rotterdam will be for them.[10]

On 30 August that year, Paul Polman is at the Wageningen University to celebrate the completion of construction of the Global Foods Innovation Centre Unilever is building there. Various media outlets have been in touch asking for interviews. These won't focus solely on this new research institute, so over breakfast in the hotel Polman talks to his communication team about whether the moment has come to say something positive about the scrapping of the dividend tax.

His friend Mark Rutte's cabinet could do with the support. Surveys show that that around 85 per cent of the Dutch public is now against abolishing the tax. Policemen, nurses and teachers have announced that they're going to gather on the Malieveld in The Hague and demonstrate against the government's decision. The recovering economy means that the expected loss in tax income will add up to €1.9 billion by 2020. They could do with that money themselves. Wide sections of the public are in support of them.

Unilever managers think that Rutte has done nowhere near enough to make it clear that this 1.9 billion isn't a gift to Unilever. The company won't profit from the cut directly. Director of communications Fleur van Bruggen points out that them trying to change that narrative will be counterproductive and seem like redundant advertising. They decide to react cautiously.

Standing in front of the skeleton of the new building, Polman uses his speech to ask why it is there are people in the Netherlands who say that big companies aren't important. 'What are they talking about? The papers obviously have no intention of actually looking into how important a head office like this is to the Dutch economy. There are 4200 companies in our value chain.'

Louise Fresco, the board chairman of Wageningen University and former Unilever director, reinforces this message as she takes the stage: 'We know that Unilever pursues top quality and is truly innovative. This is about partnerships and it's good for all concerned, it's good for the Netherlands.'

Polman is no longer sure of himself. The media have clearly turned against the relocation and the opposition is doing everything it can to bring down the Rutte government. He is still endlessly surprised that Unilever isn't being welcomed here with open arms. Their head office can only come here if the dividend withholding tax is scrapped, that's matter of simple logic, isn't it? Otherwise the British shareholders absolutely won't cooperate. You may as well try telling Dutch people that they have to start buying their beloved peanut butter from a more expensive shop, or that they have to start speaking German from now on.

It will be a crying shame for the Netherlands if this relocation doesn't go ahead. Because then Unilever will become a British company. Unilever is currently investing around €1 billion per year in the Netherlands, thanks entirely to the head office in Rotterdam. In Austria, a market of a comparable size, the company invests no more than €300 million. Polman doesn't see pushing this information as his job, it needs to come from independent, unsuspected third parties. Time is beginning to run out.

He has already warned Mark Rutte. It's looking like politics is going to ruin the whole thing. Polman thinks that Minister for Economic Affairs Eric Wiebes in particular has damaged their case by not being immediately transparent about the memos that exchanged hands while they were negotiating the new cabinet. Wiebes hadn't helped matters when he appeared a few days earlier on the talk show *Zomergasten* (Summer Guests). Interviewer Janine Abbring asked him whether he could explain, without blushing, why they should scrap the dividend tax. Wiebes replied, 'No, I can't explain it in three sentences, it would take half an hour.' Abbring then wants to know whether Wiebes, a former consultant known for justifying everything he does with clever, fact-based arguments, can get along with a prime minister whose main argument in favour of abolishing the tax is that he can feel in his gut that it's a good idea. Wiebes struggles to find the right words: 'But just because you can't quite quantify something, doesn't mean it isn't true. Rutte was prime minister for seven years, he's got a lot of experience with bringing businesses to the Netherlands. He has come to the conclusion that it's true and therefore that is a valuable contribution to the debate.'

In the Wageningen interview Polman gives to the *NOS Journaal*, the Netherlands' main TV news, he also struggles to express himself well. His rusty Dutch doesn't help him when he's accusing the media of not giving enough of a platform to the people in favour of scrapping the tax. According to Polman there are many who share that position. 'Globally, there's a tendency to reduce dividend tax. It's a double tax. But yes, in the paper it's better for a plane to crash than to keep flying. And talking to people and telling them that something is a good thing is naturally less interesting to the news. We need to keep the Netherlands prosperous, open and competitive. Therefore it's incredibly important to attract big and small businesses. I'm glad that there are a good number of people in the Netherlands who *do* understand that.'

The prime minister tries to defuse the situation by saying that he thinks the decision to scrap the dividend withholding tax is an extremely annoying restriction. 'You'd hardly choose to grant an advantage to foreign shareholders just for a laugh, would you?' But it's what's needed here, otherwise there's a very real risk that big companies and multinationals will leave the Netherlands in search of a more favourable tax climate. 'That would be to the impoverishment of this country.'

Only Mark Rutte, Hans de Boer and Sybrand Buma are still arguing for the scrap. De Boer, the chairman of the VNO-NCW employers union, sums it up thus: 'I've got no time for all these men who are concerned with getting the political upper hand, these are views without basis in fact. I'm glad to be fighting on the side of right.'[11]

But even De Boer isn't managing to keep his supporters on side. His partner organisation MKB Nederland, the union for small- to medium-sized businesses, is beginning to change its position. The newly appointed chairman,

Jacco Vonhof, says that scrapping the tax wouldn't have been his first choice. This is a signal that the community of interest for small- and medium-sized businesses is parting ways from its big brother, the VNO-NCW.

Even big, international businesses are abandoning the plan. The influential American Chamber of Commerce (AmCham), responsible for 450 companies and 450,000 jobs in the Netherlands, is speaking out against the scrapping of the tax, despite having supported it for a year up until now. 'The amount of approximately 1.9 billion euros that will be released as a result of not abolishing the dividend withholding tax should be used by the Cabinet to strengthen the general business climate, by further reducing the corporate tax rate and by preserving the 30% facility for expats', declares AmCham director Patrick Mikkelsen.[12]

Hans de Boer is already furious with the noises coming from Eumedion but sees these fresh objections as nothing short of a betrayal. The 450 members of AmCham, 60 per cent of them large American multinationals, brokered an agreement between the Dutch and US governments that means they no longer have to pay dividend tax. The people at VNO-NCW had thought that a show of solidarity with Shell and Unilever's situation would be self-evident.

But AmCham is angry. They could still just about reconcile themselves to the fact that the corporation tax reduction they'd desperately wanted had been kept at 21 per cent in the coalition agreement in order to cover the deficit of €1.4 billion created by scrapping dividend tax. But now that this has gone up to €1.9 billion and corporation tax has been pegged at 22 per cent, it's all getting too expensive for them.

There's a further issue here too. Foreigners who work in the Netherlands are given a 30 per cent reduction on income tax for the first eight years they live there. The government has announced its intention to reduce this to five years. AmCham wants interim legislation, otherwise a number of their members will face acute financial difficulties in a couple of months' time. An income of €100,000, for example, would mean that person suddenly paying an additional €20,000 in tax. AmCham warns The Hague that the Netherlands is at risk of becoming an unreliable country. A country where 'multinational' is threatening to become a dirty word. All this is terribly damaging to the business climate.

These reports are met with glee from the British media. Exactly how welcome is Unilever in the Netherlands? Why is the multinational so desperate to go there again? De Boer and Van Haersma Buma are furious. Van Haersma Buma from the CDA thinks it's completely unacceptable for a bunch of lobbyists to involve themselves in political affairs so directly. And in such an 'America First' way to boot! He sees it as bordering on Trumpian.

GroenLinks leader Jesse Klaver has yet another trump card up his sleeve and announces that he'll submit a proposal for a new economic recovery bill next year in order to ensure that the dividend withholding tax is reinstated. He doesn't like putting forward such a combative proposal, it's never been done, but you can repeal a piece of legislation that's not due to come into effect until 2021 by withdrawing it before it's entered into law. After the local elections, this coalition will probably lose its parliamentary majority, allowing them to take such a step. His colleagues in the party have already prepared the bill.[13]

While a furore of never-before-seen proportion is building in the Netherlands, Polman is in San Francisco basking in the thunderous applause of participants in a congress on sustainable pension fund investment. 'We can't protect the oceans while we're in a rat race of quarterly results. We've been warned and we know what we need to do, the only thing lacking is willpower.'

A couple of days later, he's declared the world's most influential CEO when it comes to promoting 'female leadership'. The jury raves about the growing number of women in leading roles at Unilever, 47 per cent of managers there at this point are women. There's also a great deal of admiration for the company's efforts to help millions of women in Unilever's supply chain become economically more stable, as outlined in the USLP.[14]

Back in London, the main thing people are complaining about is Polman's ongoing absence from meetings with shareholders. It doesn't help that over the past few years he's hardly shown his face at any of the innumerable exclusive gentlemen's clubs where bankers, analysts and investors meet to make deals informally. Polman has neither the time nor the inclination for such things.

Some analyses suggest that even Unilever's desire to be able to make big deals more easily – the most important reason for unification – isn't particularly popular with investors. Things are fine as they are, aren't they? The share price has tripled over the past ten years. Why should they give senior managers the freedom to embark on big, dangerous adventures to the tune of tens of billions of dollars? Research has shown time and again that the promised returns are never realised in three-quarters of cases.

Formally, responsibility for persuading the shareholders to vote in favour of unification lies with Marijn Dekkers and Graeme Pitkethly. The latter explains the reasons for the move on a video on Unilever's website. When asked why head office has to move to Rotterdam in particular, the CFO doesn't answer. In an awkward speech, he instead spends most of his time reeling off a list of all the things that are going to remain in the United Kingdom.

Pitkethly also knows that nobody wants to move to Rotterdam within his own team, the ULE. This had led them to investigate the possibility of setting up a small office in Amsterdam's business district Zuidas, just as Feike Sijbesma had done in the case of DSM. Moving to Amsterdam would likely be a touch more palatable to most Brits. But the board soon bust that bubble by arguing that it's important they be close to colleagues in Rotterdam. Isn't this part of the point?

The closer they come to the vote, the more the conviction grows that this isn't going to be a foregone conclusion, particularly in the British media. The *Financial Times* claims that 20 per cent of the top 50 PLC shareholders have now expressed significant concerns about moving to Rotterdam. The organisation behind the London FTSE has confirmed publicly that Unilever will lose its place in the index. The two biggest shareholders, who have given no indication of how they plan to vote, could make a difference, however. The index investor BlackRock owns about 7 per cent of shares through a variety of funds, the managers of each of those funds have been given the freedom to decide for themselves what they want to do. At Unilever, the assumption is that around half will vote for and half against.

The Leverhulme Trust's position is particularly tricky. This foundation manages a large chunk of Lord Leverhulme's estate. The around eighty million shares it holds in Unilever represent about 7 per cent of the PLC, with a value of around €9 billion. Niall FitzGerald, chairman of the 12-member board of trustees, has asked his fellow trustees Paul Polman, Leena Nair and Amanda Sourry to exclude themselves from the discussion. He thinks it's sad that it's come to this, and painful too. In his experience, the NV–PLC structure represents no barrier to the future of Unilever in an operational sense.

Polman is confident that the board of William Lever's foundation will support the plan to move to Rotterdam. He's had a lot of constructive advice from FitzGerald over the past few years. Not everyone is convinced. Wouldn't William Lever be spinning in his grave? There's a persistent rumour going around at head office that the Leverhulme Trust might vote against after all, or even abstain. That wouldn't help them to pull off the move, especially now that the vote is so close.

'You are a small shareholder in Unilever. You do not much care for the corporate flit to The Netherlands, but think that voting your 100 shares against the move is pointless given that there are 1,190,520,545 other shares available to vote. You are wrong. The "simplification" proposal requires a 75% majority of Unilever PLC shares voting for the resolution to pass, and it also needs a majority of voting shareholders to approve. In other words, your holding will count the same as an institutional holding, and if enough small shareholders vote No, the proposal will fail, even if the 75% majority is reached.'[15]

Neil Collins, the influential *Financial Times* columnist, has read the entire 120-page prospectus offered to shareholders and scrutinises the vote that's set to take place in London in a couple of weeks' time. In the consultations with advisors and legal experts, who on the Unilever side now consist entirely of Brits, the possible impact of the second vote, required by British law to pass the motion, has only belatedly become apparent. Nobody has brought it up explicitly until now. Many of the Unilever top brass are caught off guard. Unilever's Dutch advisors are furious about this. They suspect their British counterparts of keeping this typically British piece of legislation to themselves on purpose. They have to read through the document three times before they find it. But it's there.

A couple of days after Collin's column appears, Marijn Dekkers writes an open letter to the media, aimed at all shareholders, big and small. He seems almost desperate: 'Simplifying Unilever will also strengthen our governance. It will for the first time give each shareholder an equal voice over our future, based on a "one share, one vote" principle. In addition, the board's proposals commit the company to not having protective devices – which have been used by some other listed companies in the Netherlands – and to put our directors up for re-election every year. Contrary to some reports, dividends will not face a new form of tax under a Dutch holding company structure [...] a minority of institutional investors, which have mandates requiring them to invest in companies included in the FTSE UK Series Index, may have to reshape their portfolio or sell their Unilever shares. We are sympathetic to their concerns and made strong representations to FTSE Russell to remain in the index, but as a board we have to take a wider view and take decisions which we believe are in the best interests of the business and Unilever's shareholders as a whole.'[16]

On 28 September, the *Financial Times* estimates that around 16 per cent of shares belong to shareholders who will vote against the relocation to Rotterdam. Given the threshold of 70 per cent, they only need another 1.5 per cent to vote against the proposal in order to shoot it down in the first voting round.

A cornered animal behaves erratically. On 1 October, the company makes a last-ditch attempt to get wavering PLC shareholders over the line. The company makes a solemn promise never to make use of the 250-day 'timeout law' created by Polman's big hero Henk Kamp, the minister for economic affairs under Jan Peter Balkenende. The law, which still hasn't been ratified by the Dutch government, was conceived in order to offer companies the precisely time and space Unilever had needed after the takeover attempt by Kraft Heinz, 250 days grace in which to consider their position and prepare their defence.

CHAPTER 19

THE PIONEER FEELS MISUNDERSTOOD

October–December 2018

Marijn Dekkers suddenly loses his temper. How exactly is Unilever supposed to start suddenly leading the way in this field too? Marc Engel has just finished talking about the enormous impact plastic pollution has on the environment. He thinks that as one of the biggest users of plastics in the world Unilever has a big responsibility to combat it. Paul Polman immediately agrees with his supply chain director, he thinks Unilever needs to show itself to be taking the initiative on this issue.

This irritates Dekkers. The topic is close to his heart; he worked on finding solutions to the problem over twenty-five years ago when he was a young chemist. Unilever had been in a position to make a real difference to this very issue over the past decade, but they'd put their heads in the sand. Unilever is the second biggest purchaser of plastics in the whole world but barely started looking into changes it could make until recently. The board chairman feels that Polman has been abdicating his important responsibilities on this front for some time. A matter he regards as serious. He thinks it's too easy for the CEO to start calling for Unilever to get ahead of the curve on plastics when he himself is just about to leave.

Paul Polman reacts as if he's been slapped and tells Dekkers that people who think like him have no place in the Unilever board. For a moment, it's deathly quiet. Most of the people there were already aware that there was no love lost between the chairman and the CEO but they find the two Dutchman airing their troubled relationship so publicly in front of the group embarrassing, really embarrassing.

Unilever's board and the ULE spend the first few days of October talking over their strategy for the years to come, the post-Polman era. The

Rotterdam-London question is naturally also on the agenda. The increasingly tense *PLC* shareholder vote will take place in three weeks' time.

The awkward clash between the CEO and the board chairman gives several of those present the sense that Dekkers is trying to send the next generation of leaders a message. He's already said a couple of times that even though he finds the USLP, which is due to finish in 2020, inspiring, the biggest lesson they should take from the past two years has to be the fact that a company like Unilever needs to focus first and foremost on making money, however carefully and sustainably they're doing it. You can disagree with that, as Polman does, but that's the way of the world. Others think that this message from Dekkers is poorly timed; Paul Polman is still here. The confusion this discord is causing isn't helping anyone. In a couple of weeks' time, the members of the ULE will have to present their vision for the succession, formulated with the help of Valerie Keller, to the top 200 managers in the company.

That also applies to the four internal candidates who have thrown their hat into the ring to be Polman's successor. At the end of next month, the board will make its decision. One of them, Kees Kruythoff, finds the confrontation between his two bosses completely off-putting. What's he supposed to make of it? How can he best position himself as the logical choice to take over from Polman? He spends hours talking to Dekkers and Polman about their difference of opinion, which is about as fundamental as it gets.

There's at least one lesson the candidates can take from the row. Marijn Dekkers wants Polman's successor to give the issue of plastic packaging top priority from the jump. The issue has become unavoidable. Over the last few years, the world has been flooded with images of rivers, beaches and oceans choked with plastic. According to the United Nations, in 50 years' time, 100 million tonnes of plastic will have entered the oceans and each year sees another eight million tonnes added to problem. Unilever is one of the five biggest contributors.[1]

Every year, the company uses around 600 million kilos of plastic. According to Marc Engel, less than 1 per cent of this is made from recycled materials. If you want to halve the company's environmental impact, as the USLP set out to do eight years previously, then there's a clear task cut out for them here. However, it's also a difficult one because they are about to announce proudly that the very same Unilever Sustainable has helped the company to succeed in helping 653 million people to improve their hygienic conditions since 2010. From washing their hands with Lifebuoy soap, to brushing their teeth with Prodent and from using cleaning products like Domestos to washing clothes with products like Persil and Surf, Unilever is improving hygiene and thereby helping people to live more healthily and lift themselves out of poverty. That's an amazing thing. But pretty much all of those products are packaged in plastic.

In order to make these items accessible to as many poor people as possible and still turn a profit, Unilever started making mini packages of things like washing powder. It's been doing that for a long time now. Engel, who's just been named the most influential purchaser in Europe for the second year in a row, estimates that the overwhelming majority of the around hundred billion little Unilever sachets sold in countries like India and Indonesia end up as litter. In order to stop the washing powder from clumping, the product is packed in multilayer plastic. That in itself is a decision made for the sake of sustainability – it increases the shelf life – but the downside of using layers of different kinds of plastics is that it's really hard to recycle. These countries are hardly equipped to handle such a task. They're usually still in the process of developing an infrastructure for collecting and processing waste. The upshot of all this is that much of the plastic ends up in the ocean after being washed out to sea along a handful of big rivers.

Another thing that doesn't help is the way items are sold in the world of fast-moving consumer goods. Packaging plays a central role in establishing a brand to its best advantage. In addition to the safety and preservation requirements, Dove bottles, for example, also need to be pure white in order to empha-sise quality and of a certain thickness in order to feel reassuring. It's almost impossible to meet those requirements using recycled plastic. And it certainly wouldn't be cheaper to make. All this while recycled plastic is more expensive across the board than the 'virgin' plastic, made directly from oil.

Manufacturers of recycled plastic are pleased that Unilever is willing to pay a little bit more for their materials but that doesn't mean they're buying all they could. The prices purchasers at Unilever put forward to their col-leagues give rise to predictable resistance. The marketers concerned respond that 'their' customers won't be willing to pay for it, and they don't want to see those extra costs added to their profit and loss calculations. The same applies to buyers; they have their targets too. What really needs to happen is for the top management to make it clear that they'll be satisfied with a slightly smaller margin, but ever since the near miss with Kraft Heinz there is no chance of that happening. If there ever was. The shareholders wouldn't look too kindly on that.

This is why it's important that used plastics are collected and recycled on a grand scale. That way, the price of recycled plastic will go down automatically. An enormous help there would be a high tax on CO_2 and the use of fossil fuels, the raw materials from which plastics are derived. That would make virgin plastic much more expensive.

Paul Polman knows that the big plastics manufacturers have been struggling with this issue for years. Since the beginning of 2010, he has been a board member at Dow Chemical, the biggest producer of plastic in the world.[2] During those meetings, he's noticed how under threat the American company feels. The company wants to be part of the solution but it doesn't know how. They don't have the technology to switch to recycled plastics while still making profits that keep their shareholders happy. Since the demand for their virgin plastic remains high, it's hard to make a case for a new approach. In its last annual report, Dow didn't get much further than promising to explore how plastic could be better recycled.

Unilever can't just sit by and wait for that to happen. If they still want to keep their promise that 25 per cent of all plastics used by the company will be made from recycled materials by 2025, something needs to happen now. Initiatives are springing up all over the company. Annemarieke de Haan, the head of Unilever Malaysia, is working with local government to investigate ways of improving how they collect used plastic. In Indonesia, Unilever is investing a couple of million euros in a test lab for experimenting with ways to recycle the plastic used in those billions of tiny sachets. Unilever has pledged to share any technological breakthroughs they make with all their competitors free of charge. Since black plastic bottles are almost impossible to recycle, the marketing manager of Comfort is looking into whether the brand could switch to from black to dark grey plastic without losing customers.

Sustainability manager Anniek Mauser believes that the spotlight being shone on this plastic drama will finally convince Unilever's marketers of the importance of their sustainability mission. They need to face up to it. The statistic put forward by the Ellen MacArthur Foundation that there will be more plastic in the ocean than fish by the year 2050 could well be a game-changer when it comes to awareness of environmental issues. The customer will soon regard this as so important that the buck will pass automatically from buyers to the marketers. And that could happen very quickly, Mauser thinks. As it is European customers who are most likely to be the first to draw a line in the sand, Europe boss Hanneke Faber has made this her priority: less plastic, better plastic, no plastic at all.[3]

They daren't do it. Various legal advisors have insisted that they should only allow the vote on the move to Rotterdam to go ahead if the board is pretty much certain it will go their way. Knowingly taking a massive risk only to be voted down by your own shareholders means that the company has been mis-managed. Then everyone's in trouble.

They can't take that risk. Unilever's board decides to postpone the vote on the company's head office, which they had planned for the end of October, indefinitely. They estimate that the chances of them not getting the required 75 per cent of votes in a couple of weeks' time at 30–40 per cent.

It's also far from certain whether they'd then get the green light from 51 per cent of the shareholders physically present at the meeting. For a while, they'd thought that with their 7,000 British employees, each of them shareholders, they'd make it over the line easily. But the voting rights attached to their shares are all held by one company, Computershare, which means all of them only count as one vote. Demanding your voting right back requires messing around with paperwork, so it barely ever happens. This means that support from Unilever's own workers will be limited. Even worse: it seems that Unilever employees who *are* applying for their voting rights are the ones getting the most riled up by all this Brexit sentiment and they don't want the head office to leave. A couple of coaches full of opponents to the vote would be enough to tor-pedo the whole plan. This situation comes as a surprise to the Unilever board.

One former Unilever director is feeling relieved about all this: Niall FitzGerald. Now the committee that manages Lord Leverhulme's estate won't have to declare itself for or against leaving London.

On 5 October, Hans de Boer is just about to have his morning shave when he gets a text from Paul Polman explaining that the vote won't be going ahead. The message ends with an encouragement to call him if he has any questions. Unilever's head office will not be moving to Rotterdam. Two days previously, De Boer had called the Unilever CEO for another reason and asked him in passing about how their shared project was going. Polman had told him then that he was afraid that they wouldn't be able to pull it off after all. De Boer had immediately called the Dutch prime minister, but Mark Rutte had assured him that he had heard otherwise and that there was no need to worry.

It's been a long time since he was last had such a rude awakening. The chairman of the employers' union immediately phones Rutte. He's just received the exact same message, albeit with 'Dear Mark' at the top instead of 'Dear Hans'. The men curse as it sinks in that they're going to draw the short straw despite the enormous effort they have invested over the past few months. Fighting tooth and nail to push through the scrapping of dividend tax hasn't been enough to bring Unilever to the Netherlands. The prime minister immediately comes to a conclusion: it's over. Scrapping the dividend tax has become untenable.

De Boer is furious. He thinks Polman should have told them earlier, that way they would at least have been able to prepare for the media frenzy that's about to begin. He doesn't understand Polman's explanation that it's illegal to share sensitive information with outsiders. They were in it together, weren't they? That means you can also work on a plan together in confidence in order to keep it on the right track. People from the employers' union openly speak of Polman as having thrown the Dutch prime minister under the bus. His whole third cabinet has almost fallen thanks to Unilever.

De Boer doesn't understand the decision either. Why didn't Polman decide to go down fighting? He's supposed to be a man of principles isn't he? Working in those kinds of jobs means getting your hands dirty, of course it does, you have to be pragmatic. But there's such a thing as basic principles as well as grand ones. This was a serious matter, with a lot riding on it. In situations like this it's worth saying: I'm going to see it through to the end. That's how he would have gone about it, anyway.

At the same time, De Boer is forced to agree with Rutte. He's no great fan of Polman. The prime minister had once told De Boer that Twente's famous son was no longer a Dutchman. Polman is a citizen of the world with remarkably little interest in the Netherlands. That explains to De Boer why Polman is blowing off the vote so easily now.

The third musketeer, Sybrand van Haersma Buma, has also received the same text message. He's completely flabbergasted, having never received the slightest indication that anything might go wrong. In September, he'd asked Unilever once more whether there was any reason for him to worry, the British media's campaign to keep the headquarters in London hadn't escaped him. No, no they said, there was no cause for concern. And now this. To him, allowing your prime minister to learn of something this important from a text message is bad form.

Van Haersma Buma calls Rutte straight away. The two men swiftly arrive at the same conclusion. Scrapping the dividend withholding tax is no longer an option, they'll have to scrap the scrap. Van Haersma Buma reproaches Polman for not making the schedule, choices and risks attached to the plan much more transparent. The CDA leader thinks that they've all been taken for a ride.

Ten days later, Rutte announces that the dividend tax is here to stay. The €1.9 billion it would have cost to scrap it will now go to improving the business climate in other ways. Corporation tax is going down and the expats will be given their transition legislation. De Boer thinks this is a shame but he understands the decision: the political reality is taking precedent over the economic reality. Not least because the media perception of the alternative was unequivocal.

Jesse Klaver of GroenLinks sees this step-down as unavoidable at this point. Going ahead without being able to guarantee Unilever coming over would have been political suicide. The Christian Union and the progressive D66 party wouldn't have gone along with it now, meaning that a vote of no confidence would have gone ahead to prevent the policy.

Polman doesn't understand it. He thinks it's stupid for Rutte to immediately abandon his plans for tax reform. Backing down implies to everyone that he was a puppet on Unilever's string after all. After sending the SMS, he'd naturally spent some time on the phone with the PM. Polman hadn't thought it proper to call Rutte out of the blue first thing in the morning, before the stock exchange was even open. Hence the text message. During the call, they'd both expressed their disappointment. Rutte is furious that he's suddenly being put on the spot without being given any time to prepare. Polman explains once again that he would have faced prison if he'd given him any advanced warning. Paul Polman still regards Mark Rutte as a close friend.

In the Dutch press, news about the dividend tax is celebrated as a victory for democracy over the shadowy interests of multinationals. In the UK, the cancellation of the vote is celebrated as a victory for shareholder democracy.[4]

Marijn Dekkers's biggest feeling is one of regret. They haven't handled this well. He thinks that the Unilever board had totally misjudged shareholder sentiment. The Brits have no desire for a move, they don't want to be abandoned by 'their' Unilever, especially not now that the country is turning its back on Europe. That's why there had been such a ferocious campaign against the departure from London in the media. The campaign had meant that this dreadful Brexit, one of the most important reasons *for* the move, had become one of the biggest obstacles to Unilever leaving the UK.

Thinking it all over, Dekkers comes to the conclusion that his board chose Rotterdam because its members are first and foremost globalists, citizens of the world. They'd all left their home countries at a young age, just like him and Polman. They'd crisscrossed the whole globe for study and work and are accustomed to paying tax in more than one country. The only Brit on the board, John Rishton, had even been the CEO of Ahold for a while. This type of world-citizen has no appreciation of the now rampant desire to put one's own national interests centre stage. They've been trained to believe that an open world market, accessible to everyone, is the ideal arrangement for everyone: the global village. It doesn't matter to them whether the plane to their next meeting lands in Rotterdam or London. Feeling rather morose, Dekkers wonders whether people like himself and Polman aren't relics these days, dinosaurs from a time in which globalism was a positive thing. Will they manage to hold the line against all this nationalistic ardour?

In Rotterdam, the disappointment is overwhelming. They're ashamed of the way things have gone and think that Unilever has made the Dutch prime minister look foolish. They notice a change immediately. They are suddenly being received much less warmly in The Hague. They see the situation not only as a big defeat but as a blunder. Enormous errors in judgement were made. Internally, blame for this is mostly being assigned to board chairman Marijn Dekkers and CFO Graeme Pitkethly. This is their fault. The Dutchman and the Scot should have persuaded the *plc* shareholders. That's where it all went wrong. In their defence, the men explain that they organised at least two hundred meetings with shareholders.

Martine Zeegers is gutted that headquarters won't be moving to Rotterdam. She's disturbed by how fiercely the Brits played hard ball, and that it was the interests of the shareholders of all things that had ended up scuppering their plans. Moving to Rotterdam, that safe haven they'd talked about, should have been a magnificent and logical final note of the Polman era, in which an end to the dominance of shareholder value had finally seemed like a possibility.

Forty-one-year-old Zeegers is responsible for human resources policy in the Benelux region. She is regularly asked whether she too plans on becoming the prime minister of the Netherlands; Mark Rutte was one of her predecessors in this role. She may not share that particular ambition but she had known from an early age exactly what work she had cut out for her. Coming from a small, tightknit community of businessmen in Limburg, she'd had a lot of explaining to do when she decided to marry her girlfriend. Ever since then, she's been fearless.

The same applies to her boss Leena Nair. The Indian HR manager had survived the Mumbai attack alongside Paul Polman almost ten years previously and been brought into the ULE to take on responsibility for human resources policy. She learned her greatest leadership lesson from the young woman Malika on the night of the attack. 'When I hear people doubting whether they can do x, y or z, I think: oh my God, you've got so much more power and influence than you could ever imagine. Stand up and show people what you are capable of.' And then she tells the heroic story of the hotel employee who led the Unilever managers, all a good deal older and more experienced then her, so resolutely to safety. She had done nothing short of lead them out of hell.[5]

Women like Leena Nair and Martine Zeegers represent the future of Unilever. In that future, employees' service to society and 'purpose thinking' will take on a central role. They want to say goodbye to personal financial targets. In their vision, the organisation consists of a network of teams, people who trust each other and offer constant, honest feedback on how each other is working. That will make performance evaluations between boss and subordinate a thing of the past too, and not a moment too soon. In their vision, there won't even be any need for top-down leadership to guide strategy. Over the next few years, they want to investigate whether the company can do without a couple of the six different levels of management even as it stands. A basic requirement for this will be that all employees have a clear understanding of their purpose, not just the leadership.

For the past eighteen months, Zeegers has been organising 'purpose workshops' for the 600 marketing and sales employees based in the Netherlands. During these sessions, the aims of the individual, the aims of the brand and the aims of Unilever have to come together. Some colleagues wonder why this has taken so long, why they didn't take everyone along on this journey from the beginning, back in 2010. If this way of talking had been clear to everyone in the company from the word go, the leadership would have had an easier time implementing the USLP goals, particularly when it came to having others carry out the work.

It will be new colleagues especially who will form the basis for this new way of working. The potential to attract that talent is there; with around two million speculative applications per year, Unilever stands alongside Google, Facebook, Amazon and Apple at the top of the list of most desired employers.

The way in which Unilever tries to select the best talent from this enormous pool of workers has already undergone some drastic changes in the Benelux. Two years ago they had realised that despite the enormous diversity of this pool of applicants they were still taking too many people from the same universities and employing too many of the same type of slightly corporate, elite, often white young men. The exact same type as 25 years previously. This was often happening without them realising it. Flicking through CVs, they tended to look for things that made people stand out. This meant they soon settled on students who had already been on some kind of student board or who had studied abroad.

They decided to remove the interpersonal element from the first round of the hiring process and to stop asking for CVs. All the people who wanted to come and work for Unilever were invited to play two online games. These were designed to reveal how they view themselves and how they look at the world around them. The intention was for that to show that they were not only capable but also driven by something, and to reveal whether they already had some idea of their life's purpose and their contribution of the world. In the second round of the application process, they had to record a digital interview, which was then analysed. It was only in the final round that a real-life meeting took place in the flesh. It often happened that candidates weren't even asked what they had studied until they were being offered the job. After two years of this approach, more than 60 per cent of new trainees in the Benelux region are women.

In November 2018, members of the ULE present their concrete plans for the future of the USLP, based on their personal purpose, to the top 200, who have gathered at London head office. Polman is deeply moved by their presentations. One colleague talks about employing 8,000 people with disabilities. Another thinks that Unilever should become a social enterprise.

Marc Engel has plans to increase the use of recycled plastic by 18–20 per cent by 2019, to a total of 113,000 tonnes. This is six times the amount currently being used. He tells them about his collaboration with the waste processing company Veolia that will collect that plastic and is investing in collection centres where tens of thousands of 'base pickers' will be set to work gathering plastic from the rubbish. These pickers will be paid by the kilo. Engel is feeling relieved, for a while the ball had been in his court when it came to Unilever's insufficient use of recycled plastic because he hadn't been able to get hold of enough of it. Now he's no longer the bottleneck. Marketers of Dove who keep on complaining about the plastic he obtained not being white enough are now being instructed to use the same message about the plastic as they do for their brand: beauty doesn't have to be perfect.

Various attendees of the annual Unilever-sponsored meeting at Amsterdam's Concert Hall describe this year's event as toe curling. Polman speaks off the cuff and spends most of his speech complaining about the Netherlands and the awkward political fuss around the failed relocation to Rotterdam. He plays down the issue, emphasising that attention should be focused on the real issues of the day such as poverty and the environment. Dutch people are interested in those too, right? So why isn't Unilever being welcomed with open arms? Why is he always given so little support here? It's bizarre that the media celebrated the failed relocation to Rotterdam as some kind of victory. He's convinced that headquarters would have come to the Netherlands if there hadn't been such strong negative sentiment in the country. Paul Polman feels like he isn't understood in his native country.

During a big meeting with the Rotterdam staff, Polman had calmly explained to the employees why unification was still a good idea and why they couldn't go ahead with the new headquarters. The Benelux leadership gets the impression that their CEO has gotten over the defeat and that he's now ready for an interview with the Rotterdam newspaper *Het Algemeen Dagblad*. The aim is simple: save Unilever's reputation and save your own reputation. They prepare the interview in excruciating detail. Polman will emphasise how deeply Unilever is still connected to the Netherlands, how important Rotterdam remains to the company and that brands like Unox, the popular Dutch sausage brand, won't be sold off.

However, Annemieke van Dongen and Sander van Mersbergen from the *Het Algemeen Dagblad* don't want to talk about those things. They want to know what went wrong with moving headquarters to Rotterdam. The journalists don't think that their subject realises for a moment that they're there representing their readership, or that they've come to ask the questions ordinary readers might still have. Polman immediately loses his cool, but since they've only got an hour, the journalists press on and ask about Polman's relationship with Prime Minister Mark Rutte.

Annick Boyen, head of communications, is in the room in London head office and sees to her horror that everything is going wrong. The journalists ask Polman whether it's true that he sent Rutte a text. He sees this as a totally irrelevant question. This is probably his last interview as CEO, his departure is going to be made official within the next couple of days, he's done so much for the company and for the world and *this* is what they want to ask him about! He becomes irate and says that the journalists aren't asking the right questions. When asked about the causes behind the failed move to Rotterdam, Polman gives Green leader Jesse Klaver both barrels: 'Discussion is always a good thing in itself. But when you have an opposition party who says "we're going to repeal it as soon as we get into power and you know that governments can be overthrown just like that."'

When the journalists suggest that he might go down in history in the Netherlands as the man who wanted to get rid of a tax on foreign investors, despite all his achievements on sustainability, Polman says: 'That's completely ludicrous. I think you live in a piddly little country and aren't thinking big enough. I think that most people in the world do see what we're trying to do as a company. I don't think I have anything to apologise for.'

After they've left, the journalists exchange startled glances: What happened here? This came completely out of the blue. Doesn't Unilever have any decent explanation for why the longed-for relocation to Rotterdam didn't succeed? They've never known a CEO bear his soul like this, with no apparent concern for the share price or the impact on the company.

Polman's colleagues from the communications department are dismayed. This was a massive strategic error. Their CEO obviously hasn't processed his frustration regarding the failure of the relocation plan. This is the price they'll have to pay for their mistake.

The interview has serious consequences. For many in the Netherlands, Paul Polman has fallen off his pedestal with a crash. He's written off as a despicable member of the disengaged global elite. Can't this man get over his defeat, what does he even stand for? Sybrand van Haersma Buma can't understand why Polman is complaining about political debate in the Netherlands like this. Essentially, what he's saying is that it would be better if the opposition kept their mouth shut. Buma sees this as a naïve position. People who know Polman a bit better or are closer to him mostly just feel sorry for the CEO. Their only explanation for the interview is that it was a temporary loss of control. He didn't deserve this kind of treatment.

But Unilever didn't deserve it either. Conny Braams looks on sadly as Unilever's reputation once again collapses in the wake of the interview. Like Philips, IKEA and other trusted brands, Unilever normally has an approval rating of around 70 per cent in market research surveys. When something goes wrong, the score goes down. The furore around Polman's pay rise saw it drop to 64 per cent but this interview with *Het Algemeen Dagblad* drives it down to 60. She thinks it will take a while for them to repair the damage.

While the Netherlands is busy getting up in arms about the interview, Paul and Kim Polman are in Kenya celebrating the 10th birthday of the Kilimanjaro Blind Trust. Polman estimates that they've donated about €10 million to help blind children learn to read and write. The trust's achievements are summarised during a seminar. By funding the repair of around twenty-five thousand braille typewriters, they've managed to help around the same number of children. They've also bought around one thousand new typewriters and seventy tonnes of braille paper. This warms Polman's heart.

What will he do to help in 2019? It isn't long now until he steps down as CEO and after that he'll have about eighty hours a week to spare. The thought alone makes him uneasy. He can't end up at a loose end. His roles for the UN Global Compact and the International Chamber of Commerce (ICC) will give him the platform to keep pushing the message among his World Trade Organisation contacts that the next few years will see the final battle for the soul of capitalism. A system that can only be rescued by placing a long-term vision at the centre of commerce and showing how everyone can profit from it in the end. If they don't manage to win support from the general public to shift the horizon and embrace long-termism then something terrible might well arise in its place.

There's still time, though. Emmanuel Macron has asked him to assist with preparations for the G7 summit in Biarritz in August 2019. The French president wants leaders from the UK, France, Germany, Italy, Japan, the United States, Canada and the EU to make concrete agreements on how they will address climate change.

In Polman's personal view, none of this goes far enough. He wants to start doing new, exciting things. He has to be able to keep pushing his boundaries. He wants to try fasting for Ramadan and has plans to learn to play the saxophone, despite his lack of musical talent. He also wants to run the world's five biggest marathons next year, in a respectable time. For a while, he had seriously considered going and studying medicine. But his wife won't have it, she thinks starting a medical degree at 63 is ridiculous. Regardless of what happens, he's definitely entering the Beijing–Paris rally next summer with one of his close friends. They've been renovating a 1967 Citroen DS for a year at this point already. It's going to be a proper drive, they're not allowed to use GPS. It's going to be the fifth time the rally has run; of the hundreds of cars that set off, only seventy reach the finish line. People have died during almost ever edition of the race. No, he's not scared of dying, if it's his time to go, then it's his time to go.

Paul and Kim fly from Kenya to the United States. Unilever's board is meeting in New York for a special meeting. The only item on the agenda is Polman's successor. Feike Sijbesma wants to take Polman aside for a minute. He thinks it's terrible that Polman has given Unilever his heart and soul for 10 years, doing everything for the company, only to leave under a cloud, as many people see it. The CEO of DSM wants to know what went wrong with the journalists from *Het Algemeen Dagblad*. Sijbesma could list 20 different things Polman shouldn't have said. How did it happen? Polman gets prickly and says he doesn't care, that they were only journalists. He says their impact is negligible; they'll go back to writing about something else the next day. But Sijbesma isn't satisfied, he thinks that speaking to journalists means presenting oneself as the CEO of Unilever and steering the conversation as such. He can't just sit there as Paul Polman, hell bent on saving the world, and get offended when he doesn't get the questions he wants or feels misunderstood. That kind of behaviour just isn't on, and the journalists don't know what to make of it either. That's when everything goes wrong.

Polman realises that he never should have done the interview. He's angry with what he sees as the weak-willed executives from the communication department. He feels like he was lured into a trap and that the journalists got exactly what they wanted from him. He said so much more than he should have. But now he also blames himself for losing control and getting as angry as he did. That was foolish.

Sijbesma feels a strong bond with Polman. He understands the depth of his feeling; they both stand for the same things. But he also believes that Polman has lost his way. Even the Unilever CEO doesn't have the power to change the rules of the game. You can't tell the financial sector that you think their way of working is rubbish, or that you know better and want a different system. You can't do that, the whole world is playing their game. If you start playing checkers when everyone else is playing chess, you're going to lose. You can get as angry as you like about that but it isn't going to get you anywhere. You certainly can't ever let that emotion show to outsiders, to do so is irresponsible.

Marijn Dekkers, Laura Cha and Feike Sijbesma have conducted almost twenty interviews. This Nominations Committee now has to choose Polman's successor from among the six remaining candidates and present their decision to the whole board. Three of the candidates are external, they are number twos or number threes in big companies like Nestlé and Danone, hoping to be appointed number one somewhere else. Egon Zehnder has selected them from all different corners of the fast-moving consumer goods market. Amanda Sourry, Kees Kruythoff and Alan Jope make up the other three.

They used a pre-established profile to look for the best candidate. Alongside proven leadership qualities and a focus on results, the board is looking for an open, transparent leader who understands the digital domain and subscribes to the USLP. One of the issues the new CEO will have to get to grips with is the plastic problem. The board assumes that governments are going to introduce decisive laws on plastics within the foreseeable future. Unilever needs to be ready.

Last summer, all kinds of advisors were brought in to test the new candidates on their experience, knowledge and lifestyle. The directors agree that if two candidates come out in equal first place, they will select the internal candidate. A possible downside of that approach is that you know all their weaknesses but it also means that you know exactly who you're getting into bed with. They think Polman has done a good job on this front: there's been enough talent developed under his leadership to keep their company moving forwards.

In the end, it comes down to Kees Kruythoff and Alan Jope. The Dutchman has made it clear to them that he wants to go even further and transform the sustainability agenda more aggressively. The centrepiece of his strategy is taking over more small brands developed by activist entrepreneurs on the basis of their social mission. Kruythoff regards himself as Polman 2.0. Polman is likewise a fan of Kruythoff. He's got a big network of contacts, just like him and, even more importantly, he's got the USLP in his blood.

Alan Jope is the son of a housewife and a printer. It took until he was 60 for his father to realise that he was dyslexic, rather than just stupid. After his Bachelor's in Economics at the University of Edinburgh, Jope Junior was expected to start making money straight away. The accountancy firm Arthur Andersen was only too happy to take him on. However, Jope found marketing a much more enjoyable discipline and in 1985, he applied to Procter & Gamble and Unilever. The Americans offered him a job in Newcastle, Unilever offered him one in London. His girlfriend Rosie congratulated him on the offer from the Dutch-British giant, since there was no way she was moving to Newcastle. The two of them are together to this day and have three children. Alan doesn't call Rosie his better half, he calls her his better three-quarters.

Jope thinks that Polman's biggest service to Unilever has been rediscovering its DNA and taking the company back to its roots. The Dutchman has cleverly combined making money with a big focus on doing good. As his potential successor, Jope has committed to raising the margin to 20 per cent and sales growth from 3 per cent to 5 per cent by 2020, as promised. Whatever happens over the next 10 years to 2029, revenues have to have increased by many billions of euros. To him, €80 billion doesn't seem realistic, however.

Fifty-four-year-old Jope has made it clear that he intends to change emphasis over the coming years. He wants to concentrate on internal processes. They need to put all the Dutch versus British hullaballoo of the past few years behind them as quickly as possible. It's only logical anyway, there are more Indians at the top of the company than there are Brits or Dutch. The 14 members of his team come from 12 different countries. The fact that he's Scottish brings some advantages: he's technically British but in terms of his character he feels much more Dutch, he's just as blunt and to the point.

He won't be accepting time-consuming invitations from the UN, NGOs or other important public institutions. Where Polman spent most of his time mobilising the Unilever brand on a global scale, Jope intends to focus on consumer brands and on the market. He wants to ensure that their sustainability messages are better formulated and communicated much more clearly. At the moment, customers unwrapping a Unilever product from its packaging are given no indication of that brand's contribution to a more sustainable way of living. It isn't on there.

Jope is keen on Hanneke Faber's message that every brand should be a movement. The point of departure for all calculations is so-called brand equity, a proper analysis of the value of a brand. Shampoo, for example, is valuable because it will make your hair shine and smell nice, and because it reduces dandruff, but also increasingly because it comes in bottles made out of recycled plastic. The fact that this last value carries ever more weight with the customer means that Unilever can take it into consideration when setting its prices.

By the time he's finished, Unilever won't necessarily have a bigger share of the foods sector but it will have grown significantly overall. The brands will be known for the unambiguous, authentic and sustainable contribution they make. Jope won't try to provide a living wage to the entire world but he does intend to redefine what working for Unilever means. In his view, Unilever doesn't have 160,000 workers, it has three million. All those people earn their living from the multinational's activities, he feels responsible for that. He wants to do more with them and for them.

For board chairman Marijn Dekkers, it isn't a difficult choice. He thinks that Jope is by far and away the best option. This is his man. After Polman, he wants a CEO who has both feet firmly on the ground, someone pragmatic. The rest of the board obviously feels the same way. Alan Jope is nominated unanimously and on 1 January 2019 the board names him as the man who will take the baton from Paul Polman.

Kees Kruythoff is deeply disappointed. He believes he hasn't been chosen because he's Dutch. The most important Dutchman on the board, Marijn Dekkers, is still carrying the scars of the dividend tax debacle. That whole furore has brought the old Dutch-British animosities back to the company again. We've had a Dutchman, now it's time for someone from the UK again. It's settled, he'll leave Unilever after twenty-six years.

'Unilever chief executive Paul Polman will step down [...] months after he lost a bruising fight with shareholders over moving its headquarters out of London', the *Financial Times* concludes the next day as it shares the news, much to the annoyance of many of those involved. Now it's the paper who seems like a boxer that doesn't know when to stop going on the offensive, kicking Polman when he's down. The *New York Times* goes with the headline 'Paul Polman, a "Crucial Voice" for Corporate Responsibility, Steps Down as Unilever CEO'. The newspaper paints a complimentary portrait of the departing CEO. He was one of the first CEOs to put his money where his mouth is and engage earnestly and successfully with the big issue of sustainability and with creating a business world prepared to take responsibility for it.

Polman can't believe that he'll be delivering his last speech as Unilever CEO in Mumbai of all places. The circle is complete. Ten years on from the dramatic event that brought such profound change to his life he has to return to the same city to once again go into battle against the group of people who least understands him. He looks around the room, he's on first name terms with most of the analysts at this point. He tells them candidly that this isn't easy for him, that he's just been on the phone to his wife for advice and that she told 'when in doubt, hug it out'. If it isn't going well, try giving them a hug. Those assembled chuckle softly.

Naturally, he brings up the topic of results: 'I'm still embarrassed to tell my 90-year-old mother that we could do all these things – satisfy all these stakeholders and at the same time give our shareholders a 290% return when the cost of money was zero over a ten year period of time. She's never had that kind of return on her pension savings.' Isn't this the proof that companies like Unilever that opt for the multi-stakeholder approach will determine the future?

'How come so few companies are following our example?' That is a serious problem. 'The cost that society is incurring today for climate change alone is over $5.3 trillion. Any company that didn't think about that would be out of their minds. It's probably the biggest intergenerational crime that we're committing in the history of mankind.'

He summarises the successes of the last ten years. Personal care has grown from €12 to €22 billion. The foods division has been streamlined. 'We're now one of the few food companies that is growing and we've done that at the same time as moving our footprint from 75% developed markets and 25% developing markets only 10 years ago to a more balanced 50/50. En route, if you will, towards the direction of the rest of the business and getting to the 75/25 footprint that reflects more or less where the population is longer-term.' And, thanks to ZBB, costs are also heading in the right direction. He grins as he says that even the consultants at Accenture are impressed: 'they've never seen a company making these kinds of savings so quickly'.

'But central to what we do is purpose and we need your help there. You're as much part of that, not only by believing in it but by actively participating in it and acting on it with your own investment decisions, your own behaviour. First and foremost, we're not investors or sell-side analysts or CEOs, we are citizens of this world planet. It is very clear, and someone wise said it once, that the purpose of life is to give purpose to lives so that society thrives and the world survives. That is the essence of what we're trying to do with the Unilever Sustainable Living Plan. With the USLP, we've created a new business model that will be more imitated by other companies. We see it reducing our risks. Avoiding deforestation in your value chain, sticking to human rights and not having slave labour or child labour, moving to green energy, reducing your water footprint or plastic footprint, or driving sustainable sourcing in its broader sense all make our business model more robust. It's also keeping well ahead of changes trends in legislation, many governments and many citizens are getting fed up.'

Polman calls on his audience to give CEOs like him a bit of space to manoeuvre and above all place a little more trust in them, even if it means looking beyond the numbers. 'Look at the decent companies that you want to have around in 10, 15, 20 to 30 years, start also to look at the companies that think about the world that the people you all represent are going to be retiring in.'

An analyst asks Polman whether he's disappointed. In terms of revenue, Unilever hasn't grown for five years. Polman shrugs. 'Ah, we've done a tremendous amount. It wasn't always easy. And what you see on the global scene and the way our politicians behave, unfortunately is not really helping us. Still I was hoping for better and hoping for them as well to rise to the challenge but it's not happening.'

Another analyst wants to know what advice Polman has for his successor when it comes to dealing with analysts. Polman looks over at Jope: 'To run this company by all the wishes of the shareholders will lead to guaranteed bankruptcy. There are these intangibles that need to be made tangible, you need to provide more transparency on the real value drivers. You need to explain what materiality is in what we are doing you need to better communicate why the USLP is a value drive for the shareholders long term and all that. You cannot blame the shareholders or say they don't care it's our responsibility to be sure that that communication is had and that is better communicated. I've tried to do that, I've not always succeeded. [...] I'd also thank you. We've not always looked eye to eye, we haven't always agreed on all the things. I thank you all you have been doing, I thank you for the constructive challenges *most of the time* and I also wish you luck in your own professional and personal journeys thank you very much.'[6] The analysts clap cautiously, his Unilever colleagues clap harder. Marijn Dekkers remains seated with his arms folded.

Over the Christmas holiday, Polman and Sijbesma speak a couple of times on the phone, both men feel driven to reflect on the past year. It hasn't been easy. Sijbesma has found himself thinking that he'd like to avoid the kind of final year that Polman has had. He has been the CEO of DSM for 11 years, how much longer will he stay? He wants to leave at the top of his game, while the party's still in full swing. But what is the top? *De Volkskrant* has just named him the most influential Dutch person. Polman, in second place just a year earlier, didn't even make the shortlist of 200. That's how quickly it can all go away.

There's still so much to do. Above all, Sijbesma hope that Polman's legacy will remain intact despite the failed unification and awkward media appearances. He has done so much good work.

CHAPTER 20

PAUL POLMAN'S LONELY HIGH ROAD

January–July 2019

Their smiles are benign but they gaze boldly into the distance. Floris Maljers, Michael Perry, Morris Tabaksblat, Niall FitzGerald, Antony Burgmans, Patrick Cescau; the portraits of the bosses of the past twenty-five years hang in Unilever's head offices in chronological order. The Brit Perry, the Irishman FitzGerald and the Frenchman Cescau hang in the London office, the Dutchmen in Rotterdam.

Paul Polman has informed Unilever he does not want his picture included in any such row. Not in London and not in Rotterdam. Once you're hanging there, it somehow seems like you're finished or the job is done. And that couldn't be further from the truth. Of course, he deserves to be there, he doesn't doubt that. Unilever was a smug, inward-looking mess when he started here back in 2009. He saved the company from destruction. Unilever is headed in the right direction now, setting the tone for the whole industry, and has grown considerably into the bargain. It has won every award going.

He gives the company top marks but Polman would only give himself a C+. He still hasn't managed to bring about the change the world so sorely needs. Rescuing Unilever had only been a means to achieving that end, a way of showing that this change was possible. Sadly far too few other leaders are following his example. No, his task is far from finished.

Ten years later, the 'intern' of 2009 finds himself back in another tiny back room in London head office. He will stay on with Unilever as an advisor for another six months. On his desk, there is a stack of copies of *Imaginary Cells*, his wife's book. Sixty-two-year-old Polman likes the metaphor the book uses, the difficult but thankfully also inevitable transformation of a bloated, lazy caterpillar into a colourful, energetic butterfly. The end of the old, self-interested capitalism focused on personal gain feeds the beginning of the new, socially responsible capitalism focused on common interests.

Whenever he gives a copy to one of his guests, he sings the praises of his wife's foundation Reboot the Future. The world is going to make this turn. Companies need to show that they are creating prosperity and well-being for everyone, and that nobody is being excluded.

Sadly, things have been going in the opposite direction since 2016. The world is stuck in a negative feedback loop. Deforestation is still increasing, climate change is accelerating, poverty is increasing, both in absolute and relative terms. All of these developments are feeding the mistrust felt by many people already, mistrust of globalisation and the elites that seem to be the only people profiting from it. This is giving already rampant populism an alarming boost, which in turn keeps politicians trapped in an iron grip. Thoughts of increasing cooperation, connecting and internationalising are clearly no longer at the top of many governments' agendas. That means the business world is having to take the initiative even more.

At the moment, the general public is placing more trust in business than in politics. That's the light at the end of the tunnel in all this.[1] Polman does give himself somewhat of a pat on the back for this. He sees his greatest achievement of the past few years as the creation of the Sustainable Development Goals, his participation in the United Nations High-Level Panel. Multinationals had long been the big enemy at the UN but now they see the private sector as the most important driver of the changes the world needs. That's a win.

Back when he was appointed 10 years earlier, Polman claimed that he was glad they were in the middle of a crisis. The crisis challenged the ethics of doing business and made it clear that the financial sector had become much too dominant. The crisis gave him a mandate to change course and place the USLP at the centre of the company's activities. Right from the jump, he had predicted that at most only part of the USLP promises would be kept. He'd predicted ups and downs. Even so, he's proud of what they've achieved. Unilever has helped around 653 million people to improve their hygienic living conditions. And when it comes to their own production plants, some areas have far exceeded the target to halve environmental impact. Looking at the whole environmental impact of the over two hundred billion Unilever products manufactures each year, the outcome isn't so good. The aim to source 100 per cent of agricultural products from sustainable suppliers by 2020 is stalling, as of the end of 2018 they've only managed to make it to 56 per cent. Cutting the mountain of rubbish produced as a result of the use of Unilever products in half also hasn't happened, they've reduced it by only 31 per cent. The hoped-for 50 per cent reduction in water use currently stands at a paltry 2 per cent. They don't seem to be getting anywhere in their effort to get the people who lather their hair and wash their bodies with Unilever products to spend any less time in the shower, for example. The promised 50 per cent reduction in greenhouse gases by 2020 has actually resulted in a 6 per cent increase as of the end of 2018. When it comes to improving living conditions and tackling poverty, the picture is mixed. Almost two-thirds of all purchasing is from companies who have signed up to respect human rights in line with Unilever guidelines. They've helped almost two million of the five million women they hoped to assist in increasing job opportunities by 2020. And 2.6 million of the promised 5.5 million small farmers and retailers have been helped to make their income and working practices more sustainable.

During 2018, Unilever is also once more declared the most sustainable business in its sector, both by the Dow Jones Sustainability Index and by GlobeScan.[2] Polman actually finds that rather disappointing, it would be much better to see other companies catching up with Unilever by now. There needs to be a race to the top, with companies egging each other on to start operating even more sustainably.

Where are they? He's often said this was an issue: the USLP will have been a failure if other companies don't start following their example. Very little has changed on that front. While the urgency of the situation is only increasing. For eight years now, Unilever's annual report has contained a summary of their sustainability achievements alongside the conventional financial results. But the underlying message that they're all part and parcel of the same thing and can't be taken separately hasn't been picked up by enough people. Analysts haven't asked a single question about it over the past ten years. No, everything is going much too slowly. The flywheel isn't turning fast enough. There's still a pressing shortage of leaders who understand that as long as the value of living trees is not in their spreadsheets our ecosystem is at risk of collapsing.

Looking back on his time as head of Unilever now, a couple of months after handing over the reins to Alan Jope, he wonders what he could have done better. The consistent criticism that he didn't listen enough to the people around him and failed to make the ULE into a proper team is one he can understand.

He still knows exactly what it was that made him place himself so emphatically above all those Unilever managers back in 2009, making sure that they all had to report directly to him on a one-to-one basis. In those early years, he'd been incredible irritated by the top management at Unilever. It was all one big gossip shop, a debating society, a typically British affair in which the Dutch were also only too happy to participate. Everyone wanted to give their two cents on everything the whole time. He'd broken this down by dishing out clear responsibilities from the top down. That way, they wouldn't lose all that unnecessary time to endless discussions. That way, there wouldn't be any more scope for revisiting decisions that had already been made, as happened constantly when he first arrived.

After that, he had assumed that the logic of the USLP, the desire to make the world a better place and finding their personal purpose had been enough to bind them together. Sadly, it hadn't been enough, the connections hadn't formed. From then on, they did nothing but complain about his absence, not seeming to understand that he was busy working in their interest in the world beyond the company, trying to make their reach even bigger. Maybe he should have realised earlier that not everyone wants to or is able to work 80–100 hours per week. Maybe he should have given the Unilever management more attention after all, been more consistent in helping them to further stimulate purpose-driven thinking across the organisation.

His calling in outside help from Valerie Keller to get the top brass at the company to think about their personal investment in the future of the USLP last year had been an admission of weakness. He should really have done it himself. If he had spent more time listening to them and given them more freedom to speak publicly then it would have become much more of a team effort and the ULE would have been more effective *as* a team. In any case, he believes that he made mistakes more often than he did things well. But he also made sure that the things he did do right carried the most weight. He understands that not everyone sees it that way. That's the fate of the pioneer. Recognition only comes afterwards. Polman is well aware that he's currently five or maybe even ten years ahead of the curve. Not when it comes to NGOs or governments, they've made their support of him clear enough. But from the perspective of shareholders he's still a radical.

He thinks it's terrible that the financial markets have only become even more short-termist over the past few years. The speculative dimension of the economy has become even more dominant in comparison to the actual economy. And that means that financial results are becoming more important with every passing quarter. In order to keep investors happy, publicly listed companies on Wall Street now hand over almost 100 per cent of their profits to their shareholders in the form of dividends or share purchases. Sometimes even more. Unilever hasn't escaped this either, much to his deep sadness. Polman sees these developments as nothing short of disastrous. Companies should be using their profits to invest in their employees and developing sustainable, innovative products and services.

At the same time, he's still proud of the sharp increase in Unilever share prices under his leadership. Measuring from the low point of the share price in March 2009, Unilever's shares have since increased in value by almost 270 per cent. Over the same period, Procter & Gamble and Nestlé's share prices increased by 155 per cent and 191 per cent, respectively. However, this still hasn't quite made up for the many years of stagnating investor trust in Unilever shares in the 15 years before Polman's arrival. An investor who bought the equivalent of €1,000 of shares in Unilever, $1,000 of shares in Procter & Gamble or CHF1000 in Nestlé 25 years ago back in 1994 would have shares worth €5,900, $6,700 or CHF8300, respectively, today.

Those companies haven't achieved this increase entirely thanks to their own efforts. Obviously, the former Unilever CEO knows that the central banks have pumped an incredible amount of money into the world economy over the past few years. That money is out there looking for returns and it has to go somewhere. That goes some way to explaining the increases in share price.

This financial world now needs to pivot, quickly and dramatically. It's essential. Call him a know-it-all, call him naïve, but Paul Polman refuses to accept the system the way it is. He will keep on being provocative. At the end of January he had run into Larry Fink at Davos. He'd laughed as he asked the boss of BlackRock how he'd like to get a letter from a couple of big companies including Unilever: a 'Dear Larry' letter rather than the yearly 'Dear CEO' letter he writes himself. Maybe that will be a way for them to get him to start putting all his pretty words into practice and actually do something. When it comes to moving his company's investments into sustainable initiatives, the biggest investor in the world is still under performing woefully.

The CEO of BlackRock had been visibly uncomfortable and said that now wasn't the right time. Polman understands; he knows Fink is embedded in a culture on which Polman's way of thinking has made scarcely any impression. American politicians who make the case for a stakeholder model, like the recent Democratic candidate Elizabeth Warren, are suspected of wanting to increase the role of government and soon written off as dangerous socialists.

He's convinced that he'll be proven right eventually. The price of this vindication is only going up as time drags on. He estimates that we've only got about fifteen years left to get the climate back on track. Sometimes he worries that it'll take a couple of major disasters for the world to wake up to the crisis. Hasn't that always been the way? We obviously need to feel the pain and see the costs first-hand before we're willing to do something about it. Disasters change behaviour immediately, from one day to the next. Australians take much shorter showers overall since they had a period of extreme drought and experienced what effects a shortage of water had on their lives.

At the same time, this scenario drives him crazy. How many disasters does it take to wake people up? He estimates that around $500 billion in additional damages is already being incurred each year as a result of climate change. The only thing is that these damages are seldom labelled as such, with hurricane damage or floods instead being framed as unavoidable mishaps. This damage needs to be linked more explicitly to the climate crisis.

The predictions of investors and financial analysts, which are based on historical data, pose another significant problem. These predictions still barely take into account things like a tax on CO_2 emissions. Because those kinds of taxes are still in their infancy, they simply don't count them. One light at the end of the tunnel is the fact that various European countries, including the Netherlands, have now introduced such a tax or have plans to do so.

On this score, he'd also been pleased to see the Dutch National Bank carry out its first 'climate stress test' at the end of last year. In it, the Dutch banks and pension fund watchdog had calculated what it would mean for those industries if the tax on CO_2 emissions rose to $100 per tonne. They projected that Dutch financial institutions would lose around €111 billion in capital because of how dramatically they would have to adjust the value of investments in energy-intensive industries. The president of the Dutch National Bank, Klaas Knot, had told *NRC* *Handelsblad* that a scenario in which this 'legislative shock' was combined with a 'technology shock' seemed the most likely to him. Because obsolete technology will need to be replaced in favour of new technological advances at such an accelerated rate, around €159 billion in capital will simply evaporate. The message from the watchdog is clear: the timely implementation of climate legislation could limit the future negative effects of climate change. It's as if Paul Polman's listening to himself.

This isn't the only light at the end of the tunnel he sees. Since 2017, listed companies in Europe have had to explain how they deal with non-financial information such as their impact on the environment, human rights and diversity in each of their annual reports. These now rather short paragraphs will get longer the more that consumers, employees and investors ask to see such accounts. That will help the fund managers at big investment companies to slowly shift their course and change their behaviour.

His successor Alan Jope is of the same mind but is wary of getting too far ahead of the pack. In his first week as CEO, Jope had come to the Rotterdam head office to introduce himself. He'd found it rather tense. These Dutch colleagues have had it rather rough, the margarines division, the Dutch

Unilever-DNA, has been sold off and the single, unified head office won't be coming to the Netherlands after all. How will they receive him?

In advance of the meeting, he'd put down four main points on paper. Unilever is going to start growing again. Since the sustainable brands are growing 70 per cent faster than the rest, there will be no watering down of the USLP. The organisation's structure will remain the same. He is going to focus on increasing diversity and inclusion. But most of his Dutch colleagues' questions are about him. They want to know what kind of man he is. Jope had already emphasised that he wasn't Polman and that a 60-hour working week was more than enough for him. When Jope can't see a young female colleague who is trying to ask a question, he gestures to the hundreds of colleagues sitting before him to lean out of the way so he can see her. The Scot had been shocked at his own theatrical gesticulating and joked that he needed telling if he started getting too big for his boots.

He had promised to make good on the agreements that his predecessor had been forced to make with the shareholders. Just like Polman, he has compiled a list of nine operational indicators that will be the main focus in the constant discussions of how things are going. The only difference is that they're now called the '9 for 2019' list. However, to the relief of many of his colleagues, Jope does reverse Polman's 2014 decision not to appoint a replacement for Harish Manwani. Nitin Paranjpe will take on the role of COO.

Jope also makes it clear to his audience in Rotterdam that after the fiasco of the last few months, unifying the company doesn't even make his list of his top 10 priorities for now. The fact that it has been raised so emphatically probably means that he will have to start looking into it again next year, however. His declaration that as far as he is concerned Rotterdam is still in the top 5 options is a tiny plaster on this wound.

The next day, Jope had gone along for meetings at *Het Financieele Dagblad* and *De Telegraaf*; the relationship with the Dutch media needed repairing after disastrous closing months of the previous year. Unilever's Dutch press officers had suggested taking their time and having Jope do substantial interviews with these big papers further down the line but their British colleagues had objected to this approach. The new CEO needed to do some trial runs and get to know these media outlets first. Jope explained to editors from the *Financial Times* that Unilever's relations with the media had gotten a little bit rusty and were in need of some TLC. When the journalists told him about his predecessor's bizarre habit of complaining to them about the lack of positive coverage, Jope had nodded and told them he'd got the message.

Jope took various opportunities to thank Polman: 'As I take on the new job, I must thank & recognise Paul Polman for his immense contribution to

Unilever and to the world.'[3] He tells the *Financial Times* that Unilever will mostly be investing in expanding the personal care division going forward. This is where they have the biggest margins. 'In food, we will buy some stuff, not as much, and continue to dispose of assets that are intrinsically slower growth.'[4] At a shareholder meeting in Rotterdam, Jope says that Unilever has 'an urgent mission to provide for the desires and instincts of people and thereby make a positive contribution to the big problems facing the world'. He also emphasises that purpose cannot be given greater importance than profit in this process, but that a purpose-driven approach will lead to greater profits.

Commentators in various media outlets say that Jope's appointment represents the return of a normal CEO to the helm of Unilever, one who intends to focus on selling as many bottles of Dove and Magnum ice lollies as possible from now on. First we make money, then we do good.

Alan Jope hopes that governments will be the ones to take the lead in shaping the landscape of sustainability. It would be wonderful if, going forwards, British legislation made companies responsible for more than just the interests of shareholders. Even he sees that things are completely one-sided right now. Broadening company's responsibilities would mean that other interests could carry more weight and companies like Unilever would have space to allow themselves to be led by the goals set out in the USLP.

His 'advisor-predecessor' has rather radical ideas about what that might look like. Paul Polman thinks that Unilever should spend the next few years working on becoming a benefit corporation. A 'B-Corp', of which there are currently around 1,000, has a distinct legal status in the United States. That status offers protection against aggressive shareholders intent on making a quick buck because there are statutes establishing that their interests must be balanced against the interests of all the other stakeholders. B-Corps have made earning money formally and legally subordinate to their specific social goals, therefore also ensuring that the vast majority of their profits are invested in those same good causes.

Thus far, Polman has been laughed off the stage whenever he has suggested that they turn Unilever into a B-Corp. In order to receive this status, a company has to meet very specific criteria, and is bound, so to speak, to buying a particular kind of palm oil, tea or tomatoes at the local level because only those select products meet with the stated criteria. Experts believe that Unilever is simply too big to do this. Not to mention too publicly listed. Polman parries this criticism by stating that Danone, another listed company, around half of Unilever's size in terms of turnover, is seriously working on doing just that. Danone's American daughter company has already qualified for B-Corps status.

Along with Jay Coen Gilbert, one of the founders of the B-Corp movement back in 2006, Polman is investigating how they might accelerate this process for big companies like Unilever. He thinks that it has to be possible for Unilever to achieve this status in the next five years or so. He hopes that in the meantime governments will make more effort to facilitate this form of social enterprise through legislation. The Dutch Organisation for Economic Cooperation and Sustainable Development is hoping the same thing. This organisation has just called on the Dutch government to do something about the lack of institutional recognition for social enterprise.[5]

In the meantime, Unilever is cautiously growing in that direction from the inside out, as it were. Ben & Jerry's was one of the very first companies to be awarded B-Corps status way back when the movement started. Polman has taken over a couple of B-Corps like Seventh Generation laundry detergent, the tea company Tazo and condiments business Sir Kensington's over the past few years. Time and again, companies founded by activists – people who believe that enterprise is the best way to address social problems – have proven to have the least trouble bridging the gap between doing good and earning money.

They are without a doubt the most important motors of and inspirations for sustainable thinking inside Unilever. Polman would have liked to have taken over more of these companies over the past ten years. But it takes a lot of time to win the trust of these kinds of entrepreneurs. You need to build a reputation that convinces them their philosophy will remain intact and be elevated even further. The fact that Ben & Jerry's original philosophy is still alive and kicking after 20 years of being in business with Unilever is an enormous help on this front.

It had certainly been one of the key inducements for Jaap Korteweg, the founder of The Vegetarian Butcher, to enter exclusive talks with Unilever before agreeing to a merger in December 2018. Korteweg is convinced that a takeover by Unilever is the quickest way for him to make the greatest possible impact with his range of meat substitutes. Back when he founded the business nine years previously he came up with a business plan that he's never had to modify: he wants to become the biggest producer of meat substitutes in the world. With the marketing and retail power of Unilever behind him, he hopes for significant investment in optimising his products. Fully aware that consumers never want to pay more for anything, he assumes that Unilever's upscaling of production will bring with it a quick reduction in prices. That should enable them to reach €1 billion in sales by 2023, almost 50 times the amount he made in 2018. Any less and this pioneer will be disappointed.

The son of a farmer, Korteweg likes to summarise his dramatic school career by saying he certainly didn't learn anything and claims to have always wanted to work outdoors, ideally as a woodsman. His father had taught him at an early age that human over-consumption was killing the natural world he loved so much. And he'd seen as much first-hand. After a day spent working too intensively with pesticides, the young farmer ended up in the hospital in life-threating condition.

After the swine fever outbreak of 1999, when more than a million pigs had to be culled, 37-year-old Korteweg decided to become a vegetarian. The suffering of animals had become too much for him. Twelve years later, the entrepreneur realised that you didn't need to stop people eating meat, only to stop people eating animals. People have no desire to eat a cow or a pig, they just want a delicious steak or schnitzel on their plate. He came to the conclusion that there was only one solution for meat-addicted humanity: making something plant based so delicious that it satisfies the desire for meat. The whole world stands to profit. Around 70 per cent of all agricultural land is currently used to sustain the billions of animals destined to be consumed by people each year. You only need at most 20 per cent of all agricultural land to produce plant-based meatballs and 'chicken' pieces. This could mean a dramatic reduction in environmental impact.

No bank, not a single investor, wanted to finance his plans to develop plant-based meat. People thought it was a crazy, unachievable aim. So Korteweg ploughed his own savings into the research. He gave himself a 10 per cent chance of success but knew he had to give it a try. In 2010, he opened his shop – modelled on a traditional butcher's shop – and in 2013, his meatballs came third in a competition looking for the 'golden meatball'. Five years later, his company has an annual turnover of €25 million.

Obviously, Korteweg has received criticism since agreeing to the takeover. How can he sell his soul to a publicly listed multinational like Unilever? He's explained many times that Unilever's desire to make money from his products is a prerequisite for increasing the impact of his meat substitutes, not a disadvantage. He doesn't want The Vegetarian Butcher to remain a nice, well-meaning, 'cuddly' brand stuck in a small niche.

Jaap Korteweg was won over by the enthusiasm of the people he spoke to from Unilever. He sold all of his shares without making any stipulations in advance. He isn't employed by Unilever either. But just like with Ben & Jerry's, his face is on every pack. Whatever happens, Korteweg will spend the next five years trying to increase sales as quickly as possible. He has no reservations about the Unilever managers who will likely soon have to begin making cuts and tinkering with the quality. Just as in the case of the founders of Ben & Jerry's ice cream, Unilever will want to avoid getting into any arguments with him. They may have bought his mission outright but they'll have to keep taking him seriously too. It's in their interest to maintain a united front.

It's in his interest too, come to that. This sale could end up netting him hundreds of millions of euros. Several tens of millions are already earmarked for Korteweg's next project: making milk out of grass without cows. The first prototype of a machine to do this is already under construction. During a lecture in Breda, Korteweg told the Unilever Benelux managers that he'd be coming to them with this discovery in 10 years' time. Surrounded by Unilever managers, Korteweg had felt at ease. They surprised him too. He heard them all talking about their quest for 'purpose'. The word came up continuously. If he's being honest, he has no idea what they're talking about. Surely it's self-evident that you want to find some kind of meaning in this life? You *know* what that is, you don't just *talk* about it, you go and *do* it. Korteweg hopes that the trust many consumers have in The Vegetarian Butcher will help to compensate for the distrust that Unilever has faced over the past few years. In any case, it's clear that Unilever has a few things to learn from his company too.

Alan Jope still needs a little bit of time to get used to this idea. In the *Financial Times*, the new CEO calls the takeover of The Vegetarian Butcher an 'experimental foray'. He explains: 'Plant-based eating is a megatrend and so the most important thing is making sure vegan and vegetarian options are available across our core brands.'[6] Jaap Korteweg is reassured when he hears that his meat substitutes have been embraced as a top strategic priority at a meeting of the ULE a couple of weeks later. The Unilever managers have no doubt been inspired by trajectory of the American vegetarian hamburger manufacturer Beyond Meat's share price since it's official stock market launch that May. With sales of around $90 million, Beyond Meat is about three times the size of The Vegetarian Butcher. Investors believe in the company, it's already worth almost $12 billion just two months later. The explosion in demand for meat substitutes in the United States means that analysts are already predicting a value of over $20 billion by 2024.

Paul Polman doesn't want to say goodbye. He certainly doesn't want to spend too much time dwelling on it. That would make it seem like he was actually retiring. But he has to say goodbye, it's what you do. There are people who want to wish him well and bid farewell properly, including in Rotterdam.

In the Rotterdam head office, they've arranged a parody of the classic Dutch TV programme *In de hoofdrol*, based on the American and British show *This is Your Life*. Conny Braams is dressed up as the show's presenter Mies Bouwman and presents the farewell event together with Harry Brouwer, who's donned an orange suit for the occasion. Braams announces her guests in the breathlessly enthusiastic voice for which Bouwman was always known. Some of them appear live, others have send in video clips. Louise Fresco, Queen Maxima, Princess Laurentien, Kitty van der Heijden, Anniek Mauser, former Dutch prime minister Jan Peter Balkenende, Johan de Koning and Kees van der Waaij shower the 'retired' Polman with praise. They sing a song together. Brouwer helps Polman's 90-year-old mother onto the podium. She tells them how proud she is of her pig-headed son, who sometimes listens but mostly doesn't. The son in question can't hold back a few tears.

Some guests remember the leaving parties for Polman's predecessors. They had all been knighted on this occasion. Burgmans was made a Commander of the Order of Oranje-Nassau; Tabaksblat was made a Grand Officer of the Order of Oranje-Nassau. The organisers hadn't even thought to ask for something similar in this case. Hardly any external guests were invited either.

Some of those there find the occasion uncomfortable, sensing a touch of sadness when they see Polman's emotional reaction. They can see that these are exactly the kinds of moments in which he feels misunderstood, and there have been plenty of these moments over the past few months. Polman is still trying to insist that this isn't goodbye, and that he's going to keep on pursuing his mission. He's allergic to the word 'pension', there's still so much to be done.

Over the next few years, he'll keep on pushing to create more space so that companies like Unilever can do good. He's pleased that the rest of the world won't see him as a businessman anymore; that time is over. This one-dimensional idea about doing business will finally burden him no longer.

It's only natural that the failed coup by Kraft Heinz two years earlier comes up during the leaving party. The guests reflect on what might have happened to Unilever if they'd pulled it off. Polman takes great satisfaction in pointing out that the prediction he made two years ago is coming true. Back then, the stock markets were still trumpeting Kraft Heinz as the champion of the new business model, now it's being written off as a company that's still hopelessly stuck in a mantra of cost-cutting, a company that is no longer capable of listening to the desires of its clients at all. The 'buy-squeeze-repeat' model only works if you keep buying new things and squeezing them quickly enough. It also requires that there's something left to squeeze in the first place. Even worse, they've spent the last three years reducing expenditure on R&D and advertising by 10 per cent each year. The belief that big brands, with brand trust built up over decades, always retain their value is being eroded after all. Since the summer of 2016, the fifth biggest food company in the world has seen zero growth, remaining flat at a value of around $26 billion. Investors have lost most of their faith in the company. Just before the coup on Unilever failed, a share in Kraft Heinz was worth almost $97, now it's not worth much more than $30. The Brazilians from 3G capital have lost billions on paper and last year reduced their stake in the company from 29 per cent to 22 per cent.

Polman hopes that people will have learned some big lessons from all this and says as much to his 58,000 followers on Twitter: 'Sad to see this form of capitalism being celebrated still. Billionaires versus billions of people we should be serving. At times wonder if they would have been able to destroy Unilever as well. Millions more would have suffered.'[7]

The failure of Kraft Heinz leaves him optimistic. Trust in those kinds of companies is now so eroded that even the United States seems to be changing its tune slightly. Various Democratic presidential candidates, opponents of Donald Trump, believe in the need for radical change on this score. Jamie Dimon, the CEO of JPMorgan Chase, the bank that would have acted as guarantor for the financing of Kraft Heinz's takeover of Unilever, will soon be the first to sign a manifesto designed to challenge the prevailing agenda of creating returns for shareholders.

The CEOs of the 181 largest American companies will sign the 'Statement on the Purpose of a Corporation' saying that serving the interests of clients, employees, suppliers and communities in a sustainable way will lead to long-term value creation for shareholders. 'Each of our stakeholders is essential. We commit to deliver value to all of them, for the future success of our companies, our communities and our country.'[8]

For years, Polman has been railing against what he sees as the dated economic rules of play dominated by the thinking of Milton Friedman. For decades the business world focused on getting more freedom to operate, taking responsibility wasn't part of the main plan. That meant that the ever-demanding consumer was well taken care of but that the interests of citizens worried about the needs of society fell by the wayside. It was as if a massive separation took place. While the consumer lived the high life, the citizen began to suffer as a result. Most of the time, it was the billions of people who weren't in a position to consume very much who paid the highest price.

For Polman, this fact presents the key to change. As people begin to feel the pain of the citizen more sharply, they'll start making different choices as consumers. And that pain *is* being felt. June 2019 was the hottest month ever recorded worldwide. The need to attach a cost to these effects, so that polluters pay for what they're doing, will become ever more obvious to an increasing number of people. The tension between the concerned citizen and the penny-pinching consumer will slowly but surely decline. This will lead to the taming of the short-termist 'financial animal' in us because it will become clear that freedom and responsibility are two sides of the same coin. The lessons of Victor Frankel will finally be learnt.

Technology, especially, will be a big help in this, Polman anticipates, not least by linking production and consumption patterns more closely together and thereby making clear that there's only one world. That we've only got one world. He's placing his bets on the next generation. They have got the message. He sees as much when he talks to his three sons. They are more conscious in the choices they make and much more connected to the world around them. Young people practice mindfulness, meditation helps them to become aware of the way everything is connected together. They are going in search of their meaning, their purpose, and they're doing so en masse. This is where Polman sees the tipping point. The new generation looks for products and brands that are made by real, accountable people.

Education will also play a crucial role. Young economists are still being taught the same old message, based on quantitative analysis, that human beings will continue to increase and optimise their needs in a world defined by scarcity. It's incredibly important that the UN's Sustainable Development Goals are brought into education. That will challenge students to find out how they as economists, lawyers or business experts might be able to contribute to building a better world.

He's hopeful. Despite the cynicism he's been confronted with over the years, all those people who it turned out weren't willing to step outside their old ways of thinking, he's learned from experience that most people are willing to roll up their sleeves and work together. Nowadays he finds himself saying in almost every speech: he who wants to go fast travels alone, he who wants to go far travels with others. Polman will spend the years ahead looking for new travel companions. There's still a lot of scepticism to defeat. He's going to work harder than ever going forward.

At the beginning of July, on his last day as a Unilever employee, Polman announces the beginning of Imagine. This foundation will encourage the business world to make the SDGs the basis of their business. He and the other founders, including Valerie Keller, intend to assist heroic business leaders to get out of the comfort zone and take personal risks. He promises to invest a substantial amount of his personal fortune to get this new mechanism up and running. 'We are about to commit the biggest intergenerational crime in the history of mankind', he tells *The Guardian.* He explains how Imagine intends to prevent this. 'We are trying to create tipping points on a sectorial level.' He gives an example. According to Polman, around a hundred companies are responsible for 71 per cent of CO_2 emissions. 'Persuading a handful of these bosses to see the economic and moral benefit of changing their ways can create a race to the top. The premise is that chief executives in the private sector need to drive major change in the absence of politicians doing it right now. I tried to do the same with Unilever. It's a matter of willpower.'[9]

The same day he announces Imagine, Polman shares the news on Twitter quoting John Lennon's song with the same title: 'You may say I'm a dreamer, but I'm not the only one'.[10]

The person reading his timeline finishes the refrain almost without thinking: *I hope someday you will join us. And the world will be as one.*

ACKNOWLEDGEMENTS

Is it possible? Can a large, publicly listed company like Unilever make money by doing the right thing? Or stronger still, can businessmen allow themselves to be guided by the desire to do good and put making money second?

That is the question with which I began this journey in April 2017. The direct impetus for the project was the €135 billion attempt by the billionaires behind the American company Kraft Heinz to take over Unilever. They had calculated that with drastic cost cutting they could each make around €50 billion.

At that time, Paul Polman had been the CEO of Unilever for eight years: A controversial CEO who was promoting a message of sustainability all over the world. According to him, there was only one way to 'save the soul of capitalism': businessmen had to invest in making the economy more sustainable. Inclusive capitalism geared towards the long term is the only option. And this is a self-interested move, don't forget, because at the end of the day no one can be successful in a world that is failing. Okay, but when is that going to happen? And what do we do in the meantime? Unilever needs the consumer to come along for the ride, to keep buying their products. Because the financial markets are merciless: anyone who doesn't earn enough in the next quarter is in trouble. This crucial and complicated balancing act is what I wanted to sketch out in this book.

The great battle is raging inside many of us. We are growing more and more worried about the changing climate, about plastic in the oceans, about food shortages, increasing poverty and overpopulation. We are coming to appreciate our planet's limits. Thinking about the next generation intensifies our sense of unease. But the minute we start consuming, working or investing, these worries recede into the background. Why should I be the one to pay now for the problems of tomorrow, for other people's problems? Why should I have to make do with lower profits today? The 'economic animal' in us takes over and works out what it all costs. Because we're allowed, because we can, because we don't want to steal from our own pockets. And everyone else is doing the same. Because charity begins at home.

While we ordinary people wrestle with our double morality, we wait for leaders to help us turn this unease into a sensible course of action. In the hope that they will make the loss tolerable.

Paul Polman is one of those leaders. For ten years, he was the boss of the British-Dutch multinational. After the financial crisis of 2008, he took up the mantle and resisted the prevailing 'the business of business is business' morality. He believes that in a globalised economy, national governments by definition are falling short and multinationals therefore need to take the initiative in making the economy sustainable. Earning money is a means, it can never be the end in itself. He wants to show people that when it comes down to it even a large, publicly listed company can only make money by doing good. If the producer of Knorr, Dover, Magnum and Hellman's can grow by caring more for the world then everyone can. All it takes is a little courage, patience and above all belief.

I met Paul Polman back in 2011. When he managed to repel the attack from Kraft Heinz at the beginning of 2017, I knew he had to become the subject of my next investigation. After my books about Dutch retailer Ahold (2004) and ABN Ambro bank (2008), which focused mostly on their failing leaders Cees van der Hoeven and Rijkman Groenink, I wanted to tell the story of a CEO who was a good example. A leader who had understood the most important lesson of the crisis of 2008 and was brave enough to lead the search for a 'responsible capitalism' and was trying, with much falling and getting up again, to realise his ideal.

The Great Battle goes back further. In order to understand why the Polman-Unilever combination was so exceptional, I describe the last twenty-five years of that company's history. I make the occasional digression to decades before that to show how the company had already tried to lead the way in making a sustainable world. Not out of altruism, mind you, but out of conscious self-interest.

Over the 2 years I spent writing, I carried out 163 interviews with (former) Unilever board members, directors, employees and advisers. I also spoke with directors and executors of pension funds, politicians, civil servants, accountants, suppliers and competitors. I am sincerely grateful for their time and trouble. These meetings were highly educational and took me all over the world. In total, at least fifty requests for interviews were denied. I found out that Unilever is still made up of two companies. On the Dutch side, I was given 'passive support', because the book was going to come out in the end either way. On the British side of the company (but also among British bankers, advisers etc.) the enthusiasm was more limited and I often faced the question of what they stood to gain from helping me with my project.

With the aim of producing an accurate and inspiring history, I built my story out of a combination of my interviewees' memories and all available texts, presentations, books, articles, annual reports, published interviews and speeches. I always explained to them: We're speaking on an off-the-record basis, which means that I will use the information I receive but won't quote you directly. I also won't tell anyone that you spoke to me. I wrote the story from the perspective of an omniscient narrator in the hope that it would lead to a readable reconstruction of events and allow me to reach an optimum balance of believability and accessibility.

A caveat is necessary here. Unilever is an enormous company in which tens of thousands of managers in 198 countries have worked selling around two hundred billion products per year over the last twenty-five years. I wasn't there, and look at this history from today's perspective and with today's knowledge. *The Great Battle* is my 'impressionistic' summary, mostly based on the stories of those I interviewed. Just as with ABN AMRO in *The Prey* and Ahold in *The Ahold Drama*, I have discovered that we all favour our own memories, but that those memories all contain at their heart something that most of the people concerned would recognise. That is the story I have tried to write. The overwhelming majority of the facts are a matter of public record or were presented or corroborated by at least two different interviewees. Where two versions of events emerged, I've opted for a description that seems the most likely in light of the context of the whole situation. If any inaccuracies remain in the book then I am very sorry.

In the end, the great battle also rages inside me. As I was piecing together this puzzle I realised how brave it is to turn against the tide and challenge the present system. A lonely pioneer like Polman is constantly surrounded with scepticism, misunderstanding and suspicion. The reality is that maybe 1 per cent of people actually worry about the end of the world and the rest worry about the end of the month. I fear that we will only spring into action once the world is collapsing, when the planet's limitations really begin to hit us. Paul Polman doesn't accept that. Why should we sit and wait for even more disasters? He keeps on hammering home the point that if we continue to do nothing then the costs are soon going to be much greater. But still only very few companies and CEOs have followed his example; they fear the sentiments of the finance markets, which are just as led by short-term profit as they have ever been. Polman is right, the question is above all whether he is going to make it in time, and whether we are able to make this great course correction together in time. I hope that this story will help us to do it.

A number of people have been an enormous help to me during the writing of this book. First and foremost, my Publisher Mai Spijkers, who was immediately enthusiastic when I came to him with the idea for it back in April 2017. My thanks to Editor Marieke van Oostrom for her professional guidance. I thank Thomas van den Bergh for his sharp editorial eye and Geert Dekker for checking as many facts as possible. Roland Dorhout Mees, Martijn Bennis, Joost Kuiper and Reinout van Lennep formed my most important sounding board on content during the writing process. Four wise friends who were good enough to provide me with all sorts of good advice in a friendly but insistent tone. Without them, this book would have been twice as thick.

Darling, darling Doret, thank you so much for being willing to give me the space to be elsewhere with my thoughts. But most of all I'm grateful to you for being there and keeping me inspired when I doubted myself, when the search for this story faltered. I wrote this story for our three amazing children, Jack (15), Rover (14) and Kate (9). How could I do any different? The reason is simple, and this book is steeped in it: We were not given this world by our parents, we only borrow it from our children.

Amsterdam, 1 September 2019

NOTES

Chapter 1: Mea Culpa, We're Completely in the Wrong

1 Geoffrey Jones, *Renewing Unilever: Transformation and Tradition* (Oxford: Oxford University Press, 2005), 251.
2 'Hoe Floris Maljers het slapende Unilever wakker schudde' (How Floris Maljers Shook Unilever from its Slumber), *NRC Handelsblad*, February 25, 1994.
3 Pieter Couwenbergh and Hein Haenen, *De regels en het spel. Gesprekken met Morris Tabaksblat* (The Rules and the Game. Conversations with Morris Tabaksblat) (Amsterdam: Atlas Contact, 2007), 77.
4 Harry Meijer and Paul Wessels, 'De tragikomische soap-opera van Omo Power' (The Tragicomic Soap Opera of Omo Power), *NRC Handelsblad*, June 25, 1994.
5 Couwenbergh and Haenen, *De regels en het spel*, Chapters 8 and 9.
6 Ibid.
7 Ibid.
8 Ibid.

Chapter 2: Two Captains, One Helm

1 *Corporate Leader and Global Citizen. Een portret van Antony Burgmans in 16 persoonlijk verhalen* (Corporate Leader and Global Citizen. A Portrait of Antony Burgmans in 16 Personal Stories), book presented at Burgmans's farewell celebration in 2007.
2 C. K. Prahalad and Stuart L. Hart, 'The Fortune at the Bottom of the Pyramid', *Strategy + Business*, January 10, 2002.
3 Dirk Sampselle, *Unilever – Ben & Jerry's. A Merger for Good?* MBA Research Paper (Pepperdine University, 2012).
4 Brad Edmondson, *Ice Cream Social. The Struggle for the Soul of Ben & Jerry's* (Oakland: Berrett-Koehler, 2014), 157–65.
5 Kathryn Tully, 'My Liquidity Moment: Ben Cohen of Ben & Jerry's', *Financial Times*, June 23, 2010.
6 Observer Business, 'That's Not Sir to You', *The Observer*, February 24, 2002.
7 Couwenbergh and Haenen, *De regels en het spel. Gesprekken met Morris Tabaksblat*, 153.

Chapter 3: Mutinous Men; We Can't Go On Like This

1 *Unilever Magazine*, Issue 128, 2003.
2 Arjan Overwater and Thomas W. Malnight, 'Unilever's Path to Growth: Reflections on a Journey in Progress', *Human Resources in the 21st Century*, edited by Marc Effron, Robert Handossy and Marshall Goldsmith (Hoboken: Wiley, 2003), 203–13, 212.
3 'Unilever FitzGerald Remains on the Path to Growth', *The Independent*, February 14, 2003.
4 Larry Elliot, 'Cleaning Agent: Interview with Niall FitzGerald', *The Guardian*, July 5, 2003.
5 'Robert Polet', *De Volkskrant*, April 12, 2008.
6 'Chairmen's Report', Unilever Annual Review 2004.
7 Erik Weihenmayer, *Touch the Top of the World: A Blind Man's Journey to Climb Farther Than the Eye Can See* (New York: Plume, 2001).
8 'Nestlé Taps P&G-Veteran Polman for Key Job in Rare Look Outside', *Wall Street Journal*, September 27, 2005.
9 'Gevoel voor cijfers en mensen' (A Feel for Numbers and People), *NRC Handelsblad*, November 2, 2005.

Chapter 4: A French Bookkeeper Puts Share Price Centre Stage

1 'Patrick Cescau: Unilever's X-factor that Kills 99% of All Known Failings', *The Independent*, October 15, 2005.
2 'Strategy and Leadership in Action', Speech by Patrick Cescau, January 18, 2006.
3 Ibid.
4 Ibid.
5 Francisco S. Homem de Mello, *The 3G-way. Dream, People, Culture* (Lisbon: 10X, 2014).
6 Cristiane Correa, *Dream Big*, translated by John Fitzpatrick and Monica Pan Chacon (Rio de Janeiro: Primeira Pessoa, 2014), 30.
7 'Crisismanager', *FEM Business*, February 18, 2006.
8 Kees van der Graaf, *Defining Moments. What Every Leader Should Know about Balancing Life* (Lausanne: IMD International, 2011).

Chapter 5: Outsiders in Charge

1 *Adding Vitality to Life*, Leverhulme Annual Review 2006.
2 'Unilever Executives Embark on Soul-searching', *Financial Times*, September 12, 2007.
3 'State of the Nation', Speech by Patrick Cescau, November 27, 2007.
4 'Nestlé-topman Paul Polman vergeet zijn hoesnummer nooit' (Top Man at Nestlé Paul Polman Never Forgets Where he Came From), *Twentevisie*, June 2006.
5 'Nestlé's CEO to Wall Street: I Did It My Way', *Fortune*, February 12, 2008.

6 'In Surprise Move, Unilever Names Polman CEO', *Ad Age*, September 4, 2008.
7 Laurentien van Oranje and Jeroen Smit, *Nog lang en gelukkig. Voorleesboek voor volwassenen die de weg een beetje kwijt zijn* (Happily Ever After. A Reading Book for Adults Who've Lost Their Way a Little) (Amsterdam: Prometheus, 2016).
8 Tom Malnight, Tracey Keys and Kees van der Graaf, *Ready? The 3Rs of Preparing Your Organisation for the Future* (Rivaz: Strategy Dynamics Global, 2013), 25.

Chapter 6: Only Responsible Companies Go the Distance

1 'Polman Tears Up Unilever Targets', *Thisismoney.co.uk*, February 6, 2009.
2 Thomas Dreier, *How Viscount Leverhulme Built His World Wide Organization* (Cincinnati: Whitefish, 2012).
3 'Going from Grey to Green, Environmental Policy for Unilever efdc Companies', Unilever Report, February 1990, pp. 6–11.
4 *Corporate leader and global citizen. Een portret van Antony Burgmans in 16 persoonlijke verhalen*35.
5 'Sustainability, Unilever's Approach', Speech by Iain Anderson, March 5, 1997.
6 Hans Broekhoff and Jan-Kees Vis, *Sustainable Development and Unilever. Putting the Corporate Purpose into Action*, Unpublished Manuscript, 1997.
7 *Vrijblijvend verantwoordelijk. Ben ik vrij om onverschillig te zijn?* ('At liberty to be responsible. Am I free to be indifferent?'), De Veer Stichting Lecture, 1996.
8 Paul Polman, 'A Business Perspective on Sustainability', Procter & Gamble Sustainability Report, 2000, 5.
9 'Unilever's Updated Environmental Strategy', October 2000; internal memo with feedback from an earlier discussion with Executive Committee, November 2002.
10 N. Craig Smith and Robert Crawford, *Unilever and Oxfam. Understanding the Impacts of Business on Poverty* (Fontainebleau: INSEAD, 2008).
11 Jason Clay, *Exploring the Links between International Business and Poverty Reduction. A Case Study of Unilever in Indonesia*, Oxfam and Unilever Study (Eynsham: Information Press, 2005), 13.
12 'Beyond Corporate Responsibility', Speech by Patrick Cescau, May 25, 2007.
13 Philip H. Mirvis, 'Unilever's Drive for Sustainability and CSR – Changing the Game', *Organizing for Sustainability*, edited by Susan Albers Mohrman and Abraham B. (Rami) Shani (Bingley: Emerald Books, 2011), 41–72, 46.
14 Bradley K. Googins, Philip H. Mirvis and Steven A. Rochlin, *Beyond Good Company. Next Generation Corporate Citizenship* (New York: Palgrave Macmillan, 2007), 52.
15 Ibid., 5.
16 'Ik weet niet wat voor bos dat was' ('I didn't know what kind of forest it was'), *De Volkskrant*, November 11, 2008.
17 Christian Conrad and Marjorie Ellis Thompson, *The New Brand Spirit. How Communicating Sustainability Builds Brands, Reputations and Profits* (New York: Routledge, 2016), 85.
18 *Back to the Taj Mahal Hotel*, Documentary film by Carina Mollier, 2017.
19 https://www.unilever.com/about/who-we-are/our-leadership/leena-nair.html.

Chapter 7: Growing, Growing, Growing [...] and Doing Good

1 Brian Lewis, *So Clean. Lord Leverhulme, Soap and Civilization* (Manchester: Manchester University Press, 2008), 16–19.
2 Dreier, *How Viscount Leverhulme Built His World Wide Organization*, 13.
3 Samuel Smiles, *Self-Help* (Mineola, NY: Dover, 2016), 4–9.
4 Charles Wilson, *The History of Unilever: A Study in Economic Growth and Social Change* (London: Cassell, 1954), Vol. 1, 37–40.
5 Wim Wennekes, *De aartsvaders. Grondleggers van het Nederlandse bedrijfsleven* ('The Patriarchs. Founders of the Dutch Business World') (Amsterdam: Olympus Pockets, 1993), 261.
6 Dreier, *How Viscount Leverhulme Built His World Wide Organization*, 16.
7 W.P. Jolly, *Lord Leverhulme. A Biography* (London: Constable, 1976), 38–39.
8 Stork in the UK, and Country Crock and Imperial in the US are derived from the Blue Band recipe.
9 Wilson, *The History of Unilever*, Vol. 2, 263–64.
10 Ibid., 304.
11 Ibid., 313.
12 Ibid., 342.
13 'Karambir Kang. The Stoic', *Forbes India*, December 29, 2009.
14 Edmondson, *Ice Cream Social. The Struggle for the Soul of Ben & Jerry's*, 212–29.
15 'McKinsey Conversations with Global Leaders: Paul Polman of Unilever', mckinsey.com, October 2009.
16 van Oranje and Smit, *Nog lang en gelukkig. Voorleesboek voor volwassenen die de weg een beetje kwijt zijn*, 67.
17 William W. George et al, 'Unilever's Paul Polman: Developing Global Leaders', Harvard Business School Case 413-097, May 2013.

Chapter 8: It's Not a Job, It's a Calling

1 'Lunch with the FT: Niall FitzGerald', *Financial Times*, July 25, 2014.
2 'Unilever Leadership Development Programme, Finding Your True North', Four Acres, Alumni Manual.
3 Nick Craig, *Leading from Purpose. Clarity and the Confidence to Act When it Matters Most* (New York/Boston: Nicholas Brealey Publishing, 2018).
4 Bill George, *Discover Your True North. Becoming an Authentic Leader* (Hoboken: John Wiley & Sons, 2015), 164.
5 George et al., 'Unilever's Paul Polman: Developing Global Leaders'.
6 UN Global Compact Leaders' Summit 2010 Summary Report.
7 Christopher A. Bartlett, 'Unilever's New Global Strategy: Competing through Sustainability', Harvard Business School Case 916-414, November 2015, 5.
8 'Verantwoord Unilever is ook eigenbelang' ('Sustainable Unilever is Self-Interest Too'), *Het Financieele Dagblad*, November 30, 2010.
9 Michael Skapinker, 'Corporate Plans May Be Lost in Translation', *Financial Times*, November 22, 2010.

Chapter 9: Colours to the Mast

1 Kamal Ahmed, 'Davos 2011: Unilever's Paul Polman Believes We Need to Think Long Term', *The Sunday Telegraph*, January 15, 2011.
2 Andrew Saunders, 'Profile of Paul Polman', *Management Today*, March 2011, 42–47.
3 Jo Confino, 'Paul Polman: The Power is in the Hands of the Consumers', *The Guardian*, November 21, 2011.
4 *Catalyzing Transformational Partnerships between the United Nations and Business*, New York 2011.

Chapter 10: But We Can't Do This Alone

1 *Wetenschappelijke Raad voor het Regeringsbeleid, Minder pretentie, Meer ambitie. Ontwikkelingshulp die verschil maakt* ('Research Council for Government Policy. Less pretention, more ambition. Development aid that makes a difference') (Den Haag, 2010), 21.
2 Joseph Bower, Herman Leonard and Lynn Paine, *Capitalism at Risk. Rethinking the Role of Business* (Boston: Harvard Business Review Press, 2011).
3 Jo Confino, 'Unilever's Paul Polman: Challenging the Corporate Status Quo', *The Guardian*, April 24, 2012.
4 Robert G. Eccles, Ioannis Ioannou and George Serafeim, 'The Impact of a Corporate Culture of Sustainability on Corporate Behavior and Performance', *Management Science*, Vol. 60, No. 11 (November 2014), 2835–57.
5 'Captain Planet', *Harvard Business Review*, June 2012.
6 Rick Tocquigny and Andy Butcher, *When Core Values are Strategic. How the Basic Values of Proctor & Gamble Transformed Leadership at Fortune 500 Companies* (Upper Saddle River: Financial Times/Prentice Hall, 2012).
7 'Duurzaamheid en winst zijn niet tegengesteld' ('Sustainability and Profit are Not in Opposition'), *De Volkskrant*, April 28, 2012.
8 Sanne van der Wal, 'Certified Unilever Tea: Small Cup, Big Difference?' *ssrn Electronic Journal*, October 31, 2011.
9 Schumpeter, 'Taking the Long View', *The Economist*, November 24, 2012.
10 Rachel Wilshaw, Liesbeth Unger, Do Quynh Chi and Pham Thu Thuy, *Labour Rights in Unilever's Supply Chain. From Compliance to Good Practice* (Oxford: Oxfam GB, 2013), 5.
11 Michael J. De La Merced and Andre Ross Sorkin, 'Berkshire and 3G Capital in a $23 billion Deal for Heinz', *The New York Times*, February 14, 2013.
12 Bob Fifer, *Double Your Profits in 6 Months or Less* (New York: Harper Collins, 1994).
13 Gordon Pitts, 'Paul Polman: Rebuilding Capitalism Form the Basics', *The Globe and Mail*, March 10, 2013.

Chapter 11: Making Money Can Never Be the Goal

1 Susilo Bambang Yudhoyono et al., *A New Global Partnership. Eradicate Poverty and Transform Economies through Sustainable Development. The Report of the High-Level Panel of Eminent Persons on the Post-2015 Development Agenda* (New York: UN Publications, 2013).

2 Oliver Balch, 'Sustainable Palm Oil: How Successful is RSPO Certification', *The Guardian,* July 4, 2013.

3 Fred Pearce, 'Unilever Plans to Double Its Turnover While Halving its Environmental Impact', *The Telegraph,* July 23, 2013.

4 Jo Confino, 'Unilever's Paul Polman on Diversity, Purpose and Profits', *The Guardian*, October 2, 2013.

5 George, *Discover Your True North. Becoming an Authentic Leader*, 164.

Chapter 12: The World's Biggest NGO

1 Scheherazade Daneshkhu, 'Stiffest Competition from Local Business, Says Unilever Chief', *Financial Times,* July 31, 2014.

2 'Wie der Unilever-chef die Welt retten will' ('How the Unilever boss wants to save the world'), *WirtschaftsWoche*, August 6, 2014.

3 'In Search of the Good Business', *The Economist*, August 9, 2014.

4 David Gelles, 'Unilever Finds that Shrinking its Footprint is a Giant Task', *The New York Times*, November 22, 2015.

5 van Oranje and Smit, *Nog lang en gelukkig. Voorleesboek voor volwassenen die de weg een beetje kwijt zijn.*

Chapter 13: More Priest Than CEO

1 Lillian Cunningham, 'The Tao of Paul Polman', *The Washington Post*, May 21, 2015.

2 Bartlett, 'Unilever's New Global Strategy: Competing through Sustainability', 5.

3 Matthew 6:24-34.

4 Pope Francis, *Laudato Si'. On Care for Our Common Home* (Rome, 2015).

5 Andy Boynton, 'Unilever's Paul Polman: CEO's can't be "Slaves" to Shareholders', *Forbes,* July 20, 2015.

6 www.unccd.int/sustainability-stability-security.

7 'Bangladesh's Climate Change Migrants', *The New Humanitarian*, November 13, 2015.

8 David Wallace-Wells, *The Uninhabitable Earth: Life after Warming* (London: Penguin, 2019), 42.

9 van Oranje and Smit, *Nog lang en gelukkig. Voorleesboek voor volwassenen die de weg een beetje kwijt zijn*, 55.

10 Paul Polman – 2015 Champions of the Earth Acceptance Speech, October 8, 2015.

11 Paul Polman, 'Where Does Business End and Society Begin?" (Open letter to his first grandchild), *Unilever.com*, September 25, 2015.

12 Laurence D. Fink, Letter to Executives, April 14, 2015, reprinted *Business Insider* businessinsider.com.

13 'Het Bono-complex van Unilever' (Unilever's Bono Complex), *Het Financieele Dagblad*, September 12, 2015.

14 Michael Skapinker and Scheherazade Daneshkhu, 'Can Unilever's Paul Polman Change the Way We Do Business?' *Financial Times*, September 29, 2016.

15 Presentation by Karen Hamilton during the Meaningful Brands Conference, Havas, July 2015.

16 '195 landen sluiten historisch klimaatakkoord in Parijs' (195 Countries Reach an Historic Climate Agreement in Paris), *De Volkskrant*, December 12, 2015.

17 Gemma Tillack et al., *Testing Commitments to Cut Conflict Palm Oil* (San Francisco: Rainforest Action Network, 2015).

18 *Enhancing Livelyhoods, Advancing Human Rights*. Unilever Human Rights Report (London/Rotterdam: Unilever, 2015).

Chapter 14: Too Far Ahead of His Troops

1 Kim Polman and Stephen Vasconcellos-Sharpe, *Imaginal Cells. Visions of Transformation* (London: Reboot the Future, 2017), 8.

2 Ibid.

3 *Unilever Sustainable Living Plan, Mobilising Collective Action: Summary of Progress 2015.*

4 Skapinker and Daneshkhu, 'Can Unilever's Paul Polman Change the Way We Do Business?'.

5 Dominic Barton, 'Capitalism for the Long Term', *Harvard Business Review*, March 2011.

6 'The City and Capitalism for the Long Term' the Tomorrow's Value Lecture given by Dominic Barton, Global Managing Director, McKinsey & Company London, May 15, 2013.

7 'Breaking the Tragedy of the Horizon – Climate Change and Financial Stability', speech Mark Carney, September 29, 2015.

8 Oliver Hart and Luigi Zingales, 'Companies Should Maximize Shareholder Welfare, Not Market Value', *Journal of Law, Finance and Accounting*, Vol. 2 (2017), 247–74: 254.

9 'Unilever moet het nu zonder rugwind van de lage rente doen' ('Unilever forced to do without the tailwind of low interest rates'), *Het Financieele Dagblad*, January 30, 2017.

10 Laura Alfaro et al., *Better Business Better World* (London: Business and Sustainable Development Commission, 2017).

Chapter 15: 'Rescued' by Warren Buffett

1 Vinod Shreeharsha, 'When Warren Met Jorge Paulo: Buffett and Lemann Recall their First Deal', *The New York Times*, April 10, 2017.

2 Correa, *Dream Big*, 30.

3 Arash Massoudi and James Fontanella-Khan, 'The $143bn Flop: How Warren Buffett and 3G Lost Unilever', *Financial Times*, February 21, 2017.

Chapter 16: A Mayor in Wartime

1 Scheherazade Daneshkhu, Jim Pickard and Arash Massoudi, 'Unilever Calls for Revamp UK Takeover Code after Kraft Bid', *Financial Times*, March 14, 2017.
2 George Parker, 'Theresa May Steps Back from Tough Stance on Foreign Investment', *Financial Times,* January 20, 2017.
3 'Werkgevers: stop uitverkoop Nederlandse bedrijven' ('Employers: stop the sell-off of Dutch companies'), *Het Financieele Dagblad*, March 30, 2017.

Chapter 17: For Sale: Dutch DNA, Milked Dry

1 Wennekes, *De aartsvaders. Grondleggers van het Nederlandse bedrijfsleven*, 223–26.
2 Pim Reinders, *Sam van den Bergh (1864–1941). Steeds voor alle arbeiders aanspreekbaar* (Sam van den Bergh (1864–1941). Always Approachable to All Employees) (Amsterdam: Balans, 2016), 29–40.
3 Wilson, *The History of Unilever*, Vol. 2, 36.
4 Wennekes, *De aartsvaders*, 233.
5 Reinders, *Sam van den Bergh*, 78.
6 Wennekes, *De aartsvaders*, 238.
7 Ibid., 248.
8 Reinders, *Sam van den Bergh*, 154–55.
9 Wilson, *The History of Unilever*, Vol. 2, 306–7.
10 Wennekes, *De aartsvaders*, 264.
11 Nils Pratley, 'Paul Polman: 'I Could Boost Unilever Shares. But Cutting Costs Is Not Our Way', *The Observer*, May 20, 2017.
12 'Memorandum on Questions Concerning the Dividend Tax', Dutch Ministry of Finance, April 28, 2017.
13 'Memorandum on Unilever Talks', Dutch Ministry of Finance, June 8, 2017.
14 Memorandum, 'Cover Letter of the Submission of Unilever's Bid Book', Dutch Ministry of Economic Affairs.
15 Graeme Pitkethly, 'Companies Must Come Clean on Climate Risks', *CNN Money Invest,* June 29, 2017.
16 *Buitenhof* (Dutch TV programme), December 10, 2017.
17 'Code in bedrijf' ('Code in business'), *Economisch-Statische Berichten*, August 10, 2017.
18 Scheherazade Daneshkhu and Lionel Barber, 'Unilever Delays Decision of UK or Netherlands as Sole HQ', *Financial Times*, November 29, 2017, 16.
19 Thomas Buckley, 'Unilever CEO Loses his Cool with Goldman Analyst at Investor Event', *Bloomberg*, December 1, 2017.
20 Mark Vandevelde and Scheherazade Daneshkhu, 'Unilever Starts Search for Successor to Paul Polman', *Financial Times*, November 24, 2017.

Chapter 18: 'Rotterdoom': Mission Impossible

1 Lex, 'Unilever: Seeking Safe Haven', *Financial Times*, February 21, 2018.
2 'Topvrouw Unilever: merken moeten vijanden durven maken' ('Top Woman at Unilever: brands need to be willing to make enemies'), *Het Financieele Dagblad*, December 9, 2018.
3 https://www.youtube.com/watch?v=5NiRNkULmiQ.
4 Julia Kollewe, 'Unilever Picks Rotterdam as Sole HQ but Denies Brexit Link', *The Guardian*, March 15, 2018.
5 Ibid.
6 Jonathan Guthrie, 'Unilever has Chosen to Protect Itself from British Capitalism', *Financial Times*, March 16, 2018.
7 Scheherazade Daneshkhu, 'Unilever Shareholder Balks at London HQ Move to Rotterdam', *Financial Times*, March 22, 2018.
8 Andrew Edgecliffe-Johnson, 'Unilever Chief Admits Kraft Heinz Bid Forced Compromises', *Financial Times*, February 27, 2018.
9 'Hoe religieus is duurzaamheid' ('How religious is sustainability'), lecture by René ten Bos, April 5, 2018.
10 Attracta Mooney, 'Andy Griffiths, the Cheery Scrapper Who Keeps UK PLC in Line', *Financial Times*, October 25, 2018.
11 WNL op Zondag, September 16, 2018.
12 'AmCham against Cabinet Proposal Abolishment Dividend Tax', Press release from AmCham, September 7, 2018.
13 *Buitenhof*, September 16, 2018.
14 https://www.out-standing.org/heroes/2018-top-50-male-executives/.
15 Neil Collins, 'Why Your Vote Matters at the Unilever Shareholder Meeting', *Financial Times*, September 21, 2018.
16 Marijn Dekkers, 'Why My Company Unilever is Shifting its UK-based HQ to the Netherlands', *The Telegraph*, September 25, 2018.

Chapter 19: The Pioneer Feels Misunderstood

1 Hannah Alcoseba Fernandez, 'What are the World's Biggest Plastic Polluters doing about the Problem?' *eco-business.com*, April 20, 2018.
2 'Top 10 Largest Plastic Producing Companies', *plastics-technology.com*.
3 Kim van de Wetering, 'Hanneke Faber: "Unilever mag misschien wel iets minder bescheiden zijn"', MT/SPROUT, August 20, 2018.
4 Ian King, 'Unilever U-turn a Resounding Victory for Shareholder-democracy', *Sky News*, October 5, 2018.
5 Guy Reading, 'HR Should be Laying the Road, Rather than Filling the Cracks. Our interview with Leena Nair', *learnerbly.com*.
6 'Paul Polman Closing Remarks', Unilever Investor Event 2018, Mumbai. December 5, 2018. https://www.youtube.com/watch?v=j3BvweC8D_I&t=114s.

Chapter 20: Paul Polman's Lonely High Road

1 Eric Whan, Tove Malmqvist et al., *SustainAbility Leaders Survey 2018* (San Francisco/London: Globescan/SustainAbility, 2018).
2 David M. Bersoff et al., *In Brands We Trust? Edelman Trust Barometer Special Report 2019*, edelman.com, June 18, 2019.
3 Alan Jope, Twitter, January 1, 2019.
4 Leila Abboud, 'New Unilever CEO Jope Banks on Recovery in Sales Growth', *Financial Times*, June 12, 2019.
5 Lamia Kamal-Chaoui et al., *Boosting Social Entrepreneurship and Social Enterprise Development in the Netherlands* (Paris: OECD/EU Commission, 2019).
6 Abboud, 'New Unilever CEO Jope Banks on Recovery in Sales Growth'.
7 Paul Polman, Twitter, February 24, 2019.
8 'Statement on the Purpose of a Corporation', Business Roundtable, August 19, 2019. businessroundtable.org.
9 Sarah Butler, 'Ex-Unilever Boss Seeks 'Heroic CEOs' to Tackle Climate Change and Inequality', *The Guardian*, July 21, 2019.
10 Paul Polman, Twitter, July 4, 2019.

BIBLIOGRAPHY

Balkenende, Jan Peter. *Het woord is aan de minister-president: Acht jaar premierschap in 50 speeches*. Den Haag: Ministerie van Algemene Zaken, 2010.

Beijersbergen, Patrick. *De kleine Buffett, zijn beleggingsfilosofie samengevat*. Amsterdam: Business Contact, 2016.

Blom, Philipp. *Wat op het spel staat*. Amsterdam: De Bezige Bij, 2017.

Bruni, Luigino and Allessandra Smerilli. *De ongekende kant van de economie: Gratuïteit en markt*. Nieuwkuijk: Nieuwe Stad, 2014.

Collier, Paul. *The Future of Capitalism: Facing the New Anxieties*. London: Allen Lane, 2018.

Correa, Cristiane. *Dream Big: How the Brazilian Trio Behind 3G Capital Acquired Burger King and Heinz*. Rio de Janeiro: Primeira Pessoa, 2014.

Couwenbergh, Pieter and Hein Haenen. *De regels en het spel: Gesprekken met Morris Tabaksblat*. Amsterdam: Business Contact, 2007.

Craig, Nick. *Leading from Purpose: Clarity and the Confidence to Act When it Matters Most*. New York/Boston: Blackstone, 2018.

Cuadros, Alex. *Brazillionaires: The Godfathers of Modern Brazil*. London: Profile Books, 2016.

Dreier, Thomas. *How Viscount Leverhulme Built His World Wide Organization* (1932). Boston: Literary Licensing, 2012.

Dutilh, Chris. *De duurzame voedingsketen: Twintig jaar ervaring bijeen gebracht*. Den Haag: Academic Service, 2012.

Edmondson, Brad. *Ice Cream Social: The Struggle for the Soul of Ben & Jerry's*. Oakland: Berrett-Koehler, 2014.

Fifer, Bob. *Double Your Profits in 6 Months or Less*. New York: Harper Business, 1994.

Foroohar, Rana. *Makers and Takers: How Wall Street Destroyed Main Street*. New York: Currency, 2016.

Frankl, Viktor E. *Man's Search for Meaning* (1959). Boston: Beacon Press, 2006.

Fresco, Louise O. *De utopisten*. Amsterdam: Prometheus, 2007.

Fresco, Louise O. *De idealisten*. Amsterdam: Prometheus, 2018.

George, Bill. *Discover Your True North: Becoming an Authentic Leader*. Hoboken: Jossey-Bass, 2015.

Graaf, Kees van der. *Defining Moments: What Every Leader Should Know about Balancing Life*. Lausanne: IMD International, 2011.

Hartmann, Kathrin. *Groene leugens: Duurzaamheid als verkooptruc*. Amsterdam: Atlas Contact, 2019.

Homem de Mello, Francisco S. *The 3G-Way: Dream, People, Culture*. Sao Paulo: Qulture Rocks, 2015.

Hurst, Aaron. *The Purpose Economy*. Boise: Elevate, 2016.

Jones, Geoffrey. *Unilever: Verandering en traditie* (trans. Diederik L. van Werven). Den Haag: SDU Uitgevers, 2005.

Klomp, Kees, Stefan Wobben and Jesse Kleijer. *Handboek betekenisvol ondernemen: Het gat in de maatschappij*. Amsterdam: Business Contact, 2017.

Lafley, A.G. and Roger L. Martin. *Playing to Win: How Strategy Really Works*. Boston: Harvard Business Review Press, 2013.

Lager, Fred 'Chico'. *Ben & Jerry's. The Inside Scoop: How Two Real Guys Built a Business with a Social Conscience and a Sense of Humor*. New York: Crown, 1994.

Layard, Richard. *Happiness: Lessons from a New Science*. London: Penguin, 2005.

Lewis, Brian. *So Clean: Lord Leverhulme, Soap and Civilization*. Manchester: Manchester University Press, 2008.

Maljers, Floris. *Memoires* [unpublished], 2015.

Mayer, Colin. *Prosperity: Better Business Makes the Greater Good*. Oxford: Oxford University Press, 2018.

Mayer-Schönberger, Viktor and Thomas Ramge. *De data-economie: Waarom data geld gaat vervangen, wat dit betekent voor onze economie en hoe je hierop in kunt spelen*. Amsterdam: Maven, 2018.

Mazzucato, Mariana. *The Value of Everything: Making and Taking in the Global Economy*. New York: Penguin, 2018.

Mirvis, Philip, Karen Ayas and George Roth. *To the Desert and Back: The Story of One of the Most Dramatic Business Transformations on Record*. San Francisco: Jossey-Bass, 2003.

Ogg, Sandy. *Move: The CEO's Playbook for Capturing Value*. Charleston: Advantage Media Group, 2017.

Oranje, Laurentien van and Jeroen Smit. *Nog lang en gelukkig: Voorleesboek voor volwassenen die de weg een beetje kwijt zijn*. Amsterdam: Promethus, 2016.

Peck, M. Scott. *The Different Drum: Community Making and Peace*. New York: Cornerstone, 1987.

Polman, Kim and Stephen Vasconcellos-Sharpe. *Imaginal Cells: Visions of Transformation*. London: Reboot the Future, 2017.

Pope Francis. *Laudato Si': Over de zorg voor het gemeenschappelijk huis* (trans. L.D.M. Hedriks). Baarn: Adveniat Geloofseducatie B.V., 2015.

Raworth, Kate. *Doughnut Economics: 7 Ways to Think Like a 21st Century Economist*. White River Junction: Random House Business, 2017.

Reich, Robert B. *Superkapitalisme: En de bedreiging van onze democratie*. Amsterdam: Business Contact, 2008.

Reinders, Pim. *'Steeds voor alle arbeiders aanspreekbaar': Sam van den Bergh (1864–1941), grootindustrieel*. Amsterdam: Balans, 2016.

Riezebos, Rik and Eric Waarts. *Power play: De slag om de wasmiddelenmarkt*. Groningen: Wolters-Noordhoff, 1994.

Rompuy, Herman van. *Op zoek naar wijsheid*. Leuven: Davidsfonds, 2010.

Rooij, Martijn de and Redmar Kooistra. *Unilever Matters: A Global Company Interacting with Society*, 2006.

Sandel, Michael J. *Niet alles is te koop: De morele grenzen van marktwerking* (trans. Karl van Kleveren). Utrecht: Ten Have, 2012.

Scharmer, Otto and Katrin Kaufer. *Leading from the Emerging Future: From Ego-System to Eco-System Economies*. San Francisco: Berrett-Koehler, 2013.

Scheepens, Wouter. *Duurzaamheid in de boardroom*. Haarlem: Mauritsgroen, 2017.

Schlosser, Eric. *Het fastfoodparadijs: Een onthullende kijk op Amerika en de fastfoodindustrie* (trans. H. Braakman). Utrecht: Het Spectrum, 2002.

Schoenmaker, Dirk and Willem Schramade. *Principles of Sustainable Finance*. Oxford: Oxford University Press, 2019.

Shift Project, Oxfam and Global Compact Network Netherlands. *Doing Business with Respect for Human Rights: A Guidance Tool for Companies*, 2016.

Sitalsing, Sheila. *Mark, portret van een premier*. Amsterdam: Prometheus, 2016.

Smiles, Samuel. *Self-Help* (1859). Oxford: Oxford University Press, 2002.

Stuart, Tristram. *Waste: Uncovering the Global Food Scandal*. New York: Penguin, 2009.

Stuijvenberg, Dr. J.H. van (Ed.). *100 jaar Margarine 1869–1969*. Den Haag: Martinus Nijhoff, 1969.

Swasy, Alecia. *Soap Opera: The Inside Story of Procter & Gamble*. New York: Simon and Schuster, 1993.

Timmermans, Frans. *Broederschap: Pleidooi voor verbondenheid*. Amsterdam: Podium, 2015.

Tocquigny, Rick and Andy Butcher. *When Core Values are Strategic: How the Basic Values of Proctor & Gamble Tranformed Leadership at Fortune 500 Companies*. Upper Saddle River: Pearson, 2012.

Veer, Jeroen van der. *My A to B: Speeches, Articles and Letters*. London: Shell International, 2009.

Wallace-Wells, David. *De onbewoonbare aarde* (trans. Aad Janssen and Pon Ruiter). Amsterdam: De Bezige Bij, 2019.

Weihenmayer, Erik. *Touch the Top of the World*. New York: Plume, 2001.

Wennekes, Wim. *De aartsvaders: Grondleggers van het Nederlandse bedrijfsleven*. Amsterdam: Atlas, 1993.

Wilson, Charles. *Geschiedenis van Unilever* (trans. Dr Jane de Long). Den Haag: Martinus Nijhoff, 1970.

GLOSSARY OF NAMES

Ingram Content Group UK Ltd.
Milton Keynes UK
UKHW010617250623
423994UK00001B/35